Avery Hopwood : His Life and Plays

Avery Hopwood

His Life and Plays

by

Jack F. Sharrar

McFarland & Company, Inc., Publishers
Jefferson, North Carolina, and London

To the Memory of My Grandparents
Fred H. and Fanny Bowen Goeckel,
and for My Mother

Frontispiece and photographs on pages 8, 10, and 16 courtesy Department of Rare Books and Special Collections, University of Michigan; on pages 19, 24, 182, and 183 courtesy the Pollack Theatre Collection, Howard University; on page 10 courtesy of the Library of Congress; on pages 42, 48, 49, 85, 117, 128, 131, 134, 142, 145, 151, and 192 permission of the Billy Rose Theatre Collection, New York Public Library at Lincoln Center, the Astor, Lenox, and Tilden Foundations; on page 52 permission of the Music and Theatre Collection, Museum of the City of New York; on page 60, permission granted by George Eastman House, photograph by Nicholas Muray; on page 62 courtesy of the Beinecke Rare Book and Special Collections Library, Yale, and by permission of the Estate of Carl Van Vechten, Joseph Solomon, Executor; on page 76 courtesy of the Hearst Collection, Special Collections Department, University Library, University of Southern California; on pages 87 and 203 permission of Culver Pictures, Inc.; on page 147 from Covarrubias's *The Prince of Wales and Other Famous Americans,* © 1925, courtesy Alfred A. Knopf, Inc.; and on page 213 courtesy of the Hopwood Room, University of Michigan. The illustration reproduced on page 11 courtesy of Bruce Kellner; on page 23 courtesy of *The Phi Gamma Delta;* on page 147 courtesy Alfred A. Knopf, Inc.; on pages 162 and 163 courtesy *Vanity Fair,* copyright © 1922 (renewed 1950) by the Condé Nast Publications, Inc.; and on page 189 courtesy Dodd, Mead & Company, Inc. The cover design on page 161 permission of Warner Bros. Inc. © 1923 (renewed). All rights reserved. All other illustrations from the author's collection. Excerpts from Avery Hopwood's unpublished novel © 1989 Hollywood Plays, Inc. All rights reserved.

British Library Cataloguing-in-Publication data available

Library of Congress Cataloguing-in-Publication Data

Sharrar, Jack F., 1949–
  Avery Hopwood, his life and plays.

  Bibliography: p. 237.
  Filmography: p. 231.
  Includes index.
  1. Hopwood, Avery, 1884–1928. 2. Dramatists, American
—20th century—Biography. I. Title.
PS3515.0655Z87   1989   812'.52 [B]   88-42517

ISBN 0-89950-282-2 (lib. bdg.; 50# acid-free natural paper) ∞

McFarland   Box 611   Jefferson NC 28640

Contents

Acknowledgments

This work would not have been possible without the assistance and cooperation of many libraries, museums, and individuals. In most cases, the curators, librarians and desk clerks were most helpful in locating research materials. Dorothy L. Swerdlove, Curator of the Billy Rose Theatre Collection of the New York Public Library at Lincoln Center was especially accommodating in answering questions and requests for materials. Wendy Warnken, Assistant Curator of the Theatre Collection of the Musuem of the City of New York and her assistant MaryAnn Smith, were also diligent in finding items. Charles E. Aston, Jr., Coordinator of Special Collections at the University of Pittsburgh's Hillman Library, is responsible for uncovering Hopwood's letters to Mary Roberts Rinehart. Thanks are also due to Lucille Troph and Evelyn M. Ward of the Literature Department at the Cleveland Public Library for Hopwood's letters to Archie Bell; to James B. Casey and Peg Koebel of the Western Reserve Historical Society; to John C. Hodgson, Chief Librarian of the *Daily-News;* to Brigitte Kueppers of the U.C.L.A. Theatre Arts Research Library; Marilyn E. Mahanand, Curator of the Pollock Theatre Collection, Howard University; to Stephen C. Jones, Public Service Assistant at the Beinecke Rare Book and Manuscript Library, Yale University; and to Jeffrey Rollison, Assistant University Archivist at Case Western Reserve University. Particularly helpful and cordial have been Kathryn L. Beam, Manuscript Librarian at the Department of Rare Books and Special Collections at the University of Michigan, and her predecessor, Margaret E. Berg, whose research of the Hopwood copyrights was especially useful. Dr. Andrea R. Beauchamp, Hopwood Program Coordinator, was always willing to do some extra digging, and the materials she sent from the Hopwood Room files were invaluable. The most patient and tolerant librarian to assist in the research was Linda Burns, Head of the Interlibrary Loan Department at the University of Utah.

The original letters of Avery Hopwood in this work are permanently housed in various locations. For permission to include these letters or excerpts from them, grateful acknowledgment is made to the following collections: Bentley Historical Library, the University of Michigan, Ann Arbor; Collection of American Literature, the Beinecke Rare Book and Manuscript Library, Yale University; Department of Rare Books and Special Collections, the University of Michigan, Ann Arbor; Special Collections Department, University of

Pittsburgh Library Systems; Library and Museum of the Performing Arts at Lincoln Center, the New York Public Library (Astor, Lenox and Tilden Foundations); Literature Department, the Cleveland Public Library; and Princeton University Library.

Special acknowledgment is made to the following publishers for permission to quote from their copyrighted works. Macmillan Publishing Company for *Harvest of My Years* by Channing Pollock, copyright © 1943 by Channing Pollock, renewed 1971 by Helen Channing Pollock. Charles Scribner's Sons, for Andrew Turnbull, excerpts from *Scott Fitzgerald*, copyright © 1962, Andrew Turnbull, and for F. Scott Fitzgerald, excerpt from *The Great Gatsby*, copyright © 1925, Charles Scribner's Sons, copyright renewed 1953. Curtis Brown, Ltd., for *Intimate Memories, Vol. 3* by Mabel Dodge Luhan, copyright © 1929. Dodd, Mead & Company, Inc., for Burns Mantle's *American Playwrights of Today*, copyright © 1929. Henry Holt and Company, Inc., for *My Story* by Mary Roberts Rinehart, copyright © 1948, and *What Is Remembered* by Alice B. Toklas, copyright © 1963. Random House, Inc., for *The Autobiography of Alice B. Toklas*, copyright © 1933, and *Everybody's Autobiography*, copyright © 1937, by Gertrude Stein, and for the Hopwood letters in *The Flowers of Friendship: Letters Written to Gertrude Stein*, edited by Donald Gallup, copyright © 1953. Aitken & Stone, Ltd., for *Well, Let's Eat* by Robin Douglas, copyright © 1929. *Michigan Quarterly Review*, excerpt from "The American Writer: The American Theatre" by Arthur Miller, copyright © 1982.

Grateful acknowledgment is made to the following individuals for permission to include excerpts from works under their jurisdiction: Calman A. Levin for Gertrude Stein's letter to Roy W. Cowden; Donald Gallup, Literary Trustee for Carl Van Vechten, for excerpts from the letters of Carl Van Vechten; Joseph Solomon, Executor of the Estate of Carl and Fania Van Vechten, for excerpts from *Peter Whiffle* and Fania's letter to Carl, and as Executor of the Estate of Ettie Stettheimer, for excerpts from her book, *Love Days;* William S. Zerman, Executive Director/Editor, for excerpts from *The Phi Gamma Delta;* Professor Arno L. Bader for his collection of Hopwood materials; and to Julie Haydon Nathan (Mrs. George Jean Nathan) and Patricia Angelin Size, Executrix of the Estate of George Jean Nathan, for the works of George Jean Nathan.

Above all, this work is indebted to Hollywood Plays, Inc., Glen Rock, New Jersey, owners of the Hopwood copyrights, for lending many of Hopwood's play manuscripts and the manuscript of his unpublished novel, and for granting permission to include selections from the plays and prose writings, including the unpublished writings, of Avery Hopwood.

Inquiries were sent to contemporaries of Hopwood's, from hometown associates to actors who appeared in his plays. Responses from many of these individuals were helpful. A letter from the late Beverley Nichols was particularly insightful, as was information shared through correspondence with A.H. Woods's great-nephew Albert O. Weissberg. Actresses who appeared in plays by Hopwood and who responded to inquiries were the late Ina Claire, star of *The Gold Diggers;* Claudette Colbert, ingenue in *The Cat Came Back;* the late Hazel Dawn, star of *The Demi-Virgin* and *Getting Gertie's Garter;* the late Ruth Gordon, who toured as Blanny in *Fair and Warmer;* and the late Madge Kennedy, creator of Blanny in the Broadway run of *Fair and Warmer.* A sparkling afternoon spent with Miss Kennedy in early summer 1983 proved invaluable for recapturing the spirit of the period.

Among the many individuals who contributed to this work, special thanks to Professor Henry L. Fulton of Central Michigan University, who first implanted the idea of researching Avery Hopwood; to Professor Emeritus J. Alan Hammack of Central Michigan University for copies of Hopwood's *Theatre Magazine* articles; to Professor Edward Lueders of the University of Utah for sharing his memories and photographs of Carl Van Vechten; and to Professor Bruce Kellner of Millersville State University, for his informative letters about "Sasha" and "Buddy," for sharing his copy of Van Vechten's unpublished short story, "Undecided Sasha," and for inquiring of his "ancients," Donald Angus and the late Ann Andrews, about "Sasha." In Cleveland, sincere thanks to Thomas C. Monks for his thoughtful packet of materials, including Hopwood's birth certificate. Special thanks also to Anne Seymour for arranging the interview with Madge Kennedy. To Gerald Bordman, James Prideaux, and Craig Slaight my thanks for their active interest and helpful suggestions. To Trudie Kessler, thanks for braving the New York Hall of Records. To Richard Bowen, thanks for helping with research in Cleveland and points east. And to Michele Dostert, many thanks for the use of the self-correcting typewriter.

Finally, because this book is based upon my doctoral dissertation (Jack F. Sharrar, "Avery Hopwood, American Playwright [1882–1928]" [Ph.D. dissertation, University of Utah, 1984]. University Microfilms International, Ann Arbor, Michigan, Publication Number 8409544), I wish to again acknowledge the helpful guidance of my supervisory committee, Doctors William C. Siska, Marilyn R. Holt, and the late David E. Jones, of the University of Utah Theatre Department. Professor Jones's scholarship and skill as an editor were invaluable to the completion of the original work, while his personal interest in the research and his encouragement and friendship made the entire course of doctoral studies an enjoyable and productive experience. Thank you, David.

Introduction

In 1920, Avery Hopwood was America's most successful popular playwright, attaining the distinction of achieving four concurrent hits on Broadway — a record in the post–World War I era. He was, in a sense, the Neil Simon of his day. A clever craftsman of facile wit and unflagging energy, Hopwood concocted, for the most part, frothy entertainments that presented audiences of the teens and twenties with comic situations, representative characters, and witty dialogue that reflected the fads and foibles of the moment. He became known along the Great White Way as the King of Farce — much of it of the bedroom variety — with such hits as *Seven Days* (1909), written with Mary Roberts Rinehart; *Nobody's Widow* (1910); *Fair and Warmer* (1915); *Getting Gertie's Garter* (1921); *The Demi-Virgin* (1921), which served as a test case for stage censorship; and the four concurrent hits of the 1920 season: *The Gold Diggers,* which gave birth to the spectacular gold-digger movie musicals of the thirties; *Ladies' Night (In a Turkish Bath); Spanish Love,* written with Mary Roberts Rinehart; and the still popular mystery-thriller, *The Bat,* also written with Rinehart.

Hopwood amassed a fortune on the playmaking theory that the drama was a "democratic art,"[1] and that the dramatist was not the "monarch, but the servant of the public." He admitted that he wrote for Broadway, "to please Broadway." As a result, his plays turned greater profits than any other dramatist's of the day. But because Hopwood's talents were given to popular drama as distinct from the literary drama during the period of innovation in the twenties, his plays and his career have been almost totally eclipsed. Today he is chiefly remembered on the campus of his alma mater, the University of Michigan, as benefactor of the Avery Hopwood and Jule Hopwood Creative Writing Awards. These awards have extended a helping hand to, among others, Betty Smith, Marge Piercy, John Ciardi, Robert Hayden, Lawrence Kasdan, and perhaps most eminently, Arthur Miller. Hopwood used the wealth he had accumulated to encourage young writers at a time critical in their development to attempt, in the words of the bequest, "the new, the unusual, and the radical."

How paradoxical it must have seemed to some over the years, though, that Hopwood, a concocter of bedroom farces and similar conventional fare, should have wanted to encourage students to write creatively. Like many dramatists, however, he was not satisfied with his work in the commercial theatre; he longed instead to write the "Great American Novel." Something, he once told a newspaper reporter, "which an intelligent man can sit down and read and think about."[2] Although Hopwood worked on such a book throughout most of his career, he only succeeded in finishing a rough draft. When he died in 1928, the manuscript, which was rumored to be a "devastating theatre expose," disappeared. Now, as a result of the research for this book, the novel has come to light, and, as has been speculated, the autobiographical insights that it contains have proven significant to a full understanding of the man, his career, and why he wanted to encourage young writers.

Making use of Hopwood's unpublished novel, letters, and other primary sources, the following pages set the playwright in his historical context by chronicling his life and his career, by examining his plays — especially dramatic form, plot construction, characterization, showmanship, and the actors who performed in them — and by discussing the nature of the commercial theatre during the period. Avery Hopwood emerges as a promising young dramatist who, like so many others, was destroyed by his early success, and who was ever after frustrated in his attempts to write a work of lasting value.

The chapters advance chronologically: The Call for the Playwright and Before (1882–1905), A Dramatist Full of Promise (1906–1908), "The Play-Writing Business" (1909–1914), Skating on Thin Ice (1915–1918), Inexhaustible Avery (1919–1921), The Playmaking Factory and Final Years (1922-1928), The Hopwood Novel: The Great Bordel, or, This Is Life, and The Hopwood Awards: The New, the Unusual and the Radical. The Conclusion summarizes Hopwood's place in the history of American theatre. Appendices include production lists of his plays, a filmography, and several letters to Mary Roberts Rinehart.

Finally, a word about Hopwood's letters is necessary. As Hopwood's personal papers apparently are lost, his correspondence is scarce. Most of the available letters are to his friends Archie Bell, Mary Roberts Rinehart, Carl Van Vechten, Fania Marinoff, and Gertrude Stein. In including some of these letters, I have kept editing minimal, identifying individuals and clarifying where possible, yet leaving Hopwood's idiosyncratic style and form intact.

Chronology

1882	Born Cleveland, Ohio, May 28.
1900	Graduated from old West High School, Cleveland.
1901	Entered the University of Michigan, Ann Arbor.
1902	Transferred to Adelbert (Case Western Reserve University), Cleveland. Appointed Sophomore Editor to the campus literary magazine, *The Adelbert*. Initiated into the Fraternity of Phi Gamma Delta.
1903–1904	Returned to Michigan. Majored in the Department of Rhetoric. Contributed short stories to *Inlander*, the campus literary magazine. Worked as a cub reporter for the *Cleveland Leader* during vacations. Began writing his first play, *Clothes*.
1905	Graduated Phi Beta Kappa from the University of Michigan. Appointed special New York correspondent for the *Leader*. Moved to New York City in August.
1906	Represented by Mrs. H.C. DeMille, "playbroker." Collaborated with Channing Pollock on *Clothes*, which scored a hit.
1907	Became friend of Carl Van Vechten. Commenced correspondence with Archie Bell. Saw the failure of *The Powers That Be*, his first attempt at serious drama. Vowed to quit playwriting and devote talents to writing fiction.
1909	Considered a promising playwright by some critics, despite the failure of his second serious drama, *This Woman and This Man*. Collaborated with Mary Roberts Rinehart on the farce *Seven Days*. Achieved emphatic success.
1910	Began spending summers at Croton-on-Hudson, living and working in a tent. Commissioned by Belasco to write *Nobody's Widow*. Wrote *Judy Forgot* for Marie Cahill.
1911	Made first trip to England, the Continent and Northern Africa. Called home to prepare *Somewhere Else* for production.
1913	Represented by the American Play Company. Saw the failures of *Somewhere Else* and *Miss Jenny O'Jones*.
1914	Caught in Europe at the outbreak of World War I. Had become a friend of Fania Marinoff Van Vechten.
1915	Published *Sadie Love*, the novel. Emerged as leading American

1

            writer of "risqué" farce with the hit *Fair and Warmer*. Had *Sadie Love*, the play, produced. Joined the Authors' League of America at the request of Gertrude Atherton.

1916   Accused by some critics of "cracking the thin ice of propriety" with the production of *Our Little Wife*. Copyrighted *Just for Tonight* June 3.

1917   Contracted smallpox in the Orient. Copyrighted *Pete (Don't Be Afraid)* August 7.

1918   Copyrighted *The Little Clown* May 10. Saw the failure of *Double Exposure*.

1919   Commissioned by Belasco to write *The Gold Diggers*. Began writing bedroom farces for A.H. Woods. Collaborated with Wilson Collison on *The Girl in the Limousine*.

1920   Established post–World War I record of four concurrent Broadway hits: *Ladies' Night, Spanish Love, The Bat,* and *The Gold Diggers*. Turned down offer to join Samuel Goldwyn's Eminent Authors, Inc.

1921   Returned from Europe for the productions of *Getting Gertie's Garter* and *The Demi-Virgin*. Befriended would-be playwright John H. Floyd. Drafted last will and testament naming the University of Michigan as recipient of a trust to establish awards in creative writing.

1922   Traveled to England for *The Bat*. Wrote last solo effort, *Why Men Leave Home*. Relied on adaptation of foreign plays and collaborations from then on. Founded Avery Hopwood, Inc.

1923   Visited Gertrude Stein and Alice B. Toklas in Paris. Wrote *Little Miss Blue Beard* for Irene Bordoni. Saw the failure of *The Alarm Clock*.

1924   Made two trips to Europe. Announced his engagement to Rose Rolando, but this proved to be a publicity stunt. Collaborated with David Gray on *The Best People*. Charged with drunken and disorderly conduct in Asbury Park, New Jersey. Served as play doctor to *The Cat Came Back*, which failed. Astonished audience at the Baltimore tryout of that play by stating that he was "tired to death" of the plays he had been writing.

1925   Traveled to Europe. Wrote *Naughty Cinderella* for Irene Bordoni.

1926   Spent entire year in Europe. Did not return for the tryouts of *The Duchess of Elba*, which failed. Saw the success of Tallulah Bankhead in the London production of *The Gold Diggers*.

1927   Returned to New York City for the premiere of *The Garden of Eden*, which had been successfully produced in London with Tallulah Bankhead. Had made substantial progress towards finishing a 200,000 word novel.

1928   Sailed for Europe in April. Celebrated his forty-sixth birthday with Gertrude Stein and Alice Toklas. Died Juan-les-Pins, France, July 1. Buried Riverside Cemetery, Cleveland. Left an estate worth well over $1,000,000.

1929   Hopwood's mother, Jule, died on March 1, New York City. March 11 Archie Bell published an article about Hopwood's last work, a novel described as a "devastating theatre exposé." The novel became "lost." John Floyd purchased Avery Hopwood, Inc.

1930   The Avery Hopwood and Jule Hopwood Creative Writing Awards were established at the University of Michigan.

1982   Hopwood's "unfinished," unpublished novel was recovered.

I

The Call for the Playwright
and Before (1882–1905)

Playgoers in search of the latest in backstage gossip dined at Rector's. The Louis XIV dining rooms of green and gold were packed with *décolleté* chorus beauties and their men about town, eating lobster and drinking champagne until the early hours of the morning. Outside in Longacre Square—which was about to lose its name to a new building in the area, the Times—David Belasco might still be seen escorting his current star, Mrs. Leslie Carter, home after one of her performances. At the Knickerbocker Theatre, Julia Marlow and E.H. Sothern would soon be playing in *Romeo and Juliet,* the first of their joint Shakespeare repertoire. And not too far away at the Savoy, John Barrymore had recently debuted in a short-lived offering of Clyde Fitch's, *Glad of It.* Anna Held and Marie Dressler were performing in *Higgledy-Piggledy* for Joe Fields and Florenz Ziegfeld, Jr., John Drew was enjoying another success in a vehicle suited to his droll demeanor, and Lillian Russell, that perfection of "Golden Beauty," was scoring a hit in *Lady Teazel.*

In all parts of the theatre district, from Twenty-third Street up Broadway, through the infamous Tenderloin and along the adjacent side streets to Forty-first Street, people continued to marvel at Edison's transformation of the gas lights and the playhouse marquees—particularly above Thirty-fourth Street, where the intensity of the electric blaze had given rise to the popular advertising slogan: "The Great White Way." It was 1904.

Theatre was booming in New York and across the country. Nearly 300 productions per year were touring the hinterlands during the first years of the decade. Broadway itself offered more attractions than ever, growing from 115 shows produced in 1900 to 288 at the end of the decade.[1] In the first twenty years of this century, 53 new theatres were opened in New York, more than doubling the number of legitimate houses there. Producers knew what sold; they wanted plays that would "get over" to the vast popular audience, which included increasing numbers of middle and working class patrons.

Finding it safer to mount the successes of established British and Continental dramatists, producers did little to encourage native drama. Most American playmakers found themselves in the undistinguished, albeit lucrative, position of constructing "sure fire" vehicles for the current stars. As a result, would-be playwrights headed for New York in search of the fortunes that might be accumulated from one or two hits. After all, the average box-office gross for the period was approximately $600,000 per week.[2] The vicinity of Broadway and Forty-second Street would soon become synonymous with slick entertainment.

Avery Hopwood was still an undergraduate at the University of Michigan in Ann Arbor when he was awakened to the idea of writing plays. The January 1904 *Michigan Alumnus* ran an article entitled "The Call for the Playwright," written by Louis Vincent De Foe (Michigan '91), then Dramatic Critic for the *New York Morning World*. Young Hopwood read with fervent interest:

> Why is it that no Michigan man has directed his ablity and energy to the writing of plays? The field is wide and inviting.... The theater is no longer a luxury of the rich. It has advanced steadily and rapidly to a commanding position among the diversions of the people. Religious prejudice against it is almost eliminated. The increase of responsibility and business strain has given the amusements of the stage a place among the indispensable elements of city life.... While the demand for dramatic entertainment and facilities for presenting it have increased and improved, the plays, the corner-stone of the whole theatrical structure, are not forthcoming. Dramatic literature in this country is stagnant.... The demand for actable native plays is greater than ever before in the history of the theater. Merit is certain of almost instant recognition. The inducements offered to successful playwrights exceed those of any other branch of literature.... Clyde Fitch is reputed to realize nearly $100,000 a year for his comedies.... College men whose inclinations lead them toward literary work, cannot afford to despise the profession of dramatic writing, merely because the theater, as it is now conducted, does not aspire to the highest ideals of literature, but aims rather, to satisfy a not too lofty popular demand ... but in the ranks below greatness, men who aspire to write for the public's entertainment will find more elbow room than their fellows in the other professions, and moreover, they will find their efforts more quickly appreciated and better paid![3]

Hopwood frequently referred to De Foe's article throughout his career as instrumental in turning his interest toward playwriting. In 1912 he told a ghostwriter for *Green Book:*

> An intense admiration for the theatre, a fondness for writing, and the ambition to make money, combined to pave the way for my career as a dramatist.... Mr. De Foe told of the fabulous sums that dramatists had made, and the more I thought about it, the more determined I became to try my luck in this field.[4]

In the seven years between the time Hopwood wrote his first play, *Clothes* (1905), as a senior at Michigan, and the *Green Book* article, he had had six plays produced—three had achieved "hit" status (over one hundred performances at that time) and had earned him at least $100,000 in royalties. Within the next eight years he had attained the distinction of having four hits running concurrently on the Great White Way. Alexander Woollcott called him "Inexhaustible Avery." His plays were bringing in greater profits than any other dramatist's of the day.[5]

Hopwood had been lucky, but more than luck was involved; he had learned how (in De Foe's words) "to write for the public's entertainment," and he had learned quickly. But at the height of success, Hopwood's youthful aspirations were colored with a gay cynicism: "Mr. De Foe's article started me on my career of crime," he laughingly told a reporter. "I was not very affluent at the time and I was dazzled at the sums he mentioned. Think of the havoc he wrought in my life! I might have become a college professor!"[6]

Perhaps in the early days—before his life of "crime"—Hopwood had thought of becoming a college professor. Reports from his native Cleveland reveal him as a studious boy, preferring reading and meditation to playing baseball or "painting the town red on Saturday night."[7] He took to writing at an early age too, or in his words: "at about the same age, relatively speaking, as that at which a duck takes to water."[8] It wasn't long before tales developed about a novel he had written at nine, prophetically called *Sweet Bessie, the Lighthouse Keeper's Daughter, or Love Among the Kentish Hills*—a title not unlike the names of the "naughty" farces that would bring him notoriety 25 years later. But in 1921, Hopwood disclosed:

> [Bessie] only reached its second chapter—a curtailment which I cannot but regret when I reread one of its interesting passages:
> "One morning a few days after they married the young husband came into Bessie's room, and what was his surprise to see, lying beside her, a new-born baby daughter."[9]

Little Hopwood was also said to have edited a magazine which he supplied to the neighbors in longhand; it lasted only one issue. Greatest of his early literary feats, however, was a reworking of Shakespeare's plays, starting with *Cymbeline*. "I know," he told an interviewer in 1918, "I felt that it was something which needed to be done at once."[10] But alas, not a page remains of the early works: "Most of them [were] destroyed," he later confessed. "Not by me. I think my ruthless family did it when I was away from home."[11] Hopwood's childhood interests, Archie Bell, lifelong friend and Cleveland journalist, informed readers, "made him a 'creature apart,' or in the language of his youthful associates, 'Avery was a bit cracked.'"[12]

Hopwood, to judge by his high school studies, was a serious student, and well thought of by his teachers at least. William J. Monks, English Department head of the old West High School, "always contended that young Avery was the best pupil in Literature that he had ever had."[13] The elocution teacher, Katherine Eggleston, spoke of him in a newspaper story, recalling his membership in the Dorian Literary Society and his participation in the school plays. He was "first ranker in his class—and president too, if I remember rightly!" she

James Avery Hopwood, around ten or twelve years of age (ca. 1894), Atlantic City, New Jersey.

wrote. She also disclosed, not "violating that trust" she hoped, that Avery had sought her advice on whether "he would better be an actor or a minister."[14] Many years later, Hopwood had this to say about his decision: "I was torn between a desire to preach and to be an actor. Fate spared both vocations. I turned out merely to be a writer."[15]

The 1900 Cuyahoga County Census and Cleveland birth record confirm Hopwood's birthdate as May 28, 1882, although in later years he gave 1884 as the date. Born of James and Jule Pendergast Hopwood, he was christened in St. Mark's Episcopal Church as James Avery, taking his middle name from his paternal grandmother, Eliza Avery. From early on his friends and family called him Avery. Riverside Cemetery records in Cleveland show that Hopwood had two sisters and one brother, all of whom died at an early age: Jessie M. (1879); Olive M. (1885); and Eric J. (1886). The census also lists an Anna Wilken as residing with the family at 39 Harbor Street. Hopwood's will describes her as "a faithful servant of the family for more than thirty (30) years."

The Hopwoods were a middle-class family. James Hopwood, who listed his occupation as dealer in "Wholesale & Retail Provisions," had migrated to the United States from England in 1875, seven years before Avery's birth. By 1900, the elder Hopwood was proprietor of two meat markets on Cleveland's westside, an area some considered "the other side of the tracks." In the early years, the family had apparently lived over the shop on Harbor Street. Little else is known about James Hopwood or his relationship with Avery. It is remembered that the elder Hopwood purchased a bulldog, Jerry, as a mascot for his son's fraternity when Avery was a student at Michigan, and that in later years the dog went with him when he moved East. After Avery achieved success, he set his father up "in a nice white meat store in a promising part of town, with new cleavers and chopping blocks."[16] James Hopwood died in November 1919, shortly after the opening of his son's long-running hit, *The Gold Diggers.*

Hopwood's mother, Jule, was a native Clevelander of Irish ancestry. Protective and supportive of her son's early interests in writing, she moved her father's large walnut desk into Avery's room where it might encourage him to study.[17] Throughout his life, Hopwood remained devoted to his mother, returning to visit at least every Christmas, and lavishing on her furs and other material gifts to which she had not been accustomed. It is said that when Hopwood learned his mother had sold her diamond engagement ring to help with his college expenses, he vowed he would replace "Mother's Diamond" with the first money he made. Although Hopwood repaid the debt to his mother after the success of his first play, replacing "Mother's Diamond" soon became a joke between the two. Not only did Hopwood present his mother with a precious stone after the opening of every play, but he consoled her with another gem whenever he had engaged in some escapade of which she did not approve. Friends and neighbors often remarked that Avery's mother more than deserved the name of Jule.[18] Hopwood frequently invited his mother to live with him in the East during the summers, and she accompanied him abroad at least 35 times,[19] being en route to meet him in Juan-les-Pins, France, at the time of his death there in 1928.

Hopwood lived to be 46. Physically of average height and build by today's standards, his last passport describes him as five feet eleven inches tall with blonde hair and hazel eyes.[20] Early newspaper accounts picture him as a rather pleasant looking young man with a broad forehead, who was the "tallest thing you ever saw." One noticed the "remarkable head development," wrote a columnist, "as if brains such as his required more room than those of the average person."[21] A friend said:

> His brain seems to bulge into knots all over his head, which is covered with a thin mat of brickish-yellow hair. He is tall, rather raw-boned, somewhat awkward, baleful, witty, pale and usually bears the appearance of occupation, which successfully wards off intrusion.

When informed of this portrait, Hopwood said, "I think it's about right," but

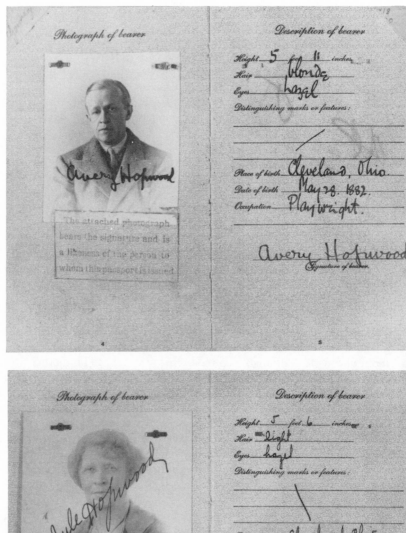

4

5

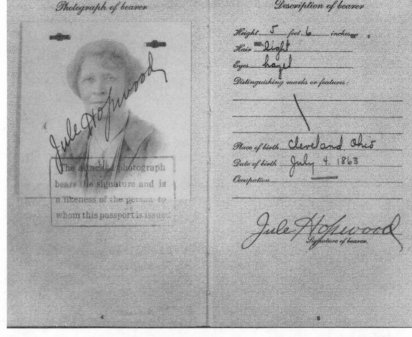

4

5

Avery Hopwood drawn by Djuna Chappell Barnes, ca. 1914. From The New York Press.

quickly added: "It reminds me of a Cleveland woman's description of an actress. She said, 'I wouldn't call her exactly homely, but she isn't exactly an Adonis.'"[22] Hopwood's sensitivity about his features are apparent in a 1913 let-

Opposite: The last passports of Avery Hopwood (top) and his mother, Jule Pendergast Hopwood; issued in London, 1926.

ter to his close friend, Carl Van Vechten. Using his nickname of Sacha, and affecting an Oriental dialect, he also reveals his sense of humor:

Hotel Woodstock
New York

Dear Mr. Slanta Claus:

Please don't plint Missy Blarnes [Djuna Barnes] plicture of Slacha. Slacha no look like that! If Bluddy plint that picture, Slacha make Hari Klari and join honorable anclestors. Missy Blarnes can dlaw velly good plictures, but she not dlaw Slacha. Oh my Jesus Clist, dlont plint that plicture of Slacha! Slacha has a nice phottyglaf. Plint nice phottyglaff!
  Slacha sends tie. Not Klistmas plesent. Just bribe. S. will give another tie if buddy no plint awful damn plicture of Slacha.

Velly wollied,
Slacha[23]

In a recent interview, Hopwood acquaintance and close friend of Carl Van Vechten, Donald Angus, recalled:

Oh, Avery had enormous charm, and his looks. . . . There was a certain soft-ness about his face, gentle would be a better word. . . . But that eye: well, it looked that way. I always wondered if he hadn't been in some sort of acci-dent or maybe even as a child that made him lopsided. It was almost [grimace here] . . . I'd say he was attractive, physically. I think he was—what's the word?—appealing.[24]

When Hopwood visited friends at the New York Phi Gamma Delta Club in 1920 to hand out complimentary tickets to *The Gold Diggers*, a brother recalled: "He still looked like a college boy although he was then 36 [38], the type of guy who doesn't change much as he gets older."[25] Hopwood retained this boyish look for a few more years and then health and personal problems began to age him beyond his years. Looking at his 1926 passport photo and later candid shots, one is struck by the deep lines of fatigue and weariness that had eroded his features. The lack of muscle tension in his right eyelid, noticeable from an early age, had become a severe characteristic of the entire side of the face, in definite contrast to the toned, albeit jaded, left. As an English Lady once told Gertrude Atherton, his appearance was that of a man whose face had been "cut on the bias."[26] But it was Gertrude Stein who formed a more telling impression of Hopwood: in the early days, "holding his head a little on one side and with his tow-coloured hair, he looked like a lamb. Sometimes in the latter days as [she] told him the lamb turned into a wolf."[27]
  Avery Hopwood, as the Registrar's Record shows, began his college career at the University of Michigan in 1901. Shortly after, however, financial burdens began to take their toll on the Hopwoods, and he was forced to return to Cleveland. His sophomore year was spent attending Adelbert, now Case

Western Reserve University. Here, Hopwood was appointed Sophomore Editor to The Adelbert, the campus literary magazine. In the course of the year, five of his short stories and several of his poems were selected for publication. Among the stories printed were "Beside the Summer Sea," a tale of a "Gibson Girl," a "Gibson Man," and "Another Man," and a short, wistful piece entitled "What Might Have Been" that captures a moment in an old man's life when he opens a long-lost letter from his only love. Besides contributing to the *Adelbert,* Hopwood pledged the fraternity of Phi Gamma Delta, becoming a member of the Xi Deuteron chapter.

Fraternity correspondent John Oberlin reported to the *Phi Gamma Delta* that Brother Hopwood was initiated into the "Fijis" on October 7, 1902, "an occasion of much rejoicing on our part and of gratification on the part of our friends."[28] The following spring of 1903 found Hopwood serving as chapter correspondent himself. "With us," he reported, "as with the college world in general, this is a busy time. There are baseball games, there are meets galore, there are hops and proms. Last of all, there are examinations looming up in distracting proximity."[29] Hopwood's attempt to join the fraternities the year before in Ann Arbor had not been as successful:

> The Freshies smiled at "Hoppy," and all the fraternities declined to admit him to membership. They all admitted him to be a fine fellow, but said they couldn't tolerate such an intellectual strain and didn't care to have his melancholy figure prowling about the "frat" houses. "You don't know him yet; he's the brightest fellow in Cleveland," said Bob Gammel, urging the election of his friend; but the vote was lost.[30]

By the fall of 1903, presumably after the family financial problems had become more manageable, Hopwood was ready to return to the University of Michigan. There, he now became an affiliate member of the Alpha Phi chapter of Phi Gamma Delta, where he also was elected as correspondent to the fraternity journal. While a Fiji at Michigan, Hopwood served on the songbook committee and as chapter pianist. As late as 1958, fraternity brothers were still in disagreement over their impressions of him. In a letter to the editor of the *Phi Gamma Delta,* Thomas Read (Michigan '06) came to his defense in reaction to an article written by another brother who had not known him personally. In "Some Notes About Playboy Playwright," Hopwood had been described by coeds in his early days as "a dishevelled student, shy, pasty-faced and a bit grimy.... Not a mixer and [with] few close friends."[31] Read responded:

> Avery was always well dressed, but not over dressed. He was neat; he was not shy; he was never ostentatious and he looked as happy as could be.... He was a close friend of every member of [our] chapter and by far the best liked of any of us in the chapter.[32]

Professor J.L. Brumm and other members of a small writing club to which Hopwood belonged recalled him as "a lonesome, rather diffident, although brilliant student," not possessing an engaging personality in the least during his college years.[33]

Hopwood's 1905 Michigan yearbook shows he was a member of the French Dramatic Club, associate editor and later literary editor for the *Inlander*, member of the Memorial Committee, and member of the select honor society, Quadrangles. He was one of only six undergraduates to have been admitted to this group that included the president of the university and other distinguished faculty members.[34] Hopwood's course of study followed French, Latin, mathematics (about which he later commented: "the time I spent on mathematics was absolutely wasted. . . . It takes no solid geometry or university algebra to add a few [royalty] figures"[35]); but mostly, he spent his time in the Department of Rhetoric taking writing and criticism classes from Professor F.N. Scott.

Scott, who had distinguished himself as one of the first, if not the first, to teach courses in Journalism at the university level,[36] taught his seminars around a big oak table, now in the Hopwood Room in Angell Hall. Here Hopwood and his classmates offered up their writing for criticism, or discussed such works as Aristotle's *Poetics* or Carlyle's *Sartor Resartus*. The five courses he took from Scott had a positive and lasting influence on him. Many feel Scott's friendship and encouragement motivated Hopwood in drafting the conditions of his will appointing the then Department of Rhetoric to carry out his wishes for the awards in creative writing.

Among the Hopwood writings that Scott no doubt read were several short stories he had published in the *Inlander*, the campus literary magazine. The first story, "The Whole Way," is a sentimental tale of a young wife who, after being beaten by her drunken husband, leaves him, only to return home filled with remorse when the sight of Easter lilies brings back the painful memory of their dead son, Jimmie. "A Comic Tale," Hopwood's next story, seems to be an attempt at Poe-esque imagination and mounting terror as a man who has just murdered a woman thinks he hears her knocking louder and louder at his library door. Another sentimental but rather charming piece is "When Alicia Played," the story of a boy who has been desperately seeking the hand of the girl he loves, only to be confounded by her incessant piano playing. The tune which Alicia has been using to vex her suitor is revealed at the end when the boy beseeches Alicia's sister:

> "What is that piece?" cried Allerton.
> Margaret's eyes, so like Alicia's, widened with astonishment, as they gazed up.
> "Of all things—"
> "Tell me," said Allerton, with clenched teeth, "you don't get away till you do!"
> "Why Robby," laughed Margaret, "surely you know it!"
> "No, I don't, but I'm going to."
> "Why—it's Mendelssohn's Wedding March—of course!" Margaret was released as suddenly as she had been caught.

"Oh, Bob, please don't," cried Alicia, a second later, in smothered entreaty, "let me finish it."

But Bob—well, put yourself in his place.[37]

"After the Hop Is Over" is a satiric college piece written in the form of a long letter from Miss Jean Brooks to Miss Annabelle Straileth in which Jean describes her "thrilling" weekend in Ann Arbor attending the J-Hop with her bid, Walton Ives Mandley, University of Michigan '06. Addended to the letter one finds a "short excerpt from the truthful diary" of Mr. Mandley himself:

> The girls have gone. I'm almost dead. So are we all. The house smells of perfume, and there's powder in the air. We haven't missed anything valuable so far. I got a crush on Miss Evans—Ratty's girl. She made Jean look like two cents. I'm in love, in love—and dead broke.... Thank God the damned thing is over![38]

The last and perhaps most interesting story, in light of Hopwood's freshman year and some of the impressions fellow students had formed of him, is "J.B. Brown, Misfit," written in 1904, the term after he had returned to Ann Arbor. Here is a pathetic story of a freshman boy who doesn't fit into the social and cultural world of the upper-middle-class students who are in the majority. Sickly and starved for companionship, Brown finds his idealistic expectations for college life crushed by unsympathetic students and faculty. Invited by accident to attend a meeting of the "Seekers After Truth," he becomes painfully aware that his homeliness has made him an object of derision. Realizing the situation, Lilian, a senior coed, befriends him for the evening out of courtesy. Several days later, when she discovers Brown has come down with pneumonia and may be dying, she and a friend visit him in his dingy little room far from campus. After witnessing the lonely boy's despair, Lilian ends the story with a plea for a more humane campus:

> "I believe there are colleges where this wouldn't have happened.... There ought to be something better to offer here, such as this boy—the misfits, ... I'd build a place for those boys like Brown, and for all the others, and one for the women, too. Places where they could all meet, without having meetings, where they could enter without anybody asking or caring what church they belonged to, or whether they were Christians or Jews; places without any mission—except to be homelike, and inviting—places where they could find friends.... And I'd have the faculty men come and mingle as often as they could with the students and try to know them, and—"
>
> They had reached State street, and turned now toward the Campus. It was near the evening meal hour, and the sidewalk was crowded with students passing in little groups of twos and threes, talking, laughing, calling one to another. From time to time there walked among them a solitary figure.
>
> As Ben and Lilian crossed the Campus, the chimes rang the hour of six. Their full-toned music died away, and in its place, after a moment, came a melody sung by young voices in the frosty distance.
>
> "Oh, Ann Arbor," said Lilian, slowly, "Ann Arbor, Ann Arbor!"[39]

Brother Avery, Michigan '05, Alpha Phi Chapter of Phi Gamma Delta.

It was at the beginning of the same semester in which "J.B. Brown, Misfit" appeared that Hopwood read De Foe's article, "The Call for the Playwright." By the end of spring semester the following year, 1905, he had completed the manuscript of his first play, *Clothes,* inspired by his reading in Professor Scott's class of Carlyle's *Sartor Resartus.* In a *Phi Gamma Delta* article two years later, Hopwood disclosed:

> I got ahead of my classes at Ann Arbor and had considerable time on my hands. I wanted to write—I didn't know what. Sometimes I thought of a novel. I still want to write a book. Then I thought I would write a play and a novel, too. I went to work and wrote a play. The task wasn't so easy as I had imagined. It took all my time before graduation . . . I wrote the thing at least ten times.[40]

Hopwood apparently shared an early draft of the play entitled *Clothes Make the Man* with Professor L.A. Strauss,[41] but his impressions of the work are not known. Roommates living in the fraternity house with Hopwood were not aware of the project until a year later when he returned for the 1906 J-Hop and told them about it,[42] by which time the play had already been picked up by a Broadway producer. In the interim, Hopwood had graduated from Michigan Phi Beta Kappa, and had returned to Cleveland to work as cub reporter for the *Cleveland Leader,* something he had done on previous vacations.

During the summer of 1905 while reporting this or that social or civic event for the *Leader,* Hopwood undoubtedly made more revisions in the manuscript of his first play. Then, towards the end of August, assigned as "special New York representative" to write a daily newsletter for the newspaper, he set out for Broadway with his manuscript and one hundred dollars. Immediately upon stepping off the Cleveland Express in Jersey City, he found himself a "New York hall bedroom," invested some money in a typewriter, pecked out several carbons of his play, and made the rounds of the managers and agents. After four weeks and considerable hounding, according to newspaper and magazine accounts, he managed to get his four-act play read by the new theatrical firm of Wagenhals and Kemper, Clevelanders themselves. *Clothes* seems to have been accepted almost at once and the producers advanced him two hundred and fifty dollars in royalties. With this money, which was more than Hopwood had ever had at one time, he bought himself a dress suit and telegraphed his resignation to the *Leader,* saying good-bye to the fifteen dollars-a-week salary. "I decided," he wrote in a 1912 article, "that I might better take a chance then than at any time in my life, for later I might be tied down in some way, and at that time I didn't care what happened."[43]

II
A Dramatist Full of Promise (1906–1908)

Channing Pollock, the playwright who initially read *Clothes* and later collaborated with Hopwood on the property, recalled in his autobiography that the play had first been submitted to the Shuberts, who declined it. Pollock, though, considered the play to have great promise. "Avery," he wrote, "had written a crisp, witty satire on the society of our day, with touches of excellent melodrama." So, when Wagenhals and Kemper phoned him some months later and asked him to rewrite it and make it "stageable," he agreed, provided that he should "share equally in the royalties and in credit for authorship, and that Hopwood should assent to the whole arrangement."[1]

It was not until midsummer 1906 when the play was being tried out by the Brown-Baker Stock Company at the Davidson Theatre, Milwaukee, that Pollock learned Hopwood had, in fact, not been informed his play was being altered. Hopwood traveled to Milwaukee and unobtrusively made his way into one of the evening rehearsals. At the end of the evening, he stepped forward out of the darkness and told Pollock: "It's not the same play, and I can hardly believe it could be so improved."[2] Apparently the fledgling Hopwood bore Pollock no resentment for reworking the script; and together, the two men took adjoining rooms at a local hotel where they collaborated to such advantage "that the first performance assured [them] of a hit."[3]

Milwaukee critics proclaimed *Clothes* a success, and predicted that the "sartorial satire" would quickly find its way to New York. "The authors," wrote one critic, "have wandered from the beaten path in conceiving this clever drama and the result is a gratefully original bit of playwriting."[4] In general, the critics found the dialogue bright and witty, the situations strong and appealing, and the characters, with the exception of the hero, drawn with "fidelity." The success of the Milwaukee tryout attracted the immediate attention of theatrical manager William A. Brady who had been searching for a vehicle for his actress wife, Grace George. He promptly negotiated controlling interest in the piece, retaining Collin Kemper as director, and set out to produce a lavish and well-tailored play that would assure his wife the metropolitan recognition for which she longed.

As the curtain rises on *Clothes,* several New York society women are revealed playing at billiards. They smoke cigarettes and banter about the latest fashions and who is wearing what. Mrs. Watling, wife of an unassuming pub-

Channing Pollock around the time of Clothes, *1906.*

lisher, Horace; Mrs. Cathcart; and Mrs. Conningsby-Lowe attempt to convince Olivia Sherwood, the character played by Grace George, that she must marry a rich man who is able to keep her in the fine clothes and surroundings to which she has grown accustomed. Olivia has fallen on hard times since the death of her father, and has been forced to live on what she believes to be the dividends from Red Rock mining stock controlled by her guardian, Arnold West. In truth, the stock is worthless, and West, who intends to divorce his unfaithful wife and marry Olivia, has been paying her way. At the end of the first act, Olivia consents to accept a loan from West drawn on her stocks so that she can purchase a beautiful new gown with which to attract the attentions of a rich,

young broker, Richard Burbank. Unknown to her, however, West has sold the
worthless shares to the unsuspecting Horace Watling.

In the second act, the unscrupulous West, who has become aware of
Olivia's intentions to marry Burbank, professes his own love for her. When she
shuns him, he succeeds in making her feel the shame of her hypocritical
desires:

> WEST. (giving way to his anger) Your heroics sound very fine, but when I
> consider what you're going to do, they are simply ridiculous. You won't let
> me help you? (Olivia shudders) You're too damned virtuous! (Goes to table
> and speaks over table.) You won't give yourself to the man who loves you,
> but you're perfectly willing to sell yourself to Burbank so long as you can gild
> the sale with that handy term, Holy Matrimony. Ha! Ha! (Laughing sav-
> agely) Oh, you women!
> OLIVIA. You've said it! To sell myself! I deliberately made up my mind to
> do that! I've tried to make him buy! I've led him on! I've made him believe
> I care for him! I wanted comforts, luxuries, money! I was thinking of myself,
> you see; only and always of myself.
> WEST. And now?
> OLIVIA. You've opened my eyes. You've given a name to the thing I was go-
> ing to do—a name I've been crowding down and denying utterance. From
> the start I've been ashamed of myself, and now—now—I won't marry
> Richard Burbank or any other man I don't love! That time's gone by! I'm
> not for sale![5]

Out of this shame, Olivia rejects Burbank's proposal of marriage. Only then
does she painfully discover that her love for him is real, and not founded on
his wealth.

In the third act, set later that night during the "circus" ball, Olivia admits
her true affection for Burbank and proposes to *him*. As the play builds to its
climax, the drunken West enters and explains he is celebrating the death of
his wife who, along with her lover, has been drowned in a shipwreck in the
Mediterranean. He accosts Olivia and she pushes him away, causing him to fall
down the stairway. Thinking him to be dead, Olivia and Burbank hide his
body behind the curtains. Just then, Watling, who has discovered he has been
ruined by the worthless stock he purchased from West, threatens suicide. In
a melodramatic scene, singled out by some critics as particularly effective in the
true "Fitchian" style, the moral of the play is brought into sharpest focus:

> WATLING. Wait, Carrie. You're wrong. It isn't I who am a thief; it's you.
> MRS. WATLING. How dare you?
> MR. WATLING. (speaks quietly but with an energy strange to him) It's you.
> Why did I speculate? Why is it that we have nothing laid by except debts:
> Your extravagance; your mad chase after social position. I've worked and
> while I've worked you've *called* and danced and played cards and given par-
> ties to people who wouldn't have come as far as your door step if it hadn't
> been for the money I was making and you were spending.

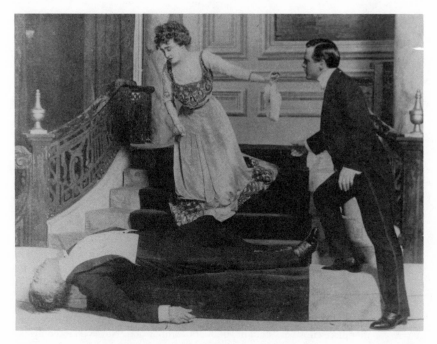

Clothes, *Act III climax: Frank Worthing, Grace George, and Robert T. Haines, 1906.*

MRS. WATLING. Listen to me.
WATLING. You listen to me. I've heard you through. You've called me a thief. I say it is you who have robbed us—me of a wife; Ruth of a mother. She's lying in the nursery now, her little cheeks flushed, her little hands hot with fever, and you've been too busy to go near her. You've lavished your affection on a dog—a dog— and you talk to me of success! You're a worse failure than I am. I've failed in business; you've failed in everything![6]

At this point the action is interrupted by revellers from the dance who pass through the room and exit up the steps. Watling, too weakened to continue, exits, followed by his remorseful wife. West, who has just come to, rises and discloses to Burbank that he has been supporting Olivia, and that her interest in him has been purely monetary; Burbank departs, leaving Olivia crushed.

Evidence suggests that in the Milwaukee tryout the play ended here. But Miss George, apparently, did not approve of Olivia's downtrodden condition, and a four-page fourth act was appended to the script to reconcile Burbank and Olivia in a conventional, happy ending.

As a vehicle for Grace George, *Clothes* succeeded in supplying all William A. Brady had hoped it would. His wife played the show 113 performances after its opening at the Manhattan Theatre on September 11, 1906, and gained the metropolitan attention she needed to reestablish herself as a "star." She had not been the featured player in a hit since Brady had starred her in a revival of Sardou's *Frou Frou* in 1902. One critic wrote: "Hopwood's play has lifted Miss George from the ranks of mediocrity to popularity."[7] Another said: "Grace George is admirably qualified to make the most of such a role as that of Olivia Sherwood, a role for which the primary requirement is delicacy rather than cogent dramatic force."[8] Also mentioned in the cast as giving his usual "truthful picture of a particularly superfluous American youth"[9] was Douglas Fairbanks, in the minor role of Thomas Smith, Jr.

The critical opinion of *Clothes* is best summed up in this quotation from the *New York Dramatic Mirror:*

> Avery Hopwood and Channing Pollock, in their new dramatic satire of *Clothes,* have not uncovered any deeply hidden or especially shocking social atrocities. The play is bright, yet it is not to be denied that much of the brilliancy is reflected from a long array of "originals"; the presentation holds the attention of the audience, yet in all critical honesty it must be classified as superficial. The authors have by no means made the most of what was truly a fine opportunity for trenchant and discriminating satire. Essentially a clever play, *Clothes* lacks the genuine cleverness to make a distinctly intellectual appeal; and it is deficient in the sincerity necessary to excite any considerable emotional sympathy. As far as the audience is concerned, the well devised farcical episodes redeem shortcomings of the attempts at high comedy; and the bits of melodrama redeem, by a certain virility, commonplace efforts at "straight" dramatic composition. However, it is only just to state that the play contains qualities which may entitle it to a New York vogue and to a reasonable success outside the city.[10]

It is impossible, today, to determine the dramaturgical evolution of Hopwood's first play. Of the two or three known copies deposited in libraries, all are attributed to the Hopwood and Pollock collaboration. One page of original manuscript was, however, printed in the 1907 *Phi Gamma Delta,* under an article entitled, "Avery Hopwood's *Clothes.* " This fragment contains the line around which the theme of the play develops:

> T-Smith
> ~~*Mrs E*~~ (comfortably) She's a has-been.
> *Mrs S.* Certainly she can't expect to go out much longer, unless she gets something new.
> ~~Ol. People used to crowd to her parties~~
> *Mrs T* ~~Oh well—when you're up you're up, and when you're down you're down.~~
>   Burbank
>   Is that so important in your world, Miss Sherwood?
> *Mrs M* ~~The (laughingly) the~~ [indecipherable] ~~and the Lord~~ [indecipherable] ~~both away—blessed be the name of the Lord~~.
> ~~Mrs S Oh, my dear!~~
>   Oh, of dominant importance, Mr(s). Burbank—
> Ol. You hear a great deal ~~about~~ in your world of the survival of the fittest. ~~In society~~ With us it's ~~seems to be a case of~~ the survival of the *Best* Fitted![11]

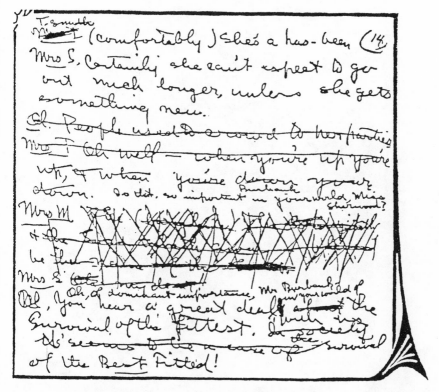

An original page from Clothes, *ca. 1905, from* The Phi Gamma Delta.

The 1906 promptbook at the New York Public Library shows this fragment remaining as rewritten, with the exception of minor word changes in the last speech: "Of dominant importance, Mrs. Burbank. You hear a great deal in your world *about* the survival of the fittest. With us *it is* the survival of the best fitted." Grace George, however, reportedly spoke the line: "Nowadays it does not seem to be a question of the survival of the fittest, but the best fitted."[12] Similar epigrams, so popular in plays at this time, are sprinkled throughout the acts, and account for much of its humor. Again, differences are found between lines as reported and as written in the promptbook. One character says, "The path of respectability is trod only by women who wear wide shoes." The less sophisticated written copy reads: "The path of perfect propriety was intended for women with big feet." A like instance finds the written line, "That woman must have a dozen silk skirts, she sounds like a rainstorm," reported as: "That creature must have on a dozen skirts, she sounds like a shower." Such evidence of fine tuning or creative criticism serves to underscore the difficulty in piecing together the dramaturgical process with any accuracy.

Newspaper critiques generally agree that the central idea, characters,

Friend, collaborator, criminal, 1907.

incidents, and "moralizing" of the play were Hopwood's, and that Pollock's contribution was purely "medicinal." Pollock gave the play a workable structure and business, something Hopwood had not yet learned much about. Ironically, most of the New York critiques of the play focused on the poor form and arrangement of material.[13] Hopwood himself never shed any light on the collaboration, and apparently avoided questions about it, simply answering: "I collaborated with Mr. Pollock on the play."[14] One newspaper interview, ten years after the collaboration, did find Hopwood making a retrospective comment:

> Mr. Kemper realized the obvious fact that *Clothes* was rather a good idea badly dressed. He called in Mr. Channing Pollock to make it over. Mr. Pollock did his best with it, and made it possible; but, with all respect to

his ability, it never was much of a play. The strange result of that collaboration was that we are still friends, Channing Pollock and I![15]

Perhaps the inscription on the photo portrait Hopwood presented to Pollock sums up the situation best: "To Channing Pollock—friend, tho collaborator, from his fellow-criminal."[16]

A fuller appreciation of Hopwood's remark may be found in the charges of plagiarism which were filed by Charles Frohman against *Clothes*. He tried to prove that the play had been stolen from *The House of Mirth*, which he had paid Clyde Fitch and Edith Wharton to dramatize from her novel.[17] This play, which opened within a month of *Clothes*, failed after only fourteen performances, as compared to the former's run of 113. It seems, however, that Hopwood had no trouble proving that the original version of his play had been written much earlier, and the charges were dismissed.[18] Another newspaper story reported that Mrs. Harry B. Smith, wife of the prolific librettist and lyricist, instructed her attorney to bring immediate action against Hopwood because of the similarities between *Clothes* and a play she had written.[19] Given the Smiths' prominence in the theatre of that time, Mrs. Smith's allegations were no doubt taken seriously, but since nothing more was heard of the case, it may be assumed that these charges were also dismissed. Cries of plagiarism and stealing were not uncommon during this period before the 1909 copyright laws went into effect.

After a four-month run in New York, *Clothes* had a successful tour through the rest of the season, playing, among other places, Hopwood's hometown of Cleveland, and scoring another success in Chicago. A German translation was made for a production in Berlin and it was seen in London shortly after.[20] *Clothes* had, indeed, succeeded in making the promises of Louis De Foe's article come true for Hopwood. At 24 the doors of Broadway had been opened to him, he had learned much about the practical world of the theatre, and he was ready to try again.

Prior to the rehearsals of *Clothes* in 1906, Hopwood had been earning a living as a freelance writer for *Theatre Magazine*. In May of that year he submitted the article "The Supermen and Superwomen of the Stage," in which he reported on the lot of those overlooked members of the profession, the supernumeraries. "The choosing of 'supers' for an important production," he wrote, "is no longer simply a question of procuring a certain number of individuals to 'fill in.'" The quality and dedication of the new "supers" had improved. This change, Hopwood noted, was a manifestation of the positive changes transforming the entire theatrical system: "It is the change consequent upon a demand for higher intelligence, special fitness and training, and dependability." The silent ranks of the "supers" were being trained in a practical school where they could "yearn, and learn, and earn, at one and the same time." Wages were not high of course—from fifty cents to one dollar a performance—but those who might land "thinking parts," roles which required acting but no speaking, could receive as much as fifteen to eighteen dollars a week. For those "supers" with the greatest ability and ambition, there might even be stardom. After all, he concluded, "not a few of our present-day dramatic celebrities, who wear purple and fine linen, and eat strawberries in December, can look back upon a time when, even with the best arithmetic, they found it hard work to make both ends meet, on super's pay."[21]

The month before, a similar article, "Where They Try Out Voices for the Operatic Stage," had appeared in the magazine. In a humorous, insightful way, Hopwood followed several aspirants through an audition process, which only resulted in their names being left among the three thousand others on file in the office. The hopes and problems of the auditionees might well be those of today's aspirants. One question on the application, "Do you object to wearing Tights?" would no doubt today read: "Do you object to appearing Nude?" but the answer would probably remain the same: "I would prefer not . . . but would do so if the exigencies of a theatrical situation compelled."[22]

As 1906 drew to a close, Hopwood began rehearsals for his second play, *The Powers That Be,* which he had written without the assistance of a collaborator. A problem play about graft and civic corruption, *The Powers That Be* was produced on the Shubert circuit in the Midwest by minor producer/director E.F. Bostwick. The play apparently met with success in St. Louis and along the way to Columbus, Ohio, where it opened February 27, 1907, at the Shubert Theatre. That night, as Hopwood sat alongside his literary agent Mrs. H.C. De Mille and the mother of the play's leading man, David Proctor, he must have been caught up in the enthusiasm with which the play was greeted.[23] The audience applauded "loud and long" at the end of each act, and there was much cheering from his brothers of the local Phi Gamma Delta fraternity, who had come to support their fellow "Fiji." At the end of the third-act climax, after the hero had delivered his impassioned speech against "bossism" directly to the audience, "the American people," from a balcony center stage, Hopwood was called upon to make a speech. He rose and said only: "I thank you ever so much; I hope some day I will have another first night in Columbus."[24]

Shortly before the play opened its Columbus tryout, Hopwood had written an article for the *Ohio Sun* entitled "On Dramatizing Life" in which he discussed his purpose in the play and playwriting in general. Calling Bronson Howard the "dean of American Dramatists," Hopwood wrote that, like Howard, he himself subscribed to the intention that drama should not merely interest, please, or move audiences, but that it should "have an idea—it should teach some lesson." Not that it should be didactic, or preachy, but it "should always have in it a something which will make people go away with the feeling that they are at least a little wiser and better for having seen it." Citing the underlying ideas of *Clothes,* the evils of materialism, and *The Powers That Be,* the danger threatening American life from the civic grafter, he pointed out that the conflict which results from the attempt to reform the situation gives a drama its shape. The difficulty in presenting such conflict arises from the selection of incident and action. A playwright must be judicious in this respect, or else the play will be dubbed "an out and out melodrama." Defending the idea of "melodrama" and attempting to clarify its usage, he wrote:

> There is entirely too much tendency, nowadays, to condemn as "melodramatic," stage scenes which are really truthful transcripts of what is taking place around us every day. American life—and, indeed, all life—is essentially "melodramatic" . . . [containing] love, hate, revenge, murder, suicide. . . . All these are material ready to the hand of the dramatist. . . . If he is to do strong and good work, he must not be confined to the depiction of boudoir comedy, and to the concoction of scenes so fragile as the afternoon tea cups around which they are built.[25]

In light of the label, bedroom farce, that was to be attached to Hopwood's later plays, one cannot help being struck by the irony in his disparaging comment about boudoir comedy. Hopwood concluded his article by talking about *The Powers That Be* in particular:

> I want *The Powers That Be* to stand or fall simply on its merits or demerits as a play. What I've tried to do is write a clean and sufficiently interesting American drama, centering about the love of a strong man for a pure woman.[26]

The enthusiasm of the Columbus opening carried Hopwood on to Springfield, where he wrote Cleveland journalist Archie Bell about some additional excitement:

> March 1, 1907
>
> Dear Mr. Bell:
>
> Behold me—in Springfield, O-hi-ho—on ruled paper. "The Powers That Be" had a really big success in Columbus, Wed. & Thur. Sunday night we open in Cincinnati.
> "Clothes" will be the counter attraction during the week, so I'll have a chance to observe the relative drawing power of the two shows. . . .[27]
>
> Avery Hopwood

Cincinnati papers did not react to either play favorably, however. Although *Clothes* met with mixed reviews, *The Powers That Be* was pommeled, receiving the most scathing notices of any play in Hopwood's career. In a moment of rationalization perhaps, he spoke about it in 1912:

> When it struck Cincinnati, a cold newspaper wave blew it out of town. I had drawn the principal character after a well known political boss, and the papers recognized the drawing and took it up with a vengeance.[28]

The very term that Hopwood had attempted to expound upon in the earlier "On Dramatizing Life" article was quickly applied to it: "cheap and claptrap melodrama."[29] According to the critics, he had drawn the character of Buntz, the villainous boss, so much stronger than his hero, Burton Clark, the district attorney supposedly fashioned after the young President Roosevelt, that the audience only laughed at Clark and applauded Buntz. Today, the dialogue between the two men leaves one critical of both:

> CLARK. Your three millions seem to have unlimited influence.
> BUNTZ. You're right there.
> CLARK. Thousands of office holders, and the people dependent upon them, look to you for their daily bread. You own these people body and soul. When you say "go" — they go; when you say "come" they come.
> BUNTZ. That's no lie.
> CLARK. You're virtually an American King.
> BUNTZ. You bet I am, and don't you forget it.
> CLARK. I don't forget it, that's why I'm after you, because it isn't right that any man in this Republic should wield the power you do. I'm going to be reelected.
> BUNTZ. Re-elected? Well, I guess not. I made you, and I guess I can unmake you, and I'll do it, too. Why, you won't get a thousand votes. I won't stop with running you out of office, but out of politics. I warned you and I'm going to make an example of you. I won't rest till you have been driven out of business, out of the city, out of the state.
> CLARK. And I warn you I won't rest until you have been driven away from the people's money; till you are out of politics; out of the city. Till you and your gang of grafters are where they belong — in the state penitentiary.
> BUNTZ. Do you know what this means? It means a fight to the finish with me.
> CLARK. That's just what I'm looking for, Mr. Buntz. A fight to the finish — and with you. (Face to face across table.)
>
> CURTAIN[30]

The third-act climax with Clark appealing directly to the audience, thus making them part of the action, did not produce the same thrill in Cincinnati that it had in Columbus; rather, the audience laughed. Further discussion of the plot does not seem warranted; suffice it to say that in the end, the hero triumphs, the girl is won, and the fallen woman is called Mother.

In spite of the scathing reviews, *The Powers That Be* did not die in Cincinnati. Hopwood retained faith in it. A new director, George Foster Platt, was called in to redirect certain scenes, implement a new third-act ending, and reshape the hero. By all accounts several days later, however, the play had not markedly improved. Yet, Hopwood continued to work on the piece, renaming it *The Grafters* in one version, *The Franchise Grabbers* in another, and in still a third version, *Masters of Men*. No version reached New York. Two other plays on similar popular themes of civic corruption had already scored major successes: *The Man of the Hour* by George Broadhurst and *The Lion and the*

Mouse by Charles Klein. According to Hopwood, though, the play continued to be performed by repertory companies, was always successful in stock, and was "pirated more than any play [he] ever owned."[31]

The immediate effects of the critical failure of *The Powers That Be* on the young playwright surfaced in an interview with *The Cincinnati Times-Star* shortly after George Platt had been brought in to fix the play. Hopwood told the paper his great ambition was to do something more substantial than to write a few plays which would fade into "oblivion, leaving nothing behind but empty memories and a bundle of ducats." Continuing, he said:

> I want to write books—fiction if you will, but I want to write something which an intelligent man can sit down and read and think about. I do not care so much about having him say: "This was written by Hopwood" as to have him say, "This was worth reading." I want to commence this work within the year. I intended to do it before, but I wrote a play, and it "went," and then I wrote another, and thus I have been switched off from my original purpose. . . . I will write two or three more and then quit—if I can. . . . This is the psychological moment for it.[32]

This appears to be the first instance of Hopwood's publicly stating his desire to be a serious writer of fiction. It is an ambition which will surface repeatedly throughout his career until eventually he will avoid discussing it altogether.

In Cleveland, expectations and support for Hopwood continued to grow. Along with other home-town playwrights, Rupert Hughes and Eugene Walters, Avery Hopwood was bringing the Forest City recognition. People wanted to know what he was up to. The old *Leader* staff chided him about adopting so quickly the badge of his theatrical tribe, the hairy fur coat. "Something microbic," they wrote, "must attack and conquer them [these writers] the minute they step from private life to 'the profession.'"[33] He had left Cleveland with a play called *Clothes* attacking sartorial extravagance, and he had returned a sartorial collaborator.

Clevelanders were also surprised to learn of Hopwood's impending marriage. Reports from early *Powers That Be* rehearsals and subsequent dispatches along the circuit indicated that the bride was to be one of the three unmarried actresses in the show. Was it "chic" Nesta de Becker, "aweing" Katherine Mulkins, or "sparkling" Caroline Newcombe? Hopwood wouldn't say.[34] The marriage never took place, and the whole story was most likely the work of a zealous publicist. On the subject of marriage, Hopwood told Archie Bell: "I will marry any nice girl who will take entire charge of me, and leave me absolutely alone."[35] To a reporter he quipped: "I would like to marry Becky Sharp. She might not always be faithful, of course, but at least she'd never bore one."[36]

Nothing is known of Hopwood's movements from early fall 1907 until September 1908. Apparently he needed some time away from his new career to make sense of his recent experiences. In September 1908, a small news release appeared in the *New York Telegraph* asking: "Do you remember Avery Hopwood?" The item reported that he had been hidden away in a cabin in a remote part of Ohio writing, and now returned "with a new play all typewritten and prettily bound in light-blue baby ribbon."[37] For an idea of what Hopwood was thinking and planning during this period of solitude, it is best to allow him to speak for himself by a letter written September 29, 1907, at his parents' home, to his former professor, F.N. Scott:

1817 W. 44th St., N.W., Cleveland, Ohio
Sept. 29, 1907

Professor F.N. Scott
Ann Arbor, Mich.

Dear Professor Scott: —

. . . .

You asked me to tell you something about myself. It's so long since I last saw you that I hardly know where to begin my Confession.

[Here follows a description of Hopwood's experience with *Clothes* and *The Powers That Be*. He says that "in most respects," *The Powers That Be* is a much better play than *Clothes*, . . ."]

I am now at work on a modern emotional drama, in five acts *[This Woman and This Man]*. I expect to finish it by January first, and it will probably be produced early next season with Miss Carlotta Nillson in the leading role. I regard Miss Nillson as by all odds the best of our younger actresses. She created the name role in Pinero's "Letty," in this country, and last season made a great hit in "The Three of Us," in which she remained on Broadway all season, and which she is still using as a vehicle.

For about a year, now, I have been gathering material, and formulating the plot, of a novel. I expect to begin the actual writing of it soon after finishing my play. According to my hopes, — which, in these matters, invariably prove too sanguine, — I'll finish the novel next September, so that, — if anyone wants it, — it may get published in the Spring of 1909.

I'm fairly bursting with ideas for plays, and novels, and short stories, and essays, and Heaven knows what else. I've decided that there's only one thing I can do, — write, — and write I shall, to the world's punishment. I'm still undetermined, however, as to what particular field of writing I'd best confine myself, — if, indeed, there is a necessity for a monogamistic wooing of the Muses. My personal inclination is still strongly toward the novel. Everyone tells me I'm a fool to write anything but plays, — which, of course, determines me more and more to try my hand at the novel. I'm sure I can do my best work there. In writing a play, I feel as if I were writing with my left hand. I can't flavor what I do with personal feeling. I'm always letting someone else do the talking, and never getting a chance to take a hand myself, and to tear things up. All this is very inelegant, and undescriptive, but perhaps, notwithstanding, you will feel something of my meaning. I can perhaps make my attitude a trifle more clear by saying that I have a strong feeling for WORDS, and that, in playwriting, this descriptive faculty gets no outlet.

So much for what I'm writing. As to what I'm thinking about, — I'll be Sophomoric, and gravely state that I spend a good deal of my time thinking about life, and trying to arrive at some definite standpoint in regard to it. Life is the most obvious thing in the world, and the most obvious task, it seems to me, for the man who writes, is to voice his attitude toward life.

My specific thinking, nowadays, is along the line of mind cure, faith healing, and the like, because my novel will concern itself, to some extent, with these phenomena. I've been reading a good deal about communistic settlements, too, — also for the novel.

. . . .

What am I going to do with myself? Just write — creatively — or, at any rate, as creatively as I can.

Faithfully,
Avery Hopwood[38]

It is clear the 25-year-old Hopwood was at a critical point in his career as a writer. Struggling with the proverbial problem of life, he continued to be preoccupied with the desire to write worthwhile fiction, particularly a novel. His plans to finish *This Woman and This Man*, initially entitled *The Woman Pays*, for production early the next season did not materialize. It wasn't until February 1909 that Carlotta Nillson played in the piece, and then it was a three-act drama rather than the outmoded five-act structure mentioned in the letter to Professor Scott.

Hopwood's growth as a playwright is immediately apparent on reading *This Woman and This Man*. Undoubtedly following the pattern of the problem play as refined by Ibsen, he builds his plot around the theme: "I think the day is coming when people won't ask a woman whether she's divorced — or married — but only what sort of life she leads, and how she brings up her child."[39] Thus, like many problem plays, it explores the emancipation of women and, in this instance, the difficulties faced by an unwed mother who must marry in order to legitimize her child. Although the psychology of the play is superficial, Hopwood succeeds, for the most part, in presenting characters who are individual, and who speak in an easier, less stilted manner than those of *The Powers That Be*. The structure attempts to break with the typical problem play by setting the second act seven years later, a gap that some critics were not ready to accept. And, with the exception of a somewhat melodramatic first-act ending in which Thekla Mueller forces the young man to marry her at the point of a gun, the action seems natural and motivated. The play's weakness lies mainly in its conventional third-act resolution which finds Thekla and Norris about to live happily ever after, and in its exposition, which, as the critics pointed out, is "bold and direct."[40] The greatest significance of the piece, however, is found in the critics' recognition of Hopwood as one of the most promising young dramatists of the day.

The first act of *This Woman and This Man* is set in Thekla Mueller's bedroom on the estate of Goddard Townsend, where she has been serving as governess to his children. Townsend's oldest son, Norris, has been away to Europe for a few months and has just now returned. Upon his arrival, Townsend confronts him in Thekla's room with the news that he has found a cable among her belongings which appears suspicious. Norris confesses that Thekla is going to have a child and that he is the father. Townsend tells Norris he must not marry her, but send her away where she can have the child put up for adoption. When Thekla returns, Norris proposes the idea. She refuses and pleads with him to share the responsibility by marrying her for the child's sake:

> Don't think I'm asking this for myself. It wouldn't mean anything to me, to go through a marriage ceremony with you—not now. If I were the only one to be considered, I'd go away, and never bother you again. —And it isn't because I'd be afraid to face the world, and say, "Yes—this is my child—conceived in love!" They could throw stones—I wouldn't care,—not for myself. But—I couldn't bear to see my child suffer, and know that I was the cause. I know how the world would treat it, if it were—born out of wedlock. Christ sometimes forgives, but man is more particular.—I couldn't bear to have it turn upon me, some day and say—"You handicapped me—you didn't give me a fair chance."[41]

Norris refuses and leaves. Thekla considers suicide, but thinks better of the idea, and sends a note to the neighboring minister asking him to come to her within the hour. She calls for Norris. When he enters, she produces a gun and tells him that if they cannot accept the responsibility together, they will die together.

The second act finds Thekla seven years later teaching in a country school in upstate New York. Mr. Johnson, a member of the school committee, presents her with a letter from a law firm inquiring whether her maiden name had been Mueller. She discloses that her husband is still living, and that she is not a widow as she had told the committee when they hired her, a fact that will jeopardize her position. Shortly before the committeeman and Thekla are about to leave, Norris arrives seeking her whereabouts. Johnson departs, and a few awkward moments pass between Thekla and Norris. Suddenly Davy enters. Upon seeing the boy, Norris's paternal instinct swells and he asks Thekla for permission to visit his son on a regular basis; he will happily provide for both of them. When Thekla shuns Norris's offer, he threatens to take Davy from her forever as would be his legal right.

The third act opens several months later back at the Townsend estate, Norris having carried out his plans to take Davy with him. Thekla has also accompanied them, and is living in another part of the house. Townsend admonishes Norris for creating a strained atmosphere in the house, and implores his son, for Davy's sake, to attempt to live civilly with Thekla. Thekla, who has not been speaking to Norris, enters the room with Davy, who has just returned from a birthday party. After what the critics called an endearing and heartfelt scene between Grandfather, Davy, and the estranged parents, Norris attempts to profess his true love and admiration for Thekla.

Davy's scene, although sentimental and stereotypical by today's standards, was apparently a welcome relief from the usual portrayal of children at that time:

> DAVY. (Plaintively) I wish I didn't have to go to be-ed.
> (He stands up on the divan and Thekla, standing in front of him assists him out of his underclothes and into his pajamas.)
> Mother — when can I stay up till ten o'clock every night?
> THEKLA. Oh — not for a long while yet, dear.
> DAVY. I wish I was big! (Pause) Father —
> NORRIS. Yes?
> DAVY. When you first got big, does it seem a awful long way from the floor? (Norris is silent.)
> Does it, Father?
> NORRIS. Why no — not particularly, sonny.
> DAVY. (After a moment's reflection) I wonder if giraffes feel a long way from the floor? Do they Mother?
> THEKLA. Why — I don't know dear — I hardly think so.
> DAVY. (After a pause) Why do giraffes have such long necks?
> THEKLA. So they can eat the leaves in the trees.
> DAVY. Oh!
> (He is now attired in his pajamas. He begins to take off his stockings. Thekla goes to the closet — gets a pair of small slippers which she brings to Davy.)
> There was a great big fat girl at the party — No wonder she's fat, though. She just gobbles all the time. (Pause) Father — can you wiggle your toes?[42]

"John Tansey," wrote one critic, ". . .plays six-year-old *David* as a real boy, unlike the traditional stage child, so often a thing of horror and of precocity far from human."[43]

This Woman and This Man draws to a rather conventional close as Norris finally convinces Thekla of his love and admiration for her, and she proclaims her "willingness" to make the marriage work.

The stage history of the play is rather short. After trying out in Philadelphia, where one critic chastised the producers for having failed to publicize the merits of the piece to advantage, it moved on to New York, and became the second offering at the new 934-seat Maxine Elliott's Theatre on West Thirty-ninth Street. The presentation of the play was in keeping with Elliott's and the Shuberts' promise to make the theatre "a home of naturalistic drama, or at least of drama put on with care and taste."[44] The production was directed by George Foster Platt, who had worked with *The Powers That Be,* and who had developed a reputation similar to David Belasco's for his attention to detail. The play, as mentioned, had been written for Carlotta Nillson, a Swedish-born actress noted for her ability to play emotional parts with naturalness. (She had played in *Hedda Gabler* in 1903.) Opposite Nillson's

Thekla was a new actor from Chicago in the role of Norris, Milton Sills. The remaining parts were filled with familiar New York character actors.

Generally, Nillson and the rest of the cast received good reviews although one critic noted that a fair judgment of Nillson's ability could not be given on opening night because "her nervousness affected her facial expression and voice."[45] Despite her efforts to continue in the piece, and for reasons which are not clear, she withdrew from it after only twenty-four performances. The main reason was probably a dismal box office. Audiences were flocking to see another play which had also opened February 22, *A Woman's Way*, with Grace George.

Critic Clayton Hamilton, writing in *The Forum* for April 1909, puts *This Woman and This Man* into perspective by echoing several critics:

> The question that should be asked of the many new plays being written by unknown authors, is not which play has been the most successful, but which playwright shows the greatest promise of worthy work to come.
>
> The best play of the month is *A Woman's Way*, by Mr. Thomas Buchanan; and this is very properly the only piece which has made any money. Nevertheless, the place of honor must be assigned, not to this deservedly successful effort, but to a play which failed to finish as a work of art and, justly enough, has made no money at all. In inherent worthiness of endeavor, *This Woman and This Man*, by Mr. Avery Hopwood, is the most significant of recent plays; and the man who wrote it is, upon the show-ing of the effort, a man whose work may be watched with high hopes for the future.
>
> *This Woman and This Man* is on the whole an ineffective play, because the author's reach exceeds his grasp; but it is important in its promise, because it shows that he is reaching earnestly toward the highest things in drama. Mr. Hopwood has made an honest effort to represent reality; and in so far as he has fallen short of his ideal, he has failed only through inex-perience and not through any faltering of purpose. He has thought earnestly about life; it is apparent that he writes not merely for the sake of writing, but because he has something to say; and it is just as evident in his worst scenes as in his best that he is striving to be true.[46]

This Woman and This Man was clearly the kind of failure out of which future successes in the serious drama might have grown. In 1912, Hopwood referred to the play as the best thing he had ever done. He was overjoyed when Archie Bell, who had just written a biography of Clyde Fitch, told him that after at-tending the opening night, the successful playwright had remarked: "If I had written it, the critics would say it was my masterpiece."[47] But by 1921, Hop-wood scoffingly referred to the play as his "drayma" in which most of the characters did impossible things. "There weren't enough Indians in the piece to make a hit with the office-boys," he told a reporter.

> I regard the whole thing now with a hostile eye. Still, Clayton Hamilton thinks it's the best thing I've done. "This Man and This Woman," [*sic*] it

was called. It taught me what to avoid and brought me food for about three weeks.[48]

After closing in New York, the play toured for two years with Minnie Victorsen in the lead, earning Hopwood $12,000 in royalties — $10,000 less than *Clothes* had brought in. Apparently, what the failure of *This Woman and This Man* taught Hopwood was that the serious drama was not profitable; for, after 1909, he put all his energy into comedies and farces.

III
"The Play-Writing Business" (1909–1914)

In the spring of 1909, shortly after the closing of *This Woman and This Man,* Hopwood decided to set up residence outside New York City, where the air was fresher and there were fewer distractions to keep him from the daily work routine that he had established for himself. Country living, camping, taking the cure, and outdoor activity in general had become popular pastimes during this period of Teddy Roosevelt.

Just north of Manhattan in Westchester County, entrepreneur Clifford B. Harmon purchased a tract of land around the old Van Cortland farm, which overlooked the Hudson and Croton rivers. Here, at the request of Madame Lillian Nordica, who desired to create "an American Bayreuth" — a rural colony where artists of all types could rest, socialize, and create — Harmon soon constructed several buildings, including a little playhouse and the Nikko Inn, where visitors on a Sunday afternoon might listen to the newest songs of Irving Berlin. The popularity of the area grew rapidly, and before long there was a festive air about the place. Gondolas with costumed gondoliers carried guests up and down the Croton, taking them to the other farms and colonies that had developed. The list of artists, stage personalities, writers and socialites who visited the area or established homes there reads like a *Who's Who.* Among the visitors were: Isadora Duncan, who brought her pupils and performed dances in the barn; Mrs. Fiske and her husband; Major Bowes and his wife, Margaret Illington; the Selwyns; Lenore Ulric; critics Alexander Woollcott and George Jean Nathan; David Belasco; and others too numerous to mention, but no less notable. Hopwood, along with Doris Keane and Edward Sheldon, often rented cottages from farce writer and producer Margaret Mayo, who owned a parcel of land at "Finney Farm." And so it was at places like "Harmon," "Laurel Hill," and "Finney Farm" that the artists enjoyed themselves, and professed to be "getting back to nature."[1]

In 1909, though, before the cottages and gondoliers had left their mark on the area, Hopwood had set himself up in a tent near the farmhouse he was renting, or perhaps owned, at Croton-on-Hudson. Within a year, Sunday entertainment sections were filled with pictures and articles about the man who wrote farce while living in a tent. Leaning on a makeshift wooden table covered with oil cloth, or sitting cross-legged on the plank floor, arm around his bulldog, Hopwood peered out from behind the canvas flaps and told

Mary Roberts Rinehart arrayed in some of the wealth earned from Seven Days *and her successful fiction, 1914.*

curious readers just how he set about writing plays. To Archie Bell he wrote:

> I have regular hours for work, — from nine to three every day. I work without intermission for lunch or anything else. I can turn easily from one thing to another, and find it somewhat refreshing to have two pieces underway at the same time, — working on one in the morning, and the other in the afternoon.
>
> — From now on I hope to divide my time equally between the novel and the drama. My preference, in the dramatic field, is for comedy. I can, if

necessary, write almost anywhere, but, like most pen-pushers, I prefer ab-
solute quiet and isolation.[2]

After some exercise, another hour of just thinking out ideas, and a light
luncheon, Hopwood would relax by swimming, canoeing, or motoring along
the Hudson. Retiring by nine o'clock, he was up by six-thirty the next morning
and ready for a short walk, breakfast, and correspondence.[3] Under these
favorable conditions, he reportedly got down to the "play-writing business"
and wrote *Judy Forgot, Nobody's Widow,* and his share of *Seven Days.*

Written in collaboration with Mary Roberts Rinehart, *Seven Days* was important in reestablishing Hopwood's credibility with theatrical managers. Initially, Rinehart's *Seven Days* appeared as a novella in *Lippincott's* December
1908 issue, but with the success of her mysteries, *The Man in Lower 10* and *The
Circular Staircase,* it was quickly expanded into a full-length novel and
published under the title *When a Man Marries.* In this form, it reached tenth
place on the best-seller list for 1910. Rinehart had been interested in the theatre
as a commercial venture before her collaboration with Hopwood, but her
earlier plays had not been too successful. Working as a play reader and "doctor"
for Beatrice De Mille, Hopwood's agent, she was undoubtedly aware of the
production possibilities for *Seven Days.* Accounts vary, but apparently Mrs. De
Mille showed the story to Wagenhals and Kemper, who wanted to purchase
the property outright; however, Rinehart, who still had a "definite fear of New
York"[4] from her previous experiences, refused the offer. In the end, no doubt
encouraged by Mrs. De Mille, Rinehart agreed to let Hopwood adapt the story
for the stage, provided she had final approval.

Hopwood later told an interviewer for *Green Book* that when he submitted a serious drama to Lincoln Wagenhals, Wagenhals had told him, "Hop,
I believe the public have had enough of the serious. Here is a story I think
would make a good play."[5] Hopwood had laughed because he and Rinehart
were already working on the idea. Soon after that the firm paid the two authors
$2,500 on account on the basis of their reading of the first two acts.[6]

Since no Rinehart/Hopwood correspondence exists until 1913, when arrangements were being made for a London production of *Seven Days,* the
nature of the collaboration can only be inferred from Rinehart's autobiography
and a few news items. It appears that the endeavor was rather rough going in
the beginning. After Hopwood had finished his adaptation, he delivered it to
Rinehart at her home in Pittsburgh but she was disappointed: he had written
a four-act comedy and she wanted a three-act farce.[7] The original story, she
felt, was totally farcical and nothing more. Essentially, her plot developed from
a situation in which a man and his divorced wife, his girlfriend, his aunt, a
number of dinner guests, a burglar, and a policeman find themselves quarantined seven days for what is suspected to be smallpox—just the kind of
nightmare from which a good stage farce might spring.

Hopwood's adaptation of the story as comedy rather than farce may have
grown from his hesitancy to deal with a form, or label, that had lost popularity

on the American stage since about 1900. American farce had flourished in the late nineteenth century with such writers as Augustin Daly, George Broadhurst, and Charles H. Hoyt, but in recent years, indelicate and raucous French and German adaptations had met with critical disfavor and public apathy. The ten years following Hoyt's death in 1899 found few successful farces on the boards. As James T. Nardin points out in his dissertation on popular American farce from 1865 to 1914, "An author who had written a farce was not likely . . . to call attention to the fact that he had written one by so labeling it."[8] Regrettably, Hopwood's first adaptation of *Seven Days* is no longer extant to compare with the farce that was eventually produced.

After the difference of opinion about which direction the play should take, Rinehart and Hopwood agreed to collaborate further on the project. According to Rinehart, she and Hopwood worked extremely well together. The relationship was strictly professional and well organized. As Rinehart said: "On everything but the play we differed diametrically, but we seldom so much as spoke of anything else."[9] Working at her office in Pittsburgh close to her home and family in Sewickley, the two writers devised a system for collaborating based on the strengths of each. Since the original story was Rinehart's, she stuck to scenes and situation, while Hopwood watched the structure and provided humor in the dialogue. "Hopwood had a rapier-like wit," she recalled. "He would take a line of mine, twist it about, and make it into a laugh,"[10] although he himself never smiled. Most of the manuscript was written by him, while she paced about the room dictating and acting the roles. When the play was finished, Hopwood proclaimed it a hit, but Rinehart remained uncertain. One reason may have been that the final scene was not decided upon and rehearsed until the afternoon of the New York opening.

The play had been a success during tryouts, but when it opened at the Astor Theatre on November 10, 1909, it was destined to break all records for attendance that year, and to establish itself as the second longest running show of the season, followed only by the Hippodrome extravaganza, *A Trip to Japan.* By the time it had begun its second season in the fall of 1910, critics had to admit that farce — good, exaggerated, preposterous farce — was back to stay. Writing in *American Magazine,* Walter Pritchard Eaton hailed the return of the genre:

> Once in so often one of those kill-joys known as dramatic critics rises to remark that farce is dead. . . . "Our respect for reality has become too great to permit the enjoyment of farce," says the critic. "There are no farces anymore!"
> It looks pretty bad for farce. Even the word becomes a reproach. As an adjective, "farcical" is the critic's most contemptuous epithet. . . . Raising the red banner of Reality, the critic dances gleefully on its grave.
> Then comes *Seven Days,* and neatly upsets all the critic's theories, along with his gravity.
> Not for more than a decade, indeed, have there been so many farces visible upon the American stage as at the present time, and not for more than

a decade, too, have so many of them been the popular plays of the hour.
Farce, sheer, simon-pure, unadulterated farce is having its innings again.. . .
Reality be hanged! Follow the crowds to *Seven Days*.[11]

As with most farces, Rinehart and Hopwood had taken an established
theme, added a few seasoned burlesque bits, and provided new twists wherever
possible; the result was hilarious. Much of the play's success was also due to
Collin Kemper's quick-paced, tight staging, and to the excellent ensemble of
actors who had been trained in earlier popular farces. "There is hardly a 'Broadway name' in the presenting company," wrote Channing Pollock in the *Green
Book Album*, "yet no play of the year is better acted than *Seven Days.*" He
added, "I'd rather have seen *Seven Days* one night than to have gone seven
times to see E. H. Sothern's unimpressive Antony and Julia Marlowe's unallur-
ing Cleopatra. If this be low-browism make the most of it."[12]

Since the success of any farce depends primarily on the style and quality
of playing, including the visual humor employed by a clever director and cast,
it is difficult to gain a full appreciation of the amusement audiences might have
enjoyed while experiencing *Seven Days*. Nevertheless, a brief, albeit complicated, description of the play's "curious circumstances" can give an idea of
what resurrected the farce spirit in pre–World War I America.

On the evening of the first day, so the program says, "we are let in on the
ground floor" of the Wilson house on Riverside Drive. James Wilson, artist,
and his girlfriend, Kit McNair, are about to share dinner with their friends,
Dallas and Anne Browne. As the curtain rises, a burglar is seen prowling about
the drawing room. Just as he is attempting to leave, Jim and Dallas enter to
have a smoke before the ladies join them. Not to be caught, the unfortunate
burglar leaps behind the fireplace screen, where he is trapped throughout the
act. No sooner do the girls join their partners than Jim receives a telegram from
his sponsor, Aunt Selina, informing him that she is coming to visit that night
in order to meet Bella, the wife he has, unknown to Selina, divorced over a
year ago. Jim is frantic, believing that Aunt Selina will never accept his present
situation, and so cut off his allowance. Kit must pretend to be his wife. Determined not to let Selina's visit put a damper on the evening, the group decides
to have drinks before she arrives. The highballs, however, hit hard on an empty
stomach — especially for Anne. The alcohol promptly strengthens her
spiritualistic belief that she has the "power." While the others are out of the
room, she is certain the noises she hears emanating from behind the shifting
firescreen — the burglar attempting to escape — are evidence of her "control."

On Aunt Selina's arrival, Jim and the others return. Selina immediately
greets Kit as his "wife," and sets out to make herself at home. Later, while Jim
and Selina are in another part of the house, Dallas and Anne are confronted
by Jim's divorced wife, Bella, who was passing by when she saw an ambulance
pulling away from the residence. As she attempts to conceal her concern that
it may have been Jim who was ill, it is learned that the Japanese valet has been
taken away suffering from what is believed to be smallpox. Complications

intensify when Tom Harbison, a friend Dallas has invited to dinner, shows up; he was once engaged to Kit. As the act draws to a close, an irate policeman, who was contaminated while removing the valet, informs this unlikely gathering that they have been quarantined for seven days.

"We descend to the source of all good things" on the morning of the second day. Kit, searching for food in the basement kitchen, stumbles upon the sleeping Bella, who has hidden there all night. Bella, desperate not to let Jim find her, runs into the coal bin when she hears him coming. Jim is about to tell Kit that he must confess to Selina, money be damned, when there is a terrific crash from the coal chute. Bella has tried to crawl out, only to get stuck and fall back down, torn and sooty. Jim is flabbergasted and insists that she leave at once. After a minor quarrel, Jim and Kit try boosting her out of the window but she gets stuck. A sample of the antics follows:

> BELLA. (Frantically) Oh, I'm stuck — I'm stuck!
> KIT. (Wildly to Jim) She's stuck!
> JIM. (Desperately) Shove hard, Kit!
> BELLA. Oh! Ouch! It's a nail!
> KIT. (To Jim) It's a nail!
> JIM. Pull her down.
> BELLA. Oh! It's running right through me.
> KIT. (To Jim) It's running right through her!
> JIM. Push her out.
> BELLA. (Screaming) Oh — you've killed me!
> KIT. We're killing her!
> JIM. (Frantically) She can't go up and she can't come down! What in hell are we going to do?
> KIT. Pull her out.
> BELLA. (Wailingly) Twist me around! (Jim and Kit business frantically twisting and pulling at Bella. Bella gives final struggle and drops back atop chest of drawers) Oh — oh — oh! (Rocking back and forth, hands to waist line. Kit excitedly pulling window down, gazing down at Bella. Jim gives cry and tumbles off chest to floor up C. by door.)
> KIT. (Anxiously getting off chest to floor) Are you hurt? (To Bella)
> BELLA. (Wailingly, sitting on edge of chest) Hurt? I'm killed! It was rusty! I knew it was! Oh — oh — (pulling out, from region of waistline, nail and holds it up) Look at it! (Throws it to floor. Jim picking himself up; limps to chair against wall just by the dumbwaiter) Jim, have you any peroxide?
> JIM. Not since you left, Bella![13]

At this point, a policeman sticks his head through the window and tells Bella not to try escaping again. They have been surrounded by guards and reporters. The remainder of the act is devoted to similar sight and line gags that find the burglar now hidden in the dumbwaiter pulling himself back and forth between floors to elude the policeman, Jim and the group attempting to make an omelette, and Jim lying to Bella that Kit is now his wife. The morning of the second day grinds to a raucous halt as the entire group makes a break for it, only to have the guards chase them back inside — all, that is, except for

Seven Days, *Act II curtain, Chicago company, 1909.*

Aunt Selina. Has she escaped? No. Tossed back in through the window, she cries "Pomona! Pomona!" and the curtain falls.

In Act Three "we go to the roof for a breath of fresh air" on the afternoon of the seventh day. The vaccinated group has made its way to the top of the house to avoid the smell of fumigation. Hungry and ornery, they set about making themselves as comfortable as possible, Anne reading her spiritual books, the policeman scrubbing the floor, and Tom attempting to get food up from down below. The burglar has now been forced to hide in the chimney. Bella, attempting to make Jim jealous, has been talking about marrying Tom, but he wants no part of such an arrangement. When Dallas suggests that they get married by phone, Tom quickly tosses the phone down the chimney, much to the discomfort of the burglar, who, by this time, has become drunk on Aunt Selina's supply of Pomona.

Before long, Tom and Kit profess their love for one another, Jim admits he still cares for Bella, and Aunt Selina, still in the dark about the relationships, is outraged. "If this is modern marriage," she says, "give me free love." Sudden sneezes from the chimney bring about the resolution when the policeman, thinking the sound to be one of Anne's spirits, fires his gun into the sooty darkness. The burglar has had it; he leaps out and angrily informs Selina that Jim isn't married to Kit, and that the woman in his arms is really his divorced wife. In the ensuing confusion, Dallas tells everyone that the quarantine has ended because the butler only had chicken pox, Anne is disillusioned at the reality of her "control," and Jim furiously exclaims: "I'll kill the chump that vaccinated me!"

The popularity of *Seven Days'* preposterous episodes soon had more than one critic proclaiming it funnier than *Charley's Aunt.* Theatre managers scrambled to find plays that would allow them to cash in on the renewed interest in farce, and by 1910, at least nine new farces were being offered on Broadway. Among the new hits were: *The Lottery Man* by Rida Johnson Young; *The Commuters* by James Forbes; and most popular of all, Margaret Mayo's *Baby Mine.* These were all farces of a new kind, employing American characters, situations and settings. Critics praised them, not only for their hilarity, but for never going too far beyond the bounds of respectability, unlike the foreign adaptations of earlier years. Farce production continued to increase throughout the decade until it reached its peak during the 1919–20 season with nineteen farces out of the 150 total plays produced, making fifteen per season the decade average.[14] Mary Roberts Rinehart had been on the right track in insisting that her story be developed as farce.

Hopwood couldn't have been more pleased with how *Seven Days* turned out. In 1922 he furnished the *New York Times* with a conservative estimate of the royalty earnings for his major plays, and those for *Seven Days* were listed at $110,000.[15] Rinehart's share was the same. The two authors had indeed collaborated well. The success of the play apparently allayed Rinehart's fear about Broadway, and in 1912 she tried her hand at a solo effort, *Cheer Up,* but it closed after only 24 performances.[16] She was not to return to the theatre until eight years later, once more in collaboration with Hopwood. This time they would offer two plays in the same season, scoring hits with *Spanish Love* and *The Bat.* In the meantime, she could return to her successful career in fiction, and continue to collect royalties from the numerous touring and foreign productions of *Seven Days.*

The success of *Seven Days* was more than financial for Hopwood, however. In the words of Channing Pollock, "his second and third works, *The Powers That Be* and *This Woman and This Man,* had not called the fire department to the Hudson River."[17] The managers, who gauge a playwright by the number of patrons in front of the box office, had begun to wonder whether Hopwood really could write a play. Pollock recalled seeing him outside the Astor Theatre in New York on opening night looking pale and truly agonized; he had not stayed for the last act. "Well, how did it go?" he asked. "A knockout!" replied Pollock. With rather pathetic sincerity, Hopwood responded: "On the level? You're not trying to jolly me?"[18] The ordeal of this crucial first night behind him, and the relish of his first major financial success before him, he quickly found new offers that would turn him away from the risky serious drama forever. As for fiction, that could wait too; he was only twenty-seven. As one commentator writing about Hopwood and playwrights like him put it in an article entitled "The Day of Young Dramatists": "One taste of the royalty cocktail makes them forget almost any other way of making a living."[19]

The winter and spring of 1910 found Hopwood preparing two plays for production the following fall: *Judy Forgot,* commissioned by manager Daniel V. Arthur for his wife, comedienne-singer Marie Cahill; and *Nobody's Widow,* commissioned by David Belasco for his current leading lady, Blanche Bates. Both plays called upon Hopwood to utilize his newly acquired farce and comedy skills, as well as to tailor the leading roles to the star actresses. Hopwood was finding himself a busy young man, even being forced to turn down contracts. Excerpts from several of Hopwood's letters to Archie Bell during the summer of 1910, when Bell was preparing an article on the playwright for *Theatre Magazine,* illustrate Hopwood's situation:

Croton-on-Hudson
New York

Dear Archie: —

I'm working my head off, & shan't stop so doing until it's time to plunge it into the none too cool peril of rehearsals.

Writingly
June 29 [1910]   Avery Hopwood[20]

Croton-on-Hudson
New York

About the article, — I'll understand whatever you said, — & let it be understood between us, always, that I shall continue to understand, — for I know you write as yr feeling prompts, — & that, to me, constitutes the only necessary, & the final explanation, of what a man writes.

Friendlily
July 17 — 1910   Avery Hopwood[21]

Croton-on-Hudson
New York

Dear Archie: —

Read the "Theatre" article yesterday, & was greatly pleased & entertained thereby. I feel that I am now embalmed among the Immortals, — I don't mean tht I'm a dead one, tho, — but I will be, if weather & work continue with equal, simultaneous strenuosity....

Yes, the play I wrote for Belasco [*Nobody's Widow*] is to be played by Miss Bates, — I signed contracts with Belasco for it a year ago last April, — He sent for me & offered the contract after he had seen "This Woman & This

Man." — The Bates piece goes into rehearsal about Sept. 20th. — Rehearsals of the Marie Cahill piece [*Judy Forgot*] begin Aug. 21st. . . .

I was so glad to read what Fitch said. Thank you, Archie. [In reference to Fitch's previously quoted comment regarding *This Woman and This Man.*]

Saturday

Rustically
Avery Hopwood[22]

Croton-on-Hudson
New York

Dear Archie:

As you may have read, the title of my play for Miss Bates has been changed to "Nobody's Widow."

I have procured a release from my agreement to do the Grace Van Studdiford opera, as the time for production — Nov. 1st — conflicted so with the Bates & Cahill productions that I wdnt have time to write & rehearse it.

I begin rehearsing the Cahill piece on Monday. The Coast Co. of "Seven Days" has opened in Frisco to enormous business.

Tuesday

Aufwiederschreiben
Avery Hopwood[23]

(Unfortunately, Hopwood's letters are not more detailed about his plays and rehearsals. If he did write such letters, Archie Bell did not retain them. No preliminary title of *Nobody's Widow* has been found.)

Judy Forgot was Hopwood's first attempt at writing the libretto and lyrics for a musical comedy. Originally entitled *My Other Eye,* the show opened in New Haven, Connecticut, following what must have been an unpleasant experience for Hopwood. While dining after the final dress rehearsal, he had contracted a severe case of ptomaine poisoning from eating soft-shell crabs. By the time the company had reached Providence, Rhode Island, his condition had worsened and he had to be taken back to New York for treatment. Hopwood was still recuperating at the Hotel Majestic when the musical premiered two days later at the Broadway Theatre on October 6, 1910.[24]

Produced and directed by Marie Cahill's husband, Daniel V. Arthur, *Judy Forgot* proved to be well suited to its star. Cahill, whose plump and jolly nature had already established her as a popular musical comedy performer, was famous for her chattery delivery, resourcefulness at comic business, and "a voice more notable for a curious penetrative sweetness than brilliancy or volume."[25] Critics agreed that Hopwood had succeeded in "plumping" together several amusing sequences that showed off Miss Cahill's talents to good advantage, but, as was usually the case with musical comedy, "a good idea had piffled out into nothing."[26] The best possibilities of the plot had been sacrificed in order to expand the "nonsensical frills." A number of the song lyrics were singled out as being rather memorable, but essentially, they had been thrown in at various times with no relation to the story. The music composed by Silvio Hein was generally thought to be unoriginal and imitative, leaving the audience asking: "Where have I heard that tune before?"[27] "Thus," wrote *Theatre Magazine, "Judy Forgot* is the same thing, but different, multiplied by the presence of Marie Cahill, with her natural humor and unconventional methods."[28] With its many striking scene changes and beautiful costumes, it had "more than ordinary appeal to that section of the public which never seems to get enough of this kind of entertainment."[29] A brief synopsis of the plot, such as it is, provides a taste of the kind of play that showed off Miss Cahill's "plump and jolly" nature to best advantage.

While on their honeymoon to Switzerland, Judy Evans (Marie Cahill) and her husband, Freddie, have a quarrel. Judy leaves and suffers a loss of memory when her train derails. Taken to Marienbad, a health resort, she soon believes herself to be comic opera star Trixie Gale, whose luggage she has accidentally picked up. The true Trixie and her husband, Dicky, who have been staying at Marienbad, have also had a falling out and have separated. When Dicky meets Judy, he is forced to pretend that she is really his wife because his uncle, who has not met Trixie, is coming to visit, and he would be most upset with the situation—a problem similar to the Aunt Selina predicament in *Seven Days*. Musical numbers, inserted along the way, lead everyone to a happy resolution. Two numbers, "The Star Factory" and "Thinky, Thanky, Thunk," which poke some fun at the theatre and its stars, are typical of the play's entertainment. "The Star Factory" is a recollection of Trixie's (Judy's) graduation from the "Dramatic School of Art." In this number, students are asked to show off their acquired skills before receiving their diplomas. They act out emotions, improvise a typical farce scenario, and sing a lyric from "The School of Manufactured Patriotism" by Mr. Geo. M. Rowen:

> I will save the stars and stripes,
> Fighting ever for the cause,
> For I find the grand old rag,
> Always wins your kind applause.
> . . . .
> D-r-a-m-a- *Drama!* Rah! Rah![30]

In "Thinky, Thanky, Thunk," which typifies the kind of patter routine that made Cahill popular, Judy suddenly finds herself at an opera wondering what everyone is thinking, and paying no attention to Caruso; she rattles on to her companion about the many celebrities who are in the audience:

> I like John Drew—don't you—or [do] you? He's always the same. . . . You
> can't tell a thing about a play anymore from the name, can you? You

know, I took the children to see a show called *The Doll's House* — and it was all about a woman who left her husband. Not that I blamed her. Nowadays it's a case of leave or be left — don't you think so? Or do you? . . . Oh, that's Jack Barrymore — you know he's Ethel Barrymore's divorced husband. . . . Oh, is that Margaret Anglin? . . . you know they say [she's] so emotional that when she sits down to eat a lamb chop she just has a good cry over it first. . . . Who's that — right across the aisle — Mrs. Fiske — or Nazimova? Listen a minute — if you can't understand what she says, it's Mrs. Fiske — if she doesn't understand what she says, it's Nazimova — Did you see Mrs. Fiske in *The Sins of Society?* You'd think they'd get tired of these problem plays, wouldn't you — or would you? I think it's problem enough to know how you're going to get the money to pay for your seats without having any more problems dished up to you when you get them. . . . That's Tully Marshall — he's a dope fiend — that's why he made such a hit in *The City*. They say the stage manager just fills him up with cocaine every night and sends him on. I think it's awful — don't you — or do you? Why he might bite somebody. . . . Oh, there's Julia Marlowe — she's my favorite actress, next to Fritzi Scheff — I wish she wouldn't play Shakespeare so much. Still, I suppose somebody has to play it. I don't think we go to the theatre to improve our minds — do you? — or don't you? — We can do that cheaper in church — Oh, speaking of churches, did you ever see *Ben Hur?* That's the kind of religious play *I* like — with horseraces and things — Well if there isn't De Wolf Hopper. You know, he's married to George M. Cohan's niece, and George M. Cohan is married to Marie Dressler, so that makes De Wolf Hopper, Marie Dressler's uncle, and De Wolf Hopper is John Drew's nephew, so that makes John Drew, Marie Dressler's grandfather.[31]

It would seem that "that section of the public" to whom *Judy Forgot* most appealed, had seen enough of it within six weeks; the musical was withdrawn after 44 performances. A successful tour followed, and most likely, Arthur had produced it with the idea of presenting his wife in a piece that would particularly appeal to her fans in the hinterland.

Just prior to the closing of *Judy Forgot,* suit had been brought against Arthur and Hopwood by popular actor, director, and librettist Charles Dickson, whose *Three Twins* had been one of the bigger hits of 1908. Dickson charged that Hopwood had used as the basis for *Judy Forgot,* the story of Dickson's novel and play, *The Simple Life.* The application for a preliminary injunction to keep Arthur from further presentation of the piece was denied on the grounds that there was not "sufficient similarity" in the two works: the theme of "sensory aphasia" had been used in many plays and stories.[32] The musical earned Hopwood $69,000, and appears to have been the first play to which he sold the motion picture rights; it was filmed in 1915, again starring Marie Cahill.

Hopwood's second play of the 1910–1911 season, *Nobody's Widow,* premiered on November 15, a little over a month after the opening of *Judy Forgot;* it proved to be his greatest success thus far, both financially, the royalties equaling the $110,000 earnings of *Seven Days,* and personally, being the first time his name appeared in lights as sole author. Many critics then, and

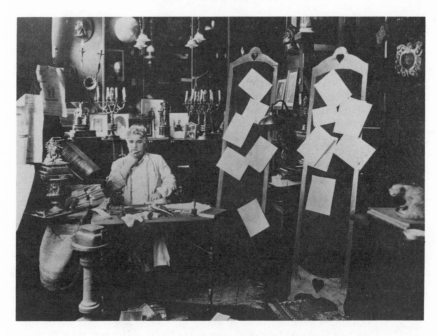

David Belasco in his workshop, 1909.

throughout Hopwood's career, would refer to it as his greatest artistic achievement.

Much of *Nobody's Widow's* success, however, was the result of David Belasco's directorial skill. It would be difficult to say to what extent Belasco reshaped the play, but the few accounts of the rehearsal process available suggest it was considerably, as with any Belasco production. In a 1920 article, Hopwood himself recalled working sessions on the production. Each night for several weeks during the Pittsburgh tryouts, Belasco, Hopwood, Bruce McRae (the male lead), and Blanche Bates (for whom the female lead had been tailored), would sit up until the early hours "discussing the play, making changes, rehearsing new scenes." The stars and Hopwood came to wish they had never heard of *Nobody's Widow,* but Belasco, filled with inexhaustible enthusiasm, kept thinking of new angles for the play. After sending the stars to bed, he would supply Hopwood with fresh paper and pencil, and insist on one more rewrite. Hopwood, finding himself locked in the adjoining room, vowed in writing: "No more playwriting — so help me God!" and affixed his name, and the date. "The worst of it is," he concluded, "I like it!"[33]

In a 1912 article, Hopwood talked about the "play-writing" business in general, and *Nobody's Widow* in particular:

> Mr. Belasco selected most of the cast for "Nobody's Widow," though I suggested Bruce McRae, only to find that Mr. Belasco had already chosen

Hopwood, a young dramatist full of promise, ca. 1910.

him for the leading role. I usually have some of the actors in mind, but leave the selection for the most part to the stage director. I think that is better, for one in his position is more competent to handle that part of the work than I am.

Mr. Belasco is a fine producer, and is not at all dictatorial. He is always open to any suggestion the actor wants to make. I hardly ever say anything to actors about their work. If they are artists, they understand the interpretation of a character without being told. Sometimes they come to me and talk over their ideas of their parts, but that is all.[34]

This is one of the few instances in which Hopwood is quoted as making any comments about his responsibilities in rehearsals. He was never known to direct or produce his own plays. The comments about Belasco coincide with later public remarks Hopwood made about the producer, and apparently the two men had a good working relationship. Belasco had most likely met Hopwood through Beatrice De Mille, whose husband H.C. De Mille had been Belasco's assistant and collaborator. Belasco once told Archie Bell that Hopwood sat on stage during rehearsals (something Belasco required of his playwrights), and when asked at a moment's notice to change a line in order to strengthen a scene, he could instantly produce one of the cleverest points in the play. Belasco said "that never, to his belief, had a playwright lived who was so facile in this respect."[35] Blanche Bates corroborated this ability: "That boy is a marvel. Belasco just says to him calmly, 'I want a witty speech,' and before he's left the counter it's wrapped up and handed to him by that kid."[36]

Blanche Bates, who had acted for T. William Frawley and Augustin Daly, first performed under Belasco's management in 1900 as Cora in *Naughty Anthony,* which was closely followed by Cho-Cho-San in *Madame Butterfly.* Regional audiences had seen her as Nora in *A Doll's House* and Hedda in *Hedda Gabler.* Although Bates continued to appear on the stage until 1933, being last seen in *The Lake* with Katharine Hepburn, many critics consider the climax of her career to have been in 1905 as the heroine in *The Girl of the Golden West.* When Belasco commissioned Hopwood to write *Nobody's Widow* for her in 1910, an attempt was being made to expand her range into comedy. Bates's previous play for Belasco, *The Fighting Hope,* had been an outmoded melodrama that had had a successful run only because of her popularity; the critics had decried the misuse of her talents in the piece. Despite the fact that *Nobody's Widow* was an improvement over *The Fighting Hope,* offering her a part "in modern dress, and joyously liberated from the melodramatic environment of the past," its success did not gratify her.[37] Many critics, however, praised her for her acting in the piece. Channing Pollock went so far as to say she "has never done anything more praiseworthy than her Roxana, a role requiring with its comedy, so much ... sincerity, emotionalism, and reality."[38] *Life* critic James Metcalfe wrote:

> Blanche Bates plays the role with vivacity and with a breezy humor that comes out over the footlights in waves. Her handsomeness of face and figure have a chance to be made the most of in conventional but stunning gowns, which are evidently fitted over a natural woman and not over a tightly laced corset.[39]

After 215 performances of *Nobody's Widow* in New York, and one-and-a-half years touring the piece, Blanche Bates married, and left Belasco's management, going the way of Mrs. Leslie Carter, his previous leading lady. Apparently Bates was never able to regain full stature as a star after this time.

Much of the play's success was also the work of veteran leading man Bruce McRae, nephew of Sir Charles Wyndham. McRae had previously distinguished himself in drama, having appeared in such plays as *Shenandoah, Sherlock*

Holmes, A Doll's House, and *Rosmersholm.* The *New York Times* reported that the "incomparably fine comedy performance" of Bates and McRae enriched *Nobody's Widow* from the beginning.[40]

Hopwood's work was also praised by most critics. The *New York Times* called his writing the freshest in theme since the comedies of Sardou "when they were still fresh."[41] Critics were in general agreement that Hopwood's sparkling and witty dialogue surpassed the plot and structure of the play. The banter arose less from a formula of words than from the effects of the situation on character. Hopwood had attempted a "romantic farce," as he called it, that drew less on physical humor, and more on humor derived from sophisticated characters in improbable situations.

The plot is set around Roxana, an upperclass American, who during a trip abroad, has fallen in love with Mr. Clayton, an Englishman. Roxana has married Clayton, only to discover him kissing another woman the same evening; distraught, she has returned to America at once. In order to save herself from embarrassment, she has told her family that Clayton died of "enlargement of the heart." The action begins with Roxana, in mourning, visiting friends in Palm Beach, Florida. Upon her arrival, Roxana discovers that Clayton, actually the Duke of Moreland, has also accepted an invitation to visit. Complications arise when the Duke, reluctant to keep Roxana's secret about his untimely death, tells her he still loves her, and that his goal for the week is to win back that love. Roxana is adamant in her opposition to his advances, until she receives a telegram informing her that the divorce she had been seeking has been granted. Suddenly, she realizes how much she really loves him. The situation is further complicated when the flirtatious Betty, at whose home the couple is staying, coaxes the Duke to her room for dinner. When Roxana finds them, Moreland pursues her back to her rooms, where he locks himself in. Roxana demands that he leave; she begs and pleads, and calls names, but he refuses. The second act ends with Roxana banging on the locked door as the Duke asks, "What are you going to do about it?" "Do?" Roxana cries, "Marry you — damn you!"

This tag line would seem to be the logical ending of the play, but a third act continues the story through the same complications as the first two. Perhaps Act Three of *Nobody's Widow* is a clear case of what Hopwood later referred to as the necessity for padding a play when the plot cannot sustain three full acts:

> Plays sometimes have to be padded, for they must be of a certain length, and in case the plot isn't big enough to fill up the time, something has to be added. A situation will, oftentimes, fall within certain lines, and will not allow of change without destruction, and if it doesn't offer enough material for the play, the only thing to do is to pad it.[42]

Doubtless, it was playwriting theory like this that eventually led critics to call Hopwood a carpenter in a play factory.

Nobody's Widow, *Act II, Blanche Bates and Bruce McRae, 1910.*

The greatest artistic flaying *Nobody's Widow* must have taken came in moralist-critic William Winter's last book, *The Wallet of Time.* Winter spent four pages lamenting Miss Bates's waste of time and talent in "one of the silliest conglomerations of twaddle and indelicacy with which the trash-ridden Stage of America has been encumbered...."[43] But, what Winter referred to as indelicacy, others called "the apex of drollery, ingenuity, pink innuendo and mezzo-tinted sentiment."[44] *Nobody's Widow* provided the first instance of Hopwood's being labeled as a playwright who "skims over thin ice with a dexterity and sureness of touch that is astonishing."[45] By 1910, Avery Hopwood had found his basic formula of presenting upper-middle-class Americans in compromising situations; for the most part, he would stick with this formula throughout the rest of his career.

Initially, the idea for *Nobody's Widow* had evolved during a dinner conversation Hopwood and Channing Pollock had had about Pollock's theory that farce was really melodrama carried to an extreme. Hopwood couldn't agree, and suggested Pollock try and make a farce from Archibald Gunther's *My Official Wife.* Pollock was so happy with his on-the-spot scenario that he took the idea to the Selwyns, agents for Gunther, who sold Pollock the rights to produce it as a musical comedy, provided no mention be made of the work's origin. Pollock and Rennold Wolf produced their musical version of the play as *The Red Widow,* which ran for an entire season. A year or so later,

In the Sahara with Hopwood (left) and friend, Robert Dempster, 1911.

when Hopwood and Pollock got together for another dinner, Hopwood paid the bill and said: "My last previous meal in your company netted me a fortune. The next day I bought from the Selwyns the right to make a play of *My Official Wife.*" The Selwyns had sold each man rights to the same work, one dramatic and one musical. The extraordinary part of the situation was that both shows played within months of each other, and neither the critics nor the public seem to have noticed the similarities between the two. Actually, Hopwood had changed *My Official Wife* so much in writing *Nobody's Widow,* that he never needed to sign the final contracts giving him the rights.[46]

When Hopwood walked out on to the stage of the Hudson Theatre the opening night of *Nobody's Widow,* accompanied by cries of "Huzza! Hopwood! Huzza!" and clasped the outstretched hand of David Belasco,[47] he made no speech; but, he may have been thinking of more than just the financial rewards ahead:

Dear Archie Bell:

"Nobody's Widow" is a smashing big hit. — We shall play close to $15,000, this week (opening). It is, of course, my biggest success, for I did it alone. The notices you have probably seen, — some of them were quite wonderful, — notably Klauber, in the 'Times';...

I am quite overwhelmed with offers of contracts, but I've not accepted any
of them, & shall not do so, — It is so much better to write for oneself, & to
be a free human being, — Don't you think so? — Well, it is, whether you
think so or not!

Adieu
Avery Hopwood[48]

Hopwood may also have been thinking of the vow he had made several weeks
earlier in Pittsburgh to quit writing plays altogether. A small notice had appeared in the *New York Telegraph* for October 26:

> With "Seven Days," "Judy Forgot" and "Nobody's Widow" to his credit, and
> with the royalties still breaking in through the transom, Avery Hopwood has
> determined to check his mad career of playwriting forthwith. In a few weeks
> Mr. Hopwood will sail for England, where he expects to devote his time to
> blowing cigar smoke scoffing at A.W. Pinero and writing novels.[49]

For Hopwood, 1911 was going to be a time to discover the capitals and out-of-
the-way places of Europe and Northern Africa, the "big story book," as he
called it, and perhaps, gather material for future works.

With royalties pouring in from five companies of *Seven Days,* Marie
Cahill touring *Judy Forgot,* and Blanche Bates still playing *Nobody's Widow,*
Hopwood steamed across the Atlantic in early March 1911 on a combination
business and pleasure trip. In early February he had met with Sir Charles
Wyndham in New York about selling the London production rights to
Nobody's Widow, and also Belasco and Wagenhals and Kemper had commis-
sioned him to view the European theatrical market for them.

On the first part of the trip, Hopwood was accompanied by a college
friend and promising young leading man, Robert Dempster. In all, the trip
took five months, the first six weeks of which were spent sightseeing mainly
in Paris, on the Riviera, and in the Sahara, followed by a visit to Vienna for
the opening of *Seven Days.* By mid–April, Dempster had had to return to the
States to fulfill a stock company contract in Milwaukee. His career as a leading
man was apparently short-lived, however, for one finds him appearing in only
two Broadway productions, *The Road to Yesterday* (1906), and a rather unconvincing Belasco melodrama, *The Case of Becky* (1912), with Francine Starr. According to Hopwood, Dempster was "always more or less engaged to
Marguerite Clark," a dainty popular actress-singer who left the stage early on
for a career in the movies, where, by 1918, her diminutive charm had succeeded
in making her Mary Pickford's closest rival as "America's Sweetheart." Dempster lost her as his sweetheart, however; she married an army officer in 1920 and
left show business for good. Seemingly, Hopwood's friendship with Dempster
was strong, as he was the only person Hopwood bequeathed a personal item
in his will, a "platinum ring set with diamonds and two sapphires." Oddly,

Dressed for the Fête des Fleurs, Nice, 1911.

though, nothing else is heard about Dempster, except for the European sojourn with Hopwood in 1911.

The two young men must have quite enjoyed themselves on their first tour
abroad. *A Theatre Magazine* photo captured them in the Sahara on horseback
peering out from behind their Arab togs, and a hometown cartoon portrayed
Hopwood costumed as he was when the two chums had marched in the Fête
des Fleurs in Nice. Westside Clevelanders, no doubt, followed the exploits of
their "Pierrot" in cerise satin with great interest.[50] In a letter of April 13, the
day after Dempster departed for America, Hopwood wrote Archie Bell
something of what he had been doing; by this time he was in London.

Savoy Hotel
London

Dear Archie Bell: —

Yr last letter was awaiting me when I reached Paris & cheered my heart, in
spite of the weather, which was devilish. — I saw Rejane, in Batailles ne piece
"8 L'Enfant de l'Amour," while I was in the city on the Seine, Rejane was
superb — the play interesting but with speeches miles long — like most of
Batailles plays.

While I was in Vienna, I conferred with Joseph Weinberger, who is to produce "Seven Days" there. It has already had a successful try-out in the
Austrian provinces.

I hd supper the other night with Wyndham. It seems quite definitely settled tht he is to produce "Nobody's Widow" in London some time this
season — he playing the Duke, and Mary Moore Miss Bates' role.

Oh, — Archie, — a manager [Henry W. Savage] has gotten hold of a libretto [*Somewhere Else*] which I was at work on a year ago — & didn't quite
complete — & he wants to produce it! — Oh wurra wurra! I don't want to be
bothered with productions. I'm still novel mad — tho I've not begun work
yet. . . .

I've "gone into chambers", on Endsleigh St., but I don't know for how
long, so address me c/o Am. Express, 6 Haymarket, Pall Mall. . . .

Pat Campbell has a big success in Besier's "Lady Patricia", — It's a
delightful comedy.

Write me soon — all the news.

April 13th–1911   Avery[51]

Before returning to the United States, Hopwood made sure he visited Marienbad, Bohemia, the setting for *Judy Forgot,* where he took the cure, and
reported: "You can imagine my surprise when I found I was apparently as well
known and as welcome as the Prince of Monaco, who was present taking the
baths."[52]

In May, Hopwood reported on his impressions of theatre in London. He
observed that in England actors and actresses were more accepted by the "society folk," and that there was much less "worshipping the personnel" by the
middle classes than in America. He also formed the opinion that the English

stage excelled in its actors rather than its actresses, particularly the "young actresses of emotional temperament." There were many charming comediennes and beautiful women on the stage, but none who gave any promise of attaining the stature of Mrs. Patrick Campbell or Miss Lena Ashwell. He speculated that this lack of female stars might have been the result of actor-managers controlling the stage; playwrights might have consciously or unconsciously written the best parts for them because they had the power to accept or reject their work. The opposite seemed to be true in America, where there were more leading women than men. Here the theatre was controlled by managers who were strictly businessmen and not actors. Their aim was simply to present a popular favorite who would make the most money, man or woman. Ultimately, there was "greater artistic gratification" in plays presented by the actor-managers than by those who were not actors. Perhaps a "blend" of the two systems would be the happiest solution. Hopwood concluded: "I have never seen such perfection of production in all my travels as I have seen in London. Musical comedies are put on with a taste and skill which is delightful."[53] (Hopwood's correspondence mainly refers to the popular theatre, and it is not known to what extent he may have visited any of the art theatres.)

A final letter to Archie Bell, written a month before Hopwood's return to New York, expresses his desire to see and do as much as he could before immersing himself in another rehearsal process:

> c/o American Express
> 6, Haymarket
> Pall Mall,
> London–S.W.

> It was funny Archie, — Yr letter — in which you mentioned the possibility of your joining a Dieppe house party — came just as I was leaving for Dieppe! (and yet people say there is no god!)
>
> I stayed in Dieppe only over night — then went on to Paris which was gloriously springy & spent ten very happy days there. Then I hied myself back to Londres, for a fortnight — & now I am staying at Maidenhead, on the Thames, for the rest of the summer, — with interludes, I hope to go to Paris again, on the 13th for a week or so, — and I'm going to Surrey — & Warwickshire — and about August 15th I shall leave Maidenhead and turn my face toward Venice. On the way I want to visit the Austrian Tyrol. — I'll probably stay in dear old Venezia till the weather breaks, and then — I don't know.
>
> I'm working, Archie, — and playing, too, as much as I can. Maidenhead, as you doubtless know, is a famous river resort. — The Thames is lovely, but rather cramped after the Hudson. One is always running into boats, & people, & swans, & things.
>
> I went to the Coronation — Procession — & enjoyed it in a sleepy fashion, — I had to get up scandalously early. The regatta is on at Henley this week, & we have a regatta of our own on the 15th — but I won't be here for that. We're only 21 miles from London, — & when the weather is bad — which is mainly the case! — I go into town & disport myself there.

It seems a thousand and one years since I saw you. Are you as nice as
ever? — I am much nicer. I am also yr

very gd
friend
July 4th — 1911   Avery[54]

By July, Hopwood's mother had joined him, on what was to be the first of her
many trips abroad. But their visit was cut short. Col. Henry W. Savage had
caught up with Hopwood; his return was announced in the *New York
Dramatic Mirror* on August 9, 1911. Work on *Somewhere Else* was scheduled
to begin.

Within two months, however, much to Hopwood's ire, Col. Savage decided to take a trip around the world in order to collect properties and costumes
for the show, and so postponed the production until the 1912–1913 season.
Hopwood would have another year to complete and rework the piece he had
started several years before. Then, too, the music had to be composed. For this,
Col. Savage hired Gustav Luders, a composer who had worked for him on such
earlier operetta successes as *King Dodo, Woodland,* and *The Prince of Pilsen,*
much in the vogue of, but not as lasting as, *The Merry Widow* or *Babes in
Toyland.*

While work progressed on *Somewhere Else* and possibly other scripts,
Hopwood was beginning to develop a minor reputation as a champion party-
goer. In November 1911, he was invited to a dinner in his honor given by in-
terior decorator William Dodd. Being on a Friday, the affair was announced
as a "fish night," and to add to the festivities, the guests were asked to costume
themselves as marine life. Hopwood's friend Carl Van Vechten, music critic for
the *New York Times,* came dressed as an octopus, and the other guests wore
similar garb. But Hopwood, apparently having forgotten the masquerade,
came impeccably attired in evening clothes. Finding himself in a room that
looked like a giant aquarium, he quickly poured himself a drink and began
weaving and staggering about. When revellers asked what sort of aquatic
creature *he* was supposed to be, he gurgled: "A sponge!"[55]

Hopwood was not always caught unaware. He and "Buddy" Van Vechten,
as Carl was called by his friends in those days, regularly sweet-talked Anna
Pollock, wife of Channing, and press agent for Oscar Hammerstein's company,
into digging through the costume closets of Hammerstein's Victoria Theatre[56]
so that they might go to the season's fancy dress parties tricked out as "the
fairest ones of all." Hopwood had met Van Vechten as early as 1906, Carl having come to New York that September; they had been introduced at a party
hosted by two maiden ladies, Edna Kenton and Mabel Reber, who lived not
far from Carl on Fortieth Street.[57] No doubt the immediate rapport the young
men shared was strengthened by their mutual friendship with the Pollocks,
whom Carl had known in Chicago, and before long the two boys considered
themselves close friends.

Van Vechten, like Hopwood, had come to New York from the Midwest.

Born in Cedar Rapids, Iowa, in 1880, he escaped at nineteen and attended college in Chicago, where he studied with, among others, Professor Vaughn Moody, author of *The Great Divide*. After graduating from the University of Chicago with a specialization in English, he began covering musical activities for the *American;* it was during this time that he became a friend of the Pollocks. In 1906 Van Vechten moved east, and shortly became assistant music critic and later Paris correspondent for the *New York Times*. By 1913, he had established himself as an important opera critic, as well as America's first critic of the dance. His varied and prolific career encompassed dramatic criticism also, and eventually he became known as an essayist, novelist, and jazz enthusiast, receiving credit for helping to generate the Harlem renaissance of the Twenties through his support of black musicians. *Nigger Heaven,* his most serious novel, was instrumental in focusing a new awareness of black culture. An earlier work, the semiautobiographical *Peter Whiffle: His Life and Works,* set in the sophisticated continental world of dillentantism, captured the ennui of a young writer who never could write a book. As Edward Lueders, author of *Carl Van Vechten,* has pointed out, some of the traits exhibited by Peter were undoubtedly based on Hopwood, among other friends of Van Vechten's.[58] Van Vechten's biographer, Bruce Kellner, also associated Hopwood with an earlier character, Sasha Idonsky (Broadwood; Doowpoh), in an unpublished short story entitled "Undecided Sasha," which was eventually reworked and expanded into *Peter Whiffle*.[59] Van Vechten had given Hopwood the Sasha nickname early on, and Hopwood continued to use it throughout his life (spelling it Sacha).

In June 1907, while on a tour to review European opera for the *New York Times,* Van Vechten married his first wife, Ann Snyder. After returning to New York the couple moved into a single first-floor room just behind the Metropolitan Opera House at the Maison Favre where they often entertained opera singers, stage celebrities, newspapermen, musicians, and writers. Hopwood and Pollock frequently attended these delightful afternoons of informal and amusing camaraderie,[60] but within a few years, the party atmosphere began to change. Van Vechten's marriage with Ann became cold and distant. Bored with her role as housewife, and often taking second place to her husband and everyone else in their group, she came to look upon many of Van Vechten's friends with suspicion, particularly Hopwood. The relationship finally reached the breaking point. In an incident Hopwood included in his unpublished novel, he described Van Vechten's scheme to have friends catch him in a hotel room with a Times-Square hooker in order to obtain grounds for a divorce under New York law. After arriving "almost too late,"[61] the friends succeeded in gaining the necessary evidence, and by the end of 1912, Van Vechten and Ann were divorced. A year later, Van Vechten's new love, Fania Marinoff, whom he would soon marry, must have wondered whether Ann's suspicions about Hopwood's influence on Carl had been well founded. In a letter to Mabel Dodge, Van Vechten recounted a recent party:

Fania Marinoff and Carl Van Vechten, photographed by Nicholas Muray, 1920.

We had dinner at the Brevoort and I got very drunk and read . . . out loud to the assembled dining room . . . The Portrait of Mabel Dodge [by Gertrude Stein] and Avery was drunk enough by that time to say he understood it. I went to Evangeline in a terrible condition but it didn't do any good; it was too dull. However, during the course of the piece, Fan and I had a rotten row and she left with authority, nor did I see her again that night. . . . She adjudged my condition to be due to my having seen you and Avery— after all not far wrong. . . . Scenes from the Younger Generation were freely enacted.[62]

Mabel Dodge, writing in her *Intimate Memories,* recalled:

Occasionally [Carl Van Vechten's] Dutch warmth went out in friendships for other men, for he was so full of dear sweet affectionateness that it had to run over. Avery Hopwood, . . . and others, I knew he had been fond of, but Fania he loved then and ever after.[63]

Despite the high life enjoyed by Sacha and Buddy, Fania Marinoff embraced Hopwood as a dear friend after her marriage to Van Vechten, and in later years husband and wife served as his closest confidants.

Through his relationship with the Van Vechtens and Mabel Dodge, Hopwood expanded his circle of acquaintances. He may even have found himself at some of Dodge's famous Wednesday evenings mixing with such disparate types as Walter Lippmann, Edwin Arlington Robinson, Emma Goldman, Margaret Sanger, Amy Lowell, and John Reed. It was through both Mabel Dodge and Van Vechten that Hopwood was eventually introduced to Gertrude Stein and Alice B. Toklas.

Exactly when Hopwood met Stein is not clear, but Van Vechten says "hello" from him in a letter to her as early as 1915, and she herself mentions having known him toward the start of his career. It may be that Stein simply knew *of* him then, because Mabel Dodge's letter of introduction of Hopwood to Stein has been approximately dated by Donald Gallup as early 1923, and Van Vechten, writing in a letter to Stein in February of the same year says: "You probably have seen Avery and I am sending you one or two others later."[64] The introduction Hopwood presented to Stein from Mabel Dodge Sterne, as she was then known, having remarried, was short and cryptic:

Dear Gertrude,

This is to introduce Mr. Avery Hopwood. I don't need to tell you about him & his pursuits because, as usual, you will know more about him in two minutes than I could in two years!

Yours,
Mabel.[65]

Gertrude Stein included a short sketch of Hopwood under the 1907–1914 section of *The Autobiography of Alice B. Toklas*. In it, she recalled that of the many people Van Vechten sent to amuse her, "The first and perhaps the one she liked best was Avery Hopwood. The friendship lasted until Avery's death. . . ."[66] Van Vechten's friendship with him lasted as long, remaining affectionate, if somewhat erratic.[67]

Between the "fish dinner" in late November 1911, and the end of January 1912, Hopwood was reported as seriously ill for a period of five weeks, but he was recovering well by January 23.[68] Shortly after he made a visit to Cleveland, where he spent time recuperating and writing the rough draft for a new comedy. An announcement appeared in the April *Phi Gamma Delta* reporting the completion of a comedy called *The Last Straw*, but nothing else was heard

Gertrude Stein, Carl Van Vechten (self portrait), and Alice B. Toklas, 1935.

about such a title.[69] *The Last Straw* was undoubtedly a preliminary title for a
play which was produced later. In the spring, Hopwood was ready to move
back to his tent at Croton-on-Hudson and finish work on *Somewhere Else*.
Savage had not yet returned from Europe, so rehearsal and production dates
for the show were still undecided. In late spring he wrote to Bell of his uncertain summer plans:

The Lambs
130 West 44th Street

Dear Archie: —

What are you doing? — I'm still at Croton, with my summer plans unformed.
Savage returns from Europe on Saturday, I'll know then when rehearsals of
"Somewhere Else" begin & can proceed accordingly.

    I'm half way thru a new comedy, which looks very good, I've not yet gone
back to work on the other comedy, of which I made a rough draft while I
was in Cleveland, — I'm also working on the long delayed novel. If rehearsals
begin in 8 weeks or so I'll probably stay at Croton most of the summer — tho
I may go to Ogunquit, Maine. — I want to go to Venice, but I'm afraid I can't
make it? [*sic*]

If you come East, be sure to let me know. I'm very well now. — How is yr mother?

Tout a toi
June 12th [1912]   Avery [70]

Hopwood spent the remainder of his summer at Croton, waiting for the start of *Somewhere Else* rehearsals and working on several new projects. An article entitled "The Play-Wrighting Business" appeared in the August issue of *Green Book* under Hopwood's name, but he later confided to Bell that the piece had been "written (entre nous)" by someone who interviewed him. "So," he told Bell, "don't hold it against me . . . if there's anything to hold!" In the interview Hopwood revealed that, aside from working on *Somewhere Else*, he had been preparing a comedy for Wagenhals and Kemper, as well as writing a script for Belasco. In addition to the three plays, Hopwood disclosed that he had begun work on a book. Why?

> The novel is good business if you are established. For instance, before a well-known author has finished a book, the publishers have probably sold fifty thousand copies over the country, and if it isn't a good book, it doesn't die in a night. But if a play is a failure, everybody knows it the next morning.[71]

Towards autumn, however, Hopwood was finding it difficult to write both plays and fiction. Three letters sent to Bell from Croton over the course of the summer show his growing frustration:

> Archie Bell — you bad thing! Why didn't you come see me, when you were East?
> My soul cries out for vengeance! — Meanwhile — isn't it damned hot? . . .
> I'm tiring of the Simple Life, but I'm going to try to stick to it till I finish the things I have under way.

Your warm friend
[July 1912]   AH

Dear Archie: —

Wht will you think when I tell you tht I've practically decided to throw over my playwriting engagements & simply stick to the novel, after all, you see, the trouble is tht when I try to novelize & play write at once, the novel gets pushed aside because there is no necessity to finish it at a certain time, while there *is*, with the plays. "Somewhere Else," of course, will go on, . . . but I think the other plays are doomed. . . .

Write me soon, says
Saturday [August 1912]   Avery H.

Here I am Archie—hard at work—on four new things—work on the novel is progressing—& I'm still playwriting. I find I can't give it up.—I guess I'll have to do both.—I wish I cd juggle the drama & the novel as gracefully as Barrie, Hervieu, et al.

I'd like most awfully to see you Archie. Perhaps I'll strike Cleveland with "Somewhere Else," which, by the way promises to be somewhat amusing. . . . Bt I've no idea that Cleveland will be on its route—& so I'm thinking now of running on for a week, early in November, before rehearsals begin. . . . Croton is heavenly, & my tent is restful, & canoeing & tennis occupy my (very few) unoccupied moments. . . . be gd to yrself—says—

Sunday [September 1912]   Avery[72]

After putting the finishing touches to *Somewhere Else,* Hopwood made a trip to Cleveland in November. No sooner had he arrived, however, than Savage wired him that one of the important characters needed an additional song to make the part more attractive. Unable to work at home, where friends demanded his attention, he took a room at the Whilom Hotel in rural Barberton and wrote out four new verses and a chorus, which he posted to composer Luders.[73] Within a few weeks Hopwood once again found himself caught up in the hectic tempo of rehearsals. He took time to scribble Bell a note and wish him a Merry Christmas:

                                                               Hotel Seymour
Dear Archie:—

Just a line—in a tearing pre-production rush— . . . "Somewhere Else" looks good (Rap on wood)—We open Xmas day, in Utica, but our appearance in Cleveland early in Jan. will practically be our premiere, as it will be the first *Great Big City* that we play.
     Merry Christmas, Archie.

                                                               Yours
                                                               Avery[74]

Hopwood's first inclination to abandon *Somewhere Else* several years earlier had been sound, for it was destined to fail after only eight performances in New York—the shortest run of any of his plays. Against Hopwood's wishes, Savage had gotten hold of the piece from the De Milles, and had doubtless made Hopwood a good financial offer. Savage, who had predominantly produced light operas, saw great possibilities in this musical fantasy. Unfortunately, he should have realized how much audience tastes had changed since his successful production of *The Merry Widow;* perhaps Hopwood had. In any case, Savage's vision for *Somewhere Else* was closer to the old musical extravaganzas one might still have found at the Hippodrome from time to time. Premiere night, January 20, 1913, was apparently one of the most dismal Broadway had witnessed that season. In truth the failure surprised Savage, as well as the rest of the company. Notices along the tryout route had been favorable. After the success the musical had had in Utica and Buffalo, "theatrical wiseacres" were predicting the show would run at least a year in New York. Newspapers had been impressed with the music, the singing, the large orchestra, the diverting story, and the spectacle.

Called "an opera bouffe in two acts," the verse on the title page of the typescript sets the tone:

> "A little nonsense, now and then,
> Is relished by the best of men."
> What here we give is nonsense sure,
> So, if our jests you can't endure,
> The fault is surely yours, for then
> We know you're not the best of men![75]

The setting in Act One is the Palace Garden of the Queen, and Act Two moves into the Playground of the Royal Children. "The time is the present, with inclinations toward The Future. The Place is Somewhere Else." The story that develops in this environment might well be material suitable for the television series *Fantasy Island*. Somewhere Else is a "never-never land" sought by many, but seldom found by any. It is an island where everything is beautiful, and where every wish is granted, providing the pleasure from its granting harms no one. Telephones are already obsolete in Somewhere Else, and exotic creatures like the Mazoopala are man's best friend. Into this paradise sails Billy Gettaway, a 30-year-old widower of a wealthy 65-year-old matron who has left him burdened with her 45-year-old overweight daughter, Hepzibah Dodds. But Billy can't "get away," Hepzibah has hidden aboard his yacht, and a chorus of his ol' college chums have followed along too.

Typical operetta songs entitled "Love at First Sight," "If I Kissed You," and "Forget-Me-Not," carry the thin plot through a series of complications that result in true love for Billy and Queen Mary Seventh; for her daughter, Chloe and Billy's friend, Rocky; and of course, for Hepzibah and the wicked stepuncle of the Queen, Villainus. The college chums, "who are taking a Postgraduate course in Feminology," happily find themselves in the arms of the island nymphs, "who believe that the proper study of Womankind is Man." Much of the stage business, like that in *Judy Forgot,* draws heavily from vaudeville and burlesque. The Second Act Finale, "Moving Pictures," must have been one of the earliest musical numbers to make use of the now timeworn effect of "quivering lighting" to produce the jerky motion of the silent movie chase scene. The *Dramatic Mirror* observed:

> Musically it was up to the best efforts of Gustav Luders, and the company is excellent. But its merits consist chiefly of the colorful effects achieved, the admirable dancing and the audacious costuming, leaving little to the imagination where the female form divine is concerned. The whole is little

better than a picturesque hodgepodge of brilliant effects and beautiful chorus ladies.[76]

Heywood Brown in the *New York Tribune* was less kind when he wrote:

> It is hardly possible to imagine a more profoundly banal assemblage of talk and tunes than are gathered together in Avery Hopwood's and Gustav Luder's *Somewhere Else*. A fantasy? A phantasmagoria.... It is a mistake to think so ill of the popular taste as to offer it anything so elaborately dull as all this.[77]

Variety reported that the sign in front of the Broadway Theatre reading, "Seats selling for *Somewhere Else*," would soon have to be changed to: "Seats selling for *something* else." The gloom of opening night was compounded at about 10:50 p.m. when actress Elene Leska "stopped the action of the already painfully monotonous progression by pausing in the middle of a vocal number and playing most amateurishly a violin solo."[78] The bit evidently required the charm Hazel Dawn had given it in her 1911 hit, *The Pink Lady*.

Two nights before *Somewhere Else* was to be withdrawn, Gustav Luders suffered a stroke and died. His obituary in the *New York Times* reported that "he had been greatly troubled by some of the newspaper criticisms of his latest opera, although the critics generally had praised the music in the piece."[79] The day before, Hopwood had written to Archie Bell:

Hotel Woodstock

Dear Archie:—

Well, "Somewhere Else" goes to the storehouse on Saturday, & I am very tired out, but not unhappy, as I never *did* expect it to succeed.... Well, it's all over now, & I'm going on to new & better things.—I don't believe I shall stay in New York long.—I'm going away to finish up the Wagenhals & Kemper play, which may have a Spring tryout....

Yours—after the battle—

Jan 23rd [1913]   Avery[80]

On January 27, Bell wrote an article for the *Cleveland Plain Dealer* defending Hopwood's situation and explaining the circumstances of the musical's failure. If Hopwood had, indeed, written the libretto to *Somewhere Else* five years earlier in 1908, as Bell explained, it must have been one of his projects during the time he had secluded himself in the Ohio cabin, also working on *This Woman and This Man*. Ironically, a glowing publicity article entitled "The Creator of *Somewhere Else*" appeared in *National Magazine* for March 1913; it was probably intended to keep Hopwood favorably in the public eye. *Somewhere Else* was the last time Hopwood devoted his energy to the libretto and lyrics of a musical comedy until 1920.

The Wagenhals and Kemper comedy that Hopwood had written to Bell about does not appear to have been produced, although a play under his name entitled *Miss Jenny O'Jones* was tried out by William Brady for Grace George in the fall of 1913. Brady may have made arrangements with Wagenhals and Kemper similar to those made when he purchased *Clothes* from them for his wife in 1906. Information on *Miss Jenny O'Jones* is scarce since the play never made it to New York, closing after a short tryout in Springfield, Massachusetts. The sketchy production history of *Jenny O'Jones* suggests that it was another case of a manager wanting to rush a play into performance.

Before working on *Miss Jenny O'Jones,* Hopwood had traveled to England in late winter or early spring to help with a production of *Seven Days* scheduled to tour the provinces. Unfortunately, by the time he arrived, the play had been ruined by bumbling, haggling, and poor playing; the entire process from rehearsal to performance had been a fiasco. Hopwood needed a rest. No sooner had he left England for Venice on the much deserved holiday, however, than a cable arrived form Brady summoning him back to America so they could rush *Jenny O'Jones* into rehearsal. Reluctantly, Hopwood returned. While on a preproduction swing through the Midwest, he wrote Rinehart and Bell from a popular health resort in Southern Indiana. The uncharacteristic four-page typewritten letter to Mary Roberts Rinehart detailing the *Seven Days* bungle has been included in the appendices (Appendix C, letter 1). His typical, hastily scratched note to Bell spoke of *Miss Jenny O'Jones:*

> French Springs Hotel
> French Lick, Indiana
>
> Dear Archie: —
>
> I meant to see you before I left Cleveland, but I went away in a tearing rush — to a very primitive spot in Northern Michigan — & from there I came here, & now, today, am leaving here for New York — where I shall stay till Oct 1st — perhaps later — but I expect to go to Michigan again, at that time. — I am going to New York to try to beg off from an early production of my play with Brady, as I want more time on it. I'm going to endeavor to persuade him to give Miss George a preliminary season in something else.
>
> I'm feeling rested & fit, & eager for something or other — life, I guess! (Archie smiles profoundly!)
>
> Yours in Sulphur,
> Saturday [June 14?] 1913   Avery[81]

A while later, in New York, he filled Bell in on some backstage "dope":

> Hotel Seymour
> Wednesday
>
> Dear Archie: —
>
> I was awfully sorry to learn that you had been laid up, but I suppose by this time the tonsils have ceased from troubling, and Archie's back on the

job? I've induced Brady to postpone the New York premiere of my play, till I can get the last act in shape. I'm going away to Atlantic City or somewhere, to work on it. Also, I have the somewhat difficult task of readjusting things, so that the comedian's role does not swamp the star! Do you get me? This is entirely confidential. And Brady prefers not to have anything published, about the postponement. I insisted on being given more time, because I think the play is a valuable property, and I didn't see any sense in rushing it into New York until things were just as they should be. When I gave him the play to read, I told him I wanted to do a month's more work on it, but he insisted upon putting it into rehearsal immediately. However, I'm having my own way about it—although a trifle belatedly.

Do write me—care of The Lambs. And don't mention anything of what I've told you, for if it got back to Brady, he would be annoyed—and I don't believe in annoying managers.

Your's [*sic*] for health,
Avery[82]

Hopwood's comment about managers should not be interpreted as a lack of spine, but, rather, as evidence of his shrewd business acumen. One newspaper article reported that he was able to stand up for his rights in financial arrangements, and that he negotiated business matters "in a way entirely foreign to other writers of plays."[83] Hopwood had learned show business, and he wasn't about to offend those who kept the wolf from his door. A number of times he publicly defended the role of the commercial theatre manager.[84] A hint of this managerial loyalty may be found in an undated letter written to Channing Pollock concerning, it would appear, whether or not to sue Frederick Belasco, David's brother, and Marcus R. Mayer, for failure to honor a contract to produce *Clothes* at the San Francisco Alcazar Theatre:

Croton-on-Hudson
New York

Dear Channing:—

I've been trying to see you, but y're always out.—I hope you won't feel that I'm a rank deserter, in the Belasco-Mayer "Clothes" affair. I feel, as you do, that we have a perfect right to demand that the contract be fulfilled, or the forfeit paid,—but I also feel, that with matters standing as they do, so far as David Belasco & I are concerned, it wd not be wise for me to enter into litigation with his brother. And it is not merely prudential reasoning, for Mr. Belasco has been exceedingly kind to me, all along, & I know that he wd be apt to consider me ungrateful, if I took any action against his brother, who, as you know, is also his very good friend.

Don't be angry with me,—please—I know that if it hadn't been for you, "Clothes" wdnt have had the stock run which it has enjoyed,—I know that you are one of my best friends, & I one of yr's—so please don't let's quarrel.—I *won't*,—so what can you do about it? . . .

In any other case except this particular one—of *course* I will stand with you, in the matter of collection.

Kindest regards to Mrs. Pollock—and please write & tell me tht you understand.

Faithfully

Sunday [1910?]   Avery Hopwood[85]

After the matter was settled, and the forfeit paid, Hopwood regretted his decision not to support Pollock, and so returned his share of the money to him. Pollock, in turn, sent back the share, and told Hopwood frankly that it had been his "lack of faith" in him that had "hurt" the most; but, he added, the matter had ended long ago, and he concluded by asking Hopwood if he might not spend part of his vacation with him. The cumulative effect of the pressures caused by loyalty to managers, loyalty to friends and family, and loyalty to self was beginning to have an impact on Hopwood's career.

These early frustrations reached a peak in late 1913 with the failure of *Miss Jenny O'Jones*, ten months after the failure of *Somewhere Else*. The circumstances surrounding the failure of *Jenny O'Jones*, however, are not as clear as the reasons for the musical's failure. For one thing, no copy of the script is available, and because the play closed in tryouts, very few news items were released. The only review of the play, appearing in the *Springfield Sunday Republican*, indicates that the story was somewhat reminiscent of *Nobody's Widow*, centering upon the complications that result when a young American girl marries, this time, a *German* Baron, only to discover that he still has interests in "an old flame," Mrs. Allingsby. It is interesting to note that the Allingsby character was listed on the program at the first performance as the Comtesse de Miraball, but Brady, witnessing the final rehearsal, had insisted that the character be assigned a less "continental" name, in order to give the play a more American appeal.[86]

When *Jenny O'Jones* opened the next day, not only did it give the appearance of being half finished, but many of the situations in the piece were thought to create a "suggestion of erotic tension" that was "obvious, gratuitous, and vulgar"; not the kind of farce that should have been "offered for the delectation of a New England audience on the most characteristic of New England holidays"—Thanksgiving.[87] Grace George and several other performers, particularly Julian L'Estrange and William Morris, received favorable notices in the work, but the play was doomed. At the end of the third day in Springfield, Miss George was taken ill and collapsed, and the play never made it to Boston, let alone New York. The columnists reported: "Advices from Springfield say the Hopwood play was entirely unsuitable for Miss George."[88] No letter to Archie Bell exists explaining the failure of the play, as in the case of *Somewhere Else,* and nothing more is heard about it under this title. Hopwood placed it in his storage vaults for use at a later time.

In the first week of January 1914, Hopwood steamed back to Europe to spend a few months in Germany, and to seek refuge from the theatrical grind. Frustrated, he reiterated his vow to quit playwriting in favor of the novel:

> To certain temperaments — and mine is one of them — impatience will result from one definite limitation of the stage, and that limitation is simply one of ideas. When a new idea has become threadbare in the intellectual world, out of which it came, it is ready for the theatre. In the drama popular ideas must be the rule. You have to write for everybody; the ability and eagerness to do this are, of course, fine things. But supposing your interests lie elsewhere? I am just a bit tired of writing for everybody — here throwing a sop of comic relief for one type of person, then another sob of sentimentality for another type, and so on. I want to write what I feel like writing, and if it happens to interest a few persons, why then, if I am writing a novel, no harm is done. Feeling this as strongly as I do, I believe that I should abandon playwriting, at least for some time....[89]

Hopwood wasn't alone in his sentiments about the limitations of writing for the popular theatre. By 1912, the Little Theatre movement in the United States had already begun to support plays not readily accepted by the commercial theatres, the Chicago Little Theatre and the Toy Theatre in Boston being among the most prominent in the new movement. In 1915, the Neighborhood Playhouse and the Washington Square Players would form in New York, as well as the Provincetown Players in Massachusetts. Professor George Pierce Baker had been addressing the issue in his playwriting classes since 1903, and by 1913 had established his influential 47 Workshop at Harvard, attracting such gifted students as S.N. Behrman, Robert Edmond Jones, and Eugene O'Neill. It is curious that Hopwood apparently never aligned himself with any of these groups. He had come from a university environment; but, in light of his own professed motivation for entering the theatre, it is doubtful that he ever considered writing plays for their literacy or artistic merits alone. His earlier attempts at the serious drama had been, of course, commercial failures, and seemingly he had not the temperament, or perhaps the ability, to forgo financial success in order to pursue purely artistic aims. For him, the novel symbolized the only chance for true artistic freedom.

Hopwood leveled the most vehement indictment against his career in playwriting to date in a *Green Book* interview for March 1914 entitled "Why Avery Hopwood Writes Plays," but it may have been masking doubts about his writing abilities in general:

> If I had had my way, I would never have written a play in my life ... It never occurred to me to attempt to become a successful playwright for the mere purpose of writing a successful play ... There was always the one ambition — to write a novel, and I still have a feeling that fiction is a matter that requires more time than I have to give it.[90]

Hopwood wrote plays, he said, in order to accumulate enough money "to permit him the leisure" he felt fiction demanded:

After each of these, particularly the successful plays, which paid a pretty royalty, I have assured myself that I had satisfied my boyhood ambition, that I had earned a little leisure and could afford to become a novelist. In fact, after looking over my bank statements . . . I thought I could afford to take about twenty years, if necessary, to write the novel that seems to have been born in my mind when I was born. I thought, however, that I would take a little journey into the world, see a few places that have appealed to me since childhood. . . .[91]

Whenever Hopwood traveled to one of those places, however, a manager's cable had brought him rushing back to New York to begin rehearsals, and consequently, he never had found the time to begin his novel. Now, it seemed to him, "about all the 'ideas' he had ever talked over with managers had been produced," and it was time to try to start the novel again. "What the novelist has to say to his public he says"; Hopwood told his interviewer, "the playwright must depend upon some actor, engaged by the owner of the production to convey his message for him." But, he added, somewhat ominously, "I am always finding myself outlining a play . . . and of course I may never be able to cure myself of this habit—consequently I shall be getting deeper and deeper into the theatre."[92]

IV
Skating on Thin Ice (1915–1918)

While Hopwood was abroad, apparently making good on his attempt to write a novel, World War I broke out, and his friends and associates lost contact with him for several months. A *New York Telegraph* item reported him missing in the war zone, having been last heard from in Alsace-Lorraine. If, they said, Mr. Hopwood knew "that a succulent assortment of royalties had accumulated in New York," he might put more effort into escaping.[1] Two letters written to Van Vechten before the hostilities began indicate that Hopwood had been enjoying himself:

Grand Hotel Continental
München

Dear Carlo: —

Sacha arrived here last night fresh from a triumphant 5 weeks engagement in Berlin. It is now noon, & Sacha is being unpacked by a valet de chambre, who has just remarked, in very *South* German German, that whoever packed my trunks, did it very badly. Puzzle picture! Find the packer!

Munchen is very merry & bright this being Carnival time. People stray abt at night in strange hired clothes. —I was told, before I came here, that all sorts of immorality flourish here, during Carnival, but I had set my heart on this trip, so I came, nevertheless....

Yours
16ten Feb. [1914]   Tommy[2]

May had found Hopwood in Baden-Baden:

Hotel Regina
Baden-Baden

Buddy dear—

Sacha is growing pink & plump here—taking the water cure, & the goat's milk cure, & all the other cures, —a different one everyday. In the baths, one is supplied with a breech-clout & conspicuously posted abt are signs, to this effect (I translate) "The clothes provided are to be worn during the entire bath, & in such a fashion that they will fulfill the purpose for which they were intended." —Evidently, Baden-Baden is not exactly naive....

72

I'm staying on here a little time more — then to Austria, I think — Vienna — & the Tyrol. I'll write you soon again....

Love to the Fan Fan & ... all my heart to Buddy

[May 19, 1914]   S.[3]

After making it back to America in a rather roundabout way, Hopwood wrote Mary Rinehart to let her know how he was, and to solicit her help in placing some fiction with a publisher:

Hotel Seymour
September 10, 1914

Dear Mrs. Rinehart: —

I just got back from Europe yesterday. I was so glad to hear from you. I was in Germany, when the war broke out, and I was shut up in Baden-Baden for three times Seven Days, and, when I did get out, had a long and difficult trip to Rotterdam. From there I got to London, and sailed, on a slow boat, for Quebec.

About "Seven Days" for Italy. We've sold it once, there, you know. The deMilles did that for us, about three years ago. I'll have to find out from them just what happened. I'll let you know. Then you can tell me what you think we'd better do.

I've almost finished a novel. It has a mystery and a good deal of comedy. What shall I do with it? I mean, principally, about trying to place it with a magazine. Does one send it first to a magazine, and then, later, arrange with a publisher? Or does the publisher arrange for the magazine rights? Will you let me know? And will you tell me — do you submit your fiction always on half-size paper? You see, I am very ignorant.

Greetings to the Doctor, and the boys....

Your's most sincerely,
Hop[4]

(Rinehart, a trained nurse, was married to Stanley M. Rinehart, a prominent tuberculosis specialist; he also served as her manager. Her sons, Stanley, Jr., Frederick, and Alan later became the well-known publishers.)

The novel that Hopwood was about to finish may have been the same one he referred to when he wrote Archie Bell a year later in the summer of 1915: "In the Sept. no of 'The Smart Set' — appearing Aug 15 — you will find a novelette by yours truly — so, you see, I have begun writing fiction at last!"[5] Mrs. Rinehart's advice on how to go about getting the work accepted by a magazine had apparently been helpful. Originally printed as "A Full Honeymoon" in the *Smart Set*, it was copyrighted in late 1915 by John Lane Company and published in book form under the title *Sadie Love*.

The novel, dedicated to his mother, follows the same formula as the romantic farce-comedies Hopwood had been writing, and indeed, he adapted it for the stage almost at once. *Sadie Love*, the play, was being produced in Los Angeles by Oliver Morosco at his Burbank Theatre the same month "A Full Honeymoon" was appearing in the *Smart Set*. By the time the play reached New York on November 29, 1915, the novelization had appeared, and the public had the choice of reading or seeing the piece, on the pattern of today's promotional tactic of "see the movie, read the book." The *New York Times Book Review* commented:

> Both the novel and the play follow the same lines and are the same sort of breezy, irresponsible, gay farce-comedy, full of ingenious and resourceful complication. . . . And it all makes an amusing caricature of the modern attitude toward marriage and divorce.[6]

The novel received no serious critical attention at the time, but Professor Arno Bader, former Hopwood Committee Chairman, has characterized the work as "curiously inept."[7] It is as though the passages between the dialogue are stage directions, rather than developed narrative.

In actuality, what Hopwood had done was to pull his earlier comedy *Miss Jenny O'Jones* out of storage and rework it for fiction and the stage. A comparison of the *Jenny O'Jones* and *Sadie Love* cast lists shows that he restored the character of the Comtesse and changed the German Baron, Von Hanau, to the Italian Prince Luigi Pallavicini, a change no doubt necessitated by the war. The synopsis of *Miss Jenny O'Jones* in the *Springfield Daily Republican* indicates that there was much similarity between the plots of the two plays. Hopwood's one published attempt at fiction found him still "writing for everybody," in a way he knew best.

Sadie Love, in the play, having been widowed and forced to live with her aunt on Long Island, has just married the romantic Italian Prince Luigi Pallavicini. Now, as a Princess, Sadie anticipates a life of adventure. Before the couple can leave on their honeymoon, however, the Prince's previous love, the Comtesse de Mirabold, arrives and insists on having him back. Sadie is furious when she realizes the Prince has married her out of pique towards the Comtesse, and now he is unable to decide which woman he loves more. Sadie and the Prince agree to obtain a divorce, but only after they take an "ostensible honeymoon," so as not to make themselves a complete laughing stock. Doubting that this nuptial trip can remain platonic, the Comtesse demands that she be taken along too. Sadie refuses to accept such an arrangement. But, when Jim Wakeley, a former beau of Sadie's, unexpectedly arrives hoping to rekindle their friendship, she consents to the Comtesse's going along, provided she agrees to including Jim on the trip. Jim has reservations about the plan because he has recently been married himself, and insists he "wouldn't know how to behave." "We *won't* behave," promises Sadie. To complicate this already mixed-up situation, Lillah Wakeley enters in search of her wayward husband, but she too has brought a new interest, the simpleton Mumford Crewe. "Just a moment!" interrupts Sadie, "I must draw the line *somewhere* on this honeymoon! It's getting—much too much! It *was* a Cook's tour—it's become an excursion! If we keep on, it'll be a *National Movement!*"[8] Sadie and Jim demand that the Prince and Lillah give them divorces as soon as possible so that they can get married, but Mrs. Wakeley and Pallavicini, piqued again, refuse to allow the new couple to even leave the house. "Very well!" counters Sadie, grabbing Jim's hand and leading him up the stairs to her bedroom, "We'll be unfaithful to them *here*.... Then [they'll] *have* to divorce us!"[9]

When the second act opens it is discovered, to the relief of many in the audience, that Sadie's Aunt, Mrs. Warrington, has locked Jim and Sadie in separate rooms for the night. Before long, though, the Prince comes to Sadie and, professing his true feeling for her, invites her to sneak away with him and enjoy a private honeymoon aboard the steamer *Santa Anna*. But, just when their confessions of love become ardent, Jim, who has been attempting to escape down a knotted sheet from his room above, stumbles through the French doors of Sadie's room and interrupts them. Sadie departs coyly, leaving the two men to share the room for the night. Later, after learning that the Prince has also made plans to elope with the Comtesse, Sadie invites Jim to a honeymoon cruise on the *Santa Anna*.

Although the typescript at the New York Public Library lacks the third act, Channing Pollock's review of the play in *Green Book Magazine* and the review in the *New York Dramatic Mirror* combine to complete the tale. Sadie and Jim arrive on board the *Santa Anna* posing as the Prince and Princess Pallavicini, and are assigned the stateroom; but, Jim's zestful wooing is cut short when a detective retained by Mrs. Wakeley informs him that he may be in violation of the Mann Act. "'A criminal offense,' exclaims Sadie, 'to take a girl from New Jersey to New York! I should call it an act of charity!'"[10] Soon, however, Sadie's heart flips back to the true Prince, and she insists on Jim's changing to other quarters. Shortly, the *Santa Anna* is halted in the bay as a tug pulls up carrying the Prince and the others, "and after various other complications Pallavicini and Sadie are reconciled. Jim makes up with his wife, and the Comtesse takes a fancy to Mumford Crewe."[11]

During *Sadie Love's* tryout in Los Angeles, Hopwood diligently ironed out some of the play's rough spots and worked on speeding up the production. By the fourth and final week of the run, he had rewritten the entire third act with "fascinating results," reported the *Examiner*. Advertisements exhorted: "lay down the war news—away with the stock market report—arm yourself with laughter." An eminent critic (so the promos boasted) counted 750 "hearty laughs," which figured out to one-tenth of a cent a laugh. Angelinos were reminded that they only needed to pay 25¢—50¢—75¢ tops to see now what New Yorkers were going to have to pay $2.00 to see in less than six weeks. Fair enough? Over 50,000 playgoers thought so, and they kept the seats of the Burbank Theatre filled for the limited run of 41 performances. In the light of this success, Morosco was understandably optimistic that when *Sadie* played

Burbank Theater

Matinee Tomorrow

From Main Street Los Angeles, to Broadway New York, Direct

—— NO WAIT ——

Marjorie Rambeau's Farewell

IN

"SADIE LOVE"

BY AVERY HOPWOOD

She
Goes
Direct
From
Los
Angeles
to
New
York

You Are
Paying
75c
Top Price
For This
Play in
Los Angeles
—Next
Time You
See It You
Will Pay
$2.00
Per Seat

MARJORIE RAMBEAU and PEDRO DE CORDOBA—both will leave for Broadway in this play at the conclusion of its run here.

YOU PAY

25c—50c—75c

to See It Now

New York Will Pay $2.00 to See This
Same Play in Less Than Eight Weeks

"GOOD BYE MARJORIE"

This will be your last chance to see Marjorie Rambeau at the Burbank. She leaves for New York as soon as "Sadie Love" closes its run here.

There's a laugh for every minute of the play.

Broadway, its run there would equal the success of his first major hit, *Peg O'
My Heart*, in 1912, which had run for 603 performances. *Sadie Love* wasn't
destined to enjoy such illustrious success in New York, however, but it was
creating somewhat of a sensation around the country, particularly on the East
Coast.

Sunday theatre columns printed more than one article about the
notorious new farce that Los Angeles critics had called "smart and vastly amusing, but risqué to the verge of naughtiness."[12] Most of the pre–Broadway excitement, though, Hopwood stirred up himself when he outraged various Los
Angeles women's groups in a series of interviews, so appalling were his comments on the nature of women and the appeal of "naughty" plays. He had proclaimed that the "average man [was] cleaner minded than the average
woman."[13] Contending that it was women who demanded "naughty" plays,
not men, he had said:

> Men may laugh at a risqué play or line or situation. Women devour it. The
> reason for this . . . is in the different way of living which men and women
> follow.
> Men's lives are much freer. There are not the same conventions binding
> their actions. They follow their own inclinations more. Whereas women's in-
> clinations and mode of living and loving are frequently hampered and cur-
> tailed by "what the world would say."
> It is this very condition which makes her so interested in the theatrical pro-
> duction which is commonly called "a bit naughty". . .
> Women find an outlet for their pentup lives in the theatre, or perhaps
> they find it in going to church where there is a popular preacher, for the
> church is often as much a dissipation as the theatre.[14]

To another reporter he had said:

> I wanted to write a risqué play, because I think that it appeals to a healthy
> instinct. I refer to the instinct of sex. Prudery and false modesty may pretend
> to be ashamed of that instinct. I'm not. And if men and women came away
> from "Sadie Love" with a certain amount of stimulation, I'm glad of it.[15]

In response to the question "Shouldn't the theatre uplift the public and give
them something constructive?" he had replied:

> The trend of future playbuilding will be toward a much wider field,
> especially in the relations between men and women. There is a great flower-
> ing season to come to the American drama, as there has been in all countries
> after a period of commercial successes. We are getting away from the old
> Puritan ideas and influences. . . . When people become conservative it is not
> because they have learned more, but because they feel less.[16]

Opposite: Marjorie Rambeau and Pedro de Cordoba (top) in Sadie Love, *1915.*

For the moment, "as women decide the fate of the average play, why not write that play which appeals to them?"[17]

The risqué appeal of *Sadie Love* must of course be viewed in the light of 1915 sensibilities, when some women still wore corsets, none had achieved the right to vote, and sex wasn't yet taken for granted. In point of fact, theatregoers might have been more shocked had Hopwood not been persuaded by Morosco to alter the background of the title character when he adapted the novel for the stage.[18] As has been mentioned, the story lines of the two works are basically the same, but the essential difference is that the Sadie of the novel, like Jenny O'Jones, is an ultramodern flapper, whereas the Sadie of the play maneuvers through her escapades under the respectability of widowhood. One might read about a free-spirited ingenue, but to see her operating on the stage is quite a different matter. This compromise, in the opinion of drama critic George Jean Nathan, ironically led to the play's limited success on Broadway, where it opened at the Gaiety November 29, 1915.

The New York production received its severest knocks from Heywood Broun, who called it "a pajama play" that "neither shocks nor stimulates" because the improprieties of the piece "are heavy-footed."[19] He criticized Hopwood for poorly blending elements of farce and romance with ugly results:

> Farce says the world is merry and romance declares that it is beautiful, while Avery Hopwood has invited into his play the divorce laws of New York State, the Mann Act, and seasickness. The divorce law of New York State and the Mann Act are stupid and ugly. Seasickness is ugly, and not one of the three has any business in farce or in romance. . . . Having been allowed to become serious in the middle of a farce, we awake to the fact that the funny parts were merely silly.[20]

The rapid shifting between boisterous farce and amorous romance split the focus of *Sadie Love*, leaving many in the audience confused as to the appropriate response. To the contrary, wrote George Jean Nathan, dramatic editor for the *Smart Set:*

> The notion — it is persistent — that a dramatist cannot succeed in mixing in a single theatrical composition the different dramatic elements is as bovine as it is popular. . . . Why should there not be sentiment in farce, as there is in Hopwood's? Who passed a law against it? . . . The critics, instead of courting progress and infusing new life into the bones of the drama, are forever yelping "You can't do this," "You can't do that," and are so constantly doing their little, if ineffectual best, to keep the theatre in status quo.[21]

The *New York Times* said: "the prime trouble lies in its gross improbability. From first to last its story is altogether too preposterous," however brightly written.[22] *Vogue* and the *Dramatic Mirror* praised Hopwood, however, for his skill at suggesting that he is about to be very "naughty," and then managing to

Labels within illustration: NOBODY'S WIDOW, DANGER, FAIR and WARMER, SADIE LOVE, APROPO, Avery Hopwood's specialty is skating on thin ice.

Avery Hopwood skating on thin ice, 1916. From Herb Roth's sketch for Green Book.

"nullify the suggestion by a surprising exhibition of good taste."[23] The *Theatre* reviewer had just the opposite reaction:

> It is not unusual to ascribe it as a merit when a dramatist manipulates the suggestive in such a way, indirectly and skillfully, that actual immorality is avoided. It is called "skating on thin ice." In this case we do not see any skating or any ice, thin or thick. Some of the incidents are laughable, but most of them are too close to purgatory or worse. What, between the war and the competition of the movies, the stage needs to exercise common sense in what it offers.[24]

This quote is significant in terms of the light the final sentence sheds on some of the causes for the sudden demand that developed for risqué plays during this period. Movies, which were often more daring than any stage play, had been slowly but relentlessly drawing the large popular audience away from the legitimate theatre since 1910. Consequently, in an attempt to regain their lost patrons, producers increasingly turned to fare they felt could compete with the films being presented. This, coupled with higher costs brought about by the war, was making the entertainment business more competitive. Farces, often utilizing stock settings and costumes, could be produced relatively inexpensively, thus keeping ticket prices lower and making them more appealing to the average theatregoer. In this respect, however, Hopwood's plays were often at an advantage. Critics agreed that *Sadie Love*, like Hopwood's plays before it, had been "smartly produced" with a better than average cast; yet, the ticket prices had remained standard.

Morosco had employed a popular West Coast actress for the role of Sadie. Tall and sophisticated in appearance, Marjorie Rambeau had gained attention with her Broadway debut the year before in *So Much for So Much* at the Longacre Theatre. Cast opposite Rambeau in the role of Prince Pallavicini was Pedro de Cordoba, an actor who had established himself acting Shakespeare with the Sothern-Marlowe Company. Critics generally praised his "neat manner of mockery" as the romantic prince, as they did Rambeau's beautiful, authoritative and refined Sadie. Yet significantly, the very qualities most critics praised in Rambeau were considered by Channing Pollock and George Jean Nathan to be counterproductive to the play. Pollock thought the story "might have seemed less implausible had its chief role been entrusted to a less sophisticated" actress, one like Billie Burke, who was noted for her "spoiled, petted, impulsive and impetuous young women."[25] (Jesse Lasky must have thought so too, for he cast Burke as Sadie in his film version three years later.) Nathan, writing under the chapter headed "The Commercial Theatrical Mismanager," in his 1917 book, *Mr. George Jean Nathan Presents*, bluntly struck to the heart of the matter:

> Every commercial manager in the land, including Mr. Morosco, has known from boyhood the ancient theatrical stratagem, of making an audience laugh by placing naughty lines in the mouth of an ingenue who is supposed to be innocently unaware of their import. Yet Mr. Morosco, seeking to tone down the tartness of the Hopwood line and situation, deliberately took a course opposite to that established from time immemorial by the box-office mariners and so obtained a result directly the reverse of that which he sought. With the casting lesson of one farce success after another literally staring him in the face and with the correlated knowledge that such risqué farces as "Baby Mine," "Twin Beds," Mr. Hopwood's own "Fair and Warmer" and so on are best to be sold to an audience with a youthful and guileless-looking little sweetie in the leading role, Mr. Morosco then went a step further and cast the widow with a one-hundred-and-eighty pounder whom, whatever her other merits, still had ceased to believe in Santa Claus at least twenty-seven or twenty-eight years ago. Of course, against these Liverpools, Mr. Hopwood, however good his farce might otherwise be,

could ride but vainly. A playwright's lines must ever fight against the physical personality of the actor reciting them. Flapper dialogue coming from the lips of a grown woman with feet firmly upon the ground becomes not merely unconvincing but entirely silly. The laugh so disappears from the dialogue and its place becomes usurped by unruly speculation as to whether the lady rolls to reduce. A big woman cannot be risqué and funny at the same time.... Imagine ... Ethel Barrymore in "Twin Beds," Sarah Bernhardt in "The Habit of a Lackey" — Marjorie Rambeau in "Sadie Love"![26]

Even though Marjorie Rambeau wasn't the ideal Sadie — P.G. Wodehouse considered her too good for the role in the first place — she went on to score a major hit the next year in *Cheating Cheaters* (1916), followed by several other successes through 1925. But it was in later years as a versatile character actress in films that she distinguished herself, playing, most notably, the wornout floozy, Bella, in *Min and Bill* (1930), the raucous Mamie in *Primrose Path* (1940), and the touching, reminiscing mother opposite Joan Crawford in *Torch Song* (1953) — the latter two roles earning her Academy Award nominations as Best Supporting Actress.

Nathan's contention about successful ingenue casting in risqué farce had, indeed, proven true for Hopwood the month before with the hit opening of his play *Fair and Warmer*. The overwhelming sensation created by the more adroit handling of improprieties in that play by the demure Madge Kennedy in the role of the ingenue had definitely prepared critics and audiences for a very different sort of *Sadie Love*. *Sadie* ran for 80 performances at the Gaiety Theatre, and it earned Hopwood a satisfactory $39,000 in royalties, but this was a mere pittance compared to the $229,000 he was to earn from *Fair and Warmer*.

The successful opening of *Fair and Warmer*, like *Seven Days*, had been crucial to Hopwood's continued career in the playwriting business. He had not scored a clear winner on Broadway since November 1910 and the hit run of *Nobody's Widow*. Producers and critics were awaiting, once more, to see if he really did know how to write plays that could "get over." So, after the curtain had gone down and the reviews had hit the street, he was a happy man again, at least financially. With *Fair and Warmer*, Hopwood had succeeded in breaking his previous pattern of continental-flavored stories by presenting a completely American set of characters in an American setting. Brady's insistence that he Americanize the *Jenny O'Jones/Sadie Love* characters in 1913 had been sound advice since audiences were turning away from Continental types. Had *Sadie Love* retained its American thrust, it may have succeeded by capitalizing on the success of *Fair and Warmer*. Ultimately, however, *Fair and Warmer's* success lay once again in Hopwood's ability to take time-tested vaudeville fare and present it in a fresh and amusing, if not hilarious, way. Following the general pattern of such previous hit bedroom farces as *Baby Mine* and *Twin Beds* by Margaret Mayo, wife of Edgar Selwyn, who produced *Fair and Warmer*, Hopwood's play succeeded in making this Americanized form of French farce a Broadway vogue. "It is a play of the 'Twin Beds' variety," wrote Woollcott, "that is a little better acted, twice as well written, and about four and a half times as amusing."[27]

Essentially, American bedroom farce was a laundered version of the French farce. Following in the tradition of Labiche and Feydeau, American playwrights tailored their situations and characters to suit the morals and sensibilities of their post–Victorian audiences. Consequently, the most successful of the American playwrights of this genre were those who were able to handle "Charlotte" situations with deftness — dancing with impropriety, but never taking her home. Husbands could never really commit adultery, ingenues could never actually be compromised, and risqué situations had better always be explained away in the final moments.

It is significant, however, that *Fair and Warmer* was not originally written as a bedroom farce. First copyrighted in June 1915, under the title *The Mystic Shrine*, the action of all three acts was set in the drawing room of Billy Bartlett's apartment. It was not until the production was on the road that the third act was relocated in the Bartletts' bedroom. Admittedly, a play need not be set in a bedroom to fall into the genre of bedroom farce, but, during this period, the presence of a bed was requisite. A brief description of the plot of *Fair and Warmer* will illustrate the significant change in direction the play ultimately took.

In Act One of *Fair and Warmer*, described in the program as "A play of Temperature and Temperament," Laura Bartlett and an old boyfriend, Phil Evans, begin to rekindle their feelings toward one another after Laura confides in him that Billy, her husband, is "so damned good!" "I thought," says she, "a husband would be an awful, wonderful, beautiful — disturbing creature, who would bring adventure, color, romance into my life!" He hasn't. Although it is 8:30 p.m., Laura and Phil decide to take in the opera and leave Billy to his safe domestic world. What does it matter if they arrive late? They're singing *Siegfried*, and "*Siegfried* always begins before you arrive, and ends after *you* leave."[28] Billy is content to stay at home and entertain Jack and Blanny Wheeler, friends from upstairs, who have just come down for a visit. While Blanny is in another room, Billy learns that Jack has been running off to a club called The Mystic Shrine, which he has been using as a cover for other diversions. Blanny is a dear, sweet wife, but Jack requires more excitement. He leaves for the evening, and the act closes with Billy and Blanny vowing revenge against their wayward spouses.

Act Two finds Blanny and Billy trying to keep awake long enough for their mates to come home and find them in a "compromising" situation. In all naivete, the pair decide to mix themselves something to drink in order to stay alert. Both being inexperienced, they concoct the most amazing drink the stage may have ever seen: whiskey, a good foundation, "makes the world go round"; some Italian Vermouth, French too, "better be safe and put in a little of each"; gin won't do any harm, "the more you put into a cocktail, the more you get out of it, they always say"; a foundation and three stories, what about an attic? Absinthe, "that goes in"; apple brandy, a roof; sherry wine, the paint. "Oh, if that's a cocktail, what must a horse's neck be like?" Wash it down with pink champagne, much milder; add apricot brandy, "that's healthful." Do they make watermelon? "I just love watermelons"; oh well, "here's some peach"; and Creme Yvette, "such lovely violet stuff!" My goodness twelve stories high now. "It's a skyscraper ... it's the Woolworth Building," better have an elevator—Creme de Menthe, "we'll put in a *green* elevator!" And "Oooh! Look at that little fat bottle, 'Forbidden Fruits.'" "That'll make us feel like Adam and Eve"; Adam and Eve—in a skyscraper— with a green elevator!" Shake well. "Now hold your glass."

Needless to say, the two teetotalers are soon seeing double. Before long Billy has passed out on the couch and Blanny has curled up at his feet under the Bearskin rug. The gadabouts, Laura, Phil, and Jack, return in short order, and are aghast to find their innocents *en situation*. Jack demands to know "what happened here tonight with my wife!" "We had a party," Blanny yawns. "Oh, a lovely little party. Lots to eat, and drink—and everything flloating around the room." She extends her arms and "floats" into Billy's embrace. "And every once in a while, Billy would compromise me." "He'd what?" rages Jack. "He'd compromise me," Blanny explains matter-of-factly. "It's something to do—with somebody else's husband!" Gasp. "And then—we went to bed!" What! "Oh. Only for a little while," sighs an angelic Blanny. More gasps. Exclamations of horror and amazement from Laura, calls for divorce from Jack, peels of laughter from Phil, and agonizing cries of dawning realization from Blanny: "Oh Billy! You've ruined me!" "You hear that, Laura," roars the triumphant Billy, "I've ruined that woman!" "Ohhhhh," growls Jack, rushing after Billy. Phil stops Jack. Laura protects Billy. Blanny frozen with fright. Picture holds till the curtain grounds.

These "goings-on" gave the audience plenty to laugh about during Intermission as they smoked their Between The Acts, took refreshment, or powdered their noses. Had they seen *The Mystic Shrine* version in early tryouts, they could have laughed at the same situations in Acts One and Two, but upon returning to their seats, they would have seen a very different Act Three. The essential difference is found in the comic thrust of the two plays. The third act of *Fair and Warmer* revolves around the misunderstanding that ensues when the "hung-over" Billy discovers a remorseful Blanny in his bedroom the next morning; she has come to apologize. But Laura returns, and Blanny is forced to hide under the bed. This predicament is complicated when Laura's movers suddenly arrive on the scene to haul away all of her belongings, including the bed. Jack arrives looking for his missing wife, and as the bed is being torn down with a protesting Billy still in it, Blanny rolls out from under. After much arguing, the play winds down to a conventional end when the Bartletts' maid, Tessie, succeeds in straightening out the entanglements so as to "ensure the future felicity of all before the final curtainfall."[29] This is clearly a third act of the typical rollicking farce of situation, sight gags and all.

The third act of *The Mystic Shrine* derives its humor from a very different thrust. The act begins with Jack joining Laura and Phil in the Bartletts' drawing room to discuss the preceding night. Billy is in the bedroom recovering. Laura informs Jack that she has asked a lawyer, Mr. Anthony Jeavons, to come this morning and help them initiate divorce proceedings. He is an excellent lawyer, boasts Laura. "He has divorced all my friends." Mr. Jeavons soon enters, and begins a series of interviews with each of the concerned parties about just what did happen the night before. As Jeavons interrogates Billy, and then Blanny, he asks questions that satirically point up inconsistencies in the divorce laws of the time. Finally, Jeavons questions Tessie, who, as in *Fair and Warmer*, supplies the answers that bring about the happy ending. Tessie's "obligatory scene" in this instance is much more believable than in *Fair and Warmer*, however, because it grows from the situation rather than serving as an obvious *deus ex machina*.

The Mystic Shrine presents a third act that is not so much a farce as a comedy, principally deriving its humor from dialogue and satire rather than action. A critic for *Harper's Weekly*, interestingly enough, sensed the incongruity of the *Fair and Warmer* third act, or perhaps had heard about the change:

> The first two acts are much the best. In the third the action becomes physical rather than mental. There we have a rapid sequence of hiding under the bed and locking of the bathroom door; both of which proceedings are common to the usual Broadway farce, and far less entertaining than the merry dialogue of the two earlier acts.[30]

Apparently the Selwyns or Hopwood or both felt that the play needed a hard-and-fast finish. One might speculate that Hopwood preferred the original version, but being the astute man of the popular theatre he was, rewrote the last act to insure a success.

The success of *Fair and Warmer* was heightened, critics agreed, by the perfect combination of witty and humorous dialogue, an "admirably" planned plot, "nicely" drawn characters, and an "adroit" interpretation of the subject. In addition, the production enjoyed "the advantage of excellent acting in every part and the utmost care and skill in stage direction."[31] *Fair and Warmer's* merit as a play was evident, wrote Rennold Wolf of the *Morning Telegraph*, because "one of the most competent companies that ever appeared in a play of this class participated."[32]

The cast included veteran comic actors Olive May and Hamilton Revelle in the smaller roles of Tessie and Phillip Evans, Janet Beecher as Laura Bartlett, and Ralph Morgan as Jack. But the stars "who ran away with most of the honors," according to Woollcott, were Madge Kennedy and John Cumberland in the roles of Blanny Wheeler and Billy Bartlett. These two performers had been brought in from their successful run in the farce hit of the previous

Opposite: Madge Kennedy in Fair and Warmer: *a look of devilish innocence, Act II, 1915. Inscribed by Robert McLaughlin, then manager of the Ohio Theatre, Cleveland.*

season, *Twin Beds*. Most of all, however, it was the young Madge Kennedy who brought just the right quality to her character to make the play work. Louis V. De Foe, writing in the *Green Book* said of her:

> Madge Kennedy proves anew that consummate art is involved even in far-cical acting. If her sense of humor were less delicate, if she were not so well aware of the limit beyond which the comic actress must not step without giv-ing offense, the "intoxication scene" which fills an entire act of this vastly amusing little play might easily repel the audiences that night after night enjoy it hugely. As it is, no other actress approaches this clever girl from California in the expression of what, for want of a better term, may be called devilish innocence. . . . The stage at the present time is singularly deficient in ingenues whose predilection lies in the direction of farce, and so Miss Ken-nedy has an open field before her.[33]

In the words of Woollcott: "Mr. Hopwood should mention Miss Kennedy in all his prayers."[34] Madge Kennedy began her professional acting career at the age of 18 in 1910, when she toured with Henry Woodruff in *The Genius*. Prior to her success in *Fair and Warmer*, she had appeared on Broadway in *Little Miss Brown* (1913) and the popular *Twin Beds* (1914). In 1916, Samuel Goldwyn lured her to Hollywood and placed her among his *femme* stars of the silent screen—Geraldine Farrar, Mabel Normand, Mae Marsh, and Pauline Frederick. Kennedy returned to New York in 1920, when she starred in *Cornered*. Leading roles in *Spite Corner* (1922), *Poppy*, opposite W.C. Fields (1923), *Paris Bound* (1927), and *Private Lives*, having succeeded Gertrude Lawrence (1931) followed. Madge Kennedy's last stage appearance was in Ruth Gordon's *A Very Rich Woman* (1965). Her later film career included character roles in *The Rains of Ranchipur*, *Lust for Life*, *They Shoot Horses, Don't They?* and *The Day of the Locust*.

The key to Madge Kennedy's success in *Fair and Warmer* and, indeed, Hopwood's, was in the clever handling of the second act. As Miss Kennedy recalled in an interview with the author:

> I tell you, I think I was very deft. Really pretty snazzy about the whole thing. Blanny wasn't a bad girl, she was innocent. You know, half the time I didn't know what they were laughing at, I really didn't. I didn't know sometimes how funny those lines were.[35]

Further evidence of Miss Kennedy's personal charm in the role may be found in her recollection of rehearsing the many girls who were to take the show on the road: "They had I don't know how many companies. And because I have a foot that turns in, all those girls had to imitate that. Wasn't that crazy?" Clearly, Madge Kennedy's particular attributes and personality had captured the character of Blanny Wheeler implicitly. What was crazy was that the managers thought all those girls could capture that charm by merely a turn of the foot.

When Selwyn and Company tried out *Fair and Warmer* at the Apollo

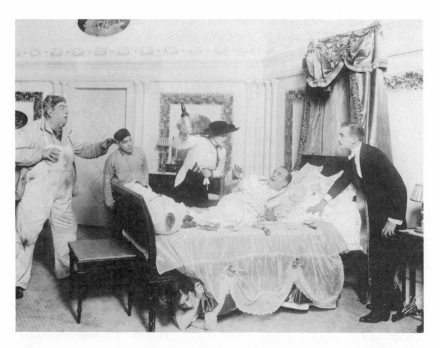

Fair and Warmer, *Act III, Robert Fisher, Harry Lorraine, Janet Beecher, John Cumberland, Ralph Morgan; Madge Kennedy peeks from under the bed, 1915.*

Theatre, Atlantic City, on July 5, 1915, it was still entitled *The Mystic Shrine.* Miss Kennedy did not recall when the play changed titles, and it may be that titles were never discussed with the company (for a short time, the play was even billed as *The Morning After*). *The Mystic Shrine* promptbook shows what appears to be Hopwood's printed insertion of what was to become the title line of the revised version:

> BLANNY. I think I'll stay for a few minutes and have a little talk with Mr. Bartlett.
> JACK. *Oh! good idea. He'll entertain you.* — don't lie awake for me tonight. I'm afraid I'll be late. I think it's going to be a strenuous initiation. *Good night Billy. Don't keep Blanny up too late.*
> BILLY. *(Reading from Paper)* FAIRER & WARMER TOMORROW *(sigh)*[36]

During the Atlantic City tryouts, Madge Kennedy and John Cumberland headed the cast, but Janet Beecher's role (Laura) was being played by Lucille Watson. Before the play reached its final tryouts in Syracuse and Buffalo in October, the supporting roles played by Ferdinand Godshalk and John Westley were recast with Ralph Morgan and Hamilton Revelle.

By all accounts, the play met with great success all along the tryout route. Premiere night in Syracuse proved to be a particularly joyous occasion for

Hopwood when his Phi Gamma Delta brothers from the local chapter at Syracuse University massed in the lobby and formed a chanting procession down the aisles of the theatre. In an interview shortly after the incident, Hopwood spoke of the boost his fellow Fijis often gave him:

> They came in New Haven once, and once in Columbus, Ohio, and both times they gave me such a welcome that it almost stopped the piece. . . . Yes, I'm proud of the fact that they come — it's one of the nicest things that happen [sic] to me. I felt pretty sure they'd be here tonight. . . . In fact, I think I'd be superstitious enough to fear for the fate of the play if it didn't open with the Phi Gamma Delta boys in the audience.[37]

After opening in New York City election night, November 6, 1915, at the Eltinge Theatre on Forty-second Street, *Fair and Warmer* continued its run until July 1916, when it was moved to the larger Sam Harris Theatre two doors down. There, despite Madge Kennedy's short absence for an appendectomy, the play continued its successful 377 performances, finally closing after a brief stint in Brooklyn. Between 1916 and 1920 there were an unprecedented nine road companies of *Fair and Warmer* touring the country,[38] the first of which was headed by Francine Larrimore, Miss Kennedy's understudy, and John Cumberland, who together scored a big success in Chicago. (Ruth Gordon, who played Blanny in the third company throughout the Midwest, gives a full and entertaining account of her experiences with the show in her autobiography, *My Side*.) On May 14, 1918, the play opened in London, where it ran an overwhelming 497 performances at the Prince of Wales's with Fay Compton in the lead.[39] A year later, Screen Classics, Inc., signed May Allison to play Blanny in the film version, which also scored a hit. *Fair and Warmer* had unquestionably established Avery Hopwood as America's most popular and adept writer of risqué farce comedy.

Earlier in 1915, when Hopwood was finalizing publication of "A Full Honeymoon," as well as working on *Fair and Warmer*, he and Mary Roberts Rinehart had been awaiting the results of another English production of *Seven Days*. In January, London theater manager Ernest Mayer had cabled Hopwood and offered him and Rinehart rather standard terms to produce the play, despite the earlier James Welch fiasco in the provinces. Hopwood wrote Rinehart:

> It seems to me that we had better accept Mayer's offer, for I am certain that it is the only chance we will ever have to get the play done in London. You known how managers are — if a play is supposed to have failed, they won't touch it with a six foot pole. So, if Mayer wants to do the play, I think we ought to let him. The terms are not opulent, but the war does make a difference, and anyhow, anything that we get out of the play in England will be "velvet" pure and simple, after the Welch contretemps.[40]

A reply from Rinehart's husband informed Hopwood that Mrs. Rinehart had sailed for Europe and was presently in England; she was about to cover the war for the *Saturday Evening Post*. Hopwood wrote to her again, and encouraged her to visit Mayer, and, should the *Seven Days* proposition go through, to oversee some of the rehearsals to make certain everything was done right this time. A sudden and disturbing realization prompted him to write yet another letter the next day — he had forgotten to inform Rinehart that he had gone ahead and accepted the terms without her approval:

> I thought you would probably feel much as I did about the matter. But now I wonder if I ought to have waited, till I heard from you. Let me know how you regard the transaction. Of course, it may not go through, but I have a feeling that it will. If I have acted wrongly, scold me, or sue me, or do whatever is proper under the circumstances.
>
> In the event that the play really *is* produced in London, I shall have to sit on myself here, to prevent my sailing, for the rehearsals.⁴¹

After a short postponement of the production by Mayer, the play opened around the first of March. Two weeks went by, and still no word arrived about the success or failure of the play. Hopwood wrote to Rinehart, Mayer "has preserved a silence which I am inclined to construe as ominous."⁴² In the meantime, he cashed the £25 advance and told Rinehart that he would soon forward her "share of the pelf," an amount of $59.87. Mayer finally broke his "ominous" silence at the end of the month, and Hopwood sent the report of another *Seven Days* failure in England to Rinehart:

> The Royalton
> 44 West Forty-Fourth St.
>
> Dear Mrs. Rinehart: —
>
> I send, under separate (fumigated) cover, the London notices of "7 Days". — I take particular exception to the one which calmly states that the play was written by two ladies. I am not at all sure that I am a gentleman, but I *did* think it was generally admitted that I am *not* a lady.
>
> As a result of these clippings, I have suddenly become violently pro–German, & the quicker the Kaiser blows up London — (Censored!)
>
> With greetings to the Doctor & to you — Hop
>
> [Late March 1915]⁴³

Unfortunately, the clippings Hopwood passed on to Rinehart have been lost, but Mayer's letter stating his opinion of why the play was "a pretty bad failure" has survived. He reported that the first night's reception, both in Birmingham and London, had been respectable, although not exactly enthusiastic. "Still," he wrote, "there was no booing, which was something to be thankful for." The press had shredded the production, however, and business as a result had fallen off abruptly. The week's London performances couldn't yield more than about £150 to £200 total. Actually, Mayer felt the performance had been "quite sound," certainly much better than the previous attempt to produce it. But, he noted, the biggest disappointment in the current production had been Lottie Venne in the role of Aunt Selina; she simply "did not justify her position as a star." In the final analysis, Mayer felt that the play could only have succeeded if an American company whose temperaments better suited the piece had acted it:

> The production was quite adequate, but it confirmed what I and the producer felt from the beginning, that this play could only have been a success if it had been acted by an American company. It wants that streak of grotesqueness running through it which American artists, whatever other failings they may have, cerainly have got, and I honestly do not think that even if a better English company had been engaged, the play could have succeeded.[44]

This appears to have been the end of *Seven Days* in England.

A successful London production of the play might have been profitable, but Hopwood and Rinehart had to reconcile themselves to enjoying the $110,000 the piece had earned in America and on the Continent. To Hopwood, the shared royalties of *Seven Days* must have seemed scant when compared with the quarter of a million he would be earning from his own *Fair and Warmer;* this money, along with the change gathered from *Sadie Love's* shorter run, had made 1915 a good year. It was time for a holiday.

Avoiding the war zone, Hopwood left for the Mediterranean just after the first of the year:

> Well, Archie boy—here I am—bound for furrin parts.—I went rather unexpectedly—sooner than I anticipated—and in my usual mad rush.—I'm bound for the Riviera—& Tunis—& Algiers—& Italy—and—and—Oh, it makes me woozy to think of it.—
>
> Do write me when you feel the impulse—& *do* feel it! I love to hear from you, Archie—because you *are* Archie—& because you know how to write![45]

A May 1916 snapshot from *Green Book* shows Hopwood smartly dressed in blazer and white trousers, hand on hip and smiling broadly under the palms at Nice, enjoying the benefits of his continuing prosperity. He had now established his pattern of rehearsing his plays in early spring and summer, and then, shortly after they had opened, of heading off to Europe, Northern Africa, or the Orient for the winter, often making countless side-trips back to the Midwest when time permitted.

After returning to the States in the spring of 1916, Hopwood wrote Bell

Piermont, New York

Dear Archie: —

I was simply delighted to hear from you, and to learn that you were back
to the U.S.A. again. Everytime I got one of your post-cards, I had such an
acute attack of home-sickness for the Far East that, if I hadn't been tied up
with my new play, I think I'd have packed up and started out for China or
somewhere.

The play, by the way, is almost finished. I think I will call it "Our Little
Wife". It opens in Detroit October 9th, and comes to New York soon after.
Margaret Illington, Walter Jones, and C. Aubrey Smith head the cast. The
Selwyns are producing it.

I've had a house, at Piermont, on the West Shore of the Hudson, since
early spring, and expect to be here until early Autumn. . . . It's really a charming old place, with fourteen acres of ground, and flowers and vegetables
and things. And Archie, I have a monkey, named Pep-Squeak, and I'm very
anxious for you to meet him. So do come to New York, and come up and
see me. . . . And be sure to tell me why you pick out Japan for my trip. I
thought China was more interesting. But I'll go wherever you say!
A riverderci [*sic*], as we say in Venice.

Avery

Doris Keane expects to produce "Nobody's Widow" in London, January.
"Fair and Warmer" has also been sold for London, and will probably be done
there about next April. It is to be played in Madrid, too, around the same
time.[46]

Our Little Wife, like *Fair and Warmer*, avoided the use of "Continental"
characters and focused on upper-middle-class New Yorkers. The plot centers
on the misunderstandings that result from Dodo Warren's "polyandrous" inclinations. Herb, Dodo's husband, seeks the aid of Bobo Brown, a friend who
has just returned from a trip to China, in discovering if Dodo's flirtations with
other men might actually be amours. Dodo loves Herb, but she just can't give
up having her previous "Tame Cats," as she calls them, regularly come to visit.
She flirts with Tommy, a young poet, and her handsome physician, Dr. Elliott,
until Herb can no longer bear sharing what he regards as "our little wife."
When Herb asks for Bobo's help in tempting his wife, Bobo refuses: "I couldn't
make love to your wife! I go slow and I don't go far!" Don't worry, says Herb,
"Dodo will supply the speed." Despite Bobo's engagement to Herb's niece,
Angie, he agrees to go along with the plan. Unaware of Bobo's recent engagement, Dodo immediately begins to flirt with him. After Herb leaves the room,
in an exchange some critics said was representative of the show's poor taste,
Dodo takes Bobo's hand and tells him: "Everyone has a vibration! But yours
is unusual . . . You positively radiate strength . . . I can feel your hidden
power." Flattered, Bobo replies: "Where do you feel that?"[47] Not to go too far,
however, Dodo quickly lets Bobo know that she is not a "bad" woman. She

would never accept an invitation to his bachelor apartment for a late night dinner — the invitation, of course, being part of his agreement with Herb to test Dodo.

Dodo leaves, and Bobo informs Herb, who has been waiting in the other room, that his wife has remained true; she has refused to dine with him. The situation is complicated, however, when Angie arrives and Bobo invites her to his apartment for dinner. She accepts; but Dodo, who has overheard their conversation, decides to break in on the party in order to protect Angie from so forward a young man. Further misunderstandings arise when Tommy, Dodo's poet friend, tells Herb that she is actually going to Bobo's. Meanwhile, Fanny Elliott, the jealous wife of the doctor who has been attending Dodo, arrives and presents a love poem she believes Dodo has written to her husband. Learning of Dodo's plans for a late-night rendezvous at an apartment, and suspecting that her husband has been maintaining a secret flat, Fanny determines to expose the shameless couple.

Act Two of the play, set in Bobo's apartment, begins with an amusing scene between Bobo and his French valet, who has prepared a perfect meal for "young lovers." It is a scene which, like other choice situations in Hopwood farces, George Jean Nathan writes, "has been bodily appropriated by him from the work of this and that European writer."[48] The remaining incidents of the act involve much door slamming as the respective characters show up one after the other and are forced to hide or escape so as not to be discovered by the other parties. Just when everything begins to settle down in Act Three, however, Dodo, who has agreed to behave herself, starts to flirt with the lawyer Herb has called in to consult about a divorce. When Dodo invites her new "Tame Cat" to join them for a picnic along the Hudson, Herb throws his arms up in exasperation.

Aside from criticizing Hopwood's proclivity for borrowing farce situations from others, a situation common among the writers of the genre, Nathan was of the opinion that *Our Little Wife* was the playwright's best work to date. Unlike other drama critics, who were critical of the play's less delicate qualities, Nathan praised Hopwood for having "a quick eye to the crazy-quilt of sex humours and a keen vision to the foibles of the cosmopolite." If, Nathan concluded, Hopwood were able to "abjure the puritanical Anglo-Saxon pettinesses that in time seem to assail the writers for our American stage," he would be "headed for high farce estate."[49]

Nathan paid Hopwood more critical attention than any other drama critic of the period. Originally working for the *New York Herald*, Nathan set about the task of improving the American theatre by introducing the plays of Ibsen, Shaw, Hauptmann, and Strindberg through his commentaries on the theatre. Fighting for the drama of ideas, he also encouraged Eugene O'Neill by publishing his early plays in the *Smart Set* magazine, which he edited with H.L. Mencken.[50] This same magazine, which also presented the works of James Joyce, Wedekind, Molnar, and Brieux, among others, had, it will be remembered, printed Hopwood's "A Full Honeymoon" *(Sadie Love)*. Never listing Hopwood among the so-called "hack" writers like Winchell Smith, Augustus Thomas, or Mark Swan, to name a few, Nathan placed him alongside Langdon Mitchell, Eleanor Gates, and the young Eugene O'Neill as attempting to rid American drama of its "strident, half-cooked, credulous, unlearned and egregious" ideas that so epitomized "mob America's view of art and letters."[51] But, if Nathan's estimation of Hopwood was encouraging in the beginning, it was not always consistent.

Criticizing Hopwood for "working in a stiff and flinty language," but nonetheless skating over thin ice more gracefully than others, Nathan later praised him for excelling in his "high cunning in the writing of naughty English, [and] for his happy knack of selecting precisely the proper word for precisely the improper place."[52] In short, Nathan observed, "Hopwood knows how to write this risqué English because, first, he knows how to write English," unlike "his Broadway farce-making competitors. . . ." Where most of the "sweating Broadway farce heavers" labored to produce laughs by combining jokes, Hopwood was able "to get a triple laugh by the much simpler expedient of selecting carefully a single peppery, appropriate verb."[53] For this reason, Nathan placed Hopwood on a level with the most prominent French farceurs, and compared him to the young Sacha Guitry in particular:

> There is always a cosmopolitan twinkle of eye, a gay phrase, an amusing — if, in truth, entirely superficial — hitting on this or that human idiosyncrasy. Taking his farce writing by and large, I suppose he intrinsically resembles the young Guitry more than he resembles any other Continental. Like Guitry, his comment on life is most frequently negligible; and like Guitry, his satiric sense, if he has such sense, remains largely invisible; but like Guitry, too, he can take a sheet of gay tissue paper and with a fancy adroitness twist it into an exceptionally jocund foolscap. . . . And he is the only man writing risqué farce in America whose work has any finish, any style, or any metropolitan flavour.[54]

Hopwood did not particularly agree with those who complimented him by comparing his work with the French. When in Detroit for the tryout of *Our Little Wife,* he spoke to the press "About the Doubtful Compliment of Calling American Farce 'Good as the French.'" Hesitating to discuss farce at all, he said most of his plays had started out as comedies, but that the public and critics had called them farces. "The truth is," he continued, "there is no clear line between the two forms in this country. Comedy and farce slide into each other, . . . You see abroad there is a clear line drawn between farce and comedy." The French saved wit, social-observation, characterization, and new situations for their comedy, whereas their farce was so tied down with convention that it was becoming stale. American writers were not concerned with these traditions, and consequently were presenting a subtler, more varied form of farce that attempted to emphasize characters over situation. At least this was his aim. For these reasons, he was frequently annoyed when critics compared his plays with the coarser French farces.[55] Nathan agreed with Hopwood in this respect:

"If anything," he wrote, "Hopwood writes his risqué farces with the two-fold delicacy of a Frenchman." Nathan continued,

> "Our Little Wife," were it rewritten or adapted by a Frenchman for the Paris stage, would be deleted of its present delicacy and made as dirty as a wash-stand in a sleeper on the Southern Railway.[56]

Perhaps Hopwood had striven for a subtler form of farce-comedy, as evidenced by his original third act of *Fair and Warmer,* but the plays that follow show that he had given up whatever aspirations he might have held along those lines. At the moment, Hopwood was trapped among those who praised him for freeing "the American theatre from the nasty French farce," those who condemned him for copying the nasty French farce, and those who chided him for laundering the nasty French farce. It might have been best had Hopwood heeded the advice given him by a writer for *Vanity Fair* who commented on *Our Little Wife:*

> Avery Hopwood is in the unfortunate position of having to top *"Fair and Warmer"* every time he writes a racy farce. He would be a wiser man if he steadied the public with a melodrama or a tragedy or something before he took up farce-writing again. His trouble is that he insists on writing pieces of the same *genre* as that triumphant success, and it is impossible not to be disappointed when they suffer in comparison. There was an elusive quality about "Fair and Warmer" — its name was Madge Kennedy — which he was not able to recapture in "Sadie Love" and misses considerably over a mile and a half in his present play. Margaret Illington is not the right heroine for a Hopwood farce. She smiles bravely, but she is not happy in the part of *Dodo Warren*, the maintainer of tame cats.[57]

Margaret Illington, once married to Daniel Frohman, had first appeared on the stage in 1900 as Michel in *The Pride of Jennico* for Augustin Daly, later playing Juliet for his company in Los Angeles. Between 1903 and 1916, she acted in many of the popular melodramas, both in New York and in regional stock companies. An "uncommonly handsome" actress, who could "bring undeniable dynamic force to the thunderous emotional roles," the *New York Times* called her "our most tear-stained actress."[58] Her attempt at a farce role, like Blanche Bates' in *Nobody's Widow,* had been designed to broaden her appeal; but, as Dodo, she was "never sufficiently alluring, never the outrageous flirt that the author intended."[59] Closer in type to Marjorie Rambeau, who had missed the mark in *Sadie Love,* Illington was not able to keep *Our Little Wife* running past 41 performances.

Samuel Goldwyn, who filmed *Our Little Wife* two years later, had considerably greater success with the piece when he engaged Madge Kennedy, the "ideal" Hopwood heroine, to play Dodo. Certainly Illington's apparent unsuitability in the characterization was not the only reason for the farce's limited run, but this reaction of the critics serves to underscore the fact that farce, more than any other form of drama perhaps, is rarely able to rise above its performers. Since farce has little literary value, and makes no significant attempt to comment on life in any lasting way, the performers must be well suited to, and masterful in, putting over the only value the form has to offer — entertainment.

It is not known what Hopwood thought about the consensus that Margaret Illington was wrong for the character of Dodo, but it may be assumed that he shared the opinion of his friend, Carl Van Vechten, who wrote a short piece about Hopwood in his book *The Merry-Go-Round,* and mentioned the failures of *Sadie Love* and *Our Little Wife:* "An utterly absurd allotment of actors . . . and the heavy hand of an uncomprehending stage director . . . played havoc with the delicate texture of his fabric."[60] Countless playwrights have felt that their plays have been ruined under similar circumstances, but this hazard of commercial theatre must have been an increasing frustration for Hopwood. In an interview shortly after *Our Little Wife* opened in New York, he declared that his experience in playwriting led him to believe "that the author is not exactly sure what his play is going to be until the manager produces it and the critics have got through with their portion of the work."[61]

Autumn 1916 found Hopwood exercising some control over a production. Oliver Morosco had written him in September attempting to exercise the English rights to *Sadie Love,* which he thought Hopwood had given him during a conversation on a train trip to Washington, D.C. Hopwood may have publicly defended theatre managers, but he didn't allow them to coerce him:

Piermont, New York
October 18, 1916

Oliver Morosco, Esq.,
Tilden Bldg.,
New York City.

Dear Mr. Morosco: —

I am in receipt of your letter, in regard to the English rights of "Sadie Love." I think that you must be mistaken about my having given you these rights on the way to Washington, as I've never been in Washington. Besides, it was not necessary to give you the rights, as you had a sixty days option on them, under your contract. You did not exercise the option, so I thought that you were no longer interested. And, as a contract was not drawn up for the English rights, the option lapsed.

However, if you should wish, at some future time, to produce the play in England, I would be glad to take the matter up with you. But I do not think that "Sadie Love" ought to be done in London until theatrical conditions there have improved. And until they have, I would be unwilling to consider any proposition for England.

Your's most sincerely,
Avery Hopwood[62]

Morosco answered the next day by admitting Hopwood was half right in one respect; the agreement had not been made on the way to Washington, but on the way to Wilkes-Barre. However, Morosco did agree with Hopwood that the play should not be produced until war tax and income tax and "other things" had become more settled. He hoped Hopwood might stop in the office some time so that they could discuss the matter further. It was this kind of shrewd business dealing that added to Hopwood's success in the commercial theatre.

Shortly after the opening of *Our Little Wife,* Hopwood headed for Cleveland and then Chicago, where *Fair and Warmer* was in its sixth month at the Cort Theatre. While in his hometown, the *Plain Dealer* ran an article about him entitled "Erstwhile Clevelander Keeps Far Away From 'Gay Life' — Except in Plays." Hopwood's outwardly retiring manner had people asking where he got his "inspiration" for the "near-naughty" farces he concocted:

> In private life, he is one of the quietest, most reserved writers for the theatre in America, . . . and if ever he spouted an epigram or ever said a clever thing to a friend . . . it is yet to be recorded.[63]

Hometowners still pictured Hopwood as the young man with the "amen expression" who had headed for Michigan with the "avowed intention of becoming a minister of the gospel." Evidently, they hadn't heard him admit: "It gradually dawned on me that to become a clergyman I had to believe in things, so I gave up the idea."[64] Writing to Miss Ettie Stettheimer, one of three sisters he had met in Germany before the war and to whom the arts and literature were of vital importance,[65] he expressed a similar skeptical view towards life:

> I admired yr philosophic aspect in yr Thesis, — inspite of the fact that "The Will to Believe" has always represented for me, the Jumping Off-Place, for the reason — I've never been able to jump.[66]

Rather than jump, he might escape. While in Chicago, visiting the *Fair and Warmer* company, he wrote Archie Bell of his latest travel plans:

Hotel La Salle

Dear Archie: —

I shall be here until about Thursday noon of this week, . . . and now Archie — l-i-s-t-e-n — I'm sailing, Dec. 28 from Vancouver for Japan — on the "Empress of Asia," — I expect to go to China too — and *so* — if there's *any* information you can give me abt those two countries, I wish you'd send it to me here, special delivery — or to the boat. . . . Please don't tell anyone that I'm going until after Xmas, as I don't intend to tell my mother until then. I wish that yr "China" book were out now! Best to Archie.

Avery[67]

At Vancouver, Hopwood penned Bell a thank you for the information that was awaiting him:

Archie dear, you have the real touch, which only aptitude & enthusiasm can give, & I'm so glad that y're finding the opportunity to delight others, with yr narrative of the things & places & peoples that have delighted *you*.[68]

Two days before Hopwood sailed for the Orient, Rennold Wolf, writing in the *New York Telegraph,* announced: "Avery Hopwood to Globe-Trot and Produce Play in London."[69] It was Hopwood's plan to finish his China trip in Manchuria, where he would take the Trans-Siberian to Petrograd and Moscow and then go on to England for the *Fair and Warmer* production; but, as he informed Mary Rinehart at a stopover in Honolulu:

As you see, I did not go any of the places that I expected to. The production of "Fair and Warmer" was postponed until Spring, and, as I found myself feeling more and more rocky, I decided to come out here for a few weeks, and get in better shape, for whatever work lies ahead of me. I expect to return in March, and shall probably go to England soon after, if they want me.[70]

Although Hopwood regained enough strength to continue his journey to the Far East, he never did make it to London for the *Fair and Warmer* production. Shortly after arriving in Shanghai, he was overtaken by an illness that was quickly diagnosed as smallpox, which may have been the cause of the rockiness he had been experiencing earlier. Placed in a detention hospital for six weeks, he returned to New York about May 12, 1917, "having recovered without showing any facial marks of the disease."[71] During the filming of *Our Little Wife* in 1918, Miss Kennedy recalled that Hopwood frequently mentioned his experiences in the quarantine hospital, and said that he hoped the handsome young man with whom he shared a room had recovered without scars as well.

By June, Hopwood was back at his summer house in Piermont, New York, regaining his strength and planning new projects. He wrote to Mary Rinehart about one of her new novels that she had recently sold to the movies:

June 24, 1917

Dear Mrs. Rinehart: —

Why, Oh Why, did you put "Bab" into the movies? I have been in the Orient, and I didn't know that Bab existed, until a manager sent me the book, the other day, because he thought it would make a good play. It would, and it's deliciously amusing. And you had to go and let them make a fillum of it! O tempora! o mores!

The manager was John D. Williams, late of the Frohman forces, and the producer of "Our Betters", "Justice" and "Erstwhile Susan." He did not know that the book was being turned into a moving picture, and, oddly enough, he had thought of Marguerite Clark for the part of "Bab" — And now I read that she is the Bab of the picture.

Williams, though, somewhat jolted by the news, was optimistic enough to think that the picture would not hurt a play based on the same story.

I'm not so sure. What do you think? Are you making a play of it—or is anybody else?

Greetings to you and the Doctor and the boys. And thanks for "Bab". When I read about Carter watching Bab, and looking exactly like a cat, and how "If he had taken his hand in it's [*sic*] white glove and washed his face with it, I wouldn't have been surprised"—when I read that, in the Hudson Tube, I almost *died!*

Sincerely your's
Avery Hopwood

P.S. Of course, it wasn't the tube that did it! P.S. again.—If you want "Bab" dramatized, would you like to do it with me—maybe—perhaps? If you think the movie won't hurt it.[72]

Rinehart dictated an immediate response to Hopwood in which she told him that in spite of "Bab" being in the movies she still thought it was possible for the stage. The book had proven so popular that letters were pouring in daily about the character she had created, and movie audiences were so different, she felt, from theatre patrons, that a play could work. Despite Rinehart's involvement with war work and camp visiting, she was tempted to "try for another 'Seven Days.'" "Why don't you make a rough sketch to see if it works out as well as you think it will," she wrote, "and then let me see it?" She concluded:

If the prospects look bright, we might get it on late in the fall. You will remember that it was through "Seven Days" being sent to you by a manager that it had its initial push. Williams sending this to you may be a good omen.[73]

But, on the fifth of July, Hopwood wrote back and told Rinehart that "an unexpected complication" in his plans for the next few months would make it impossible for him to take on any new work. He regretted having to give up the idea of doing anything with "Bab," but, he said, "I've no doubt . . . that some one else will grab her up, & I'm sure that if she has any sort of chance, she'll be a great success."[74] He closed by inviting Rinehart and her family to come visit him and his mother at his "nice old house" at Piermont.

Later in the summer, Hopwood reestablished contact with Archie Bell:

Piermont, New York
August 17, 1917

Dear Archie:—

I think of you as cool and cucumberish (I *like* cucumbers)—and I hope that you are! I have vegetated all summer, on the banks of the Hudson, and it has done me a lot of good, and I haven't liked it particularly. I mean the process—not the result. And now, I'm thinking of going on a trip West

—to the Yellowstone or somewhere—but probably I won't, as I love the Autumn here.

I am going to town tomorrow, and I am going to get a copy of our book on "China"—at least, I hope that I am. I suppose it will make me acutely homesick. I liked China better than Japan—not the port cities, of course—but the country—and Peking. I simply *adored* Peking, and I want to go back there. . . .

I have finished a play for the Selwyns, and am writing another for them. They will both be done within the next six months or so—produced, I mean. The Selwyns are also going to make a musical comedy of "Our Little Wife", and Morosco is performing the same operation upon "Sadie Love". I am not assisting at these two transformations, having decided that it would be more amusing to sit back and do nothing, and take in my share of the royalties—if there *are* any.

I have also agreed to accept royalties from my early loves, Wagenhals & Kemper, but they assist [*sic*] upon my doing something to earn them, so I have promised to write them a play.

Doris Keane still postpones "Nobody's Widow", as "Romance" runs on and on. If she ever does get to producing my play, I'm going over [to London] for it. . . .

"Fair and Warmer" was played [in Shanghai] recently, by an American repertoire company, conducted by T. Daniel Frawley, which is going all over the Far East. It has also been successfully produced (my play, I mean)—in Australia. And the dear, sturdy breadwinner is to be done in the States by three companies, this season—so that will help keep the Wolf unsatisfied.

That's all my scandal. Send me some more of your's.

Greetings to your sister. Very much your's, my dear Archie.

Avery[75]

Sadie Love, the musical, book by Tommy Grey and music by Harry Tierney, was not announced for production until January 16, 1920. It was scheduled for a Los Angeles premiere in February of that year, but nothing more is heard about it.[76] *I'll Say She Does,* the musical adaptation of *Our Little Wife,* was produced on the East Coast in late summer of 1920. After a successful Washington, D.C., stock run with Lynn Overlord in the title role, it apparently failed in tryouts at Stamford, Connecticut, and Wilmington, Delaware, before its scheduled New York opening in October.[77] The play that Hopwood had recently finished for the Selwyns was most likely *Pete,* copyrighted August 7, 1917, which he later revised as *Don't Be Afraid.* Although a press release announced that this "comedy drama" was being readied by the Shuberts for a June 21, 1920, opening at the Crescent Theatre in Brooklyn, it never reached Broadway. Described as "away from Hopwood's customary farcical style," it treated the theme of "reincarnation in a serious way."[78]

Pete is a curious departure from the plays Hopwood had been turning out, and it may be that he was responding to the suggestion made by the *Vanity Fair* writer who had encouraged him to attempt something that would not be directly compared to *Fair and Warmer*. The play, called "A Miracle Comedy" on the title page of the typescript, is a sentimental mixture of melodrama and moral instruction. The story centers upon the relationship between gentle Jacky Adams, who loves animals, and his gruff, impersonal father, John Adams. During the three acts, time advances rapidly, and the scenes shift between the Adams' home, a dog and pony show, and "The Judgement Gate."

One evening while John Adams is reading the paper, he becomes annoyed with his wife, Emily, who has brought home a kitten for Jacky. Constantly irritated by the meowing of the cat, Adams insists that his wife get rid of it. When Jacky protests, his father sends him up to bed. Hurrying back down to the living room, Jacky tells his father he has seen burglars outside the house, and that he doesn't want to go upstairs alone. His father belittles him, saying: "Don't want to! You mean you're afraid. What sort of a man do you think you'll ever make—you little coward!" Emily admonishes John for talking to his son in this way, but Adams says he only wants to put a little courage in the boy. Emily responds:

> You'll never do that by bullying him! Talk to him first—convince him that there isn't anything to be afraid of—and then send him upstairs! I've told you before, you'll never accomplish anything by being brutal with Jacky. He's nervous, and high strung. The only way to influence him is by sympathy, and kindness.[79]

It is soon revealed that the supposed burglars were Bertha Wendell and her young daughter, Judy, who have come seeking aid from the Adamses. Bertha, once married to the brother of John Adams, divorced him because of his drinking and vice, and shortly thereafter, he died. Bertha remarried, but her second husband died too, leaving her penniless. John Adams shows Bertha no sympathy. He tells her: "That morning, when I found my brother, I swore that if I could ever make you suffer as he had, I'd do it. If that time has come, I'm glad! Get out of my house!"[80] As Adams is forcing Bertha and her child from the house, he is bitten by the Wendells' dog. Adams, enraged, runs back into the house and gets a revolver with which to shoot the dog, but in the process trips and falls, killing himself when the gun discharges.

The next scene reveals Adams standing in the presence of the Unseen, who is about to judge his soul. The Unseen tells Adams that he has lived before and that he will live again, but this time he will return to Earth and shall suffer, "be athirst," shall "hunger, and be accurst—not in the form of Man, but as a dog!"[81] Adams cries out in horror, "Ah! No no! Oh God! Not a dog! Not a dog!" He "falls prostrate, shrieking out in terror, groveling before the Unseen." Later, Adams returns to Earth as Pete, a dog in a carnival show. He finally makes his way back to his home, where Jacky and Judy, now much older, have become good friends. Pete has been abused by the evil Sandro, owner of the carnival, and, after additional incidents, Jacky and Judy attempt to take Pete away from him. During a violent struggle with Sandro, in which the now eighteen-year-old Jacky attempts to free the suffering dog, Sandro produces a gun and tries to shoot the boy, but Pete, rushing to protect Jacky, is killed instead. Cradling the dying dog, Jacky tells Pete that not only has the dog saved his life, it has shown him that he is no longer afraid. In the last scene, Adams finds himself before the Unseen once more, who tells him that he has learned much through suffering as a dumb beast, and that now he will be born again as a child, to grow and prosper. "For those who chill and stunt the soul must sink, and rise again — But those who strive with upward face, ascend, to heights beyond."[82]

In *Don't Be Afraid*, the version the Shuberts apparently attempted to produce, the ending of the play is drastically different. Pete is not killed, but is taken home by Jacky and Judy, whom we find in the next scene costumed as much older parents with several little children. The play assumes a dreamlike quality, and we see the character of Emily, now a grandmother, reading to all the little ones, as Jacky and Judy bid goodnight, and leave the house to attend a party. Shortly after Grandma and the children have gone to bed, the house catches fire. Pete saves the family, but he himself is burned to death in the flames. Going before the Unseen, Adams is told that he has been redeemed; but, this time, he returns to earth as his former self. In the last scene, Adams awakens from his delirium, having recovered from the effects of his gunshot wound, and calls everyone to his bedside for a speech of repentance. Jacky tells his father that he has learned much about courage from him during the ordeal. Adams invites his brother's wife, Bertha, and her daughter, Judy, to live with his family, and, much to everyone's delight, the play ends with Adams gently petting the dog that bit him.[83] Perhaps the *Don't Be Afraid* ending was substituted in an attempt to make the play's fantasy more plausible, as well as to appeal to the sentimental tastes of the popular audience. Whatever the rationale for the revisions, they appear not to have made the Brooklyn tryout a successful one, and the play was withdrawn.

An absence of correspondence and newspaper articles makes it impossible to know much of what Hopwood was doing from the fall of 1917 until the summer of 1918. He did continue writing plays, however, for a script entitled *The Little Clown* was copyrighted on May 10, 1918. An unidentified clipping of September 1918 announces that this play was written for Billie Burke, although no production is known to have taken place. *The Little Clown* was produced as a film in 1921, but the role of Patsy was played by Paramount's "blonde bombshell," Mary Miles Minter, not Burke.[84]

Another unproduced play, *The Sideshow*, which also deals with circus characters, may be attributed to Hopwood. Although no copyright date is found for this script, and nothing seems to have appeared in the trade newspapers about its production, the typescript donated by the American Play Company to the Theatre Collection of the New York Public Library at Lincoln Center does bear Hopwood's name. The basic relationship between the leading characters in *The Little Clown* and *The Sideshow* are similar, but the tones and plots of the two plays are quite different.

Essentially, *The Little Clown* is a Pygmalion story centering upon Patsy, the star performer of Anderson's one-ring circus. Patsy, whose specialty is the trained dog act, is loved by Dick Beverly, a handsome young equestrian, who has joined the circus in order to escape the aristocratic world of his parents. This relationship is complicated by the fact that Pete, an acrobat, also loves Patsy. When the circus is playing near Beverly's home, his parents come to visit and try to persuade him to leave this artificial life and study to be a lawyer. He agrees, provided they will allow him to marry Patsy. Shocked that their son would bring such a common girl into the family, they reluctantly agree, provided she live with them for six months and attempt to become accustomed to their manner of living. Despite Patsy's beauty and charm, she fails to learn the social graces necessary to convince the Beverlys' friends that she is actually a girl of breeding. Having shocked everyone with her naiveté and her circus manners at a dinner given in her honor, she returns to the circus without telling anyone. Several months later, Dick, who hasn't been able to put Patsy out of his mind, and his parents, who have grown to miss the "little clown," seek out the circus and ask Patsy to rejoin their family. Much to the Beverlys' joy, they discover that Patsy has become a changed person after all.

The Little Clown, like *Pete*, is sentimental, but in a more convincing way. It also offers an important role for a child, as was the case in Hopwood's *This Woman and This Man*. But significantly, as comedy, it is closer to the simple and natural style of humor being written by playwrights like Clare Kummer, whose *Good Gracious Annabelle* (1916) had helped establish fresh standards for the genre. Here was comedy that emphasized character and dialogue over situation in a way that would later be taken up by writers like Kaufman and Connelly.[85] It may be that Hopwood had so firmly established himself as a writer of risqué farce by this time, that managers were not interested in producing fare under his name that did not conform to expectations.

Unlike the sentimental comedy of *The Little Clown*, *The Sideshow* is darker in theme. The central character, Beauty, the Lovely Head with the long golden hair, is loved by John, a handsome, double-jointed young man known as Apollo to Sideshow patrons. Like Dick Beverly of *The Little Clown*, Apollo is actually an aristocratic young man who has joined the circus environment to escape the outside world, a situation somewhat similar to Andreyev's *He Who Gets Slapped*, which had premiered in 1914. Apollo professes his love for Beauty, who is supposed to marry the manager of the sideshow, and the two elope. After several months together, Apollo tells Beauty that he can no longer remain a part of the show. Not only has he grown weary of the daily grind, but he is no longer certain it is best that he and she remain together. Beauty, emotionally crushed by Apollo's feelings towards her, does not tell him that she is expecting their baby. After Apollo departs, the manager takes care of Beauty, treating her as if she were one of his own family.

Later in the play, when it is discovered that the marriage between Beauty and Apollo had not been legally performed by a licensed justice of the peace, the manager offers to marry Beauty, but she declines. Apollo eventually returns to the sideshow; he needs Beauty in his life. When he arrives, he discovers that he has become the father of twins. After much coaxing by Apollo and resisting by Beauty, the two agree to marry again. Interspersed are incidents involving such colorful characters as the Human Bone; Sal, Queen of the Cobras; Mighty Maggie, the fat lady; the Chinese Giant; the Turkish strong man, Sandow; and numerous other nonspeaking sideshow oddities.

Like *Don't Be Afraid, The Sideshow* also contains a dream sequence, but although the visual elements for the scene are extensive and complex, they remain conventional. All in all, *The Sideshow* is a curious mixture of "realistic" carnival life, sentimental melodrama, and fantasy. Expressions such as "Gad!" and topical references to a younger Lillian Russell in one scene, tend to indicate that the play had been written at an earlier time. In general, the dialogue is less sophisticated than in Hopwood's later works. In any event, *The Little Clown, Pete/Don't Be Afraid*, and *The Sideshow*, although departures from Hopwood's typical form of writing, show little in the way of progressive dramaturgy, but they do, like his earlier social problem plays, possess moments of sincerity that give evidence of his continued desire to produce something serious. It may be that these plays were all works from that remote period prior to *This Woman and This Man*, taken out of storage, and then reworked during his summer of convalescence.

It seems unlikely that Hopwood made any extensive foreign trips during late 1917, or early 1918, particularly to Europe, where the hostilities continued. In a much earlier letter to Mary Rinehart, he had advised her against traveling to the war zone:

> I am moved to say "Don't," in regard to your idea about going abroad. My own experience was that I saw little of the acutely interesting side of the war & I had to put up with all the minor discomforts & restrictions which it entailed. Living conditions in all the countries concerned are growing steadily worse, prices are bound to be high (especially for non-residents), & there is a general depression in life & spirits which wd be bound to react on you. However—I don't want to stand between you & the writing of a "War & Peace."
>
> A grind organ is playing the "Marseillaise"—& now it stops suddenly, &, after a discreet pause, indulges in "The Wearin' o' the Green." Oh la la![86]

If such a devastating event as the Great War had had so little impact on Hopwood as to seem just an inconvenience to travelers, it had been a profound experience for Rinehart, whose eldest son was stationed in France. In this context, one is able to more fully understand Rinehart's comment: "On everything but the play we differed diametrically, but we seldom so much as spoke of anything else." Hopwood seems to have shown little interest in social issues either, once telling a reporter that he had never voted in an election because there had been nothing of concern to him, that is until the question of suffrage for women, but, on that issue he refused to say "which turn" his vote would take.[87]

Although Hopwood and Rinehart had little in common in their personal lives, they remained amiable colleagues in collaborating on the plays. By the summer of 1918, the two were beginning to talk about a project that was to become their most successful venture — the writing of a mystery-thriller, *The Bat*. But, at the time Rinehart approached him with her idea for the mystery, he was in tryouts for a new farce, *Double Exposure:*

Piermont, New York
June 14, 1918

Dear Mary: —

The play went very well in Washington, and is to open in New York late in August. We begin rehearsals again in two weeks, and I'm busy making various changes. However, I've time to read that MS., if you have succeeded in finding it. . . .
  I saw some mutual friends of ours, in Washington, and I may do some Government work, in the Autumn.
  I also saw Dr. Rinehart, and we had several pleasant chats.

Sincerely,
Avery Hopwood[88]

Like *Our Little Wife, Double Exposure* was produced by Selwyn and Company. Despite the previous play's failure, they still had faith that Hopwood could give them another hit like *Fair and Warmer*. In order not to take any chances of miscasting *Double Exposure*, Selwyn reassembled most of the original company of *Fair and Warmer*, with the exception of Madge Kennedy, who had gone to work for Samuel Goldwyn in Hollywood the year before. Critics soon agreed that the play boasted one of the most proficient ensembles of farce actors of any show to open on Broadway during 1918, but, curiously, it whimpered to a close after only fifteen performances.

Borrowing his central premise from the German Von Scholz's farce *Vertauschte Seelen*,[89] Hopwood had attempted to move away from a situation built solely around the usual "innocuous misunderstandings,"[90] and to explore an improbable idea that might offer fresh and unlimited merriment. What he did was to present the audience with a farce that gave them both— misunderstandings that grew from situations they were not fully able to accept. Speculation about the play's failure, which, needless to say, surprised the entire company after the successful out-of-town runs, is more interesting than the piece itself.

In *Double Exposure*, Tommy and Lecksy Campbell live in the same apartment building as their close friends, Sybil and Jimmie Norton, an arrangement like that in *Fair and Warmer*. Tommy, a painter, doesn't feel his wife appreciates his talents fully, and he longs to spend time with Sybil, with whom he has an "artistic" affinity. Sybil, who is tired of her husband's "underground alcoholism," finds Tommy attractive. The play opens as the couples are about to go out for the evening, but before the Nortons arrive, Lecksy is visited by the Baba Mahrati, a Hindu holy man, who has been treating her for nervousness. When she confides to him that her husband has been showing signs of straying, he asks to speak with Tommy alone. The Mahrati tells Tommy that through hypnosis he can make his "astral" body enter the body of Jimmie Norton, thereby allowing him to experience Sybil as his wife. Tommy, at first skeptical, succumbs to the Mahrati's argument. Before long, Tommy-as-Jimmie begins to realize that life with Sybil would not be an improvement over his relationship with Lecksy. In fact, he comes to appreciate Lecksy more. To complicate matters, Jimmie's "astral" body has entered Tommy's physical self, and the resultant "insinuating evil" that develops from the new husband-wife pairings is amusingly handled. When the Mahrati appears in the last act, it is discovered that the entire proceedings have transpired during the fifteen minutes Tommy has been under hypnosis — it was all a dream. Coming to his senses, Tommy is happy to be back with Lecksy.

Critical reaction to the farce was mixed. In Buffalo, the critics had said: "In 'Double Exposure' Mr. Hopwood has far outdone his 'Fair and Warmer' and 'Seven Days.'"[91] Washington, D.C., had apparently liked it too, but in New York critics once again said that Hopwood had not lived up to his previous hit. Broun allowed that it was more discreet than *Sadie Love* or *Our Little Wife* but that the idea was not "pliable." "Of course," he added, "even when Hopwood cannot think up funny situations he can carry his audience along to a certain extent with clever dialogue."[92] Woollcott, calling the piece a "High Moral Farce," said Hopwood's excursion into the fourth dimension was "a false lead," for it "proved the same old stage of slamming doors that lead nowhere, of the safest of all situations pretending to be risque." He conceded, however, that although the central situation had gone wrong, "Many of the details of characterization, and many a wayward quip, showed the hand that penned *Fair and Warmer*."[93] The play's greatest praise came from an unidentified reviewer, who wrote:

> Mr. Hopwood managed his supernatural element adroitly. His skill in contriving all the situations in which his characters appeared made the action move with a naturalness and probability rare enough in the run of native plays of this kind. . . . There is unusual wit in the language of the play, which has another quality rare in the work of American playwrights in that it springs from the situation. . . . No other playwright works with such finish as Mr. Hopwood in this field.[94]

Ironically, the play's failure to convince the audience of its central idea may have resulted from the very thing the Selwyns had attempted to avoid when they brought together the veteran *Fair and Warmer* cast — actors who were not believable in their casting. Edgar Selwyn had once told George Jean Nathan that for a farce to succeed in America, it was essential that the play's first act "convince its auditors of the sincerity of the farce [*sic*] and win the hearts of its auditors to the cause of its thematic protagonists." Nathan admitted that Selwyn was

> undoubtedly correct: But imagine such an imposition as 'sincerity' upon a writer of farce—farce, a something designed merely to make people laugh and be merry. Imagine critical rules for such a thing![95]

Nathan's reaction to farce rules seems justified, but successful farce had long been defined as: "possible people doing improbable things." Hopwood had written characterizations that required the male leads to faithfully imitate one another, and, despite the skill of John Westley and John Cumberland in the roles of Tommy Campbell and Jimmie Norton, neither was able to juggle the demands the mimicry imposed. New York audiences apparently never believed for a moment in the mystic exchange of personalities between the two hypnotized husbands:

> The change in identities put the cast to a severe strain, particularly since Hopwood conceived the ego as carrying voice and manner with it into the new astral home. Thus for a whole act John Cumberland, one of the most amusing farce personalities in the theatre, disappeared utterly. His astral body was on view to be sure, but he was busy trying to imitate the voice of John Westley. On the other hand John Westley was trying even harder to imitate the voice and manner of John Cumberland.... Their switch back to their own personalities was one of the factors which made the conclusion of the play effective.[96]

The question here is, could this problem, which appears not to have surfaced during tryouts, been remedied by casting actors who were closer in physical and vocal type than Westley and Cumberland, or should Selwyn and Hopwood have trusted the audience's ability to accept the exchange of souls without the external physicalizations? Apparently, by the time the third act rolled around, and everyone learned that the whole evening had been a dream anyway, nobody cared. After opening August 28 and playing two weeks at the Bijou Theatre, the play closed.

A month later, in another bit of irony, the Bijou housed a twenty-week run of a disinfected translation of Sacha Guitry's farce *Sleeping Partners*, starring French actress Irene Bordoni. This was also a season which paired up Marjorie Rambeau and Pedro de Cordoba (*Sadie Love*) in a successful war drama, *Where the Poppies Bloom;* introduced the popular Irving Berlin song "Oh, How I Hate to Get Up in the Morning" in the revue *Yip Yip Yaphank;* and had Mae West vamping an innocent young Ed Wynn for 283 performances in the Friml musical *Sometime*. This last play, which opened October 4, also starred Francine Larrimore, who had apparently wasted no time in finding work after playing Lecksy in *Double Exposure*. In retrospect, *Double Exposure's* chance for a respectable run may have been dampened by the premiere two days earlier of the Frank Bacon and Winchell Smith smash-hit comedy *Lightnin'*, which was destined to achieve an unprecedented run of 1,291 performances — the first play in America to top the 1,000 mark.

Almost immediately following the closing of *Double Exposure*, Hopwood got back in touch with Mary Rinehart about the manuscript of her thriller:

Piermont, New York
Sept. 16th 1918

Dear Mary: —

I was delighted to hear from you, & to learn that you have a good idea for a "Thriller", & I will arrange to see you, very soon, to talk it over with you. I think that Wagenhals & Kemper will be glad, too. We have kept them waiting a long time, for the play that we promised them after "Seven Days". —

I like "The Hidden Room" for a title but I like "The Bat" better. — But, whatever we call the play, I shall be happy to get to work on another play with you, & I think that, if we put our united efforts on a mystery play, there is no reason why we shouldn't make it a corker. — I'll wire you or phone you within a day or two, & make an appointment to talk things over.

Your's, sincerely
Avery Hopwood[97]

Hopwood couldn't have been more right in his prediction that the play would be a corker, but a series of delays due to Hopwood's other play commitments, Rinehart's war correspondence, family concerns, and other novels, kept the play from being produced until the 1920–1921 season.

Rinehart had been attempting to dramatize her mystery novel *The Circular Staircase* since 1917. She recalled dining with Edgar Selwyn and asking him his opinion as to the success of a play that would keep the audience "completely mystified . . . until practically the drop of the curtain." Selwyn responded: "It would be worth a million dollars" — he had no idea how low his estimate was.[98] As Rinehart continued working on her script, she realized that the plot of *The Circular Staircase* was too involved, the solution seemed inappropriate for a play, and the action was spread out over too long a time. She would have to abandon the book and write a completely new piece. It was then that she hit upon the idea of inventing a master criminal called the Bat and of setting the action during one night; she would keep the idea of stolen money hidden in the secret room of a rented country house. By the fall of 1918 Rinehart had finally been able to complete the rough drafts of the first two acts and an outline for the third. Still unsatisfied with the last act, however, and under pressure to leave on assignment in France, she contacted Hopwood to write a solid third act and make suggestions where he thought the play needed fixing:

Piermont, New York

Dear Mary: —

I've read the play a couple of times, & like it as much as ever.... I think
that the character of Cornelia & the idea of her solving the mystery is the
biggest asset in the play, from the standpoint of novelty....
    I think that in the First Act, the audience should be put more explicitly
in touch with the situation—I mean abt "Brooks" predicament, & the
necessity for finding the money, in order to clear himself.—I don't believe
that this is made quite clear enough.
    What shall I do with the MS.?...

[Late Sept., 1918]   Hop[99]

Then suddenly, for reasons which are not known, Hopwood cooled on the
project; he offered a veiled excuse:

Piermont, New York
Oct. 2. [1918]

Dear Mary: —

I've decided, finally, not to tackle the play. I can't get away from the feeling
that comedy is my best bet, and that when I do anything else, I am writing
with my left hand. But I do still think that you have the material for a very
good play, and if I can be of assistance to you, unofficially, do let me know.
I hope that you do go on with it. It would be a pity to give it up.

Sincerely,
Hop[100]

In the time between Hopwood's decision not to work on *The Bat*, and February
25, 1919, Rinehart had been in Europe covering the Armistice and he had remained near the East Coast keeping his eye on a musical adaptation of their
earlier collaboration, *Seven Days*.
    Tumble In, produced under the management of Arthur Hammerstein,
adapted by Otto Harbach, with music by Rudolf Friml, offered such catching
tunes as "A Little Chicken Fit for Old Broadway," and the popular "Wedding
Blues." After traveling down to Philadelphia to catch a tryout performance of
the show, Hopwood clipped a review from one of the papers and attached it
to a letter to Mary; it said:

> There is charm in every aspect of the performance and, with gowns of the
> newest sort and with plenty of lingerie of the flimsiest and filmiest sort, and
> with attractive settings, it would be a captious person indeed who would not
> be delighted by the gay and breezy entertainment.[101]

In the letter, Hopwood also reopened the possibility of working on *The Bat*
(*The Hidden Room*):

2 East 81st St., New York City
Feb. 25, 1919

Dear Mrs. Rinehart: —

I am enclosing this clipping, so that you may see that time is avenging you, in the matter of credit for the authorship of "Seven Days". They've forgotten me entirely!

I went over to Philadelphia, last evening, to see "Tumble In", and I like it very well, though — I think that there is work to be done upon it. Mr. Harbach told me that you had come to see the play in Washington. I had thought that you were in Europe.

When are you coming to New York — and where will you be, when you do come? I want to see you.

Have you done anything with "The Hidden Room?"

I have taken an apartment, at the above address, and expect to be here until summer.

Sincerely,
Hop[102]

Rinehart, perhaps still somewhat irritated with Hopwood's backing away from the mystery play, answered him promptly, but tersely. Yes, she had attended *Tumble In* in Washington, but she could not see a New York hit in it. And, no, she had done nothing with *The Hidden Room*, although she still thought it had great potential. Yet, despite the perfunctoriness of the letter, it appeared the collaboration on *The Bat*, or *The Hidden Room*, as they were now referring to it, could be salvaged. At least Rinehart hadn't shut the door. Hopwood, in his next letter, took their partnership for granted, and wrote: "I know that 'The Hidden Room' has a very good chance & I look forward to our next confab about it." Then he informed Rinehart that John Rumsey, their agent, thought Wagenhals and Kemper should get only one-third of the royalties for *Tumble In*, instead of the one-half they wanted. Hopwood wasn't as generous:

I don't think they should get any at all — but perhaps the ⅓ ratio will look as if we were putting something over on them, since we shared the stock & moving picture rights. — Still, they're so damned rich, — & Wagenhals hasn't even been interested enough in "Tumble In" to go see it — & they certainly did nothing for it — I don't know what to do. — What do you think? . . .

P.S. Our names have been omitted entirely from all the principal billing of "Tumble In" — I have protested.

AH[103]

The musical had not been particularly well received by the critics in New York, but audiences were dancing into the Selwyn Theatre to the tune of "eighteen hundred a night." "If that keeps up," Hopwood soon wrote Rinehart, "you can afford to buy a few new hats, and I may be able to buy gasoline, out of our respective pittances."

In spite of the London fiasco, *Seven Days* had proven to be a sturdy bread-winner for the playwrights, on the road, in the movies, and now as a musical, but, under the jingling of the royalty coins, some were beginning to hear the worn rumblings of the farce machine that had produced such rewards:

> A good many of us remember Mary Roberts Rinehart's and Avery Hopwood's *Seven Days* from which *Tumble In* has been devised and thought it very funny in the olden days. But since the appearance of the original farce much flotsam and jetsam of its ilk have floated under theatrical bridges. . . . All these ingredients of *Seven Days* have seen service in the cause of farce so frequently of recent years that they no longer stimulate laughter as of old.[104]

But if the critics were growing tired of the old farce formula, audiences, caught up in post war enthusiasm, weren't. Rinehart and Hopwood were about to cash in on their most successful season on the Great White Way.

V
Inexhaustible Avery (1919–1921)

In the months following the end of World War I, the Broadway theatre began to flourish as it had never done before. Renewed optimism brought audiences back into the playhouses in unprecedented numbers. Not only did the standard comedies and musicals benefit from this resurgent prosperity, but the "new movement" in theatre started to make its impact on Broadway. American plays were beginning to be thought of as having literary worth. Just the year before, Jesse Lynch Williams had been awarded the first Pulitzer Prize in drama for his play, *Why Marry?* In April 1919, the Theatre Guild, an outgrowth of the Washington Square Players, established itself. Within months, they had produced their first important offering, St. John Ervine's *John Ferguson,* which furnished them with a firm financial base upon which to grow. The Theatre Guild was well aware that their survival depended upon box-office success, but they were dedicated to offering audiences the finest American and foreign plays as an alternative to the usual Broadway entertainment. But, if the future looked brighter for the new movement, the established managers and playwrights found themselves working harder to compensate for the increased challenges of the motion pictures and the dwindling popularity of the road show. Increased railroad costs and the war tax made standard tours prohibitive. By 1920 there would be only 42 legitimate production tours in the country, compared to the 392 tours in 1900.[1]

The steady collapse of the touring circuit also had an important impact on the writers of popular plays. Dramatists found themselves increasingly suiting their works specifically to the tastes of New York audiences. As a result, many pieces, particularly comedy farces, took on "a more blasé, sophisticated, urban viewpoint."[2] This appeal, coupled with a relaxing moral code, found some playwrights attempting to probe adult themes forthrightly. In the case of the bedroom farce, writers became quite daring, and often sacrificed skating on thin ice for a smirkier, more vulgar humor. This shift, partly motivated by theatrical managers attempting to match the increased naughtiness of Hollywood, eventually led to renewed efforts by antivice groups to impose censorship on the drama. Although Hopwood's *The Demi-Virgin* was to serve as a rallying point in this controversy, for the moment he was riding a crest of theatrical enthusiasm that moved him even closer to his goal of five plays running on Broadway at one time.

By March 30, 1919, six days after *Tumble In* had opened on Broadway, Hopwood and Rinehart were preparing to resume writing *The Hidden Room*. Offering to have a copy made of the original draft of the mystery, he told her:

> I'd like to brood over the play, in my spare moments, and then, when we next see each other, perhaps we could map the thing out entirely. If you do send it, be sure to enclose that tentative draft of the new third act — or rather, the scenario — which you made, last Autumn. . . .

Best Wishes
Hop[3]

Within a few weeks, however, Hopwood was too busy to meet with Rinehart:

2 East 81st St.
New York City,

Dear Mary: —

> I find that I am so engulfed with work still to be done, on the Belasco play [*The Gold Diggers*] & my other productions, that I won't be able to get to Pittsburgh in May, but when you are out here . . . we can have a couple more sessions, if you are not too rushed, & then later on, we can probably get together for a week or so of work & shake the play into shape. — I've been thinking about "The Hidden Room", a great deal (N.B. — Transpose those two phrases!) — & I'm sure that it is a good thing, & that we can make it a champion thriller.
> I think that I will have a copy made of our labors thus far & send it to you, so that you can refresh yr memory with it.
> Greeting, and all good wishes,

Hop[4]

Throughout the busy spring and summer of 1919, the collaborators attempted to get together to work on the script, but a meeting scheduled for July had to be postponed: "I have 3 sets of rehearsals, in August — the first beginning Aug. 4," wrote Hopwood, and "I believe y're working on a novel." Later, he wrote Rinehart that it was just as well they were not attempting to put the play on this season, "as two detective plays [had] gone on already, and two more [were] to open shortly." In August, an unexpected turn of events found Hopwood with some spare time to work on the project, but Mary had already written him of her plans for a necessary trip to California to settle a dispute with Goldwyn over a motion picture scenario she had written.[5] Hopwood replied:

2 East 81 St., New York City.
August 11, 1919.

Dear Mary: —

> Strangely enough, when I got your letter I was just about to send you words that I could come to Glen Osborne, to work on "The Hidden Room", as the

theatrical strike has postponed all my productions, and no one knows just when the trouble will end. However, we are hoping for the best.

I think that October will be all right for me, to work on the play. I am not usually so overwhelmed with work, as I have been this summer, and I do not think that we will have any trouble about going on with the work, and finishing it, if your plans permit.

We might very advantageously get the play ready for Boston, for this season, and Chicago, and then bring it in to New York the first thing next season. In any event, let's get the MS. in shape as soon as possible....

Sincerely,
Avery Hopwood[6]

The actors' strike was another result of the precariousness of the road show. In many instances, unconcerned producers would indiscriminately break wage agreements, leaving whole companies of actors stranded in remote parts of the country when a show no longer turned a profit. Calling for fairer treatment in all areas of their working conditions, the actors demanded the establishment of a central bargaining unit to arbitrate cases in which their theatrical contracts had been broken. Tensions increased until on August 7, *Lightnin'*, the hit of Broadway, struck. Banners reading, *"Lightnin'* Has Struck!" were carried up and down the Great White Way by resolute actors, and before long many other companies refused to perform.

As might be expected, there was much division among the actors, managers and playwrights, particularly on the question of whether Equity's demand for a closed shop should be met. The actors, of course, were hoping the dramatists would give them a strong show of support by presenting a solid front to the managers, but a consensus among the writers could not be reached. A reception committee formed by the Authors' League, headed by Hopwood, James Forbes and Louis K. Anspacher, welcomed producers David Belasco, George Broadhurst, Arthur Hopkins, and Winchell Smith to a meeting at which the managers tried to discourage any support for the actors. Pointing to George M. Cohan's offer of $100,000 to establish a new union, Actors' Fidelity League, the producers asked the writers for support. In the beginning, the vote had been neutral. But, when it was discovered that the playwrights had agreed to back Equity, provided that the organization drop its demands for a closed shop in the coming agreement, an "icy chill" fell over the managers' attitude towards the dramatists.[7]

On August 18, Hopwood and Eugene Walter sent a telegram to all of their colleagues requesting a meeting the following day at the Hotel Astor to consider the formation of a "Stage Writers' Protective Association," which would act independently of the Authors' League. Sensing the divisiveness of such an action, Channing Pollock argued against the establishment of a new group, and eventually succeeded in gaining support for a Dramatists' Committee within the League. This body was organized as the Dramatists' Guild in 1926.[8] Recalling this turbulent period in a 1950 *Theatre Arts* article, Ward Morehouse observed:

> The strike brought laughter, tears, songs, speeches, parades, drama, and a bit of melodrama here and there; it provided the Broadway area with an extraordinary spectacle, a great, big, free show.... Old loyalties were smashed, old friendships were severed, new enmities were created, and during the uproar twenty-three of the Broadway theatres, including the mighty Hippodrome, were closed. It all resulted in the overwhelming victory for the actors and in recognition of the Actors' Equity Association as their bargaining representative in all matters.[9]

When the strike finally ended on September 6, 1919, the triumphant actors returned to work, the curtains went up on schedule, and the "theatre-starved" public lined up in droves in front of the ticket windows. Broadway was about to enjoy a booming and varied season.

The first show to open the Lyceum Theatre after the strike was David Belasco's production of Hopwood's newest and brightest comedy, *The Gold Diggers*. Hopwood had gotten the idea for his latest work almost a year before while sitting in the Ritz in New York with a charming, and "apparently authentic blonde," Kay Laurel. As the two sat waiting for a mutual friend, Miss Laurel called out to a girlfriend who had just entered the bar: "Hello, Gold Digger." "Gold Digger?" asked Hopwood. "Yes," responded Miss Laurel, a quite heavenly smile on her lips and a dancing little devil in her eyes,

> "That's what we call ourselves! You men capitalize your brains, or your business ability, or your legal minds—or whatever other darned thing you happen to have! So why shouldn't we girls capitalize what nature has given us—as our good looks and our ability to please and entertain men? You men don't give something for nothing—why should we? It's an art to amuse men—to thrill them, to fascinate them, to make them happy. Why shouldn't we be paid for it. We've got to live—and what's more, we've made up our minds to live darned well! Men like to be with us—and to be seen with us."[10]

Jotting the idea down, as he often did, on his clean, starched cuffs, Hopwood later filed the comments in his "fat black note-book" for future development. It wasn't until David Belasco had summoned him to discuss possible ideas for a young actress under his management whom he intended to promote as a "star" that the idea actually began to take shape. After reading several possibilities from his "family Bible," as Hopwood called his notebook, he came upon the gold diggers scribble. "I'll take it!" said Belasco, instantly, "Go ahead and write that play—I'll take it!"[11]

By all accounts, Hopwood worked on the scenario and dialogue of the play for five weeks; and, in the end, with the benefit of "D.B.'s unfailing interest and sympathy, and ... his rich suggestfulness," he succeeded in giving the American theatre *The Gold Diggers*, a comedy that would eventually serve as the generator of countless motion pictures and movie musical spectaculars. Now a popularized slang term found even in the dictionary, there was a time when Belasco's advance men advised him to change the title because audiences expected a play about the forty-niners. *Variety* announced: "The piece does not concern the mining of precious metal, but rather the 'digging' of it in cities."[12] The plot and the character of the stereotypical chorus girls that seem hackneyed today, were probably not much fresher in 1919, but the entire production effervesced and sparkled with such champagne qualities that it was assured of an immediate popular success.

The star Belasco featured in *The Gold Diggers* was Miss Ina Claire in her second play under his banner. First appearing on the stage in vaudeville in 1907 at the age of twelve, she had gained popularity through her mimicry of Sir Harry Lauder. Her sprightly ways had soon carried her through such plays as *Jumping Jupiter*, *The Honeymoon*, and *The Quaker Girl*, and in 1913, she had made her first appearance in London as Una Trance in *The Girl from Utah*. After returning to America in 1915, she had entered vaudeville once again, this period of her career culminating in her appearance as Juliet in *The Ziegfeld Follies of 1916*. By 1917, not long after signing a contract with Belasco to learn more about acting, she had appeared in his production of George Middleton and Guy Bolton's popular comedy, *Polly with a Past*. Now, with *The Gold Diggers*, the "Bishop of Broadway" put her name in lights over the title, and proclaimed her a "star." Joining Miss Claire in *The Gold Diggers* was her leading man from *Polly with a Past*, the distinguished Bruce McRae, who had appeared opposite Blanche Bates in *Nobody's Widow*.

McRae played Steven Lee, whose nephew Wally has fallen in love with the innocent and demure Violet Dayne, played, somewhat ironically, by Mae West's sister, Beverly. As *The Gold Diggers* opens, Violet, who has been taken under the protective tutelage of popular chorus girl Jerry Lamar (Ina Claire), is attempting to wake up Mabel Munroe. The man-hunting Mabel has just spent the night on the sofa of Jerry's apartment after leaving her "John" stranded. Throughout the morning various types of show girls come and go talking of the problems and pleasures of trying to make it in the business, until at last, Jerry makes her entrance from the bedroom. "Hello!" she says from the doorway, "What man is on the pan now?" Getting the girls to join with her in some morning exercise, she lectures them on the facts of life in a sequence that is representative of the whole:

> Well, it's just like this—men will do a good deal for us now—but, oh, girls—lose your figures or your complexions—get a few lines in your face— get tired out and faded looking, and a little passé—and the fellows that are ready to give you pearls and sables now—well—they'd turn the other way when they saw you coming!... I know what I'm talking about, honey!... For it's one of two things—either you work the men, or the men work you!... They've got the coin to burn, most of them—and we're hustling

> to pay our rent and dress the way we ought to ... There's hardly a girl in
> the show business that isn't helping to take care of somebody beside herself.
> Believe me, we don't rob anybody! . . . We take from them that have, and
> give them value received.
>
> MABEL. Maybe some of us don't give as much as the men think they ought
> to get.
>
> JERRY. But lots of others give them more than they ought to—and so far
> as I can see, it's just about fifty-fifty! Just about!
>
> MABEL. And the moral of the story is—"Dig, sisters, while the digging's
> good!"[13]

Jerry, who clearly is not as demure as Violet, but who, nevertheless, is "equally
pure in heart," agrees to help her friend convince Wally's uncle that the chorus
girls don't deserve the "hard knocks" they have to take. Stephen Lee soon arrives on the scene with the idea of saving his young nephew from the machina-
tions of the gold diggers. Once inside their lair, however, he immediately
mistakes the beguiling Jerry for Violet, just as planned. Jerry, upon meeting
the attractive but stuffy Lee, decides to have as much fun with him as she can.
She plays her game a new way, using a bit of reverse psychology; she vamps
"Uncle Steve" hard and fast, hoping that he will be so shocked by her behavior
that he will be more than happy to have his nephew marry the first "nice" girl
who comes along—the real Violet.

Jerry is too good at what she does, however. After a "tantalizing" dance,
some snatches of a few songs that were never "written for trying over the family
piano," and a champagne toast, Lee is completely becharmed. Jerry is in a
panic. Realizing the folly of her game, she quickly tries to put Lee off by
pretending to be drunk and concocting tall tales about her shame-riddled past.
But the enamoured Lee is most benevolent; he offers to forgive her if she will
become his wife. Now Jerry is in a real fix; she has no alternative but to expose
the entire lie. She confesses everything, and, in what is the most conventional
touch in the play, calls Mother (who has arrived only that morning, and who
has been napping in the other room) to corroborate her story. Lee, more hurt
than angered by the trick, leaves. All works out to the good, though; he returns
the next day and woos Jerry in high style. The play ends with the customary
matchmaking between all the parties concerned, and as the curtain falls, the
gaiety is brought back into proper focus when a somewhat bewildered Stephen
Lee asks: "Jerry—what are you doing to me?" "You know what I'm doing," she
says, kissing him, "I'm gold digging!" "Toodeloo!"

Luxuriously produced in a one-piece set that captured the "realistic" atmosphere of the typical chorus girl's habitat in the "Eighties, between Broadway and Riverside," *The Gold Diggers* presented audiences with beautiful
women, the latest in Bendel fashions, and the most breathtaking sunlight yet
seen on the American stage. Belasco's new $80,000 lighting system created a
"strange exotic atmosphere" that spread through the theatre "like a perilously
fragrant vapor released from a magic urn."[14] It is clear that the excitement of
the total production did much to make the play the hit it was. One

The Gold Diggers, *Act II, Ina Claire and Bruce McRae, 1919.*

reporter commented that those who laughed through the performances admitted that the experience was something like taking a gold digger out to "breakfast, lunch, dinner and supper, without the ordeal of paying the checks when food is worth so much more than money." Reclining in her dressing room after a matinee performance, still wearing her third-act tea dress of "flesh satin . . . embroidered with pearls and lace," Ina Claire told the same reporter: "It is a fact that every gold digging incident in the play has happened in New York."[15]

But if most of the critics agreed that Belasco and Hopwood had hit on a comedy that was sure to dig them plenty of gold, they didn't necessarily agree that the gold-digging incidents and the portrayal of the chorus girl were particularly accurate. Surprisingly, however, Heywood Broun felt that, despite a somewhat sentimental, and at times burlesque treatment of the characters, the "essential spirit" of the girls was "quite the most accurate portrayal of the type, which the American stage [had] known."[16] (*The Chorus Lady* [1906] had been a successful predecessor on the theme.) "But why," asked Courtenay Savage in the *Forum,* did Mr. Hopwood write the play about chorus girls of this type, when the real story of a chorus girl who attempts to live on her thirty-five dollars a week, would be so much more typical and possibly interesting?"[17] "Maybe some day," answered the *Variety* reviewer, "when he forgets the box office, Mr. Hopwood will."[18] Clearly, Hopwood, who had always been a

gold digger himself, so to speak, knew where his strengths lay. Belasco had
asked for a starring vehicle, and that is what he had been given. In an interview
two years later, Hopwood confessed it had been something of a job:

> No cinch to put a girl into that circle, keep sympathy for her, keep her clean,
> get her "a good man in marriage" at the end and still let the thing be a fairly
> true picture of that life. I worked myself woozy over that scenario.[19]

Although there is still some question about whether the play was actually
written for Ina Claire, Woollcott's scenario seems appropriate:

> If *The Gold Diggers* was not written to order for Miss Claire, it was probably
> rewritten for her, and if it was not altered to fit, it looks as if it were. It plays
> as though it had grown out of the following letter:
>
> Dear Old Avery Hopwood:
>
> Kindly write for Miss Ina Claire a three-act comedy along the following lines
> of specification:
>   1. Leading part must be that of a chorus girl.
>   2. Leading part must have a chance to wear three startling gowns and one
>   or two startling negligees.
>   3. Leading part must have one dance and two songs.
>   4. Leading part must have one scene of intoxication and two dialect op-
>   portunities, French and Yiddish.
> Kindly deliver same at once and oblige.
>
> > Yours ruthlessly,
> > David Belasco[20]

Ina Claire and the rest of the cast received good notices in the comedy,
and were credited with contributing much to the overall success of the piece.
Although Miss Claire was generally praised for her "naturalness and grace and
understanding," one critic noted that her work was "still somewhat obscured
by a tendency toward . . . imitation of other actresses." "We are still anxious
to see the real Miss Claire," he wrote, "and not her haunting suggestion of Jane
Cowl."[21] Of special note was Jobyna Howland, "the six-foot Gibson model"
who "genuinely" and "irresistibly" played the part of Mabel Munroe, the man
chaser. Bruce McRae turned in his customary solid and sophisticated performance, as did H. Reeves Smith as the friend. A sentimental chord was struck
on opening night as audiences burst into "thunderous" applause when Pauline
Hall, a veteran actress who conjured up memories of the old days when
photographs of Lillian Russell and Fay Templeton were still smuggled in
cigarette packages, made her appearance as Cissie Gray, the ex-chorus girl
reduced to selling perfumed soaps in her old age.[22]

Everything about the production had been designed to make it an entertainment of immense theatrical appeal. The capacity audiences seemed to

grow even larger as the play moved into 1920. When Prohibition struck on January 18, the crowds at the Lyceum began to revel in the champagne atmosphere that surrounded the performance. Before long, it was billed as the most "sparkling" comedy in town. By May, *Variety* was reporting on the play's remarkable ability to draw "repeaters," and speculating that a large number of musical comedy performers in the cast had developed a loyal following that would keep the show running well into the next season.[23]

As the play moved into 1921, rumors began to circulate about the star: James Whittaker, drama correspondent for the *Chicago Tribune*, announced that Ina Claire had recently become his wife, and that she intended to leave the show and the Belasco management that summer. In Whittaker's opinion, *The Gold Diggers* was "aimless," and asked nothing of his wife "that was more than skin deep."[24] It was even said that if Miss Claire had known Belasco was going to put her into the piece, she never would have signed an acting contract with him in the first place. Doubtless the star had grown weary of the vehicle after almost two years. Towards spring 1921, the rumor was made official; Ina Claire would leave *The Gold Diggers* due to a severe throat condition. On May 20, vaudeville and musical comedy performer Gertrude Vanderbilt stepped into the role of Jerry Lamar.

Ina Claire continued to play light comedy roles throughout the twenties, emerging as a more serious actress in 1932 as Marion Froude in S.N. Behrman's *Biography*. In an interview with Helen Ormsby in 1938 she spoke of her early years:

> *The Gold Diggers* was pretty rough stuff, and that was as far as I had progressed when Edgar Selwyn talked to me. After that I began to study comedy—really study and work hard. I married and gave up the stage for two years . . . but, believe me, I couldn't get back fast enough. In those two years, though, all the phony values in the theatre had faded out for me; I was only interested in what was genuine and true.[25]

A viewing of Ina Claire's flirtatious performance as Jean in the 1932 film *The Greeks Had a Word for It* (later, *Three Broadway Girls*), gives a delicious taste of what her Jerry Lamar of *The Gold Diggers* might have been like, in contrast to her sophisticated yet no less alluring and beguiling Duchess Swana of 1939's *Ninotchka*.

"Rough stuff" *The Gold Diggers* was when compared to the best of the later comedies of Behrman, Barry, or the Kaufman collaborations, but it caught the fancy of the public. Audiences kept the show running for three months after Ina Claire departed, achieving a total of 720 performances during its two-year run. A successful tour followed. Hopwood couldn't have helped but nod in cynical agreement had he lived to hear the lead lyric from the most famous of his play's movie musical spinoffs: "We're in the Money" from *Gold Diggers of 1933*. The original property earned him at least $236,000 in royalties.[26] *The Gold Diggers* made its last professional appearance on the Broadway Television Theatre, December 29, 1952.[27]

Three days before the premiere of *The Gold Diggers*, Mary Rinehart wrote
Hopwood to say that she had been working on a new novel, and that her
mother had been seriously ill. Consequently, she had not been able to do any
more writing on their thriller, but she thought she could give a good week's
attention to it in late October before she had to return to California on
business. Admitting that she would have to steal this time from the novel, she
asked Hopwood to work up a "tentative last act," in order to save them "a lot
of trouble and time later." It would be best if she came to New York for the
work; there would be fewer family distractions there. Her letter caught up with
Hopwood on the road, and he sent her an immediate response:

The Washington
Washington, D.C.
October 2, 1919.

Dear Mary: —

I have launched "The Gold Diggers" successfully in New York, and am here
with "The Girl in the Limousine", which opens in New York next Monday,
October 6th. From about October tenth, on, I will be free to work on "The
Hidden Room". If you prefer, I can come on to New York, if that would
fit in better with your plans....
I was so very sorry to hear about your Mother. I trust that she is better.

Sincerely your's,
Hop[28]

The Girl in the Limousine, or, *Betty's Bed*, as the script was originally entitled,
was Hopwood's first play to be produced under the management of A.[lbert]
H.[erman] Woods.

"Saint Al," as Percy Hammond dubbed Woods, was a colorful and self-
educated man of the commercial theatre. Able to hit a brass spittoon across
an uncrowded room, he was rarely without a large cigar clamped between the
teeth of his wide mouth that often let fly with some of the most descriptive
profanity in show business. He addressed everyone as "Sweetheart," and,
although a shrewd businessman, he was known for his benevolence. An incident that occurred during the recent actors' strike was typical of his character.
He stopped in front of a theatre one day and told a group of rain-drenched
pickets:

There's a store open down the street. You go on down there and buy some
raincoats, and I'll pay for them. I don't want you to get pneumonia, because
when all this is over, I'm going to need you again.[29]

Woods's early career was built in partnership with P.H. Sullivan and Sam H.
Harris producing lurid pieces such as Theodore Kremer's *The Bowery After
Dark* (1902) and *The Evil That Men Do* (1903), which offered working-class

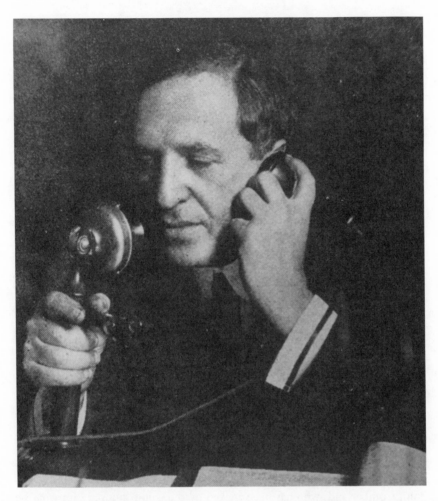

Al Woods, King of 42nd Street entertainment, 1922.

audiences plenty of thrills for 10-20-30 cents a ticket. A series of reworked "villain-pursues-working-girl" melodramas continued to build Woods's success; there was Kremer's *Bertha, the Sewing Machine Girl* (1906), followed by the creations of a young man from Harvard, Owen Davis, who could turn out formula plays at assembly-line speed: *Edna, the Pretty Typewriter; Nellie, the Beautiful Cloak Model;* and *Convict 999* were but three of the scores of plays Davis cranked out for Woods before audiences had had enough of this kind of entertainment and the two decided to part company. Davis went on to write more serious drama, as will be seen, and Woods left his partnership with Sullivan and Harris and moved uptown to Broadway, where he scored a tremendous hit with the scandalous *The Girl from Rectors* in 1909.

Now, in 1919, Woods was sitting in an office high atop his own theatre on Forty-second Street, The Eltinge, named for his lucrative client, the popular female impersonator, Julian Eltinge. From this theatre, Woods continued to amass a fortune following his proven dramatic theory: "Write me a play to fit the title and match the poster."[30] Only now, he was cashing in on the post-war enthusiasm for bedroom farce, and Avery Hopwood would "fill the bill."

Betty's Bed was originally the work of Wilson Collison, an ex-druggist from Kansas City, who had come to New York, like Hopwood, in search of vast royalties. Collison had had his first success for Woods earlier in 1919 with *Up in Mabel's Room*, which Otto Harbach had reworked. For *Betty's Bed*, however, Woods had called in Hopwood to re-vamp the script.[31] Eventually, Hopwood's name became attached to *Up in Mabel's Room* also; and, although according to Van Vechten, Hopwood may have done some doctoring on it, the piece was clearly credited to Collison and Harbach. It is easy to see, however, why Hopwood's name became associated with the title, since his name was practically synonymous with bedroom farce by the end of his life.

When Hopwood presented Woods with the rewrites of *Betty's Bed*, Saint Al flipped through the pages and said: "We'll call it *The Girl in the Limousine*." Hopwood agreed that the title seemed "fetching" enough, but that unfortunately "there was no reference in the play to any such girl and none to a limousine." "That's easy," replied Woods, "you can put that in." Hopwood told Archie Bell that that is exactly what he did—"scratched out a few lines, wrote in a few more, accounted for a limousine offstage," and added "a new air of mystery."[32] The play opened two months later, and scored a hit.

Destined to be the "most bed-ridden" bedroom farce ever to hit Broadway, *The Girl in the Limousine* was typical of the more flagrant exhibitions Hopwood was to concoct for Woods. The plot, as Woollcott observed, "doesn't matter"; noting, with the names of Collison and Hopwood attached to it, the title might have read: "In Mabel's Room and Warmer." Calling it "bedroom farce to the limit," he did concede that the laughs were new and real."[33] The play centers on a situation involving Tony Hamilton, innocently played by John Cumberland, who has been tricked by thugs into stopping for what he thinks is a girl stranded along the road. The girl, unfortunately, has turned out to be one of the crooks. After knocking Tony unconscious, the two thugs have brought him to a nearby house, where they strip him down to his "silks," and dump him in a darkened bedroom off the garden. Earlier, Betty, played by film actress Doris Kenyon, had left a party she was giving in another part of the house to come in and lie down. When the thieves discover there is a woman in the bed, they hurriedly roll Tony's body underneath and out of sight.

Before long, Tony, who had been on his way to the party, is behind the bed, in the closet, under the covers, in the clothes hamper, and in countless other places, trying to keep from being discovered. The complication comes when Betty's Aunt Cicely (Zelda Sears) arrives, mistaking Tony for Betty's husband, whom she has never met, and who has left on a business trip. Betty tries to explain, but well-intentioned Aung Cicely, perceiving that Betty has come down with a cold, forces her back to bed, and insists that Tony crawl in too, for he has started to sniffle. When Cicely finally realizes what she has done, she exclaims: "I have never sworn in my life, but, by God, I hope I haven't poulticed her lover!" "Where am I," she asks in disgust, "in Greenwich Village or Sodom and Gomorrah?" As Woollcott commented, why did she need to ask, "when her locale is so easily recognized as the middle of an Avery Hopwood farce."[34]

The Girl in the Limousine was acted by an outstanding group of farceurs, and the critics appear to have enjoyed it for what it was intended to be: "an effective combatant against the common enemy called gloom."[35] Doris Kenyon's performance "decorated" the production well enough, but John Cumberland was outstanding in his character of Tony, his performance earning him the epithet "an immoral little Jack-in-the-box." Medals for the most hilarious characterizations went to Zelda Sears as the aunt and the rising young comic actor Charles Ruggles as Jimmie Galen, the family doctor who thinks he is hallucinating. The piece gained hit status, but predictions for a full-season run did not materialize — the show lasted just 137 performances.

Kenneth Macgowan, one of the champions of the new movement, and co-editor with Sheldon Cheney of *Theatre Arts Magazine*, noted the limited run of *The Girl in the Limousine, Nightie Night, Breakfast in Bed,* and like farces with a renewed optimism for the development of the American theatre. The melodramas, farces, and pallid comedies that could have expected a full-season run in any of the earlier seasons, were beginning to close after only three or four months. Clearly, the "emotional" and "mental" tone of the popular audience was changing. A "growing audience of intelligent and sensitive folk," he observed, "have begun to find the theatre a place worth their attention." Strictly commercial managers were even contributing enough worthwhile productions "to make it plain that there was a distinct shift in public taste."[36] Productions of such plays as Booth Tarkington's *Clarence* with Alfred Lunt and Helen Hayes, John Drinkwater's *Abraham Lincoln*, Gorky's *Night Lodging*, St. John Ervine's *Jane Clegg*, and Andreyev's *Sabine Women* were solid evidence of the new direction the New York theatre was taking.

Ironically, the week of February 1, 1920, which saw the closing of the epitome of the bedroom farce, *The Girl in the Limousine*, also witnessed the opening of *Beyond the Horizon*, Eugene O'Neill's first Broadway production. Emerging when he did, O'Neill represented a revolutionizing force in the American theatre, and he soon took his place "as the leader in a general playwriting revolt against the artificiality of the American drama."[37] Winning the first of four Pulitzer prizes for O'Neill, *Beyond the Horizon* marked the beginning of a theatre for the dramatist and the end of a theatre for the playmaker. Describing the "American Drama Mid-Channel," Macgowan capsulized the transition:

> These months the American theatre is passing through the most interesting and significant period of its history. It has come out of a

century of Colonial dramas, history plays and minstrel shows, frontier melodramas, Civil War melodramas and Wall Street melodramas, small-town comedy from Broadway to Oshkosh, crook plays and bedroom farces. It has passed through the stock company, the Daly-Wallack-Frohman organizations, the star, longrun and touring systems. To-day—thanks to a more or less mystical combination of the war, economics and the uncharted surge of the creative spirit—the American theatre is rushing ahead at a break-neck (and pocketbook) speed into the most picturesque and most active professional theatre in the world. It seems about to bring forth theatre organizations to match its producers and designers. And there are signs of plays and playwrights to justify them all.[38]

For Hopwood, in this spring of a new decade, changing "mental" tones, and "shifting" public tastes must have seemed inconsequential abstractions in the face of his busy work load. Or, did he view the situation through Mabel's moral: "Dig, sisters, while the digging's good"? An April note to Archie Bell revealed something of his plans for the future:

Life holds glorious surprises, as well as tragic ones.—I know it will all be wonderful.—

I have been away with "I'll Say She Does"—the musical version of "Our Little Wife"—It opens in Boston Monday.—

I expect to have 4 *more* productions in the next four months, so you can imagine how busy I am going to be.[39]

The early months of 1920 also found Hopwood and Rinehart continuing their work on *The Hidden Room*. He telegraphed her at Glen Osborne, Pennsylvania, about plans for their next meeting:

February 18 1920

Will stay William Penn Hotel because am having my mother come to [Pittsburgh] for two or three days and will spend evenings with her . . .

Avery Hopwood[40]

Rinehart recalled she and Hopwood followed a serious work schedule, using the same methods as during *Seven Days*. Writing the last act together, they soon found that changes were necessary in the first two acts. Since *The Hidden Room* was a "stop-watch" play, everything that occurred in the plot had to be carefully accounted for, and the proper offstage time allotted for its happening. After much writing and checking, and rewriting, Hopwood returned to New York with a script that was still not polished. Within a week he read the play to Wagenhals and Kemper, who had expressed an earlier interest in producing it. Hopwood informed Rinehart of the reaction:

2 E. 81 –

Dear Mary: –

Kemper likes it very much. – He thinks tho, that the 2nd act needs strengthening, & that the whole play will be greatly improved by building up Cornelia & Liddy [*sic*], from the comedy side, – I'm inclined to agree with him. – If you come to New York again, let me know & we'll have another whack at the MS.

I think Kemper wd like to try it out in the late Spring. – I'll let you know further details when Wagenhals returns from Europe – I mean, details abt the business end.

Greetings to you all

Hop[41]

Towards the middle of March, Rinehart took her manuscript to New York for a final drafting session. Within a week or two, she and Hopwood had almost polished Act 3, but again they found that Act 2 required more work. After another five days, the play finally seemed in satisfactory shape. Now came the time to begin revising for humor. On April 2, Rinehart wrote to tell her husband that these revisions were proceeding especially slowly. She only hoped that she could hold out until the end.[42] Ten days later, at five o'clock in the afternoon, Hopwood scrawled at the bottom of a page: "The Curtain Falls." Rinehart recalled the time well because just as the two were shaking hands across the table, a telephone message arrived that she was about to become a grandmother; she departed immediately, her active participation in the production completed.[43] Within a short time, Hopwood mailed her the theatrical contract for *The Bat,* as they had resumed calling it:

2 East 81st St.
New York City.

Dear Mrs. Detective: –

I am enclosing the W&K agreement. If it is satisfactory, sign it, & return it to Wagenhals – or perhaps simply write saying that you find it O.K.

"The Bat" is booked to open June 14th, in Washington. – It plays there for a week, then goes to Atlantic City for a week. – W&k. are both very enthusiastic, & working hard to get a fine cast & production.

If you go away, please let me know where I can reach you, if we have to consult you about anything.

It will, of course, be necessary for you to see the final rehearsals, & the opening performance of the play.

Greetings to you & the Doctor, & to Alan.

Sincerely
Avery Hopwood[44]

Hopwood and Rinehart were so convinced they had a solid success in *The Bat,* that they each invested $5,000 towards the $20,000 cost of the initial production. Wagenhals and Kemper also owned 25 percent each. Net profits from the play were to be split among the shareholders, and stock, motion picture, and other rights would be divided in the same way. Wagenhals and Kemper would each be paid $200 a week for the New York run, with road companies paying them an additional $200 per week, provided the weekly gross ran over $5,000; otherwise, they would receive only $100. The royalties paid to Hopwood and Rinehart were based on the gross profit, and were fixed for the initial run and for any future companies (Appendix C, letter 2). The collaborators would receive 5 percent of the first $4,000 in weekly receipts, 7.5 percent of the next $2,000, and 10 percent of all weekly earnings over $6,000.[45] With six companies eventually touring the country, it is easy to see why *The Bat* was the authors' greatest financial success.

Rehearsals for *The Bat* got under way at the end of May, but Rinehart would not be able to attend; she was planning a much-needed vacation out West. Hopwood wired her that she wouldn't have to be at the first rehearsals because she "simply would have to listen to people learning lines," but he thought it would be "nice" if she could attend the final ones. He reported that Kemper, who was directing the play, had assembled a most promising cast. According to Rinehart, Kemper's direction and meticulous attention to the weaving of the plot contributed significantly to the play's success. His astuteness in gaining the desired effects was remarkable, if not cagey. A synopsis will make it clear why careful direction was necessary to the play's success.

Cornelia Van Gorder, an elderly unmarried lady, has rented a summer house belonging to a New York banker who is believed to have been murdered on a trip to Colorado some days before. Van Gorder soon discovers that the house is thought to contain a hidden room where the banker may have secreted a large sum of money. Undaunted by warnings that the house and surrounding area have been the target of a thief known as The Bat, she refuses to leave the premises. After repeated attempts by someone to enter the house, Van Gorder calls in a detective to help catch The Bat. Some suspect that The Bat may even be the banker himself. Three other people soon arrive looking for the money: Brooks, a gardener, who is eventually revealed as Jack Bailey, a young bank cashier who has been accused of embezzling the funds; his girlfriend and apparent accomplice, Dale Ogden, who is Van Gorder's niece; and Doctor Wells, who had been a friend of the missing banker. Mixed into this group, among others, are an Unknown Man; Lizzie, Van Gorder's flighty maid; and The Bat. Before the mystery is solved there is a series of mysterious happenings, including broken windows, gleaming eyes that float about in the dark, two bloody murders, and the sudden appearance of the shadow of a bat on the doors and windows. Flashes of lightning and the eerie sounds of thunder and of flapping wings heighten the thrills, keeping the audience in suspense until the final moments, when it is revealed that the man whom everyone has supposed to be the detective is actually The Bat.

Since the entire success of the mystery depended on the audience's acceptance of this twist, Kemper knew that the actor playing the detective could not belie himself. Early on, he had decided not to let the cast see the ending of the play until just before dress rehearsals, when they would be given the brief final scene. Harrison Hunter, the actor who portrayed the detective, was outraged when he discovered that he was The Bat. He indignantly informed Kemper "he did not want to play criminal parts." But Kemper's tactic had worked perfectly. "Set in his lines and business by that time," Rinehart tells us, "Mr. Hunter played the straight part of the detective so well that his identity with the Bat astounded the audience."[46] It is difficult in these days, when so many whodunits have come and gone, to appreciate the impact of this realization on the audiences of 1920, but surprised they were. Although the device had been used once before in Gaston Leroux's book *The Mystery of the Yellow Room*, *The Bat* was the first play to introduce the ploy.[47] A program note that asked patrons not to divulge the ending apparently worked, for the play ran over two years. One newspaper called the solution "the best-kept secret in New York."[48]

The success of *The Bat* had been mounting since its June tryout in Washington, when it was being billed as *A Thief in the Night*. Spurred on by substantial increases in the nightly box office, enthusiastic theatre owners from New York City actively bid for the piece. The Morosco Theatre finally won the honors, and the play opened there on August 23, 1920, to an immediate popular success under its original title, *The Bat*. A portion of Robert Benchley's review in *Life* captures the general audience response:

> From eight-thirty to eleven you are leaping about in your seat in a state bordering on epilepsy, pressing moist palms on the sleeves of the people on either side of you, reassuring yourself with little nervous laughs that this is only the theatre, and then collapsing into the aisle at the end of each act. Fortunately, you are not at all conspicuous, as the aisle is full of similar casualties.[49]

Certain critics who had dismissed the play as "hokum" on the first night, were praising the play a week later. Finding something to pick at, several critics condemned the humorous touches that Rinehart and Hopwood had spent so much time adding. The laughable hysterics of Lizzie, played by comedienne May Vokes, were considered incongruous with the primary tone of mystery and suspense; but the majority of reviewers, like the audience, welcomed these bits of comic relief. Woollcott, writing in his "Second Thoughts on First Nights" column several months later, expressed his opinion of the authors' intentions:

> Not real thrills, but a state of bogus, self-conscious excitement — that is [the] game. The mood of ghost stories told around the fire in a darkened room, hair-raising tales related in a sepulchral voice to the accompaniment of much jumpiness and all manner of half-smothered laughter, that is the mood *The Bat* invites and most cunningly achieves.[50]

But if Woollcott had succeeded in analyzing the play's effect, he was not prepared to give Hopwood much credit for its overall success. In his initial review, he had said that nowhere was Hopwood's "touch recognizable." "Probably all he brought to the joint product," Woollcott wrote, "was a consultant's special knowledge of the stage, its tricks and its manners."[51] Undoubtedly Hopwood performed these tasks, but, as Rinehart's autobiography and the correspondence between the two indicate, they worked together much more closely. By 1922, Woollcott still had cause for mentioning *The Bat*. He admitted that the play had established a vogue for mystery plays, just as the collaborators' earlier *Seven Days* had revived a taste for obvious farce in America.

Within a year of the Broadway opening of *The Bat,* there were six touring companies of the show breaking box-office records in every region of the country. A one-night stand in Americus, Georgia, alone earned $1,343.[52]

The fall of 1920 had found Hopwood following the Chicago Company as it played its way through the Midwest: Wilkes-Barre three nights, Syracuse three nights, Detroit for a week, and then on to the "Windy City." Jotting Doctor Rinehart a note from The Lambs before joining the company in Wilkes-Barre, Hopwood had told him: "The Chicago 'Bat' Co. looks to be in very good shape, . . . I shall be in Chicago for the opening, Dec. 26. I'll let you know . . . how the performance goes."[53] But when Hopwood wrote again, he had a rather pathetic tale to tell:

> 2 East 81st St
> New York City

Dear Mary: —

I am glad that you will have a chance to see "The Bat" in Chicago. — When you get there, Katharine Gray will be playing Cornelia. — The company seems to me to be good in the main — & certainly it is doing wonderful business. — I'm glad you didn't attend the Xmas premiere, — I never passed such an agonizing event in the theatre, — watching poor Mrs. [Lizzie Hudson] Collier trying to articulate the long words that we gave Cornelia. — I think Mrs. Collier had a slight stroke — certainly, there was an embolism, which affected the speech centers. — I would have liked you & the Doctor to lean *on,* that night (I stood up — it was a sell-out) — but I think you would have collapsed, before the end of the evening. — The agony continued — tho diminished — through the next two or three performances. — The terrible thing about it, the first night was that many people in the theatre thought that the poor woman had been drinking — & she *knew* that they thought it because there were titters when she would struggle with a word. And yet — the wonderful part of it all was, — that tho it affected the notices, somewhat, it apparently made nary a crink in the business, — and bear in mind — the rest of the company were so upset the opening night, that they *all* gave their worst performance. It was rather marvelous, though, — to see the play

Opposite: The Bat *company around 1921, Act II climax, Morosco Theatre.*

weathering it through.—for all the world like a stout ship, riding the
storm. . . .

Sincerely
Hop[54]

The Chicago *Bat* Company may have "weathered" the opening performances
well, but the ultimate popularity of the show soon gave rise to a new kind of
problem.

By September 1921, a motion picture adaptation of Rinehart's *The Circular Staircase* was being shown in Chicago billed as *The Bat*. Rinehart had sold
the rights to *Staircase* to movie producer William N. Selig as early as 1915, but
she had bought back the rights in the spring of 1920 in order to protect her
interests. When Hopwood and Wagenhals and Kemper realized that Selig's
rerelease of *The Circular Staircase* as *The Bat* was cutting into *The Bat's* box
office, they immediately contacted Rinehart to seek her support in suing Selig
for false advertising.

Hopwood appealed to Rinehart to make it clear that *The Circular Staircase*
and *The Bat* were two distinct works. Rinehart replied: "To say I am upset is
putting it mildly. . . . THE CIRCULAR STAIRCASE is not THE BAT (as who should
know better than you and I?)"[55] Supporting Hopwood and Wagenhals and
Kemper, Rinehart encouraged them to get an expert lawyer who knew "all the
tricks Selig would try to pull," and have an injunction issued preventing the
motion picture from being shown while the case was being settled. "There is
no use in losing one hundred thousand dollars," she told them, "to save a thousand" (Appendix C, letter 3). Hopwood and Rinehart eventually had *The Bat*
novelized (anonymously, by the young Stephen Vincent Benét),[56] undoubtedly to make their point clear that the play was distinct from the earlier
mystery. Motion picture rights to *The Bat* were later sold for $50,000; the col-
laborators had not lost much money.

Although Hopwood's financial records are not available, one is able to
form an accurate idea of his earnings by looking at Rinehart's, who shared a
like amount. Rinehart's share of the total royalties by the end of 1923—not
counting foreign productions, stock performances, and movie rights—
amounted to $200,902.35. Add to this total the $275,326.18 in profits from
the shares owned in the production, and the final income for each of the
playwrights approached half a million dollars. By 1946 it was estimated that
over ten million people had seen the play, and that it had grossed well over
$9,000,000.[57] Its New York run of 878 performances made it the longest run-
ning mystery play during the twenties and thirties, despite the inevitable
number of thrillers that were patterned after it. The success of *The Bat* was the
culmination of Hopwood's triumph during the 1920—1921 season.

While working on *The Bat*, Hopwood and Rinehart had also been preparing an adaptation of *Aux Jardins de Merci* by José Felice y Codina, Carlos de
Battle and H. Maurice Jacquet, which Wagenhals and Kemper had seen in

Spanish Love, *Act II, William Powell (leans forward center) and cast, 1920.*

Europe and wanted to produce in America. Hopwood prepared the first draft of *Spanish Love,* as the American version was called, in New York, and Rinehart worked on polishing the script from her office in Pittsburgh, sending rewrites to Hopwood as she finished them. With the play set to open six days before *The Bat,* they had to work at an exhausting pace. Rinehart remembered having to remove long asides and lengthy speeches by the leading characters. "The dramatic values of the story were almost completely lost in a mess of talk, incident and a type of crude peasant humor which was probably obsolete in Spain, and was certainly of no value in America," she recalled.[58] Woollcott wasn't exactly certain why the "Avery Hopwood Playmaking Factory" and Mary Roberts Rinehart had been called in to reconstruct the tale, since "vivid and violent melodrama" was clearly a departure from their regular fare; but he assumed it was simply because they had given the producers a hit in *Seven Days.*[59]

The success of *Spanish Love* hinged largely on its colorful and innovative production values. Wagenhals and Kemper had spent several weeks in Spain gathering properties, buying fabrics, and making plans for an elaborate and unique setting. An imported troupe of Spanish dancers, plenty of castanets and voiced chimes, beautiful sunset effects and gorgeous native costumes would all combine to seduce the audience into empathizing with the tale's age-old theme of passion and revenge.

The play was produced at Maxine Elliott's Theatre, where Kemper altered the acting space for increased intimacy by covering the orchestra pit for use as a forestage, the first in a Broadway theatre. Kemper then used the aisles and lower boxes of the theatre as acting areas, directing characters to enter and exit through the auditorium.[60] In the end, this manner of playing annoyed many of the critics, who thought the technique only suitable for a Winter Garden musical. But the public, after the initial nervous reactions, enjoyed the concept immensely. Sometimes, reported Broun in the *Tribune,*

> this method contributed to the effect. There was, for instance, a thrilling first act curtain, when Pencho came back from outlawry and gazed straight over the heads of the audience at the crowd of the village folk who were fleeing up the aisle. . . . On the other hand we were startled entirely out of our attention for a certain scene upon a darkened stage when a voice just behind us exclaimed, "Come on, old lazybones!" We looked back angrily at an inoffensive old man in Row H only to discover that the comic father of the heroine was making an unexpected entrance down the center aisle. We have often found that something of the illusion is lost when the playgoer comes face to face with the player. When actors are not on the stage they ought to be in The Lambs or some other quiet fastness safe from prying.[61]

In short, "a Spanish love affair," wrote Robert Benchley, "like a Spanish bullfight, ought really to be kept within the confines of the arena."[62]

Critics were unanimous, however, in their opinions that the acting of the play possessed a fresh vitality in keeping with the emotionalism of the piece. "It bids the players cut loose from all the restraints that modern plays have taught them," said Woollcott, "and some of them break free as if they had longed for just such freedom all these days in the theatre."[63] Young William Powell, in his first major speaking role on Broadway, gave the young lover, Javier, an engaging spirit and sense of humanity. Equally effective was James Rennie as Pencho, the rival suitor for the hand of Maria del Carmen, played by Maria Ascarra. But Miss Ascarra's talents failed to measure up to the requirements of the heroine's role. Aside from her Spanish blood and appearance, Woollcott was hard pressed to think of any reason for casting her in the part. A first-rate actress, "even if she had been born in Chicago and named Margie Gilhooley," would have been preferable in his opinion.[64] The most telling moment in the acting came at the end, after the intense rivalry between Javier and Pencho had been resolved and their hatred had died away: the two men embraced silently before the weakened Javier slipped dying to the floor.

"Looking back over my experiences in the theatre," observed Rinehart in her autobiography,

> and over that highly successful combination of Wagenhals and Kemper, Avery Hopwood and myself, I believe that if we made our stars, our stars in turn made us; a bit of credit which might be given more often than it is.[65]

Spanish Love wasn't "A Babe Ruth Home Run," as one telegram was to describe *The Bat's* big hit six days later, but it did very well, playing for 307 performances, and earning the authors $87,000 apiece.

On August 31, 1920, Hopwood wrote to Rinehart to bring her up to date on all the news and the excitement she had been missing:

> First of all – ain't it a grand and glorious feeling – about "Spanish Love", and "The Bat"! – I think that the latter play will wear out the edges of the chairs, in the Morosco. No one sits anywhere but on the edge, during the performance. When I was in Washington, with Spanish Love, I found out that the natives were still arguing about certain episodes in "The Bat". A man in one of the departments told me that whenever he heard a row going on in his office, he knew that it was about the "Doctor" or "The Unknown" – or about who went up-the stairs, or who was behind the couch.
>
> Before I left New York, [R. Larry] Giffen, of the Kauser office, called me up to inquire about the film rights to "Seven Days". I told him that they had been disposed of. I believe that the best policy is to keep absolutely mum about these rights, until next February, when they revert to us. I am sure that we can dispose of them again, for a very big sum, for the title is a highly valuable one, for the movies. I would not let Giffen in on this piece of information for the present, for it might leak out to the present holders of the rights, and if they chose to revive the original film version, or prepare another one, we would be left waiting at the church....
>
> When will you be in the East again? You must be sure to go to New York, and see the two plays in action. I wish that you could have been there for the premieres. It would have done you good to see them both go over with a bang....
>
> I hope we can move [*Spanish Love*] from the Maxine Elliott, to some larger theatre. The M.E. is too small, and, like the other theatres below Forty Second Street has no window sale. If we move to Forty Second Street, or above it, we will play to much larger business....[66]

Hopwood's third offering of the 1920 season was more in keeping with the pastry he was used to serving up on Forty-second Street: *Ladies' Night (In a Turkish Bath)*. This farce, written in collaboration with Charlton Andrews, opened at the Eltinge Theatre on August 9, before *Spanish Love* or *The Bat*. It was said that in producing this play, Woods was attempting to get away from the bedroom farce, but all he succeeded in doing was to move the actors out of the bedroom into the baths. Critics called it a case of going from "bed to worse." At one point, it was rumored that Woods had even innocently suggested that Hopwood should adapt *Othello* for him and call the piece "Up in Desdemona's Room."[67] Clearly, there was still money to be made from risqué farce. But *Ladies' Night* carried the usual situations a step further; it seemed to be an exercise in testing how far a farce could go without bringing in the police. The play apparently disappointed no one who enjoyed being shocked, for it presented "all the old thrills and a few more – bare legs, the shimmy, jokes with double meanings, vampires, bathroom scenes, underwear, and

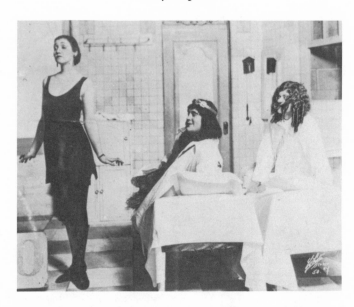

Ladies' Night, *Act III, Judith Vosselli, Edward Douglas, and Charles Ruggles, 1920.*

infidelity."[68] Although no reading copy of the play is available, one is able to form a good picture of the piece from the opening night reviews.

The story centers on bashful Jimmy Walters whose embarrassment over the scanty attire affected by the ladies of the "smart set" keeps him a recluse. His wife complains that they never have any amusement in their lives, and his friends laugh at his prudish, old-fashioned ways. Deciding to cure him once and for all, two of his chums trick him into attending a costume ball at a notorious club in town where they hope he will overcome his inhibitions. A police raid on the club forces the men to flee, their identities concealed by the female dresses they don. Jumping through the first open window they see, the chums suddenly find themselves in a Turkish bath on ladies' night. Jimmy's horror at seeing so many "unadorned" women is compounded when he discovers his wife, who has come there to forget her domestic troubles. The remainder of the plot revolves around the compromising and embarrassing situations that occur as Jimmy attempts to escape from the bath.

John Cumberland's portrayal of the injured and innocent Jimmy won him the dubious but lucrative distinction of having acted consecutively in more bedroom farces than any other actor in New York. Winner of most of the evening's laughs was Charles Ruggles in the broad comedy role of Fred Bonner, while Claiborne Foster, Allyn King and Evelyn Gasnell were good at *not* concealing their shapely figures. Or, as Broun put it: "The women led in physical attractiveness; the men in acting."

Arthur Hornblow found the piece "entirely unworthy of the talents of the two gentlemen implicated in the authorship":

One is sorry to find Mr. Andrews, author of *The Drama Today* and other works dealing with the intellectual theatre, fathering such a mental defective. If our college trained men do not hesitate on occasion to descend into the morass, we may well despair of the future of the American stage. Mr. Hopwood, it is true, specializes in this sort of dubious gaiety, but heretofore even he has been rather careful of his trademark. One expects better than this from the author of *Nobody's Widow* and *The Gold Diggers.*[69]

"Is the Undraped Drama Unmoral?" This was the question posed by Hopwood in a January 1921 *Theatre Magazine* mock interview in which he discussed *Ladies' Night:*

> I wrote "Ladies' Night" last year. My collaborator was, and is, — don't gasp! . a college professor! A paradox? I don't think so, for if you will really look at the play dispassionately, you will see that it is meant for nothing more than satire . . . on *outré* fashion, and fashions nowadays, as you may have noticed, are remarkably *outré.* That is all my collaborator suggested, and all I have done. . . . You may say I have gone too far. I don't think so. . . . I have simply forced audiences to face ridiculous facts, and, if these savor of immodesty, that is the fault of Fashion, and not my fault. . . . This play is neither immoral, nor is it unmoral in the present state of society. A girl will allow you to gloat over her charms in a scanty bathing suit, whereas she would shriek her life out, were you to see her in a somewhat similar state of nudity in her bedroom. People go to the theatre to be amused, not shocked, and a travesty of fashion combined with a display of rustic modesty is much more likely to amuse than to shock. . . .
>
> Any manager, or any actor, will tell you that nastiness won't carry any farce. People love a touch of the *risqué* just as they love a cocktail before dinner — if they can get it in these curious times. In a play like "Ladies' Night" there is no trace of sexual feeling, because the whole thing is carried out in a comical way. . . . In a really comic play, as this is acknowledged to be, one is never conscious of the presence of Aphrodite. . . . One cannot be amorous, and laugh one's self to death. . . .
>
> I am of the opinion that this is a play, which the middle-class — meaning the majority of people — enjoy hugely. The prurient come to be shocked, though why they should come at all I can't conceive. The play is not meant to appeal to those people who cover up the legs of their pianos and veil their eyes at the sight of a well-turned ankle. . . . What is my hero but a man of the Victorian type, who has to be brought up to date by a series of — well, make the adjective *outré* — shocks?[70]

As Ethan Mordden points out, Hopwood thought of his farces as "arch and suave, not *hot.*" But surely in the early days of Freud's impact, Hopwood was not so naive as not to realize that audiences *were* aroused by the presence of Aphrodite, even in the midst of a raucous farce. Hopwood was clever enough to capitalize on the smart set's suppressed desires for 375 performances, or a total of $89,000 in royalties. In light of Hopwood's success to this date, it must have been difficult for him to appreciate Woollcott's comment: "The effort to stage such lewdness is part of every season's history, yet the experience of the last ten or fifteen years has proved it one of the less profitable forms of theatrical enterprise."[71] Such was not the case if you did it as well as Hopwood.

With *Ladies' Night, Spanish Love, The Bat* and *The Gold Diggers,* which was now in its second year, Hopwood distinguished himself as the first American playwright in post–World War I times to have four concurrent hits on Broadway. Not since the days of Clyde Fitch, when, according to Woollcott, that author had six plays running in New York, had a native playwright been as successful as Hopwood was in this season.[72] But, "there are certain dismaying indications," the critic observed,

> that he has only just started. It seems altogether likely that Mr. Hopwood will break the Clyde Fitch record this season. Probably some of his friends wish he wouldn't. Probably the best of them think it is high time he stopped dashing off plays with both hands and went into retirement for two years, to emerge blinking with a really fine and enduring comedy under his arm. But perhaps he will not be content to do this until he has fulfilled just once his obvious ambition to have all the plays in New York at one time bear his name on the program.[73]

Hopwood's professed ambition had surfaced as early as 1910, when Archie Bell reported that his goal was to "eclipse the London record of Somerset Maugham, who had had five plays running simultaneously in the British metropolis. 'Five plays in New York next winter or the season following; anyway, before I'm thirty.'"[74] Reaching this objective was taking more time than Hopwood had planned. He was now thirty-eight. Had Hopwood's musical version of *Our Little Wife, I'll Say She Does,* and *The Great Illusion,* (his adaptation of Sacha Guitry's) *L'Illusioniste,* made it past their out-of-town tryouts during the 1920–1921 season, he would have had six properties going at once.

It wasn't long before Hopwood's Broadway successes attracted the attention of the Hollywood moguls. October 1920 found the playwright heading to Los Angeles. A telegram sent to Carl Van Vechten during a brief stopover in Ann Arbor informed his friend: "If anyone asks you where I am just say I have gone west and you don't know my address which will be quite true. In fact I don't know my own address. Love to you and Fania. Avery."[75] Actually, Hopwood had sold several properties to the movies prior to 1920. *Clothes* had been filmed in 1914, *Judy Forgot* in 1915, and adaptations of *Our Little Wife, Fair and Warmer,* and *Sadie Love* had soon followed. Although Hopwood had not written the screenplays for these treatments, he reportedly had a hand in writing a scenario for Samuel Goldwyn in 1918 based upon a lost unproduced work, *Just for Tonight* (Appendix B).

Goldwyn, who had long thought of the writer as the prime element in a movie's success, had been attracting many of the most prominent writers in America and Europe for several years to be a part of his Eminent Authors, Inc. Channing Pollock, Mary Roberts Rinehart, Gertrude Atherton, Somerset

The blasé Mr. Hopwood asks "Is the undraped drama unmoral?" 1921.

Maugham, Sir Gilbert Parker and Rupert Hughes were among those Hopwood might soon join.[76] In most cases, however, these writers had not found their talents suited to motion picture writing. Consequently, their scenarios often required the work of a "hack" to make them acceptable for filming, something which the authors very much resented. Pollock recalled that he and Hopwood had sold *Clothes* to Famous Players–Lasky, only to have it reworked and filmed with the entire climax of the play left out. Financially, this had worked out well, because they were then able to fashion another scenario around the unused episode and sell it again.[77] In the end, though, the idea of writing for Hollywood did not appeal to Hopwood.

Perhaps Hopwood recalled some of the problems Rinehart had encountered in her movie writing prior to the opening of *The Bat*. After returning to New York, he dropped her a note:

> I have been negotiating with the movie people — or rather, they have been negotiating with me — but I have about made up my mind that playwriting is much more satisfactory, in every way, than motion picture work.[78]

A letter written to Van Vechten while Hopwood was still in California indicates that despite his disinclination towards working in the film business, he was, nevertheless, "having a gorgeous time." The Hotel Hollywood was playing host to everyone who was anyone. But, he concluded, in language more revealing than his lines to Rinehart: "I don't think I'm going to write movies. — I am too high priced a whore for that."[79] Buddy understood. Hopwood returned to New York, where his reputation as a moneymaker was still surefire.

In late November, Hopwood elicited the help of Mary Rinehart's husband in an attempt to encourage her to collaborate with him on one more hit:

> I know that Mary has numerous demands upon her for fiction, but I do not think that any line of work would bring her in as much financial return as another play — and when we work together, the chances of success are so much greater. I do not mean that she should commit herself to going on and writing indefinitely, with me, but I do think it would be bully if we could put over at least one more big knockout. It would be enough to make us both financially independent.[80]

Dr. Rinehart answered that it was altogether likely his wife would be able to work on a new play, but not until after she had finished her current novel. Of course, he added, all future plans depended entirely upon her health, and if the writing of the present novel wore her down as much as the writing of the previous one, she would require a long rest after she had finished it.[81] The successful Rinehart/Hopwood collaborations had come to an end. Within a year, the correspondence between the two writers dropped off, and then stopped completely.

By the spring of 1921, Hopwood was able to make his first trip to Europe since the war. Sailing the week of March 20 on board the R.M.S. *Aquitania,* he managed to get a last-minute note off the ship to let Archie Bell know about his plans:

> As you see, I've went & gone an done it! — I expect to be gone 8 weeks, & shall be principally in London & Paris. — I want to review my acquaintance with the London stage, so as to be able to select casts for "The Bat" & "The Gold Diggers", when they are done in London, in the Autumn. — I am leaving in a great rush.[82]

Although *The Gold Diggers* was not produced in London until 1926, *The Bat* did open there in February 1922. It achieved immediate success at the St.

James's Theatre, where it broke all records for attendance, playing for 327 performances.

Aside from affording Hopwood the opportunity to reacquaint himself with the theatres of Europe and England, this trip abroad served as a much-needed holiday. Several seasons of working straight through with the kind of schedule Hopwood had imposed upon himself were beginning to take their toll. He needed a release from the demands of the theatrical grind. Then too, he longed for the kind of personal freedom and diversions that only the Continent could provide. But, if the personal freedom Hopwood could pursue in the capitals and resorts of Europe was exhilarating, it was also self-indulgent, even frenetic. Accompanied on the trip by his secretary and close friend, H. George Brandt, Hopwood undoubtedly shared the same pleasures with him that he and Robert Dempster had enjoyed on their trip to Europe in 1911. Almost nothing is known about Brandt himself, except that he was working for Hopwood by 1918. He apparently aspired to work in set decoration, and he may even have assisted on several of Hopwood's plays. In any case, one imagines him fulfilling the duties Hopwood had written to Archie Bell about as early as 1910:

> My very greatest ambition is to have a wonderful valet, who will feed, and wash and clothe, and brush and shave and etc. me, without my ever having to think about him. — It would be nice if I wouldn't have to pay him either, but I suppose I musn't demand too much. — My second very greatest ambition is to have a secretary, who will read to me while I'm being fed and washed and clothed and etc'd, and who will answer all my letters — except the ones I get from you![83]

By the middle of May, Hopwood had worked his way down to Monte Carlo, where he wrote to Van Vechten and confessed that he had been leading his customary full and varied life abroad. Writing the letter in a mixture of English and idiosyncratic French (inconsistently accented), Hopwood enjoys the bisexual double-entendre he is able to achieve by playing with the grammatical gender:

> Hôtel de Paris
> Monte Carlo
>
> Yes, Buddy mia — me voici — & how I miss Buddy, in Monte — not to mention Carlo! — and *Oh* how I miss Fania & Mabel Dodge! . . .
> — votre chere amie, la preceuse [*sic*] biche Georges Brandt est a Berlin — et le Sacha est ici, with the accent on the see.
> Il y a des grandes choses a voir — et à avoir, a Monte Carl' — J'en ai vues, & j'en ai eues, plusieurs —
> Mais pourquoi le feminin? — demande le petit Buddy — Eh heu — c'est la guerre!
> Je reviens aux Etats Deshabilles vers le 11 Juin. (par l'Aquitania) — et —

je l'espere—je reviendrai seule—(Cette fois le petit Buddy ne demande pourquoi le feminin!)

Je pars demain per Firenze—where I 'opes to 'ave many h'adventures—and probably shall & will not (When in doubt, include all available forms of the verb)

I thought of you, in Paris dans la rue du chat qui peche.

And now I must away to the gambling well, & sell myself to the lowest biter.

A rivederci, Carlo mio.

Mille baisers—partout—pour ma Fania adoree

May 13 [1921]   Avery[84]

While Hopwood was away, *Variety* reported that his royalties for the 1920–21 season would approach the half million mark, more than any other playwright's of the day. The only writers who came close to his take for the year were Otto Harbach, Guy Bolton, Samuel Shipman, the prolific writer of melodrama, and James Montgomery, whose *Irene* had achieved international success.[85] When Hopwood returned to the States in June, he had it in mind to make even more money. Taking rooms at the Ambassador in New York, he quickly resumed a disciplined work schedule during the day in order to get two new plays ready for the coming season: *Getting Gertie's Garter*, another potboiler collaboration with Wilson Collison, and *The Demi-Virgin*, the idea for which he had brought back with him from Paris. He informed Archie Bell that here he was "working like the devil as usual," although he wasn't sure he knew just why. He was certain, however, that he couldn't leave New York until the things he was "scribbling on" were finished. "The first day that I was back," he confessed, "I was rebellious—but now I've become resigned." Admitting, "I even *like* New York again."[86]

The title *Getting Gertie's Garter*, like *Up in Mabel's Room*, has come to epitomize the flagrant bedroom farces that were still being written in the early twenties. Although Hopwood, as has been pointed out, was not openly involved with the concoction of *Mabel*, he apparently did enough work on *Gertie* to warrant co-billing with Collison. Al Woods's personal copy of the script in the Pollock Theatre Collection at Howard University lists only Collison's name on the title page, which would indicate that Hopwood was called in to doctor it. "I am here with 'Getting Gertie's Garter,'" he wrote Archie Bell from the Hotel Traymore in Atlantic City, "which looks as if it wd make money—which is why I am connected with it—so I hope it does!"[87] The play had actually had its tryouts as early as April 1921, while Hopwood was still in Europe. Playing under the title *Gertie's Garter*, it apparently was in desperate need of reworking from the beginning. A *Variety* news item reported that the play's star, Hazel Dawn, was dissatisfied with her role, and that she intended to quit the show after its run in Boston.[88] Although she was still with the piece when it played Chicago two weeks later, her opinion of it hadn't changed much: "The garter," she told Percy Hammond, "has lost its carnal significance, and there is no more interest in [it] as a naughty thing than there is in a virgin's wimple."[89] Dawn had played the lead in *Up in Mabel's Room* also, and as far as she was concerned *Gertie's Garter* was the same thing but duller. However, for one reason or another she stuck with the piece, and opened it in New York on August 1, 1921.

Getting Gertie's garter is exactly what the play is about. Gertie, who has just married Teddy Darling, spends the better part of two hours attempting to return a diamond-studded garter to her old boyfriend, Ken Walrick, who had given it to her the previous year. If Teddy, or Ken's wife, Patty, ever learned that Gertie was wearing a garter that contained a picture of Ken, there could be trouble. Unlike the typical bedroom farce, the chase in *Getting Gertie's Garter* leads not to the boudoir, but to the nearest hay loft. Patty, attempting to get back at Ken, leads Teddy's sister's husband, Billy, to the barn, where she hopes they will be discovered in a compromising situation. Things get warm when Patty, hidden under the hay with Billy, removes her rain-drenched clothing, only to have the others arrive at the opportune moment. Before long, the running and hiding become so frantic the drunken butler exclaims: "The barn's getting like the house, slammier and slammier." In the end, all the risqué situations are explained away, and the proper couples go off to their respective bedrooms to enjoy their second honeymoons.

Gertie's Garter is definitely old school farce-making. As Robert Benchley remarked: "As a farce, it has its moments, but they are moments which nearly every farce has had for the past fifteen years."[90] As for being risqué, Heywood Broun commented:

> *Getting Gertie's Garter* has in it not a line nor a situation to shock a modern audience. Radium, relativity and the sub-electron have all come and passed by Al Woods.... The ... trouble is that Mr. Hopwood made his reputation as a farce writer back in the days when the favorite sport was skating on thin ice. Since then audiences have learned how to swim.[91]

But, for those who were still entertained by the titillations of this kind of slapstick sex humor, the play was good for at least a handful of nudges and twice as many titters. "Sigmund Freud," wrote Benchley, "could spend an interesting afternoon at a matinee ... taking notes on the ladies who giggle."[92]

As to the performances, critics agreed that Hazel Dawn was appropriately charming and innocent in her portrayal of Gertie, but that Dorothy MacKaye was brilliant in her comic playing of the scene in the hay mow. Walter Jones, "even noisier than usual," as the drunken butler, and Donald MacDonald and Lorin Baker as Ken and Billy, worked hard to maintain the breakneck pace the show required. Although Hazel Dawn left the piece in early September to begin work on *The Demi-Virgin,* the rest of the cast was able to keep it on the boards of the Republic Theatre another two months, for a total of 120 performances.

Getting Gertie's Garter may not have shocked the critics, or the sophis-

Getting Gertie's Garter, *Act II, Eleanor Dawn, Adele Roland, and Hazel Dawn, 1921.*

ticated theatregoers, but to the antivice societies, it was simply another example of the immoral and impure plays that were too frequently presented. As the producers of these plays continued to pander to that segment of the public who enjoyed this kind of humor, they became increasingly daring in what they put on the stage. In effect, they were tempting the authorities. There seemed to be a rush to see how far the plays could go and still remain within the law. Finally, refusing to look the other way any longer, the clergy and moral leaders of New York City demanded a cleanup of the Broadway stage. *The Demi-Virgin,* which opened in October of 1921, provided the fuel they needed for a new crusade for stage censorship.

Although Hopwood is credited with being sole author of *The Demi-*

Virgin, he loosely based his idea on an adaptation of the then-popular novel *Les Demi-Vierges* by Marcel Prévost. The only aspect the two stories seem to have shared, however, aside from the title, is the daring, risqué attitude of the female characters. Hopwood's tale is set at a motion picture studio in Hollywood, shortly after the newlywed stars of the film currently in production have been divorced. The exposition reveals that on their wedding night, Gloria Graham and Wally Dean separated about one a.m., just before their honeymoon had really begun. It seems that Wally had received a phone call from his former sweetheart at the most inopportune moment, and Gloria, outraged, promptly left him and applied for a divorce in Reno. Since then, the tattle sheets of Hollywood have begun referring to her as the "demi-virgin."

As the play opens, Gloria and Wally have been forced to return to the movie capital and finish filming the picture they had started before the separation occurred. When Gloria arrives on the set with an English nobleman tagging along as her newest lover, Wally's jealousy is instantly piqued. Not to be made a fool of, he grabs the first pretty extra who walks by and announces that they are engaged to be married. The rest of the play centers on the games Gloria and Wally play to rouse resentment and jealousy in each other. In the play's most humorous scene, the movie director, surrounded by a bevy of sycophants, talks the estranged couple through a love scene that culminates in one of the longest movie kisses ever filmed — certainly longer than the seven feet of film limitation imposed by the Hays Office on actual movie kisses. From this point on it is obvious Gloria and Wally will get back together somehow.

The second act is set during one of those notorious Hollywood parties where everyone who has been bored all day decides to orgy all night. Starlets parade about in frocks that are the last word in fashion and daring, sipping outrageously named cocktails. One vamp entices a boy into dancing an audacious rendition of the "loop the loop," but this is the extent of the carrying on. During the evening, Gloria has decided on a plan to get even with Wally. Luring him back into her room after the revellers have gone, she plans to arouse him, only to drop him cold when he has reached full boil. But the plan backfires; Wally informs Gloria he knew about the plan beforehand. Giving her five minutes to prepare herself for bed, he locks the door and tells her she owes him "a marriage debt and he is going to collect."

Act Three picks up the action a few minutes later, but the foolish Wally has left the room for a moment with the door unlocked while Gloria is at her toilette, and in come all Gloria's girlfriends for a late-night chat. In an episode clearly built into the play to sell tickets, Gloria and the girls pass the time by playing "stripping Cupid," an ingenue's version of strip poker. After the girls have managed to get down to the skimpiest French lingerie the producers thought the law would allow, they discover that Wally has been hiding behind the door, much to his delight. The girls scurry out, leaving Gloria and Wally to finish what they had started. Reviving a device from *Nobody's Widow,* Hopwood has Wally produce a telegram from his attorneys informing Gloria that her Reno divorce is not legal in California. It isn't long before the two are reconciled and decide to start their honeymoon right there.

Although tame by today's standards, *The Demi-Virgin* had been incurring the wrath of the leaders of morality since its tryout in Pittsburgh. Its run at the Pitt Theatre had been cut short after the police received several letters of complaint from the local antivice societies. *Variety* reported that the risqué features of the play had been "too embarrassing even for the blasé."[93] Woods called the piece back to New York and asked Hopwood to remove about an hour's worth of material, as well as to change some of the characterizations.[94] Apparently the changes that were made prior to the New York premiere were not sufficient to placate the societies in that city, for within two weeks of the opening the local authorities were being pressured to close the show. Dr. Royal S. Copeland, Commissioner of Health, acting at the urging of a Long Island magazine editor, reported to the City Magistrate:

> The dramatic corruption of certain plays is as surely undermining the public health of impressionable theatregoers as an exposed sewer would if it were placed in the middle of the auditorium.[95]

Copeland called attention to the healthful effects of such current plays as *The Silver Fox, Dulcy, The Green Goddess,* and, ironically, *The Bat.* The most wholesome play, for his money however, was the Winchell Smith and Tom Cushing comedy *Thank You,* about the tribulations of a humble smalltown minister. Copeland had entered the theatre where it was playing "depressed and fatigued and left 'heartened and refreshed.'"[96] He encouraged the public to attend more plays that offered this stimulating effect, concluding:

> If those good plays make for health, it must be equally true that those which are based upon salacious appeal make for disease.... All good citizens believe in the protection from those plays that admittedly appeal only to the baser side of human nature.[97]

City Magistrate and Democratic presidential hopeful William McAdoo seized this opportunity to strengthen his appeal with the leaders of the antivice groups, particularly the Reverend Dr. John Roach Straton and Rabbi Stephen Wise, by indicting A.H. Woods on a charge of presenting an "immoral and impure show." "This play," McAdoo told the District Attorney, "is an intentional appeal, for the profit of the box office, to the lustful and licentious, to the morbidly erotic, to the vulgar and disorderly minds."[98] Police Lieutenant Albert Duffy took the stand during the hearing and explained that the most objectionable scene occurred during a game of "stripping Cupid," when one performer took "about everything off but 'two moles and two freckles.'"[99] Woods attempted to defend himself by explaining that further changes had been made in the script since the New York opening: he had had the offending "mole" line cut, as well as the suggestive "you should have seen the right

The Demi-Virgin *"stripping Cupid"* scene, *Hazel Dawn (stands right) and the girls,* *1921.*

people coming out of the wrong rooms" and the salacious second-act wower about collecting the "marriage debt," but to no avail. Before long, John F. Gilchrist, Commissioner of Licenses of New York City, ordered Woods to withdraw *The Demi-Virgin* or forfeit his license for the Eltinge Theatre.

Suddenly, the controversy over the morality of *The Demi-Virgin* got lost in the larger issue of whether one man had the power to revoke a theatre's license. On the advice of his lawyers, Woods refused to close the show, and applied to the courts for an injunction to prevent the forfeiture; *The Demi-Virgin* had become a test case. After a long-drawn legal action ending in May 1922, the Appellate Division of the Supreme Court sided with Woods in declaring that "the Commissioner of Licenses had exceeded his authority in issuing the order."[100] Woods had won the case, but in the fracas, he had come to believe that his fellow managers of the Producing Managers' Association were not giving him the support to which he was entitled, and he resigned from the organization in protest.[101] But if Woods lost some friends in the fight, he succeeded in enriching himself with royalties.

The Demi-Virgin had continued to run throughout the entire proceedings, most likely spurred on by the aid of the court publicity. At one point, Woods told the *New York Times:* "My goodness, I have been planning all along to take this show off . . . but all this talk has kept the 'Demi-Virgin' going."[102] His clever press agentry had also kept it going. Since the *Times* had refused to print the title of the play in its columns, the Woods people had concocted tantalizing little queries for each day. The final one read: "Are you one of the 209,354 persons who have already seen the most talked of play in

America, now at the Eltinge Theatre?"[103] The result was a run of 268 performances, or, eleven more than Commissioner Copeland's healthful *Thank You*.
In all likelihood it had been the Woods publicists who had started talking
about the vices of the play in the first place.

The critics were unanimous in their opinions that *The Demi-Virgin* was
not as shocking as the public had been led to believe — a vulgar bore perhaps,
but not shocking. Kaufman of the *Dramatic Mirror* had his doubts whether
all the material was actually Hopwood's. "The idea and any number of laughs
sound Hopwood-ey," he wrote, "but as much of the text doesn't. It is too obvious, too dull. . . . This type of entertainment is built, not written."[104] Benchley's only complaint was that Hopwood gave no credit to the "generations of
Bowery comedians and small town drummers" who had been dishing up the
bits since they were first written. "Most of [the] stuff," he observed, had come
out of "the trunk marked 'Grover Cleveland's Second Administration.'"[105]
Woollcott characterized the performance as a series of musical-comedy gags,
with the actors all behaving "in a musical-comedy manner."[106] Hazel Dawn
had helped this impression along by picking up a violin at one point and playing the "Beautiful Lady" waltz, just as she had done in her first hit, *The Pink
Lady*, a decade before. Kaufman summed up the performances:

> Charles Ruggles, Kenneth Douglas, Glenn Anders, Constance Farber, Alice
> Hegeman, and Hazel Dawn seemed to me to deserve mention in the order
> mentioned. But only Mr. Ruggles was at all remarkable. He is.[107]

What was Hopwood's opinion of all the fuss generated by *The Demi-
Virgin?* One suspects he simply smiled and deposited the royalty checks. He
makes no mention of the play in his available letters, and the newspapers appear to be free of any interviews with him on the subject; but, in a 1924 article
he wrote for *Theatre* entitled "Why I Don't Write More Serious Plays," he
made these comments about morals and good taste:

> The question of what is, or is not, *risqué*, is of course, a very debatable one.
> Even at the risk of being excessively bromidic, I must pause to remark that
> morals are largely a question of geography. . . .
> But though there is not, and there cannot be, a definite moral standard
> for everyone, there is, it seems to me, a fairly definite standard of good taste,
> and against this I have tried not to offend. . . .
> I remember, in the case of *The Demi-Virgin*, no one found anything par-
> ticularly reprehensible in the play, until the censorship excitement and the
> effort to suppress the play had begun. Then the people in the audience . . .
> found *double entendre* in lines which were absolutely innocent in their in-
> tent. And I remember . . . a magistrate took exception to certain lines. . . .
> I could not see what he thought they meant. I was half amused, half hor-
> rified. He was, I suppose, a man of irreproachable character, but he had the
> mind of a reformer — which, so often, is a moral garbage can. And when he
> told me that he had gone over the play with his wife and his daughter, and
> they had all of them found the same meanings in those innocent lines, I
> thought, "My God, what a family!"
> Cases of this sort, of course, are fairly common, and are perfectly

Covarrubias's Avery Hopwood, 1925

understood by the students of Freud and the modern psychiatrists. I would suggest that before anyone is allowed to sit in judgement upon a play or novel, he should be psychoanalyzed, to find out whether he is morally competent to give an opinion.[108]

The controversy over morals and good taste continued to plague Broadway throughout the twenties. Aside from settling the question about the authority of the Commissioner of Licenses, *The Demi-Virgin* case had had a more profound impact by focusing attention on the question of whether or not there should be a commission established for censorship of the stage, just as Hollywood had accepted checks upon itself in the form of the Hays Office. Some Broadway managers seemed willing to have their shows scrutinized by a public jury similar to the one that had passed judgment on *The Demi-Virgin*, but others, including Woods, preferred the idea of a state censor. At least, argued Woods, a state censor could decide what material was objectionable before a play went into production, thus preventing the financial losses that would result from a jury system, if the jury decided that the play ought to be closed. In the end, the jury system prevailed as the lesser of the two evils, although it was seldom invoked. The danger was that any censorship intended to clean up the popular entertainment must ultimately stifle free expression in the serious drama. In what was perhaps Hopwood's last interview before his death, he insisted that the stage "should be strongly defended from the encroachments of 'censorship.'"[109]

As 1921 drew to a close, Hopwood still had three plays running on Broadway, and *The Bat* had scored a big hit in Chicago, yet indications are that he was becoming "depressingly bored with his own witticisms"[110] in the theatre. "I'm fed up with work," he told Archie Bell, but "no one pities me, except my self—but I do it extensively."[111] At 39, Hopwood had achieved the financial success he had wanted, but his ambition to produce a work of lasting value continued to be thwarted. Before sailing to England in early 1922, on the threshold of his fortieth year, his thoughts must have turned to mortality and the human need to pass something on. Revoking his last will and testament of 1918, he had his lawyer draft a new will bequeathing six-thirtieths of his estate to the Regents of the University of Michigan, Ann Arbor, for use in establishing "The Avery Hopwood and Jule Hopwood Prizes" to be awarded annually to those students "who perform the best creative work in the fields of dramatic writing, fiction, poetry and the essay," especially "the new, the unusual, and the radical."[112] With the accumulated royalties from his slick farces, he would encourage others in the kind of writing he had not been able to produce himself.

Hopwood seems to have kept his final wishes private, only telling his mother about the bequest on one of their last voyages together the year before he died. One evening in mid–Atlantic, while taking an after-dinner stroll on the promenade, Mrs. Hopwood asked her son: "What if the boat would sink with both of us on it? What would become of the money?" "Michigan gets it," her son replied.[113] Jule Hopwood had long known of Avery's affection for his alma mater, but this was the first that she had heard of his intentions in establishing an award for creative writing.

In January 1922, when Hopwood sailed for England to attend the London premiere of *The Bat,* he still harbored the desire to create a work worthy of serious consideration. The idea of writing his novel had not left him; he had just quit talking about it in public.

VI

The Playmaking Factory
and Final Years (1922–1928)

Hopwood's trip to London proved invigorating. Not only was he escaping all the commotion over *The Demi-Virgin*, but he was celebrating another *Bat* success as well. The mystery was doing a sell-out business at the St. James's, where it would play for 327 performances. Then there was the first English-speaking revival of *Fair and Warmer* that he had seen in three years.[1] Before long, production arrangements were being made for several of his other plays, and in a cablegram sent to New York, he informed Broadway that he intended to use London and Paris to try out some of his new plays.[2] Perhaps Europe was where he needed to be just now. Business accomplished, however, it was time to go on holiday; he set out for the Continent and beyond: there was a postcard to "Dearest Fania" from Cairo, so "very stange & queer," another from Luxor to his "little Cleopatra (or worse)," then one more from the "House of the Moorish King" in Ronda, Spain, "where my Fania rightly belongs," and finally to "Dear Mr. Buddy," there was a note from Paris:

> I went to a bullfight in Madrid . . . & I wish you would find out why Richard Strauss hasn't written a Tone Poem del Toros. He could be much bloodier than in "Salome" or "Elektra" – & much more perverse. – When I return, I shall give you & my Fania all the delicate details. . . .[3]

To Archie Bell, Hopwood had written the same and more:

Hôtel Plaza Athénée
Paris

Dear Archie: –

I had a quite wonderful time, in Tangiers & Spain, & kept wishing that you were along. – If I wrote you every time that I thought of you, Archie, you would be inundated with Hopwoodian letters.

I had a pretty strenuous time – traveling so much & working on two plays – & now I'm settled here for several weeks, to try to get in a stretch of good work.

I saw Marie Dressler in Monte Carlo, & had a very jolly time with her.

149

She was simply surrounded by the British nobility—& by some very nice Americans, too.

"The Bat" is still doing sensational business in London.—I got word yesterday that "Fair and Warmer" has been accepted for production in Germany, & the translation was made by a very good German friend of mine, Bertha Pogson, who also adapted "Raffles"—Fitch's "The Truth,"—"Cousin Kate" & several of the Barrie plays.—If the play is done soon enough I shall go to Germany for the rehearsals & the production. I think that would be good fun....

Somerset Maugham was in London, & I saw a great deal of him.—He has a very big, & very beautiful old house in Wyndham Place. These English writers certainly do themselves well.... Maugham was in Indo-China & Burma & other little places like that while "The Circle" was running in London—so he has never seen it played—one of his very best comedies.

I told you all about John Floyd in my last letter.—I'm glad he had the chance to come abroad. He's a thoroly [sic] nice boy, & I think he has ability.

My God, what a long letter! I shall probably be back in April—& shall come to Cleveland.

My very best love to Archie....

Your's—even in Paris,

March 10 [1922]   Avery[4]

Hopwood shared the rigors and pleasures of this tour abroad with a young friend and protégé, John Henry Floyd. Floyd was a 23-year-old actor/playwright from Hopwood's hometown of Cleveland, where his father had been postmaster for many years. After working as an actor, stage manager and director at the Cleveland Play House and Prospect Players, Floyd had come to New York with the hope of enrolling at Columbia University to study playwriting with Professor Hatcher Hughes.[5] Most recently though, he had been learning his craft by playing the minor role of Rex Martin in *The Demi-Virgin.* Undoubtedly it was through Hopwood's support and encouragement that Floyd wrote his first play, *The Wooden Kimono,* which was produced in 1926. This mystery-farce ran true to formula and enjoyed a run of 201 performances. Floyd's second play, *Mrs. Cook's Tour* (1929), failed in tryouts, and his third and final offering, *Queer People* (1934), a disjointed farce-melodrama about a Hollywood press agent, made it to Broadway but ran only 13 performances.

Although Hopwood's relationship with John Floyd might best be characterized as ambivalent, his affection for the young man manifested itself in his will. Floyd received the income from a $100,000 trust and $10,000 in cash. In addition to these benefactions, Floyd's sister disclosed that Hopwood gave her brother $250,000 some months prior to his last trip to Europe in 1928.[6] Very likely it was from these funds that Floyd purchased the Hopwood copyrights in 1929 for a sum of $40,000. Much of John Floyd's life is a mystery, aside from the fact that he was confined to Pilgrim State Hospital (now Psychiatric Center), Long Island, on December 1, 1939, where he remained until his death in 1961.

John H. Floyd: "handsome, strong, impulsive Johnny," ca. 1921. Inscribed to his agent, the influential and demanding Chamberlain Brown.

Paris was especially pleasant in the spring of 1922, and Hopwood and Floyd extended their stay through April and into May. Arriving back in New York around the first of June, Hopwood was ready to greet Broadway once more.

It had been eighteen years since Avery Hopwood had read Louis Vincent De Foe's "Call for the Playwright" in the *Michigan Alumnus* describing the vast fortunes earned by Clyde Fitch. Now in the spring of 1922, he found himself the example many column writers used when *they* wanted to inspire the novice playwright; but the Hopwood success was calculated to thrill more than inspire. The "bestseller theatre" that had produced "clever entertainers like Avery Hopwood," wrote Sheldon Cheney in *Theatre Magazine,* "and clever plays with racy titles or, pretty humor, with intriguing sex glamor," and with "stirring crime interest,"[7] was fast becoming outmoded in the spirit of innovation of the twenties.

The season that had just witnessed *Getting Gertie's Garter* and *The Demi-Virgin,* had also seen Eugene O'Neill's second Pulitzer prize–winning play *Anna Christie* produced, as well as his *The Hairy Ape.* Andreyev's *He Who Gets Slapped,* Shaw's *Back to Methuselah* and Kaiser's *Morn Till Midnight* had also found select audiences in 1921–1922. The success of Kaufman and Connelly's *Dulcy* showed managers that audience tastes in comedy were also changing. George M. Cohan's all–American farces still remained popular, and there was no doubting that a wholesome, sentimental piece could run forever: *Abie's Irish Rose* had just begun the first of its 2,327 performances. Sex farce, to be sure, retained its devoted following too, as witnessed by the long run of Belasco's *Kiki* with Lenore Ulric. But gradually, in all forms of drama, audiences were turning to a new generation of playwrights. Picking up the June issue of *Theatre Magazine,* Hopwood could have read that even Al Woods was moving with the times:

> "The Demi-Virgin" is the last so-called "bedroom farce" which I shall put on for seven years. I am calling a halt on this kind of play, not because of the adverse criticism which has come from certain sources, but because I believe it would lose in popularity if continued indefinitely. All things travel in cycles.... The bedroom farce has had its day.[8]

The question the critics continued to ask was whether Avery Hopwood could abandon the bedroom formula.

In an article published in the May 1922 issue of *Theatre,* historian Montrose J. Moses discussed "The Metamorphosis of Owen Davis," specifically his conversion from formula melodrama writer for Al Woods in the early years of the century to serious dramatist. Davis's *The Detour* had recently achieved critical acclaim, and in another year his *Icebound* would be awarded the Pulitzer prize for Drama. Unlike most of the potboiler-best-seller playwrights, Davis had joined the new generation of dramatists, making a successful transition from the old dramaturgy to the new. To this discussion of Davis's conversion Moses added: "How one wishes that a sudden light might descend upon Avery Hopwood ... and turn his clever pen to material more worthy!"[9]

Critics continued to echo this sentiment throughout the next few years until Hopwood barked back: "If people don't stop asking me to write a serious play, maybe I will. And then maybe everyone will be sorry!"[10] Admitting the need, however, to give more specific reasons why he hadn't attempted such drama in recent years, he offered the comment:

> I do not write more serious plays, for one thing, because it is too easy. I mean, too easy to write the sort of serious plays with which our stage,

lately, has been inundated. They are written, mostly, by men who think that they think, and who pretend to solve, in the course of a couple of hours, one or more of the great problems which confront humanity. I could not do that sort of thing, and retain my intellectual honesty.[11]

Earlier he had said:

> I admit I do write for Broadway, to please Broadway. I want my plays to be successes. I hate failures, and to my thinking, any play, however remarkable, is a *Failure* if it plays to empty benches around Times-Square. There may be a field for book-drama, literary drama . . . but that isn't my drama. Mine's the theatre of the show world. . . .[12]

A more telling appreciation of Hopwood's attitude towards his plays at this time may be gained by looking at some passages from Carl Van Vechten's 1922 novel *Peter Whiffle: His Life and Works,* in which Hopwood figures as the title character. Towards the end of the book, as Peter is attempting to come to some understanding of himself and his work, he tells Carl:

> There are two ways of becoming a writer: one, the cheaper, is to discover a formula: that is black magic; the other is to have the urge: that is white magic. I have never been able to discover a new formula; I have worked with the formulae of other artists, only to see the cryptogram blot and blur under my hands. My manipulation of the mystic figures and the cabalistic secrets has never raised the right demons. . . .
>
> But, . . . if I had found a new formula, who knows what I might have done?[13]

In the Preface to the book, Carl quotes Peter's farewell letter in which he says:

> I have begun many things but nothing have I ever completed. It has always seemed unnecessary or impossible, although at times I have tried to carry a piece of work though.[14]

Hopwood had certainly completed many plays, but he had hardly regarded them with the same literary respect as his idea of writing a novel. But, as far as anyone knew, he wasn't writing on that regularly. Aside from the short stories of his college days and the fictionalization of *Sadie Love,* he had produced nothing literary. In a final moment of realization, Peter says:

> I have tried to do too much and that is why, perhaps, I have done nothing. I wanted to write a new Comédie Humaine. Instead, I have lived it. And now, I have come to the conclusion that that was all there was for me to do, just to live, as fully as possible.[15]

It would be inaccurate to suggest that Van Vechten's Peter Whiffle speaks solely as Hopwood might have, for, indeed, Van Vechten uses Peter as his own alter ego, but clearly there is an affinity between the realizations of Whiffle and the sentiments of Hopwood.

It is a curious coincidence that in 1922, the same year as the appearance of *Peter Whiffle,* Hopwood made his final attempt at a play with a serious bent. *Why Men Leave Home* might have been the worthy departure the critics had been looking for.

Set at the country home of Tom and Fifi Morgan on Long Island, *Why Men Leave Home* finds Tom lamenting his fortune because Fifi has been touring Europe all summer without even sending him a cablegram asking for more spending money. Just as Tom is baring his soul to Grandma, in comes Fifi, straight off the boat. Tom is delighted to see her, but his attitude quickly changes when he learns that she has invited her two "gadabout" traveling companions over for the weekend. Nina and Betty arrive in short order accompanied by their abused husbands, Artie and Sam, followed by Sybil and her boyfriend, Billy, along for the fun. While the women are off planning what to do next, the men get into a discussion about their sorry fates as neglected and misused husbands. "Say," asks Tom, "Just what do you think of The Great American Wife?" The verdict is that she is extravagant, gives nothing in return to her husband, and won't have children. But travel, that she does.

The men agree that Grandma was right when she said that "SHE wasn't for equal rights for women—but equal responsibilities." "You know," Tom muses, "It would make a good title for a play." "Why men leave home! And the answer would be—'Because their wives leave home first—and the man hasn't any HOME to leave!'" Small wonder, concludes Sam, that we seek "companionship"—"happiness"—and "warm breakfast somewhere else." The men soon confess that they have not been sitting home doing the washing while the wives were away. But, by letting this cat out of the bag, Tom, Sam, and Artie have quickly turned the tables on Fifi, Nina, and Betty.

The remainder of *Why Men Leave Home* is devoted to the women's attempts to win back their husbands' affections. Fifi suddenly has a good opportunity to slip into her new Parisian nightie and dance about in front of Tom, all snug in his twin bed. Tom's response is less than amorous, however: he demands that Fifi give him an immediate divorce so that he can marry the woman he loves. It isn't long, though, before we learn that Tom's other woman is Doris, a lonely child from across the way whom he has befriended. Sam and Artie's other women have also proven to be just as harmless, so everyone is safe and happy at last.[16]

Produced by Wagenhals and Kemper at the Morosco Theatre on September 12, 1922, immediately following the closing of *The Bat* after its two-year run at that theatre, *Why Men Leave Home* proved to be the usual Hopwood formula, slightly modified to reflect the moral temper of the moment. Audiences enjoyed the familiar Hopwoodian escapades, mixed this time with just the right amount of preaching about the waywardness of "The Great American Wife"; but, for the critics, who had been hoping Hopwood might produce something newer than a thesis play, and less superficial than his usual fare, there was only disappointment. Robert Benchley observed:

> Avery Hopwood has performed an interesting experiment in *Why Men Leave Home.* Stung to the quick by the taunts of this department at his lewd farces and chagrined that his royalties cannot possibly reach the two-million mark until several weeks after Christmas, Mr. Hopwood has taken the ingredients of what would ordinarily have been another bedroom farce and has made them into a bedroom problem play by having the hero get out of bed in his pajamas to deliver a short talk on the shortcomings of the modern American wife.
>
> Everything is in *Why Men Leave Home* that was in *Ladies' Night* and *The Demi-Virgin.* There are the same leering jokes, the same double and triple entendre, the same scurrying in and out of doorways, and a couple of beds. It looks as if the thing had been all crated and ready to ship off as another Hopwood farce when the author, walking by Grace Church in the cool of the evening, had heard the choir inside singing *Rock of Ages,* and, stricken with remorse, had rushed back to the factory and inserted a tablespoonful of moral into the tank.[17]

Lawrence Reamer of the *New York Herald* agreed, saying: "Avery Hopwood's Problemism is only a piece of pretense."[18] Although he chided Hopwood for not allowing the central theme of the play to stand on its own, he concluded:

> He is one of the few American playwrights who seem to work with technical certainty. He makes his effects and he knows how. He does not bumble into them.... Maybe Mr. Hopwood just can't help being Mr. Hopwood.[19]

Most critics found *Why Men Leave Home* well directed and handsomely mounted, even if they didn't accept Hopwood's mixed mood of farce and sermonizing. Effectively acted by a relatively unknown cast, the play featured Florence Shirley and John McFarlane as Fifi and Tom Morgan, and Jessie Villars as Grandma. Apparently the most amusing character of the evening wasn't cast in the play at all, however.

Towards the end of the second act, the Morosco stage cat purred its way into the negligee scene, and then, behaving as any self-respecting animal would when caught in such a compromising situation, crawled over the footlights and hid under the seats.[20] It was sheer coincidence that this little comedienne had taken its cue from Tom's line: "Do you think that the most exciting thing I ever did, before I went to bed, was to let the cat out for the night! Well, the cat HAS been out, and so have I!" Stepping before the curtain at the end of the act, Hopwood apologized for what he called someone's "carefully calculated" efforts at disrupting the scene just ended, but then quipped: "Though the Bat has flown from the Morosco, the cat has come back."[21] First-nighters were thoroughly amused by the proceedings, as well as by the play, even if a majority of the critics were not. Although the show ran an additional

134 performances, it is doubtful that the cat made any more cameo appearances.

It is also doubtful that Hopwood took the moralizing he had inserted into *Why Men Leave Home* as seriously as some thought. Very likely, he gained personal amusement from donning the clerical collar of the moralist, so to speak, only to lead his followers to a cynical justification of why men leave home. Since Hopwood seems not to have declared his intentions in writing *Why Men Leave Home* other than to make money, it is difficult to say whether he was attempting a serious transition in his dramaturgy, or not. If he was, the critical reaction to his efforts must have been particularly dismaying to him. The play opened in London the following year under the title *Bachelor Husbands,* but critics there dismissed it as a complete failure, and it closed after thirteen performances. Hopwood *was* a Peter Whiffle: he had learned to write formula during an earlier time, and now he was incapable of moving on. Writing to please Broadway had become more than a reliable public defense for his plays; it had become a personal excuse as well. Inasmuch as Wagenhals and Kemper did its best to publicize *Why Men Leave Home* as a comedy rather than a farce, it seems certain that an attempt was being made to influence audience perception of the piece. Be that as it may, *Why Men Leave Home* was the last original play that Avery Hopwood wrote. From 1923 on, he relied exclusively on adaptation and collaboration, working with material that only attempted to move with the times to the extent that it mixed a topical emphasis with the proven formulae of risqué farce.

While in Europe during the first half of 1923, Hopwood set about obtaining the American rights to three foreign comedies: *Le Retour* by Robert de Fleurs and Francis de Croisset, *Der Gatte des Fräuleins* by Gabriel Dregeley, and *La Sonnette d'Alarme* by Maurice Hennequin and Romain Coolus. Little is known about Hopwood's process in translating and adapting these plays, although an indication of his attitude towards adaptation in general is made clear in some earlier correspondence with the office of Lee Shubert. In 1919, Hopwood had been negotiating with the Shuberts and Selwyn and Company about adapting a German play whose English title was "Miss Lily's Husband." Writing to Shubert on the subject, Hopwood told him:

> I would prefer to work from the original German MS., which I read several years ago, when Mr. [Henry W.] Savage had the play. The so-called adaptation, which has already been made, is no adaptation at all, but merely a translation, and not a good one.[22]

A few months later, after being informed that the original manuscript of "Miss Lily's Husband" could not be found, Hopwood was obdurate:

> I cannot believe that anyone would be guilty of the gross carelessness of mislaying the only original copy of a foreign play. I think that if the matter is put up strongly enough to Mrs. Hesse, she may be able to refresh her memory, and remember what she did with the MS.

> I do not care to work from the translation. There are various points in it
> which are obscure, and which can be cleared up only if I have the original
> play.[23]

Apparently the original manuscript was never found, for no adaptation entitled "Miss Lily's Husband" has been attributed to Hopwood. Actually, Hopwood's adaptations were closer to loose reworkings of the central incidents of
the originals, as in the case of the previously mentioned borrowing of the situations in *Our Little Wife, Double Exposure,* and *The Demi-Virgin.* As George
Jean Nathan pointed out, many American playwrights borrowed freely from
foreign sources during the First World War because of the "incidental abroga-
tion of copyright laws,"[24] but beginning in the twenties due credit had to be
given to the authors of the originals. Since the year before (1922), Hopwood
had been copyrighting his plays in the name of "Avery Hopwood, Inc." Not
only did incorporation offer him certain tax advantages, but it protected him
personally from any litigation that might have been filed against him for
plagiarism. It is known that Hopwood shared one-half of the royalties for his
adaptations with the original authors, as was the general practice.

Along with gathering foreign plays, Hopwood's 1923 excursion to the
Continent seems to have been particularly devoted to his appreciation of the
opera and music. From Milan he wrote to Van Vechten and recalled their
bygone days:

Hôtel Cavour
Milano

Carlo, mio carissimo: —

I've been to the Riviera, & to Venice, but I had to come back to Milano,
because I just *must* have my music. And one hears such *good* music here.
Toscanini is conducting at the Scala, & they give quite wonderful things, like
"Lucia di Lammermoor" — Fancy that! . . .

In Paris, one night, I went . . . to our favorite opera — your's & mine,
dear — "Le Mariage Secret", da Cimarosa. How we used to amuse ourselves,
scaling its melodies & with what passion we discussed whether it was more
Mozartian than Mozart was Cimarosian. Dear dear — how far off those days
seem, now. . . .

Ah — music — music! — My love to Fan. — She is not musical poor dear but
then you did not fill her with musical enthusiasm in yr extreme youth, the
way you did me — Yours in Italian Falsetto —

[March 31, 1923]   Avery[25]

After traveling to England in April, Hopwood stopped in Paris again before
revisiting Italy. He informed Van Vechten that his plans for returning to the
States had changed:

Hotel Majestic
Paris

Dear Carl: —

I had intended to return to your great country in May but since Mabel Dodge
has married an Indian [Antonio Luhan], I suppose there's not much use of
my returning until June....

Avery[26]

Hopwood also made plans through Van Vechten to sublet a brownstone in
downtown Manhattan from a friend of Van Vechten's, but, when he returned,
he found that his usual arrangement of living in hotels was much better suited
to the busy season that lay ahead.

The first play Hopwood attended rehearsals for in the 1923–24 season was
The Return (Le Retour), adapted in collaboration with Charlton Andrews and
produced by Al Woods. Since this comedy never made it past its Washington,
D.C., tryouts, almost nothing is known about it, although "Gossip on the
Rialto" had it that, "On all sides there was manifest evidence of a greater desire
to see Mr. Hopwood, personally, than to give really serious consideration to
his new play."[27] Even though the story of *The Return* has been lost, one
presumes the obligatory twin-bed scene of old was conspicuously missing; after
all, Woods's seven-year moratorium on the bedroom farce had hardly begun.
If, however, *The Return* followed the style of *The Alarm Clock,* which Woods
also produced for Hopwood in 1923, one is safe in assuming that it contained
its share of risqué humor nonetheless. Woods and Hopwood undoubtedly
dropped *The Return* in order to put all their efforts into making *The Alarm
Clock* a success; but, although *The Alarm Clock* made it to Broadway sporting
a polished cast led by Bruce McRae, it failed after only 32 performances.

Essentially, *The Alarm Clock,* adapted from *La Sonnette d'Alarme* by
Hennequin and Coolus, is the story of the country cousins who come to the
big city, only to lose their simple, godly virtues at the hands of their pleasure-
seeking city relatives. Hopwood's sometime supporter of earlier days George
Jean Nathan wrote:

> Hennequin and Coolus are witty and engaging comic artists of the popular
> theatre; some of their risqué exhibits are gorgeously funny; but their *Son-
> nette d'Alarme* is as dull a sentimental comedy as an attempt at French
> naughtiness by an American.... The original dullness has not been
> diminished in Mr. Hopwood's transposition of the text. [He] has cluttered
> up that text with obvious vaudeville jokes, allusions to Flo Ziegfeld and
> Greenwich Village, and wheezes on Prohibition, Jazz and ladies'
> undergarments, and otherwise vulgarized a manuscript whose only small vir-
> tue lies in its comparative abstention from such barbarisms. The comedy is
> further damaged by the staging of Mr. David Burton who, in an attempt to
> inject life and speed into the text, has caused the actors to run around, shout,
> and rattle off their lines as if the piece were a farce.[28]

The closing of *The Alarm Clock,* the second Hopwood/Woods failure for the season, proved to many that the duo's money-making magic had been spent; the two men never worked together again.

In between tryouts for *The Return* and the late December 1923 production of *The Alarm Clock,* Hopwood had also been following the rehearsals of *Little Miss Bluebeard (Der Gatte des Fräuleins),* as well as collaborating with David Gray on the rewriting of Gray's *Goodness Knows.* The Hopwood playmaking factory seemed as inexhaustible as ever.

Little Miss Bluebeard, billed as a "song-play," was developed for French actress/vocalist Irene Bordoni, the wife of the play's producer, E. Ray Goetz. Bordoni, as much associated with the singing of risqué lyrics as Hopwood was with the writing of bedroom comedy, had first appeared on Broadway in 1912 in the revue *Broadway to Paris.* From then on she became noted for her piquant interpretations of the heroines in plays especially written for her. Hopwood seems to have been taken with Bordoni's charms from early on, and had long wanted to write a piece for her. He had once told Archie Bell that "she's the one star for whom I would sit down to write a play."[29] On the whole, Hopwood had grown tired of writing plays for "stars" *(The Gold Diggers* with Ina Claire had been the last "star" vehicle he had constructed). Submitting an article to the *New York Times* entitled "A Change of Mind," Hopwood told readers that he had sworn, as so many playwrights before him had done, that he would never write another play for a star—"especially feminine stars." He had had too many experiences with "ladies possessed of a disputable amount of talent and a superabundance of temper." At last he had turned, "as even a playwright-worm will turn," and had declared for all the world to hear, "No more stars for me!" But then he met Bordoni—accent and everything. She smiled, and in an instant he found himself "hurtling dozens of ideas for comedies at her astonished head." The next day he signed a contract with her to write *Little Miss Bluebeard.*[30] He continued:

> I came to rehearsals prepared for anything—for anything, that is, except what happened. The first day passed tranquilly, so did the second, but on the third I prepared for an explosion. I had decided that the play was too long, that cuts needed to be made, and some of them were in scenes which concerned Miss Bordoni. I approached her with cautious diplomacy. Would she mind very much if, here and there, I cut down some of her dialogue?
>
> "Mais, non!" responded Bordoni and she beamed with satisfaction. "The more you cut the better I like."
>
> And then further astonishing phenomena began to transpire. She gave away lines to her leading man, she was delighted because the girls in her company were so pretty, she did not find fault with her dressingroom, nor with the billing, nor with the number of electric lights with her name. I walk into the Lyceum Theatre night after night, and gaze upon her with growing wonder.... "Can this extraordinary creature really be a star?"[31]

At the end of August 1923, while Hopwood was still on the road with the tryouts for *Little Miss Bluebeard,* he wrote to Archie Bell to tell him about the status of a song Bell had written for Bordoni to sing in the show:

New Monterey Hotel
North Asbury Park, N.J.

Dear Archie: —

I'm down here with "Little Miss Bluebeard", which has been doing splendidly on the road. Of course, New York may think differently of it, but we shall know very shortly, as we open there Tuesday next.

All four of Bordoni's songs got over very well, so there was no chance of making a change. As I wrote you before, we all liked "Just One More Kiss" very much, but there is no place in the comedy for more than one downright sentimental number, and it is a number of this sort, "So This Is Love", by Rae [sic] Goetz, which has made the biggest hit of the four songs which Bordoni sings. I am sorry — not because it would mean such a Hell of a lot to you, if the song went into the play, but because it would have been sort of nice for all of us to have been in on this production. If the song had come along a few weeks sooner, it would undoubtedly have been taken, as the melody which Victor Herbert wrote did not please them, and they were looking around for something else. Failing to find it, Goetz wrote the song himself.

I expect to come to Cleveland very soon after the New York opening. I look forward to seeing you.... Bordoni asks me to send you her greetings. She is wonderful in the play — and out of it!

Faithfully,

[August 21?, 1923]   Avery[32]

In *Little Miss Bluebeard,* Bordoni played Colette, a French governess who has just married Bob Talmadge (Stanley Logan), but Talmadge, already a married man with a family, has married Colette under the name of his best friend, composer Larry Charters (Bruce McRae). Stricken with remorse for what he has done, Talmadge has taken Colette to Charters's apartment to ask his friend's help in straightening out the predicament. Charters, who immediately succumbs to the charms of his French visitor, suggests that Colette live with him for a week, and that then they go through the ceremony of a divorce. Colette takes up residence in a spare bedroom, and spends the remainder of the play entertaining Charters and his bachelor friends by appearing in pajamas, eating breakfast in her negligee, and singing, along with "So This Is Love," several other songs, one of which is entitled "I Won't Say I Will, But I Won't Say I Won't."

In the last act, the whole affair is revealed as a practical joke concocted by Colette and all the other characters to determine whether Charters would ever give up bachelorhood. He does.

Little Miss Bluebeard scored a sound hit for Bordoni. Hopwood had succeeded in adapting a piece that critics agreed was an admirable vehicle for her talents. Corbin of the *Times* said: "A world without such pieces would be

Irene Bordoni sings "So This Is Love," 1923.

appreciably duller, and it is by no means certain that it would be more aus-
terely moral."[33] "As a dramatic opus," wrote Benchley in *Life*, it is "barely
distinguishable on a clear day from some fourteen million others of its class."
Clearly, he concluded, it had been written "for the exclusive use of Miss Bordoni's eyes."[34] The *Theatre* critic called Bordoni delightful in her ability to convey the double meanings of her songs, but he wondered if all French
governesses wore Poiret, Patou and Chanel gowns and cloaks.[35] Bordoni ad-
mirers seem to have enjoyed themselves; the play ran 175 performances — 79
more than the average for farce that season.[36]

The opening night of *Little Miss Bluebeard* afforded Hopwood a satisfyng
experience, after he had overcome his "first night palpitations." Writing in an

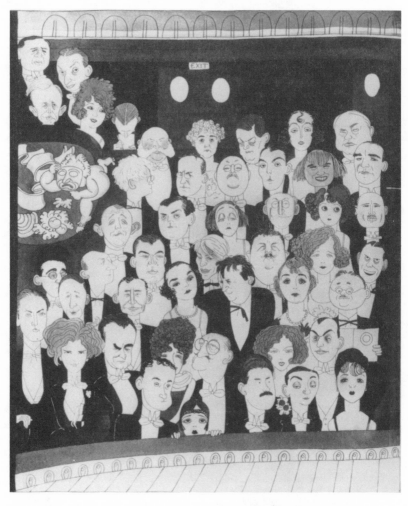

Ralph Barton's 1922 Vanity Fair *sketch, "Another Opening, Another Show...": A Typical First-Night Audience in New York: The Scene Which Invariably Confronts the Actor. UPPER LEFT BOX—A.H. Woods, Avery Hopwood, Florenz Ziegfeld, Jr., Billie Burke. LEFT LOWER BOX—John Barrymore, Michael Strange. FIRST ROW—John Emerson, Anita Loos, Fritz Kreisler, Irving Berlin, Irene Bordoni. SECOND ROW—J. Montgomery Flagg, Mrs. Leslie Carter, John Drew, Leonora Hughes, Maurice. THIRD ROW—Robert C. Benchley, Franklin P. Adams, Mrs. Lydig Hoyt, Heywood Broun, Neysa McMein, Alexander Woollcott. FOURTH ROW—George S. Kaufman, Marc Connelly, Herman Tappé, Max Eastman, Victor Herbert, Marilyn Miller, John V.A. Weaver. FIFTH ROW—George M. Cohan, J. Hartley Manners, Laurette Taylor, Alan Dale, Bird Millman, Rockwell Kent. SIXTH ROW—Oliver Herford, Herbert Swope, Nicholas Murray Butler, Ring Lardner, Molla Bjurstedt, Mallory Devereaux Milburn. SEVENTH ROW—George F. Baker, Anne Morgan, Joseph Urban, Elsie Janis, Percy Hammond. BACK FOYER—Ralph Barton—sketching.*

Ingredients in the Mixed Grill of Metropolitan Life. A Social Panorama, Sketched on the Spot, by Ralph Barton UPPER RIGHT BOX—Dorothy Gish, D.W. Griffith, Lillian Gish. RIGHT LOWER BOX—Clare Sheridan, Samuel Goldwyn. FIRST ROW—Charles Dana Gibson, David Belasco, Lenore Ulric, Daniel Frohman. SECOND ROW—Geraldine Farrar, Dr. Frank Crane, Kitty Gordon, Dr. John Roach Straton. THIRD ROW—Dolores, Charles Hanson Towne, Irene Castle, Otto H. Kahn, Zoë Atkins, Elsie Ferguson. FOURTH ROW—George S. Chappell, Margaret Severn, Condé Nast, Don Marquis, Elsie de Wolfe, Baron de Meyer, Irvin S. Cobb. FIFTH ROW—Gilda Gray, Kenneth Macgowan, Robert E. Sherwood, Constance Talmadge, Louis Untermeyer, Arnold Genthe, Willard Huntington Wright. SIXTH ROW—Reginald Vanderbilt, Alma Gluck, Efrem Zimbalist, Mrs. Harry Payne Whitney, Robert W. Chanler, Frank Craven. SEVENTH ROW—The Fairbanks Twins, Theodore Roosevelt, Jay Gould, Fannie Hurst. BACK FOYER—George Jean Nathan—leaving the theater in the middle of the second act.

article for the *New York Herald*, he confided to readers that he had spent premiere night sitting backstage, as was his custom on opening nights — particularly at the Lyceum, which offered a peephole in the wall above the auditorium (courtesy of Daniel Frohman), through which he could watch the audience:

> I watched them file in, that momentous gathering, whom out-of-town newspapers love to call "the blasé first nighters." In a theatre the size of the Lyceum, about one-quarter of the orchestra chairs, at a premiere, are occupied by the critics and their wives, and by George Jean Nathan and one of his overcoats. On this particular evening, however, it was too warm for an overcoat, so he brought a young lady. . . .
>
> Almost the remaining three-quarters of the chairs are sat upon bitterly and defiantly: (1) by actors out of a job and firmly convinced that they can do much better work than anything that they are liable to see on the other side of the footlights; (2) by playwrights with an unprintable opinion of the works of the dramatist whose latest offense they are about to witness; (3) by theatrical managers, heroic souls, who are ready to bear with smiling composure the failure of a fellow manager. This charming three-quarters of the first night audience are known to Broadway as "the murderers." From my point of vantage I observed that they were all present. Here and there among them sat, isolatedly, a few Human Beings. They are easily distinguishable from the rest of the first night audience. The Human Beings are quiet, sometimes almost sad, before the performance begins, but once it is underway they cheer up, they laugh, they even applaud. The "murderers," on the other hand, do all their laughing before the play commences. Once the curtain rises they settle into an abysmal gloom, which deepens as the evening progresses. They only rouse themselves, from time to time, to stare indignantly at some one who has the temerity to enjoy himself. . . .

Hopwood gazed long and "sinkingly" at the "murderers" before *Little Miss Bluebeard* began. Then the curtain rose. As expected, the comedy seemed to be evoking "all the hilarity attendant on the production of a Shakespearean tragedy," but suddenly someone laughed. It was the woman next to George Jean Nathan. Then someone else laughed, and the laughter became contagious. Then Irene Bordoni came upon the stage, "and the ice in the orchestra gave a despairing crack, and broke up helplessly, for the rest of the evening." Before Hopwood's astonished eyes a remarkable metamorphosis was taking place. "On all sides reluctant individuals were being transformed into Human Beings." A distinguished fellow playwright looked down worried. "'My God,'" Hopwood could almost hear him say, "'Do they actually like this thing?'" At the end of the second act the playwright arose indignantly and went home. "Then," concluded Hopwood, "I knew my play was a success!"[37]

Towards the end of November, a month before the opening of the previously mentioned *Alarm Clock*, Hopwood wrote Bell and told him of his fourth project of 1923:

475 Fifth Avenue
New York
November 27th, 1923

Mr. Archie Bell
The Cleveland Leader News,
Cleveland, Ohio.

Dear Archie:

I have been even busier than usual lately and am still very much rushed . . .
I have just returned from two weeks in Chicago with the play "The Best People". This, as you may know, is a revised version of David Gray's comedy "Goodness Knows", which was tried out in Cleveland last spring. Everything went splendidly in Chicago and although we were supposed to stay there only three weeks, our run has been lengthened to eight weeks and we may be able to continue there even longer provided that an arrangement of some sort can be made about a theatre. . . .

My love to you. . . .
Avery[38]

The Best People proved so successful in Chicago that it played to record-breaking business for five months. David Gray, whose original play it had been, praised Hopwood in a newspaper article for making the script work. As far as he was concerned, Hopwood ranked alongside George M. Cohan in his knowledge of the theatre and the American public. Both men regarded the theatre primarily as "the temple of laughter and entertainment," and as a result they had consistently provided shows where the "care-oppressed" forgot their worries and went home "refreshed and grateful."[39]

The Best People had first appeared as a short story by Gray in *The Saturday Evening Post*, entitled "The Self-Determination of the Lenoxes." It had gained the immediate attention of D.W. Griffith, who had telephoned Gray and had offered to buy the picture rights, but Gray had already determined to write the dramatization himself. Soon after *Goodness Knows*, as Gray had entitled his dramatization, had opened for a tryout in Cleveland during the spring of 1923, he realized the third act wasn't working. Avery Hopwood was called in to "fix" the piece, and before long the two men were collaborating to good advantage. It was while the two were working on the script during the Chicago tryout in November that Gray began to understand why Hopwood had become one of the most successful "modern" writers of comedy.

> Above all, there is his gift for line. No one living can put things in the mouths of his characters that convulse great audiences as he can, but there is more to a successful play than this. As we worked together I began to note not only his amazing industry and an almost infinite capacity for taking pains, but so generous and sympathetic an understanding of what I had tried to do that I was speechless. I saw my characters and scenes develop as if by magic into what I had dreamed of but could not realize myself. . . .

As a writer of entertainments he believes that his plays should entertain. With him the test of the audience is the final test. Lines that failed to get a response were ruthlessly cut whether they were his or mine, whether we thought they were good or not. Scenes that dragged were cut or rewritten till they went swiftly and smoothly. In the first thirteen performances [The Best People] was in effect again rewritten and twenty minutes of its acting length cut out. And this is the method employed by Mr. Hopwood in all his plays.

The highbrow calls it catering to the audience. Is there any other honest method of writing entertainments?[40]

After *The Best People's* five-month run in Chicago, the producers put the play to rest, awaiting the opening of the 1924–25 Broadway season. When the comedy finally premiered in New York at the Lyceum Theatre on August 19, 1924, it scored only a moderate success. Shortly after the opening, Hopwood wrote Archie Bell and told him that the play had not been as well received in the "Big Apple" as in the "Windy City" the year before, but that business had "jumped $2,000" in the second week, so things were looking better for a run;[41] it lasted 143 performances.

The Best People builds its humor from the strained relations between Mr. and Mrs. Bronson Lenox and their precocious children, Marion and Bertie. Marion, bored with life, has become a "jazz-loving" flapper; she refuses to marry Lord Rockmere, a "silly-assed Englishman" dear to the heart of Mrs. Lenox. Instead, she falls in love with the handsome family chauffeur, Henry. The Lenoxes' son, Bertie, is the stereotypical prodigal. Drunken and debauched, he becomes infatuated with a chorus girl. Despite the scandal the children bring upon the "best people," they go through with their plans of marrying the people they really love. Marion marries her chauffeur, the only man who is able to control her, and together they anticipate a simpler life back on a farm in Birdville, Missouri. Bertie gets his little "gold digger," the only girl who has ever pretended to be controlled by him. Mrs. Lenox is distraught. But in the end, Father seems inclined to think "new blood is what the Bronson Lenoxes need." As one critic wrote:

> We must not forget that it is only in a Hopwood farce that this social millennium is reached. It is all about as untrue to actual life as anything could be, but to furnish an idle evening's entertainment the nonsense serves its purpose.[42]

George Jean Nathan summed up *The Best People* in this way:

> It is the one hundred and eighty-first play about the unruly generation, the 269th play in which the irate father starts out to bribe and unmask the girl his son is engaged to and learns that she is really a very decent sort, the 352nd play in which the aristocratic daughter is pulled off her high horse by a man of the people, the 474th play in which the leading characters are flabbergasted to find that they are occupying neighboring private supper-rooms

in the same midnight restaurant, the 513th play in which the heroine rejects a title for the poor young American whom she truly loves, the 623rd play in which a son, the worse for liquor, coming upon his father in the company of an obvious woman tempestuously accuses his father of doing the very thing which his father has accused him of, the 746th play in which one of the curtains falls upon the ejaculation, "Well, I'll be damned!" the 819th play in which comedy is extracted from a scene in a cafe between an old beau and a flashy actorine, the 976th play in which a snobbish woman is confounded and put to rout by a simple and unaffected woman, and the 1995th play in which the daughter, called to accounts by her parents, retorts that she didn't ask to be born.[43]

The chief merit of the comedy, as the *Theatre* critic saw it, was in its handling of the otherwise overworked material. *The Best People* did not take the subject of the "younger generation" too seriously, but, in the "spirit of burlesque," handled "amusingly and deftly" a problem that was causing "concern in every American home."[44] The veteran cast featuring James Rennie as Henry, the chauffeur, Charles Richman as Bronson Lenox, and Florence Johns as the gold digger was praised for its spirited and skillful delivery. But, in the opinion of Stark Young, "none of the parts were good enough to play very badly."[45]

Although the New York production of *The Best People* did not run as long as the Chicago tryout, the play eventually proved itself to be one of Hopwood's more successful collaborations. In 1925, the San Francisco company of the comedy broke all records at the President Theatre, running for 342 consecutive performances—the greatest number of performances known in that city at that time.[46] A year later, the London production of *The Best People* at the Lyric Theatre more than doubled the New York run, playing a total of 309 performances.[47] Milton Waldman writing in the *London Mercury* for March 1926, noted:

> Mr. Avery Hopwood—one of the two authors of *The Best People*—is the proprietor of what is perhaps the most successful, unfailing and efficient machine for the manufacture of farce-comedy now existing in America, or perhaps anywhere outside of Paris.[48]

Hopwood's second offering of 1924 opened in December; into a season that had already seen three adaptations of plays by popular Hungarian dramatist Ernö Vadja, David Belasco decided to add Hopwood's adaptation of Vadja's *Der Harem*. Roughly speaking, *The Harem* was a variation of Molnar's *The Guardsman*, which the Theatre Guild had opened a month before with Alfred Lunt and Lynn Fontanne. In *The Harem*, however, it was the wife who was jealous of the husband instead of the other way about. Stark Young commented in the *New York Times:*

> There will be people who will find Vadja's play gayer, looser and warmer and faster than Molnar's and people who will prefer *The Guardsman* with its

subtlety and finish, its prismatic record of an actor's egotism, and its charming study of the wife.[49]

In *The Harem,* Carla, played by Belasco's most recent star, the sultry Lenore Ulric, decides to test her husband, Roland, played by William Courtney, to determine his fidelity. Carla follows her husband to a salon infamously noted for its Turkish Harem decor, where he is supposed to have a rendezvous with a young girl he has recently met. Before long Roland is being entertained by the "Sultan's" favorite, veils, beads and less. The courtesan seduces Roland for half an act, and then the two run off to a nearby hotel. The next morning, back home, Carla confronts her husband about his whereabouts the night before. When he concocts a yarn about attending a duel, she tells him she knows he has been unfaithful. She has been unfaithful too. Carla puts on her Harem outfit, and Roland, startled at first, bursts into laughter and exclaims: "I knew it was you all along."

The success of *The Harem* was the result of the "pulsating" playing, as one critic put it, of the show's starring players. William Courtney was generally thought "competent and satisfactory," but Lenore Ulric's spirited characterization kept the show moving. Stark Young observed:

> She had a good deal to do by way of variety, first as the golden-haired wife, then as the Turkish princess in tissue and beads and jeweled mask, and then as the loving, rearranging wife. She played with an unbroken naturalness even in the midst of farcical points and forced scoring of lines. She bound her audience to her with an unbroken bond all through her performance. And she kept giving us the impression that she has a great deal more than this part called for, when she gets a play that gives her a full scope.[50]

Lenore Ulric went on to play, most notably, Lulu Belle, Dot Hunter *(Pagan Lady),* Patsy Shaw *(The Social Register),* Anita *(The Fifth Column),* Sadie Thompson (in a revival of *Rain),* and Charmian opposite Katharine Cornell in *Antony and Cleopatra.*

The heavy-handed approach to sex humor in *The Harem* soon led to a call for censorship similar to the *Demi-Virgin* case two years before. Belasco was hauled before the District Attorney and threatened with grand jury action but he promptly agreed to cut out any offending passages. Ironically, the same censorship action called in the producers of Eugene O'Neill's *Desire Under the Elms,* which was found to be more offensive than *The Harem;* "it was too bad to be purified by a blue pencil."[51] But the *Desire* people remained defiant, and vindicated themselves by inviting teachers, executives, and producers to a special performance of the play, after which the audience protested any censorship of the piece. *Desire Under the Elms* eventually ran for 203 performances compared to *The Harem's* 183; *The Guardsman* ran 248.

Three weeks after the opening of *The Harem,* Hopwood was busy doctoring a farce entitled *Pretty Little Pussy* by Larry E. Johnson and Beulah King.

When the play tried out in Baltimore Hopwood had retitled it *The Cat Came Back*. Little is known about the history of this project, except that it failed almost immediately after opening in Chicago on December 29, 1924. Apparently Hopwood's reworkings and the talents of May Vokes, who had played Lizzie in *The Bat*, and a young Claudette Colbert could not save it. Chicago drama critic Fred Donaghey commented in the *Tribune* that Hopwood had done all he could with the piece, but finally advised the producers to "throw it into the lake."[52]

More significant than Hopwood's work on *The Cat Came Back*, however, is the uncharacteristic curtain speech he gave while the play was still in Baltimore. After being called before the curtain at the end of the second act, Hopwood made a few perfunctory remarks, then, under the influence of drink, as it seemed to some, he began to talk about profanity on the stage — perhaps in reaction to the current *Harem* charges. The popularity of such vulgar entertainments was on the wane, he said. American theatregoers were looking "to other types of drama to succeed the multitude of current plays."[53] Soon, a feeling of uneasiness began to move through the audience as Hopwood confessed in this most public way what many of his friends had known for some time: "even his own plays bored him." He pronounced *Getting Gertie's Garter* and *The Demi-Virgin* the "dullest" plays he had ever sat through, and frankly attributed their success in New York and elsewhere to the publicity generated by police interference. Bringing his confession to an abrupt end, Hopwood further dumbfounded the audience by stating that he was "tired to death" of writing the sort of plays that were the "fad of the moment"; he was quitting. He had made this vow several times before, but not in such a manner.

Many people had long thought Hopwood's character and personality incongruous with the kind of risqué farce he turned out, but they had no idea of the extent to which the work palled on him. Hopwood's increasing boredom with his work had, however, begun to capture the attention of the column writers, one of whom observed that he behaved at opening nights "with the air of a minister officiating at a funeral," an analogy which was not entirely new. The writer further observed:

> He goes to the theatre with the most unamused, I'll-bear-it-but-don't-think-for-a-minute-I-like-it look you ever saw in a Broadway theatre. I know he has made millions laugh . . . but I've never seen him do more than faintly, boredly, smile at the most shrieking farces. . . . Avery Hopwood is on Broadway, but not of it. He is the recluse of the Rialto.[54]

Now, that ministerial air was beginning to change into one of "extravagant dissipation." Hopwood's attendance at New York parties had been noted since the early days of his friendship with Carl "Buddy" Van Vechten and the notable "fish night" masquerade, but those days of innocent excess were gone. As for Hopwood's foreign escapades, the public had no idea. The drunken curtain speech between the second and third acts of *The Cat Came Back* may well have been the culmination of many events during 1923 and 1924.

In January of 1923, Hopwood had once again sailed for Europe unexpectedly and "in a great rush," but this time his reasons for sailing were clearly linked to personal difficulties rather than business or merely holiday. Before sailing, he confided to Fania Marinoff that complications in his relations with John Floyd had begun to make staying in New York difficult:

On Board S.S. Olympic

Fan darling—I hate to ask *anyone* anything—but I don't mind so much with you, for I adore you.

My parting with Johnny was like going thru a death, for both of us.—Will you be an angel, & call him up, right away—Biltmore—room 747—& make some sort of date with him.—Except the people he has met thru me he has only one friend in New York—& he adores you, Fan, & Carl Too.

I'm all tired out, & I'm disgracing myself in the waiting room, by penning [these] few lines in tears—so you know how I feel—and Carl must be nice to Poor Johnny, too.

I do love you Fan.—& Carl knows what I think of him.

[January 22, 1923]   Avery[55]

After arriving in France, he wrote to Fania once again:

Claridge's Hotel
Paris

Darling Fania: —

It was sweet of you to write me again, about Johnny.—I'm afraid I inflicted a rather grievous wound—I'm sorry—but it just had to be.—I don't believe I shall live with people any more.—It makes things so complicated.—And yet, living alone is complicated too....

Next week I'm going to Monte Carlo, & perhaps Italy—then back to Paris—England—home—at least those are my present plans.

I shall have many things to tell you & Carl when I return—Most of them things which I can tell *only* to you & Carl.

I've just this moment come from Gertrude Stein, of whom I've seen considerable....

Do write me daily darling.... Salutations & Showers of golden love to you & our Carl

Paris—March 15, 1923   Avery[56]

During 1923 and 1924, the combination of Hopwood's dissatisfaction with his career in the theatre and the frustrations over his sexuality had begun to take its toll. He was increasingly turning to drink and other stimulants in an attempt to flee from himself. And by summer 1924, this self-destructive escapism had become frenetic.

In early June of that year, prior to resuming work on *The Best People,* which had been set for its pre–Broadway tryouts in August, Hopwood made his last trip to the campus of his alma mater in Ann Arbor. He visited with Professor Scott, who took him down to the Quadrangle Club to have a look at the redecoration that he and other successful past-members had made possible, and then it was over to see the current tribe of Phi Gamma Delta "Fijis," where he threw a send-off party for the graduating brethren. Everyone wanted to know: had he really been suspended or expelled from the University at some point, as the editors of "The Michigan Chimes" had reported? "No such distinction came to me in my undergraduate career," Hopwood told the boys. Those zealous undergrad editors simply acquired me a notoriety, which, "at the time of my Michigan sojourn, I did not even remotely aspire to." A toast to "The Chimes." After a full night of revelry, Brother Hopwood stumbled majestically down the steps of the big house on Oxford Street, and tightroped his way to an awaiting taxi. "If you never see me again," he shouted, waving his silk hat out the window, "remember me this way boys!"[57] He departed, little more than a stranger to the young men waving back.

Several weeks later, in July, now only a month before the first tryout of *The Best People,* Hopwood telegrammed Van Vechten: "Don't wait for me for dinner"; he was sailing again for Europe. To Archie Bell he wrote:

Dear Archie: —

I was disturbed because you & Jim couldn't go abroad, so I decided to take a second trip, to make up for it. — I sailed on 3 hours notice, & found it much easier than when I have known about it 3 weeks ahead.

I can't be gone very long, probably because of "The Best People" production.

I think I shall go to Italy — While there, I shall continue to try to represent you & Jim, as well as myself. . . .

Faithfully

July 9th [1924]   Avery[58]

From Southampton, Van Vechten received a letter that more than explained the three hours' notice:

On Board S.S. "Olympic."
[July 11, 1924]

Dear Carl: —

I think it was very cruel of you not to stay & have dinner with me Fourth of July night. — I was very hurt — that was why I decided to sail, & end it all. — I've been thinking things over, however, & I've decided that God is love — tho' God is not a dinner — & I've decided to forgive you, on condition that you entertain sumptuously for me, when I return, & provide me with ocean passage at every meal.

Will you, & especially Fan, be very nice to our dear, handsome, *strong* impulsive Johnny? Ask him up, occasionally & go see his apartment, & convince him that I am an impossible person to live with. — And for Gawd's sake put him in a forgiving frame of mind toward me. — But for Gawd's sake, not *too* forgiving. — I don't want to be attacked, when I return, but neither do I want him to live with me. I'm really afraid that, if he does, it may end up in something disastrous.

Of course you won't breathe a word to him about this letter, . . .

Expect to see me at any moment, or not at all.

Unfaithfully
Sacha

P.S. The whole thing was yr fault anyhow. You are very Saturnine, & you always disrupt my peaceful little households.

P.S. If you have anything especially to report, . . . you'd better be sure that John is in America before you write me.

P.P.S.S. My Gawd! — Don't write unless yre sure! — I just got a cable from New York (in the Black Hand Manner) as follows: —

"You Will See Me. Floyd"

Carl, you've simply *got* to keep that boy in New York. — I will *not* be murdered in Europe. — I don't care what means you use, but *keep him there!*

Introduce him to some *nice girl*. . . . Or convince him that his career & his whole life will be ruined, if he *sails*.

More violent means of persuasion suggest themselves, but, I leave them *to yr* discretion.

By the way, I got an unsigned wireless, the other day, — "What shall I do about Johnny?" — I didn't know who sent it & if I had it would have beggared me to answer it adequately.[59]

Within five weeks, Hopwood had returned to America for the out-of-town tryouts of *The Best People.* He wrote Bell to fill him in on the European trip, particularly the highlight: he had met Max Reinhardt in Venice and had "had some good talks with him." But "Oh," he scrawled, "I *must* tell you about my [recent] Asbury Park encounter with the Police. — it was a scream."[60] Hopwood saved his telling for later, but newspapers had already reported it.

At about 4:30 on the morning of August 15, 1924, Hopwood and several others from the cast of *The Best People* were at a Main street restaurant eating their after-the-show breakfasts and sobering up, when in came an unsuspecting patrolman, Officer Fred Aguero. Hopwood reportedly cried out, "Look at the damned cop!" Aguero ignored the drunken Hopwood at first, but Hopwood continued to assail him with "a stream of unprovoked profanity." Aguero left the restaurant and met a patrolman Kerr on the street. When the two went inside, Hopwood renewed his abusive behavior. Aguero and Kerr took Hopwood outside and placed him in the sidecar of Kerr's motorcycle, but Charles Adams, a 22-year-old actor who was playing the footman in *The Best People,* interfered, "attempting to take Hopwood away from the police." Both Hopwood and Adams were arrested and taken to headquarters, where Hop-

Texas Guinan's El Fay Club: the "Left Bank" on Broadway, 1924, operated by gangster Larry Fay. Front and center, Tex Guinan, exmovie cowgirl and performer in Shubert Revues. Mixed into the gaiety see Frank P. Adams, Julia Hoyt, Johnny Dooley, Gallagher and Shean, Barney Gallant, Rose Rolando, Avery Hopwood, Hugo Riesenfeld, Dagmar Gadowsky, Ann Pennington, Eddie Cantor, Earl Carroll, Peggy Joyce, Richard Barthelmess and Mary Hay, Bebe Daniels, Gloria Swanson, Harold Lloyd, John Barrymore, John Murray, and the artist himself, George Wynn, under the table.

wood continued his abusiveness and refused to give his age. After considerable commotion, the two men were charged with "being under the influence of liquor, resisting an officer and disorderly conduct." Hopwood, once sober, bailed Adams and himself out by paying one hundred dollars bond. Later in the day the two returned to the court and pleaded guilty; they were each fined thirty dollars.[61] Hopwood's Asbury Park "Clash with Police" was apparently typical of several incidents that occurred later in his life.

In mid–December 1924, when Hopwood stepped onto the apron of the stage at the Auditorium Theatre in Baltimore during *The Cat Came Back* and told the audience he was "tired to death" of the kind of plays he had been writing, he was doubtless condemning himself as well as the theatre to which he had become an ambivalent slave. Within two months he sought refuge across the ocean. "My plans are vague," he wrote Van Vechten from the Savoy in London, "but I don't believe I shall return to America for a long while — & when I do I shall not stay. — So there you are — & there I am not."[62]

It wasn't long, however, before Hopwood was enticed into another project. Irene Bordoni brought *Little Miss Bluebeard* to London in early 1925 hoping to repeat her New York success. The show opened at Wyndham's April 15 to "generous" applause, according to the *Times,* but audiences quickly dwindled; too much good competition, some said. Playgoers were humming "Tea for Two" from *No, No, Nanette* and heading to see *The Vortex,* the controversial offering of that suave, young member of the postwar generation, Noel Coward. A seductive Tondeleyo was pulling in record numbers to see *White Cargo,* and just about everyone who hadn't seen John Barrymore's *Hamlet* at the Haymarket was lined up for a closing-week ticket. So, despite Bordoni's piquant and sparkling manner, her fans only kept *Little Miss Bluebeard* going for thirteen performances, not even close to her New York success.

Ray Goetz met with Hopwood shortly after the closing and talked him into developing another vehicle for his wife — one that Broadway would appreciate. As Bordoni was still Hopwood's favorite *femme* star, he lost no time in locating a merry piece of intrigue just across the channel, René Peter and Henri Falk's *Pouche.* Hopwood cleverly tailored the property ·"far from the French," called it *Naughty Cinderella,* and the show opened at the Lyceum Theatre in New York on November 9, 1925, in time for the holidays. Billed as a "romantic song-farce," critics agreed that Avery Hopwood and Irene Bordoni "could find questionable material even in the realm of the fairy tale."[63] Bordoni wore her elaborate gowns and sang her saucy songs and played her daring tricks with just the right amount of audacity and charm to push *Naughty Cinderella* to the 100 mark and 21 more. Hopwood and Bordoni had done it one last time.

With this little project out of the way, Hopwood headed home to Cleveland for one of his brief Christmas visits. When he returned to New York, according to Leonard Hall, dramatic critic for the *New York Telegraph* and Hopwood's friend since their boyhood in Cleveland, Hopwood resumed a glum habit that he had been practicing since at least the early Twenties.

He locked himself into his hotel room for days, living on salads and chewing gum, working on this or that and turning it over to his managers, and emerging suddenly — a puzzled look on his face as he wandered away to Europe in a "strange, wilful way."[64] Early 1926 was no different:

Eden-Hotel
Berlin

Dear Archie: —

I suppose you may have wondered where the Hell I was. I came abroad without telling anyone — not even my mother — although she knows it now.

I've been in London for the production of "The Best People", which has proven a really big success. — a tremendous ovation from the audience, & every critic enthusiastic. — That was not the case in New York, where Woollcott called it "a very gritty bit", or something of the sort. However, chacun a son gout.

Would you like to be in Berlin instead of Cleveland? (I'm too far away for you to punish me for my flippancy).

I've had business matters to attend to here, so I've not had time to do any sightseeing. . . .

Do write me, Archie, & give me all yr news. . . .

Best to you & Jim
Avery[65]

March 23, [1926]

Hopwood wrote Fania Marinoff the same day, and told her, as she was probably already aware, that he had decided not to remain in the States for the production of *The Duchess of Elba,* his adaptation of Rudolph Lothar's and Oscar Ritter-Winterstein's *Die Herzogin von Elba;* he had little interest in the piece anyway (it soon failed during its Chicago tryouts). Continuing, he told Fania:

Unless something unforeseen occurs, I don't believe that I shall be back in America for many moons.

London was wonderful to me, but a trifle fatiguing. I've never had such a crowded life — &, as you know, mine has been a bit full at times. — Berlin seems a perfect rest cure, in contrast.

I've never had a word from Johnny. — Don't tell him anything about me, but if you know anything of him, let me know.

It is much better that things should be as they are, but often I am saddened by the way that I left him. It seemed rather cold blooded — a quarrel would have made it seem all right — still, that may have been for the best, too. . . .

I have plans, after Berlin, but they are very elastic.

My love to my Fan & to my Carl. — and do write.

March 23, [1926]   Avery[66]

The "full" life Hopwood had been living caught up with him while he was visiting with Gertrude Stein in Paris in May 1926. Talk of at least two incidents circulated at the time and have passed down; Gertrude Stein and Alice Toklas were involved in one, the young and successful British writer Beverley Nichols figured into both.

As Nichols tells it, the first time he ever encountered Hopwood was at the Ritz. Avery approached him in the bar and introduced himself by way of inviting him to dine at Larue's. Nichols hedged, a bit put off at the stranger's appearance, his "purple" face, and that singular right eye, almost "independent" of the left. "I don't know you," he started. Hopwood countered in an instant, "That's why I'm asking you." "If you did know me, you'd certainly refuse." Such endearing frankness won Nichols over, and after a little conversation the two men were off to dinner.

The meal was an agonizing bore. Hopwood was drunk when it began and even drunker when it finished. Afterwards Nichols insisted on escorting his soused acquaintance home, but to no avail. Hopwood had more pleasurable pursuits in mind. They were going to a *bordel* where they would cut capers that would have made Nero's orgies seem like a gathering of the Vestals. Fortunately, Hopwood passed out before they reached their destination, and Nichols was able to lug him home, undress him, and steer him into bed. In the doings, a little gold box filled with white powder spilled to the floor. Hopwood became crazed: he fumbled from his bed and fell upon the carpet, "clawing" at the stuff, "sniffing it—sobbing, blaspheming, giggling, wisecracking." Repulsed, Nichols escaped into the night.

Several days later a remorseful Hopwood made amends by sending Nichols a large arrangement of white and yellow orchids along with a charming and witty note apologizing for his "outrageous" behavior. Would his young friend show all was forgiven by dining with him the next evening? He need not fear any "regrettable" conduct this night, as Gertrude Stein and Alice Toklas were to accompany them, and, he added, "Gertrude always makes me stinking sober." Not to pass up a chance to meet the great Stein and Toklas, Nichols accepted. Then, too, he couldn't help feeling that Avery was really a "nice gentle creature *au fond.*" The outcome was, alas, more disastrous than Nichols's first dinner with Hopwood.[67]

Once again the scene was the Ritz. The party was to meet in the bar, then move on to a private room, but the "regrettable" happened. Hopwood arrived late and very drunk. The reserved room had been let go. The guests were tired. As they made their way out into the lobby, wondering what Hopwood might have in store, they made for a curious sight: Stein in a man's cap and a black dress, Toklas close behind her in a pale green kimono, with Hopwood the sudden center of attention, looking a bit disheveled in a loud tweed suit, and Nichols off to the side, humbly attired in a *démodé* dinner jacket. Along the way, Stein, much to Nichols's relief, talked Hopwood into going to a quiet, rather remote restaurant.

Once there, however, the evening deteriorated quickly. Conversation of any kind was impossible. Alice Toklas remembered that early on Nichols contradicted Avery "on some point of no particular importance." Hopwood became peevish. "Hush young man," he scolded, "you and your opinions mean nothing in my young life." He dug about in his pockets and pulled out the little gold case filled with cocaine, poured some into the palm of his hand and licked it up. The ladies were horrified. Stein apparently knew more about Hopwood's problem than Toklas, and she said to him: "Oh Avery, you must not." But it was too late. The dinner party wore on, everyone attempting to ignore Avery's "obscenities." When at last the maître d'hôtel arrived with the check, Hopwood dismissed him with a wave of the hand. "Is that effective, Avery?" Stein humored. "Well not always," he scoffed, "but I always do it."[68] By this time Hopwood was becoming quite ill. Pitching his brandy snifter onto the floor, he lurched across the table and shoved the little box of cocaine towards Nichols. Stein and Toklas had had enough. They rose and asked to be shown to their car. Nichols was more than happy to comply. He recalled:

> When I had put them in the taxi I went back to Avery. He had been sick on the floor. I poured the cocaine into the coffee, got hold of him and drove him back to the hotel. My few memories of him are much similar. He was always drunk or drugged, often both.[69]

A few days later, Hopwood feebly scrawled them a note of apology:

Charlton Hotel
Champs-Elysées Paris

My own dear Gertrude & Alice, how wonderful of you to forgive me. I have been so ill that only now have I been able to read a letter, much less write one. — I'm terribly shaky, but I'm getting better & should love to come one day soon for tea — nothing but tea! — I should like to see Beverley too. — He talked to me on the phone, & was most kind.

Thank you again my dears — thank you always

[May 1926]   Avery[70]

Stein and Toklas, as Bruce Kellner has shared, "fiercely resented bad behavior of any sort."[71] Even Carl Van Vechten, although he hadn't seen the women since 1914, always made certain he was on his best when he was with them. Since Stein and Toklas "adored" Hopwood, there is every reason to believe that he had also been on *his* best behavior in the past. It is not clear to what extent Hopwood may have figured in with the rest of the "lost generation," for his plays were far from the literary contributions of a Hemingway or a Fitzgerald, but clearly his taut intellect and salty wit found its place in Stein's heart. Three years before, in 1923, she flattered him when she wrote *A List (Inspired By Avery Hopwood)*, a short abstractionist play that attempted, in her words, to "capture the liveliness" of her favorite Hopwood farce, *Our Little Wife*.[72]

July 1926 found Hopwood recuperating from his spring escapades at his favorite spot in the Mediterranean, Capri. He wrote to Stein:

> Dear Gertrude: —
>
> If your thoughts ever wander in my direction, you may wonder, while they wander, whether I have gone into The Great Silence. — On second thought, however, you probably no longer associate silence with me.
>
> I was ill again, in Paris, then my mother arrived, & we went off to Aix-les-Bains — from there to Venice — & now we're here in Capri — for a few days more — then I'm going to Perugia, to superintend the 700th anniversary of St. Francis, at Assisi!
>
> I shall be back in Paris, briefly, in September, & if you & Alice are there, then, I hope that I may take advantage of your invitation to take "tea — *just tea"!*
>
>   My love to you both
>
> July 6th 1926   Avery[73]

Also from Capri, he had written "Carlo mio":

> I am down here, as you see, in the land of "South Wind". By the way, I became friends, in London, with the son of its author — a very nice, rather naughty boy, who, also, has written a book, although he is only twenty two. He is writing another one, and, although I like to be in my friends' books, I have reasons for hoping that I shall not appear in this one! I believe it is to be very frank, and *revelatory....*
>
> (You will note that I am very vague about things. I have learned so much about the Law of Libel, since I've become Anglicised, that I'm afraid to say anything — let alone writing it!)
>
> Oh my God, I have so *many* funny things to tell you, and I know that I shall forget them before I return — which, D.V., won't be for a damned long time. Really, you had better come over....
>
> Write me Carlo carissimo. Love to you and the Fania.
>
> July 5, 1926   Sacha[74]

Hopwood's concern over appearing in the book by Robin Douglas, son of Norman Douglas, the author of *South Wind,* turned out to be an unjustified exaggeration; in fact, had Hopwood lived to read the book, he might have been disappointed.

Douglas's book *Well, Let's Eat,* published in 1929, a year after Hopwood's death, was a connoisseur's guide to the author's favorite restaurants. Hopwood was "frankly revealed" at the Eiffel Tower restaurant on Charlotte Street, London. Located in a "not too savoury" area, the restaurant catered to patrons of the arts: "those who [could] afford to pay high prices for exquisite food and good wines." Robin Douglas noted that "vivid personalities" always filled the room:

I call to mind one supper party given by that eccentric genius, the late Avery Hopwood. Other than my very unimportant self, there was Kay Laurel [Hopwood's gold digger friend] — also dead, alas! — Dorothy Dickson, two young actors, Epstein and his then-model, a strange chorus boy, startling with his effeminate mannerisms, and a gruff Society columnist. What a mixed bunch! Celebrating the successful opening of a new show of Avery Hopwood [The Best People].[75]

Along with being mentioned in *Well, Let's Eat,* and appearing as a composite character in Van Vechten's *Peter Whiffle* and the earlier drafts of *"Undecided Sasha,"* Hopwood is known to have appeared as a character in one other of his friends' books: *Love Days [Susanna Moore's]* by Henrie Waste (Ettie Stettheimer), 1923.[76] Drawn as Claude Ewart, an "intriguing man . . . seriously searching for solidities, and who wrote the most frothing and flippant of farces," he is Susanna Moore's enigmatic confidant, "a cynic by nature and circumstance," though it is difficult to discern whether Ewart is "disgusted with the world . . . or with his own cynical certitude, or with the necessity of having to assert it against an accepted hypocritical faith."[77] At one point, Ewart is concerned that Susan is being transformed into a cynic herself:

Ewart gazed uncomfortably at Susanna with his peering, pseudo-worried eyes, and the expression that his old young face wore when he was drawn further into the heart of things than he cared to go. And Susanna understood his expression; she realized that he recoiled from the intimately personal; that such incursions vitiated the purity of his singleness; she understood how he prized it, his independence, — it was for this she found him so pleasant, so satisfying.[78]

Often entertaining Susanna with tales of his "strange," "grotesque," "macabre," and "freakish" friends, he confides to her that he has taken drugs. In the end, Susanna wonders what could have extinguished this man's love for life; he has called himself "a burnt-out volcano."[79] These fictional impressions of Hopwood from 1923 are significant in the light of the similar characterization seen in Van Vechten's 1922 work, corroborating what may have been the onset of Hopwood's chronic disillusionment and ultimate dissipation.

Later in July 1926, shortly after leaving Capri, Hopwood wrote to Fania and made some attempt to tell her why he no longer cared about returning to the States:

July 20th, [1926]
Albergo La Pace Grand Hotel
Montecatini Bagni

How is the dearest darlingest and only & wonderfulest Fania-est?
The Sascha bird is reposing here for a fortnight — then going on to some new resting place. — Montecatini, as The Carlo One can tell you, is about an hour from Florence.

I haven't much news, tho considerable is brewing. — I've decided to stay abroad indefinitely. — I lived so isolatedly, in America, for so long a time, that I have only a few intimate friends there now, & it seems to me that I know everyone in London. — What a difference! — And when I think of the causes — I mean, for the way I loved in New York — it all seems so terribly foolish. I had almost forgotten what it was like to go about, & have a good time. — I've been like some one let out of prison, since I got away. — But I try not to think about it — so why should I write about it? — Except to explain why I don't want to come back — tho I guess you understand well enough. It's rather difficult, so far as my work is concerned, but I'll have to do the best that I can.

Darling Fan, I miss you very much, & Carl, & my own dear Lenore [Ulric]. I must get a castle in Spain, or somewhere, & have you all come and adorn it. Do write me. Embrace the Carl for me,

                                                              All my love
c/o Guaranty Trust Co.   Avery
1, rue des Italiens, Paris[80]

At the present, Hopwood's plays were gaining more attention in London than in New York, partly because of a sensational new actress from Alabama, Miss Tallulah Bankhead. The doors of the Lyric Theatre were closed just long enough after the successful run of *The Best People* there, to allow this seductive vamp to polish her jazzy interpretation of Jerry Lamar in *The Gold Diggers*. When the play opened on December 14, 1926, the critics immediately took up sides. Some said that the play, which had scored so heavily in New York seven years before, was "calculated to shock," others that the performance was "racy, funny and brilliant," while the *Times* quoted from the lines themselves: "If this is life give me death." The *Outlook* reported that *The Gold Diggers* was a "cocktail comedy" sure to please the galleries for some time to come, which it did for 180 performances.

Although the play's success came nowhere near the success of the New York production, critics agreed that what popularity it did enjoy was the result of its star. Bankhead, who had already begun to acquire a kind of cult following with her performance the year before in *They Knew What They Wanted*, turned *The Gold Diggers* into "an extravagant comedic tour de force."[81] Her husky voice and energy gave Jerry Lamar qualities Ina Claire may never have thought possible — or wanted to. Introducing a "scandalous" second-act Charleston, Bankhead regularly repeated the dance five or six times a night to the persistent cheers of the gallery. She recalled in her autobiography:

My Charleston . . . was hot stuff! Adele Astaire said she had never seen a better dance. She was ecstatic about the cartwheel I flipped at the finish.[82]

A *New York Times* correspondent reported that the public seemed mad for Tallulah:

The cheers began some time before her first entrance; when she entered they became deafening, mechanical and persistent; there seemed to be reasonable possibility that the play would be prevented from proceeding further.[83]

Hopwood wrote to Fania Marinoff from the Ritz:

> I've been very busy with "The Gold Diggers", which is an emphatic success—with Tallulah scoring over Jobyna [Howland], which I think is rather remarkable—& Oh, darling, Tallu & I have had a *grrrand* time—& are still doing so.[84]

Beverley Nichols was sharing in Hopwood's *"grrrand"* time once again, apparently willing to chance another "regrettable" incident or two, and Rosa Lewis of the Cavendish Hotel was also on hand to add to the festivities, as was matinee idol Ivor Novello. Mixed in with all of the celebrating, Hopwood and his party friends found some time to spread a little propaganda for Carl Van Vechten's latest book, *Nigger Heaven;* but by "Xmas day" the excitement in London had worn thin. Hopwood wrote to Fania:

> I'm off to the South of France & the North of Africa on Jan. 4th—tho I hate to leave London.—I'm going to Ireland, in the Spring, & later, perhaps, to Sweden & Syria. Best love . . . & the bloomingest of New Years,
>
> Avery[85]

When Hopwood arrived in Northern Africa in early 1927, still accompanied by his mother, he was "thrilled" to learn that Fania might be coming to London in the spring, "with the idea of debutting [*sic*] on the English stage." She had appeared on the New York stage as early as 1903, but critical recognition didn't come to her until 1905, when she played in the first New York production of Shaw's *You Never Can Tell.* In 1915, after some work in films, she had also received critical recognition for her role as the Bulgarian chambermaid in a revival of Shaw's *Arms and the Man.* And in the following two years she had achieved further notoriety for her roles as Ariel in Walter Hampden's production of *The Tempest* and Wendla in the first English-speaking performance of Wedekind's *Spring's Awakening.* Although her early career had been devoted to repertory acting, noncommercial theatre and cinema, the twenties had found her performing in more lucrative, popular Broadway fare. About coming to London, Hopwood told her:

> You are right—you are a type that is different from the general run of actresses in London. If you can once get a start in a good part, you ought to do *very* well.—But you had better come prepared to stay for a long time—so that you can wait until the right thing comes along.
>
> Of *course,* my angel, I shall do everything that I can to help you, & so will yr other friends in London.—Everyone who met you, when you were over, liked you so much.

Above: Miss Tallulah Bankhead in The Gold Diggers: *"The rejected millionaire" is Charles Carson. Opposite: "The end of her sensational Charleston" is designed to shock Ian Hunter and Fred Kerr (seated), London, 1927.*

Theatrically, in London, more is accomplished thru introductions than thru agents....

I'm so glad that Johnny's play [*Wooden Kimono*] has gone on. — We don't write to each other, but of course I'm interested in his progress.

Do come to London Fania darling & we'll have a grand time.

Best love

[Early 1927]   Avery[86]

Fania Marinoff traveled to London several times without Carl, but she never appeared on the stage.

On May 30, 1927, the Lyric Theatre in London housed its third consecutive Avery Hopwood play, *The Garden of Eden,* and once again the star was Tallulah Bankhead. Hopwood adapted the vehicle for her from a notorious German work by Rudolph Bernauer and Rudolph Oesterreicher. In it, Bankhead played Toni Lebrun, a dancer in an obscure cabaret in Paris "where terrible things happen." After Toni shuns the "amatory" overtures of Rosa, the proprietress of the cabaret, she loses her job. She heads for the Riviera and the Hotel Eden. There she meets and falls in love with the rich, young Richard Lamont. Lamont soon proposes marriage, but just as the ceremony is about to take place, Richard's father arrives and questions Toni's purity. Furious, she strips her wedding dress from her and walks out. Later, in Paris, Toni gets even with Richard and his father by agreeing to marry their royal relative, the 75-year-old Prince de Santa Rocco.

Bankhead and *The Garden of Eden* caused quite a sensation in London, where the daily press "demanded to know how much further nudity could be carried before the Empire crumbled."[87] Tallulah was not particularly pleased with the reputation she was acquiring for always taking off her clothes onstage either, but her fans went wild, keeping the play on the boards for 232 performances. The critics, as might be expected, were not as enthusiastic. R.D. Charques, writing for the *New York Times* London bureau, cabled:

> I do not propose to say very much about Avery Hopwood's *The Garden of Eden*.... I do not know and cannot imagine how successful it will be in America. It seems to me to be a clumsy and foolish piece of cynicism, designed to appeal to the mentality of the people who queue up for twenty-four hours or more at first nights. As the Cabaret girl who undresses every now and then ... and who ... finds all that money can buy and a delirium of sentimentality can conceive, in Monte Carlo, Tallulah Bankhead has no occasion to practice the art of acting.[88]

When the play was produced by Selwyn and Company in New York in September 1927 with Miriam Hopkins in the role of Toni Lebrun, the critics reacted to it in much the same way the London critics had. But, New York audiences were hardly shocked by the play's disrobing scene, and Miss Hopkins, although a fresh and delightful personality, did not possess enough of the brazen "to pull off the dramatic excesses" of the play; the show lasted only 23 performances.

New Yorkers may not have been shocked by Hopkins standing "as nude as an underwear photograph in the Sunday Rotogravures," but the producers knew that the lesbian element in the play's first act was risky business. The New York changes, designed to get *The Garden of Eden* past the authorities who had just the year before closed *The Captive* for its implied lesbian theme, had transformed what had been billed in London as a drama, into a traditional, hackneyed comedy. Rosa, the proprietress, became a kind old charwoman who was actually a down-on-her luck baroness. Protecting Toni from the cabaret cads, she takes her to the Riviera with her on her annual vacation. Richard's father is replaced by one of the cads, who shows up on the wedding day and threatens to expose Toni's past unless she agrees to be his mistress. Toni refuses, confesses all to Richard, and when he balks at forgiveness, she tears the wedding gown off. The two versions then draw to a similar conclusion. It is not difficult to see why the play failed in such short order and Percy Hammond remarked "there are no surprises in *The Garden of Eden*, for Mr. Hopwood in his other exertions has well night exhausted the store of phenomena."[89] Hopwood's last play failed in a season that saw the success of such shows as *Good News*, *Dracula* with Bela Lugosi, the Theatre Guild production of *Porgy*, *Show Boat*, Philip Barry's *Paris Bound* with Madge Kennedy, and Kaufman and Ferber's *The Royal Family*.

Hopwood had returned to the States for the rehearsals of *The Garden of Eden* rather than remain in London for what looked like another ill-fated attempt to produce *The Duchess of Elba,* which turned out to be the case; the play quickly went the way of the Chicago production. But Hopwood had been more optimistic about *The Garden of Eden* because of its London success, and during the pre–Broadway tryouts he had written to Archie Bell from Washington, D.C., to let him know that the show was doing rather well in the capital; in fact its run had been extended a second week. "I don't expect good notices in New York," he told Bell, "but if they don't hammer us, I think we may do some business."[90] Now that the hammers had done their work, there wasn't much reason to stay in New York. Hopwood traveled to Cleveland, which he had not visited for two years; playwriting was no longer on his mind.

Writing from his mother's house at 5902 Clinton Avenue, N.W., since burned down, Hopwood sent an invitation to "Buddy":

> Listen, Big Boy, if you *come my way,* I sure hope that you will stop off in Cleveland, & I sure will be glad to see you, & I sure will try to give you a Good Time. — My phone no. is Evergreen 5658 — (Now, don't get Personal about that Evergreen) —
>
> If you do decide to come my way, why not drop me a line in advance? I'll have the Girls all washed & ready for you. — also Mama's Monkey Le Fils du Grand Eunuque est tres amusant. — Merci, mille fois.
>
> Tell Marinova to keep up the good work in my behalf, & convince everyone what a Nice, Quiet Boy I am at heart.
>
> Greetings to you both, my angels.
>
> Avery
>
> — If you haven't mentioned my book to Knopf, I think it might be as well not to do so until it is finished. — People get tired of things, sometimes, if they wait too long for them.
>
> No, ducky, *I* haven't got tired.[91]

Hopwood had, at long last, made substantial progress towards completing the novel he had talked of writing since the beginning of his career.

He returned to New York with the manuscript, and within a month, George Doran issued a preliminary announcement referring to a "200,000-word book from the pen of the famous playwright." Hopwood apparently told the publisher that he intended to cut down the length of the book, but, "Not one word of a cut," was Doran's reply.[92] Nonetheless, he continued to revise the work, but before long, as he divulged to Bell, he was "leading the usual over filled (no, not overfull) New York life." In what appears to have been Hopwood's last letter to his friend, he wrote:

Mar 13 – '28
Hotel Elysée
New York City

Dear Archie: —

I've been having a very pleasant, but rather excessively occupied time — working pretty hard — & going about a good deal.

I've been away from New York so much, the past few years, that I really enjoy being here again, & I have no plans for going abroad, tho I suppose that I shall do so later on.

Did you ever meet Bob Chanler...? He's doing my portrait—in fact, it is finished—& the sittings—& Bob's circle of friends—have proven amusing—at times incredible.—He is the last of the Rabelaisians.

Mother is staying here, probably, until after Easter. — She sends her love to you & Jim.

Carl Van V. is in the West, but returns on Sat.—Did you know that he has inherited about a million dollars from his brother, the Chicago banker? If Carl should die before Fan, she gets the money (which is in trust) even if she and Carl should be divorced. —Life is unexpectedly generous at times, isn't it?

Best to you & Jim
Avery [93]

Robert Chanler, who coined the phrase "Who's loony now?" was, as Bruce Kellner recounts, "probably better known for his parties than his paintings." Van Vechten once told him that to be painted by Chanler "was a career and a social experience and an education."[94] It had been after one of his "ribald soirees" on the top floor of his house on East Nineteenth Street, "adjacent to the Van Vechten's sixth-floor apartment," that Ethel Barrymore stumbled forth and hit off the phrase: "I went there in the evening a young girl and came away in the early morning an old woman."[95] It was about this kind of frenetic living, characteristic of the period, that Scott Fitzgerald observed:

> The restlessness approached hysteria. The parties were bigger. The pace was faster, the shows were broader, the buildings higher, the morals were looser, and the liquor was cheaper; but all these benefits did not really minister to much delight. Young people wore out early—they were hard and languid at twenty-one. Most ... drank too much—the more they were in tune to the times the more they drank. The city was bloated, glutted, stupid with cake and circuses, and a new expression 'Oh yeah?' summed up all the enthusiasm evoked by the announcement of the latest super-skyscrapers.[96]

From the earliest days Hopwood had written Archie Bell, "I want to do stacks and stacks of good works, and go everywhere, and see everything, and meet everybody, and experience everything, good, bad, and indifferent, and live till my nose trails on the ground."[97] But now, his attitude seemed to reflect Daisy's turn of the phrase in *The Great Gatsby* when she laughed with thrilling scorn, "I've been everywhere and seen everything and done everything ... Sophisticated—God, I'm sophisticated!"[98]

Despite the fact that Hopwood was closer to accomplishing his true goal of writing the novel, and had renewed his interest in living in New York, he appears to have experienced a period of depression in early April 1928, shortly after his mother had returned to Cleveland.

When Hopwood had first arrived back in New York the previous summer, he had contacted his old friends, Channing and Anna Pollock, and had told them that he was "back in the land of the fairly free — but not for very long,"[99] and that he wanted to see them when they came to town. He and the Pollocks had gotten together a number of times, and, according to Pollock, all seemed to be going well with Avery; the friends had even talked of going to India together. Then, a few days past Easter 1928, Pollock recalled:

> Avery appeared at my flat in Ninety-eighth Street to announce his departure for Europe. He had been drinking, but stayed for dinner and afterward followed me to my study. "I'm sailing tomorrow," he said, "and I'm never coming back."
>
> "You intend living abroad?"
>
> "I don't intend living anywhere," Avery blurted. "I'm sick of it!"
>
> I advised him not to be a damned fool. "You've got everything a man could want."
>
> "Yes," Hopwood answered, very calmly, "I've got everything," and he recited a list of tragic habits and maladies that left me speechless. "Now," he added, "I want to leave you a power of attorney, and I'll dictate it to you at the typewriter."
>
> I protested, of course. Hopwood had a very large fortune, and it was absurd that I should be in control of it. He insisted, nevertheless, and signed the document, which I destroyed as soon as I found that his will was properly drawn and named his executors.[100]

Shortly after, Pollock read that Hopwood had sailed for Europe.

Once in London, Hopwood attended the first production of *Our Little Wife* to be staged in that city. He made a little speech at the end of the play to the enthusiastic opening night crowd, and then went out to celebrate. His comedy hadn't been too successful in New York twelve years before, so the next morning he may not have been surprised to read in the *Times* that "the whole thing is not unlike what used to be called 'French Farce' 20 years ago . . . made tiresome by the insistence on the proprieties."[101] Exactly what Hopwood himself might have said about most of his plays, and indeed his career: "made tiresome by the insistence on the proprieties." *Our Little Wife* only ran for six performances, but Hopwood didn't stay around to see; he traveled across the channel to Paris, where he informed Gertrude Stein and Alice Toklas that their little "lamb" had returned and that he wanted very much to see them.

Hôtel Chambord
123 Avenue des Champs Elysées

Dear Gertrude & Alice: —

> Monday, the 28th, is my birthday. — That date has also, this year, been made Whit-Monday, in my honor. My natal day, however, will assume it's [*sic*] true splendor only if you will both dine with me, that evening. It will be a nice, *quiet* dinner (I am once more "un agneau") — & there won't be

any other guests, unless you wish to bring someone — & you dn't have to give me any presents, as you yourselves will be gifts enough.

Do say that you will come, & tell me at what time I shall call for you.

Your nice, quiet little

Wednesday [May 23?, 1928]   Avery[102]

But, when Hopwood called for Stein and Toklas to join him in celebrating his forty-sixth birthday, he was not alone. He told Stein "that he had asked some friends to come because he was going to ask her to do something for him." Hopwood had always had a great "fancy" that she and Alice should go to Montmartre with him. "I know it was your Montmartre long before it was mine," he told her, "but would you?" Stein laughed and said, "Of course Avery."[103] After they had dined, the birthday entourage rode in taxis to Montmartre. They went to "a great many queer places" and Hopwood was very "proud" and "pleased." Stein and Hopwood always rode in a separate cab and Avery talked more "openly" and "intimately" than ever before. At one point a chill came over the conversation, as Alice Toklas recalled, and Hopwood, speaking of a friend, said: "He will get the best of me yet. He will kill me." Alarmed, Stein responded, "Do not talk like that, Avery, you do not have to be killed." Hopwood replied, "He is pursuing me and he will kill me."[104] A moment later the cab pulled to a stop and they were off to another little mill-cafe. At the end of the evening Hopwood put the ladies into another taxi and he told Gertrude Stein, "it had been one of the best evenings of his life."[105] He left the next morning for the Riviera and they for the country; the friends never met again.

By mid–June, Hopwood had settled himself at Juan-les-Pins, a small, quiet village located between Antibes and Cannes, noted for its pleasant sandy beach, so unlike the rockiness and glare of the surrounding coastline. This resort, which had been virtually created by American financier Frank J. Gould, who lived there and owned most of the property, had recently become a fashionable watering place for socialites in search of respite from the party clamor in nearby Antibes. Here Hopwood answered a questionnaire that critic Burns Mantle had sent him in connection with a book Mantle was writing, *American Playwrights of Today*. About his "early inclinations toward the drama," Hopwood told Mantle that he "wanted to be an actor, but after careful consideration of [his] physiognomy decided that [he] had better write for the stage rather than appear on it"; and, "as to the state of the drama, the theatre, and, if you like, the state of Denmark," he responded:

> I think that the theatre, in America, has reached, at the present moment, its highest level of achievement which has yet been recorded in our country and it is the most prosperous and vital theatre in the world. It should be stoutly defended from the encroachments of "censorship."[106]

A letter soon caught up with Hopwood from Van Vechten who had written that he might be "coming over in September: so don't come back too soon."

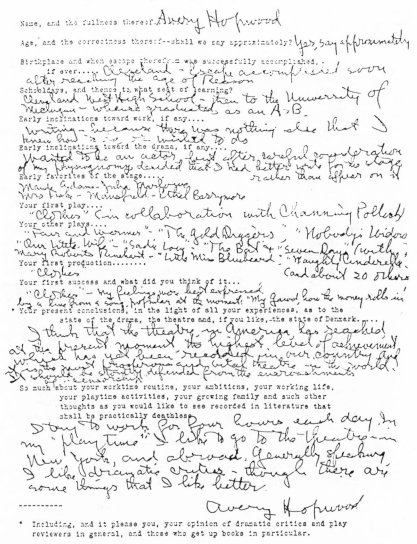

Name, and the fullness thereof. *Avery Hopwood*

Age, and the correctness thereof--shall we say approximately? *Yes, say approximately*

Birthplace and when escape therefrom was successfully accomplished, if ever.... *Cleveland - Escape accomplished soon after reaching the age of Reason*

Schooldays, and thence to what seat of learning? *Cleveland West High School - then to the University of Michigan - where I graduated as an A. B.*

Early inclinations toward work, if any.... *writing - because there was nothing else that I knew how to do and wished to do*

Early inclinations toward the drama, if any.... *I wanted to be an actor, but after careful consideration of my physiognomy decided that I had better write for the stage rather than appear on it*

Early favorites of the stage..... *Maude Adams - Julia Marlowe, Mrs Fiske - Mansfield - Ethel Barrymore*

Your first play.... *"Clothes" (in collaboration with Channing Pollock)*

Your other plays.... *"Fair and Warmer" - "The Gold Diggers", "Nobody's Widow", "Our Little Wife," "Sadie Love," "The Bat" & "Seven Days" (with Mary Roberts Rinehart - "Little Miss Bluebeard", "Naughty Cinderella", - and about 20 others*

Your first production........ *"Clothes"*

Your first success and what did you think of it... *"Clothes" - my feelings were best expressed by a line from a song, popular at the moment "My gawd, how the money rolls in"*

• Your present conclusions, in the light of all your experiences, as to the state of the drama, the theatre and, if you like, the state of Denmark.... *I think that the theatre, in America, has reached at the present moment the highest level of achievement which has yet been reached in our country and I think it has a prosperous and vital theatre in the world! It should be stoutly defended from the encroachments of censorship*

So much about your worktime routine, your ambitions, your working life, your playtime activities, your growing family and such other thoughts as you would like to see recorded in literature that shall be practically deathless. *I try to work for four hours each day. In my "playtime" I like to go to the theatre - in New York, and abroad. Generally speaking, I like dramatic critics - though there are some things that I like better.*

Avery Hopwood

• Including, and it please you, your opinion of dramatic critics and play reviewers in general, and those who get up books in particular.

"Probably the last life story the late Avery Hopwood wrote," 1928. From Burns Mantle's American Playwrights of Today.

Van Vechten thought perhaps that he and Hopwood could join Fania, who was already in France, "in a motor tour of the principal cities." He closed by quoting a letter he had recently received from Gertrude Stein: "'We did see a bit of Avery,' she told Carl, 'and he is sweeter and more delightful than ever.' And so he is, bless him!"[107] Hopwood had written to Van Vechten too, in great anticipation of Van Vechten's next book, *Spider Boy*. "I shall remain abroad in restless exile," Hopwood told him, "until that event occurs." He had just

missed "the bad, beautiful Fania"; he had had no idea that she was coming
to Europe. Hopwood concluded his letter:

> I saw Gertrude S. — She & Alice T. came to my birthday party, & I took them
> to Montmartre — but they behaved very nicely.
> I think that I'll be back in September.
> Love to the one & only Carlo.

June 12, 1928   Sasha[108]

About this same time, Hopwood sent what was his last letter to Fania:

Le Provençal
Juan-les-Pins

> Fania, my darling, me voici, & life, even here, is full of surprises. I hadn't
> been here an hour when I ran across Russell Medcraft (Co-author of "Cradle
> Snatchers"). He acquainted me with certain facts — still — it *was* rather star-
> tling when I opened my door, the next morning, in response to a knock, &
> was confronted by Mr. Johnny Floyd. — He hadn't any idea that I was in
> Juan-les-Pins — he had just arrived — & he was located on my floor. — Well,
> my dear, I give up — almost! Talk about Fate — with an extra-capital F! —
> Medcraft had told me that John was in London trying to get "Wooden
> Kimono" on. I had sworn Medcraft to secrecy, as to my whereabouts — & the
> very next morning, voila Johnny!
> He *says* that he's leaving on Thursday — mais nous verrons. I don't mind
> his being here so long as he behaves — but you know our John. — By the way,
> he arrived with a black eye!
> It's lovely here, & will be very gay, in a few weeks, when the season
> begins. — If you should decide to come here, I would of course fairly rupture
> myself with joy.
> I'm being very quiet — working a lot — reading — bathing, & going to bed
> every night at eleven.
> We couldn't have had the same kind of night in Paris that we had...,
> the police have closed practically all those places!

Love to my own Fania
Avery [109]

[P.S.] Our friend Julie [Hopwood's mother] will probably join me about July
1st.

It would seem almost certain that John Floyd was the "friend" that Hopwood
had told Gertrude Stein had been pursuing him, and would kill him. On Sunday, July 1, 1928, within perhaps a week of when Floyd had shown up in Juan-
les-Pins, Hopwood died while swimming not far from the beach of the Hôtel
Provençal. Although there has been much speculation about the circumstances
surrounding his death, no evidence exists that the cause was anything other
than accidental, or that Floyd was implicated in any way. Interrogatories
presented to eyewitnesses of the death as part of a 1929 court action between

Mrs. Hopwood and the Globe Indemnity Company, which attempted to prove that Hopwood had drowned as a result of "acute intoxication," help to piece together the events of his final hours.

Early that day, according to Jules Pacciarella, the general manager of the Hotel Provençal at Juan-les-Pins, Hopwood motored to Nice where he planned to take lunch at the Hôtel Negressco. At three o'clock in the afternoon, the Negressco telephoned Pacciarella to ask if they should extend credit to Hopwood for his luncheon, as he had no money with him; Pacciarella gave his approval without hesitancy. At five o'clock in the afternoon, as Pacciarella was entering the Provençal's casino he met Hopwood, who was then on his way to the beach. Hopwood had just come out of the lavatory "and had a very red face and the appearance of a man who had drunk too much." Pacciarella overheard the chasseur at the door tell him to be sure to wait before swimming and Hopwood apparently replied: "Oh, it does not matter."

Yves Le Bihan, the teacher of swimming at the Provençal, was at his lifeguard station when Hopwood came to the beach. He arrived with a young man, who was later identified as a soldier of the Twentieth Battalion of Chasseurs. The three men talked awhile and Hopwood offered Le Bihan a drink of a beer he had brought with him. While they were sharing the beer, Le Bihan noticed several "bluish marks" on Hopwood's chest, neck and face, as if he had sustained "blows of a serious nature," but Le Bihan did not inquire about them. After Hopwood finished the beer, he waded out into the surf, following his companion, who had entered the water some minutes before.

Le Bihan recalled that Hopwood seemed to be swimming quite well, but that all of a sudden he doubled over and sank out of sight. Le Bihan immediately sounded his alarm. He then ran into the surf and swam out to the spot where Hopwood had disappeared. After several quick dives in the chest-deep water, he grabbed hold of the playwright's lifeless body and pulled it to the surface. Almost at once, a man in a boat arrived, and together, he and Le Bihan lifted Hopwood from the water and took him to the shore, where they began to administer resuscitation. Le Bihan, his wife, Mr. Barnaud, an architect at Antibes, and Mr. Joseph, the proprietor of the bar on the beach, continued artificial respiration for fifteen minutes, but Hopwood revived only momentarily. Shortly after, two doctors arrived. Jean Marie Turrillot, the resident physician at the Provençal, continued "artificial respiration, traction of the tongue and different injections such as tonicardiac" for another hour before pronouncing his patient dead at approximately seven o'clock p.m.[110]

Although no postmortem seems to have been performed, Dr. Turrillot conducted a routine examination of the body prior to embalmment and concluded that the "bluish marks," particularly the ones on Hopwood's upper chest and arms, were nothing more than superficial bruises. As to the cause of death, he concluded: "In my opinion the cause of death of Avery Hopwood was cerebral congestion," perhaps brought on by acute intoxication.[111]

The first news releases listed the cause of death as drowning, but later obituaries reported the cause as heart failure. Fania Marinoff, who traveled

AVERY HOPWOOD DROWNED AT NICE

Riviera Crowd Sees Prolific American Playwright Sink During After Dinner Swim

CO-AUTHOR OF "THE BAT"

Nice, France, July 2 (AP).—Avery Hopwood, American playwright, was drowned within sight of life savers, and while the crowd in the beach watched last night at the Juan-Les-Pins on the French Riviera.

Mr. Hopwood, apparently in good health, went swimming at 8 o'clock, soon after dinner. He collapsed when far from the shore and drowned before help could reach him. The playwright had been resting here after a short tour of Europe. He intended to leave for Paris in a few days and then return to New York.

Graduated from the University of Michigan in 1905, Mr. Hopwood went to New York as a special correspondent for the Cleveland Leader and almost immediately sold his first play, "Clothes," written in collaboration with Channing Pollock and produced in 1906. He was twenty-four at the time, having been born in Cleveland in 1882.

From that time forward Mr. Hopwood was one of the most prolific playwrights, although in the last two or three seasons he had been an infrequent contributor to the Broadway stage. Many of his farces were adapted from the French, and he was known for his invention of diverting of compromising situations for his heroines.

His best known plays were "Fair and Warmer," "The Gold Diggers" and "The Bat," written in collaboration with Mary Roberts Rinehart. "The Bat" was one of the biggest money makers ever staged.

Hopwood's plays were so universal in appeal that they were played with equal success throughout America, Canada, Europe and the Orient in the native tongues. Many of them were written in collaboration with others, including "Getting Gertie's Garter" and "The Girl in the Limousine," both with Wilson Collison, and two others with Mrs. Rinehart, "Seven Days" and "Spanish Love."

His other successful plays included "The Demi-Virgin," "Naughty Cinderella," "The Powers That Be," "This Man and This Women," "Our Little Wife," "Double Exposure," "The Great Illusion," "Why Men Leave Home," "Little Miss Bluebeard," and "The Harem."

Mr. Hopwood never married. He leaves his mother, Mrs. James Hopwood of Cleveland, who is on her way to Nice where she expected to meet her son. He had spent much of the last two years abroad. When in New York he made his home at the Lambs Club.

AVERY HOPWOOD, WRITER OF PLAYS, DIES IN SURF

American Stricken While He Is Bathing in France; Prolific in Work.

PRODUCED BIG SUCCESSES

Nice, France, July 1 (A.P.). — The American playwright, Avery Hopwood, was taken suddenly ill and died while bathing in the sea at Juan-les-Pins, on the French Riviera, where he has been visiting recently.

Avery Hopwood, one of the most popular and prolific of American dramatists, gained world-wide note with his farce comedies, many of which were adapted from the French. Among his most popular plays were "Fair and Warmer" (1915), "The Bat," written in collaboration with Mary Roberts Rinehart in 1920; "Gertie's Garter," which he wrote with Wilson Collison in 1921; "The Demi-Virgin" (1921), and "The Naughty Cinderella." His first play, "Clothes," in which he collaborated with Channing Pollock, was produced in 1906 and won him instant public favor.

He was born in Cleveland, Ohio, in 1882, was graduated from the University of Michigan and for a time was a reporter on the Cleveland Leader.

His long list of plays includes "The Gold Diggers" (1919), "The Powers That Be" (1907), "This Man and This Woman" (1909), "Seven Days" (in collaboration with Mary Roberts Rinehart, 1909), "Our Little Wife" (1916), "Double Exposure" (1918), "The Girl in the Limousine" (with Wilson Collison, 1919), "The Great Illusion" (1920), "Why Men Leave Home" (1922), "Little Miss Bluebeard" (1922) and "The Harem" (1924).

AVERY HOPWOOD DIES ON RIVIERA

Author of Famous Farces Stricken While Bathing Near Nice

WAS BROADWAY FAVORITE

Nice, France, July 1.—(AP)—Avery Hopwood, the American playwright, was taken suddenly ill and died while bathing in the sea at Juan-Les-Pins, on the French Riviera.

Avery Hopwood, one of the most popular and prolific of American dramatists, gained world-wide note with his farce-comedies, many of which were adapted from the French. So successful was he that in 1925 his income was reported to be $250,000, making him one of the wealthiest dramatic authors in the world. Among the plays of the risque-farce classification for which he was famous were "Ladies' Night," "The Demi-Virgin," "Getting Gertie's Garter" and "Up in Mabel's Room."

Wrote Many Successes

The public favor which his plays found was best measured in 1920 when, at the same time, "Ladies' Night," "The Gold Diggers," "The Bat" and "Spanish Love"—the last two written in collaboration with Mary Roberts Rinehart—were playing to capacity audiences in Broadway theatres. It was with this achievement that Hopwood broke a theatrical record for simultaneous successes long held by Clyde Fitch and the comic opera writer, Harry B. Smith.

Hopwood, born in Cleveland, O., in 1884, and a graduate of the University of Michigan with the class of 1905, went to New York after leaving college as a special correspondent for the Cleveland Leader. In his trunk was a play, "Clothes," written in collaboration with Channing Pollock. He sold the play almost immediately on his arrival in New York to William A. Brady.

Wrote "Naughty Cinderella"

Thereafter Hopwood's record of theatrical successes steadily mounted to astounding proportions. His first play to be classed as an artistic triumph was "Nobody's Widow," in which David Belasco starred Blanche Bates for two seasons. It was produced in England as "Roxana," and enjoyed a great success there. Other successes which followed included "Fair and Warmer," "Sadie Love," "Our Little Wife," "Double Exposure," "The Girl in the Limousine," "Why Men Leave Home," "Little Miss Bluebeard," "The Best People" — in collaboration with David Gray—and "Naughty Cinderella."

During his residence in New York, Mr. Hopwood gained a reputation for lavish entertainment as well as for the ability to work unremittingly on his plays.

to Antibes towards the end of July, wrote to Van Vechten to clarify the circumstances. She had recently had tea with the Otis Skinners, who had been vacationing at Juan-les-Pins when Hopwood had been stricken:

> Cornelia Skinner was an eye witness to Avery's collapse. He was only to his shoulders in the water, suddenly he gave one piercing shriek and sank. They took him out immediately, but he had turned black almost instantly. Four men tried to revive him but he went in the second after the shriek. He didn't drown. It was a clear case of heart failure. He had been going it very strenuously in London Mercedes [d'Acosta] told me, who saw him frequently in Paris, and Eddie [Wasserman] said yesterday he had gone to Nice a couple of days before he died and had said his mother was arriving and that he wanted to go on a last spree before she came. Mercedes said that he was in such a bad and weakened condition in London, that he had to have constant injections of camphor to keep him going, he was drugging himself so. They used to laugh because he smelled like a camphor closet. Poor darling Sacha, I think of him nearly all the time. They took him to a convent nearby, and the nuns persuaded Julie not to see him, but by now you know about everything....
>
> When I think of Avery and Bob [Chanler] and countless others! You just can't beat that sort of game darling. It gets everyone sooner or later, and please god I don't want [it] to get my baby.... Let's be together on this Earth as long as we can, without deliberately destroying ourselves, since life itself destroys us day by day and from minute to minute.[112]

Earlier, Van Vechten had written to Gertrude Stein and told her, "Avery's death nearly knocked me flat. I don't think anything before has ever affected me so much."[113] To Alice Toklas' way of thinking, "Avery Hopwood and Carl Van Vechten together had created modern New York. They changed everything to their way of seeing and doing. It become as gay, irresponsible and brilliant as they were."[114] After Hopwood's death, she observed, "Carl was a reformed character." Those days had come to an end.

Hopwood's body was held at the convent at Juan-les-Pins pending notification of Jule Hopwood, who was en route from New York City to join her son. Sadly, Mrs. Hopwood learned of her son's death through the management of the Provençal as she was checking in. The general manager also had the grim responsibility of informing her that many of Hopwood's belongings had been pilfered; his rooms ransacked before they could be secured. Several of the playwright's friends, the colorful and politically eclectic Dudley Fitts Malone, Alexander Woollcott, and actor Rex McDougall, had fortunately stepped in and taken charge of what was left of his possessions. McDougall showed Mrs. Hopwood particular kindness and attention, not only by comforting and protecting her from everyone who attempted to take advantage of her vulnerability, but by attending to all of the details necessary for shipping the body out of France. In some respects, Hopwood's death was a relief to Jule Hopwood. She no longer had to worry about where her son was, or which of

Opposite: Avery Hopwood dies in France, 1928.

his recent escapades would be detailed in the daily papers.[115] Mrs. Hopwood
had been possessive of her son, and now her possession was complete.

Within a day or two, many other of Hopwood's theatrical friends then
vacationing in Europe started a movement to hold a memorial tribute in Paris.
Hopwood's success was regarded as "little short of phenomenal" in French
dramatic circles, and "discussion of his earnings always brought forth exclamations of amazement."[116] One critic speculated that if Hopwood had been born
in the land where he died, "the state would have honored him and all of Paris
would have turned out for his funeral."[117] Nevertheless, the playwright's close
friend Hannen Swaffer, dramatic critic for London's *Daily Express,* declared
Hopwood "an Englishman in all but birth."[118] The French could not claim
him.

Back in the States, the United Press obituary noted that Hopwood was
"one of the most popular dramatists that Broadway had known." Associated
Press observed that his "plays were so universal in appeal that they were played
with equal success throughout America, Canada, Europe, and the Orient in
native tongues." Hopwood's hometown *Cleveland Plain Dealer* reported:

> One of the ironies of Avery Hopwood's life was that he set out for New York
> to be a serious dramatist, but he found his forte was comedy, mostly of the
> bed room variety, and it so pleased the public and enriched him that he
> never wrote his "great opus."[119]

Cleveland dramatic critic William F. McDermott recalled that Hopwood was
often "scotched" by the critics "not because he was less skillful than other men,
but because he was innately so much superior to them that one minded when
he failed to reach the mark of which he was obviously capable." He concluded:

> That counts little in the final summing up. Hopwood gave amusement to
> millions, he wrote one or two of the wittiest contemporary farces, he was an
> uncannily sure theatrical craftsman. He knew his job and he made the sad
> world in which he lived a little gayer. That is not a bad epitaph for any
> man.[120]

Hopwood's body reached New York around July 19. Transferring the remains from the shipping line to the rail station required a full work day. As
Jule Hopwood insisted on accompanying the body home, she was forced to
wait over a day before making connections West. She spent the afternoon and
evening with Carl Van Vechten, who spoke of his deep love for Avery. In turn,
Mrs. Hopwood was most sympathetic and she confided in Van Vechten the
terms of her son's will, that all of his property came to her in the form of a trust,
and that upon her death it would be dispersed. Before, Mrs. Hopwood told
Van Vechten, she had wanted to die, but now—now she wanted to live
forever.[121] About this same time in another part of the city, customs officials
made a grisly discovery. Hopwood's remains were protected only by the rough

wooden crate used for transporting the coffin; the coffin itself and the playwright's expensively tailored clothing had been stolen.[122]

On July 23, 1928, James Avery Hopwood was buried in Cleveland's Riverside Cemetery. Jule Hopwood chose not to bury her son in the family plot, however. She had selected a new, more prominent location for the gravesite, a plot in which she herself planned to be buried one day. After the interment, Mrs. Hopwood, Archie Bell, and a few close friends and neighbors returned to the family home, where the funeral services had been held an hour before. Exhausted by the events of the past few weeks, Mrs. Hopwood excused herself and retired to her bedroom. When the last of the mourners had gone, she rose and went to the back room her son had used during his Christmas visits. She was preoccupied and distracted, but not with grief alone. Her thoughts fixed upon the packing crate standing in the middle of the room which contained her son's personal effects recently forwarded from Juan-les-Pins.

Several days later, Mrs. Hopwood asked Archie Bell, now her closest friend and confidant, to come to the house. Together they pried away the boards of the crate. Bell opened the steamer trunk inside. From among the hastily packed items he lifted out a mass of jumbled papers, Hopwood's "great opus."[123]

VII

The Hopwood Novel:
The Great Bordel, or, This Is Life

According to Archie Bell, the only source for the history of Hopwood's novel, Jule Hopwood had found the manuscript of her son's book scattered about his rooms at the Hôtel Provençal in Juan-les-Pins. She and others had gathered it together and shipped it back to Cleveland. In the weeks following the funeral, Mrs. Hopwood began reading bits and pieces and in October of 1928 she asked Bell to "attempt to untangle the mass and put it into a readable condition." Bell discovered that the writing contained many episodes that went on for thousands of words, "without an error." Other places in the manuscript were incomplete. Some scenes had been written in "as many as five versions." But, in Bell's opinion, the novel had been "'finished,' because four different endings were available...."[1] Hopwood had apparently written one of the endings three days before his death.

On the afternoon of June 28, 1928, Bell reported, Hopwood had come into the lobby of the Provençal looking unusually pleased. The maître d'hôtel remarked: "'You look happy today.'" "'I ought to be happy,'" Hopwood responded, "'because I have just completed the greatest work of my life.'" It seems Hopwood had recently taken a portion of his work to Somerset Maugham, who was vacationing at nearby Cap Ferrat. Maugham had finished reading the selections and had invited Hopwood to luncheon with him to discuss the work. To Maugham, whose literary opinion Hopwood respected, the novel was a "frank self-revelation that would be pronounced a master-piece."[2] "Overjoyed," Hopwood had begun to celebrate; shortly after he was dead.

In the beginning, Jule Hopwood had been so shocked at the candor of her son's revelations that she threatened to destroy the work. But Bell persuaded her to continue preparing it for publication. "Later," Bell recalled, "she referred to it as her son's 'monument,'" although she still maintained great secrecy about the contents. Three different typists were hired to transcribe the original so that no one except she and Bell "should know the story." In late January 1929, Bell delivered the completed manuscript to her, and the following week she took it to New York in search of a publisher.

Once in New York, Jule Hopwood quickly found herself beleaguered with the problems of settling her son's estate, so she placed the typescript in a deposit vault for safekeeping. Mrs. Hopwood had inherited the bulk of Avery's fortune, well over one million dollars, in the form of a trust; but, as he had made no provision of personal property in his will, she was required to purchase "Avery Hopwood, Inc.," of which Hopwood had owned 90 percent of the stocks. Until the legal problems concerning the disposition of the corporation and Hopwood's literary rights were settled, it was impossible for her to sign a contract to have the novel published. In addition to settling the purchase of her son's copyrights, Mrs. Hopwood and her lawyer were involved in suing the Globe Indemnity Company for $15,000 on Hopwood's accidental death policy, which named her beneficiary. Before long, the stress of the past few months began to take its toll on Mrs. Hopwood's health, and by the end of February she was seeing a doctor. In January she had written the Van Vechtens a note thanking them for the "lovely Christmas remembrance" that had "arrived in time to be placed upon Avery's grave for Christmas day." She wished Carl and Fania well, and added: "I am just as unhappy as I was in the beginning."[3] On March 1, 1929, shortly after learning she had lost the motion against the Globe Indemnity Company, Jule Hopwood died as a result of myocardial degeneration and facial erysipelas;[4] she was 72. To all intents and purposes, the Hopwood novel became "lost."

After Jule Hopwood's death, friends of the family inherited a few of Hopwood's personal papers. The largest collection of material went to Hopwood's childhood friend, Elsie M. Weitz. In a letter of July 31, 1933, Weitz referred to the items she had acquired.

> The estate of Mrs. Jule Hopwood, Avery's mother, included his complete prose writings, as well as his many successful plays.
> The prose-writings, in turn, embrace his full-length novel, his short-stories, many letters, and a *complete diary,* from the early age of eleven years, his motto happened to be "Nulla die sine linea."
> You may be interested to know that the diary & letters are being carefully gone over, & will soon be published.
> Not alone the most minute revelations of the growth of his genius are at hand, but also the indications of his wit, and the charm of his personality.
> His many friends and associates will doubtless find here a mine of anecdotes, and his very definite conception of our American Stage & Theatre in clearest form.[5]

Unfortunately Weitz died before completing her project, and her Hopwood materials (about one cubic foot) lay packed away until as recently as 1975, when the holders destroyed them due to a lack of interest in the subject. Very likely the manuscript of the novel Weitz had acquired was the original that Archie Bell had helped to put into readable form before having it typed.

In 1982, as a result of the research for this work, a typewritten copy of the Hopwood novel was discovered among the files of Hollywood Plays, Inc., formerly known as Hopwood Plays, Inc. It may be that this manuscript is the one Jule Hopwood took with her to New York and placed in the deposit vault

Manuscript of Hopwood's unpublished novel, 1982.

for safekeeping until legal restrictions prohibiting its publication could be overcome. The manuscript consists of five separate carbon typescripts labeled as Book One, Book Second, Book Third, Book Fourth and Book Fifth. The complete manuscript numbers 883 pages, all of which are paginated in pencil. Aside from occasional renumbering, the consecutive pagination is complete. Book One contains sixteen chapters (225 pages), Book Second eight chapters (pages 226-351), Book Third fourteen chapters (pages 352-567), Book Fourth six chapters (pages 568-675), Book Fifth six chapters (pages 676-883).

Books One, Fourth and Fifth are complete. Only the second and third books are lacking portions of the text. The second book, although paginated consecutively, is missing a leaf between pages 320 and 321, undoubtedly an error made during collation. Book Third contains a pencil notation on page 558: "Page evidently missing in original mss." These missing portions may well be the ones Archie Bell referred to in his article. Book Fifth contains two instances of narrative passages which have been repeated: page 794 repeats page 756 and page 856 repeats page 852. Otherwise, the narrative of the novel does appear to be "finished" and Book Fifth draws the plot to a definite conclusion. But, if the original manuscript contained as many as five versions of certain scenes and four possible endings, as Bell reported, one is left to wonder to what extent Bell himself may have shaped the plot and tone of the extant copy. For this reason alone, Hopwood's novel cannot be evaluated as a "finished" work. In later years, Carl Van Vechten, writing to Hopwood Award Chairman Roy W. Cowden concerning the whereabouts of Hopwood ephemera, said: "He wrote a very long novel which exists in manuscript and which I read once and advised against its publication as I think Avery would have done considerable revisions before he would have wanted it published."[6] And Gertrude Stein, writing in her *Everybody's Autobiography* about her visit to the University of Michigan in 1933, reflected: "Poor Avery he had always wanted to write a great novel he did write something but they destroyed it, probably it was nothing but confusion at least so he said when I used to ask him about it. . . ."[7]

Rumors about the destruction of Hopwood's "autobiographical novel" surfaced as late as 1940. Sol Jacobson, a Broadway press agent ghostwriting for the Walter Winchell column, submitted a story he had been told by a Shubert director and friend of Hopwood's from England, Roland Leigh. Leigh had spoken of Hopwood's "serious" and "biographical" novel which his mother was said to have burned because she was so horrified at its revelations. Many of Hopwood's friends suspected that the book had been destroyed because it contained episodes involving homosexuality.[8] Since the subject was only dealt with tangentially in those days, even its mention would have been considered "shocking," particularly by Hopwood's mother. Thus the rumor persisted that the novel must have been destroyed, and Winchell's column concluded: "So Avery Hopwood's claim to immortality will have to rest with his frothy farces."[9] Actually, the novel contains few references to homosexuality, but in the case of the central character, Edwin, the implications are clear.

In 1929, shortly after Jule Hopwood's death, Archie Bell had reported that the novel was "the most devastating exposé of the American theatre as an institution imaginable." Furthermore, he wrote:

> It calls a spade a spade. All that remains hidden is the actual names of the characters in the book; but these are so thinly veiled that anyone who knows the celebrated personages of Broadway will quickly recognize them.
>
> Hopwood made over a million dollars in the American theatre; but he pictured it as a fascinating and horrible idol that draws people into its flaming maw and devours them, or throws them out destroyed and mentally, morally and spiritually broken.[10]

Bell went on to call Hopwood's novel "horrific and startling in its realism . . . a Zolaesque report of theatrical conditions in America as he found them." Apparently Hopwood had thought of naming his book after an idea from Zola's popular *Nana,* in which a theatre manager says: "Ne dites pas mon théâtre, dites mon bordel." Towards the end of Book Fourth of the novel, the central character says: "It isn't just the theatre. That's what life is, too—a bordel."[11] Bell says Hopwood initially wanted to call his book "The Great Bordel," but later referred to it as "This Is Life."

Book One opens on a day in the life of Edwin Endsleigh, a student at the
University of Michigan, who has fallen in love with actress Julia Scarlet, an ingenue performing at the local touring house in *The Only Way,* a dramatization
of Dickens's *A Tale of Two Cities.* Edwin visited her at her hotel, and she con-
sented to go for a stroll with him along the banks of the Huron River. When
the young couple reached "the Lookout," they lingered and enjoyed the beauty
of the pleasant valley before them and confided in one another their hopes and
ambitions. Julia wanted to be a great actress without compromising her prin-
ciples, and Edwin, who had "hovered between the desire to be a preacher and
an actor," now yearned to be a successful writer, but he wanted the kind of
success that he could see, and feel—and spend! Before Julia left Ann Arbor
to continue her tour, she asked Edwin to contact her if and when he came to
New York.

Edwin resolved to write a play that would make him a success and enough
money to be able to marry Julia. The narrator informs the reader:

> Edwin Endsleigh . . . began his career with quite boundless ambitions. He
> was conscious himself of their fine sweep, their aspiring reach. It had not oc-
> curred to him, however, that among these ambitions were some which
> clashed, one with the other. He had not, in short, come to realize that an
> immediate material success, and the production of really worth while work,
> may not be consonant—that they may, indeed, be dissonant. . . .

Having finished his college course work a semester early, Edwin was able to
devote his full attention to writing a rough draft of a comedy, which he called
The Glass of Fashion. Then, "suddenly and appallingly," as he began to work
on its revision, he realized that his play was "third rate. It was piffle—drivel."

> Instead of asking himself how he could bring forth that which was finest and
> best, he had set himself the inferior task of imitating the dramatic "best
> seller." . . . He was filled with shame. . . . Here, at the very outset of his
> career, he found himself making base capitulation. . . .

Edwin drew inspiration from reading James Huneker's *Iconoclasts: A Book of
Dramatists,* but soon he was faced with the dilemma of how to make enough
money to give him the leisure in which to do really fine work. After reading
about Clyde Fitch's success in an article entitled "The Call for the Playwright,"
he compared his comedy with several of Fitch's. "Then came a surprise . . . it
was not so hopeless, after all!" His play "seemed, indeed, surprisingly good—
after its manner. . . ." By the end of the summer, Edwin was ready to go to New
York.

This synopsis of Hopwood's novel to this point is sufficient to establish the
extent to which it is autobiographical. Many of the events and characters are
identifiable and parallel Hopwood's career closely, while certain episodes and
characterizations are clearly composite fictionalizations. The following listing
of the major characters indicates the network of relationships and something
of the development of the story:

EDWIN ENDSLEIGH, the aspiring young playwright whose artistic aspirations are frustrated by the desire for material success.

AMORY VAN DUSEN, Edwin's first and closest friend in New York.

DANIEL MENDOZA, the prominent theatrical director/producer who is secretly married to Adelina Kane. He declines Edwin's script when he discovers that Edwin and Adelina are falling in love.

DANSON STREATOR, a playwright who writes *Thekla Bodnar* for Julia Scarlet, from whom he demands sexual favors.

MATTHEW LEWIS, a theatrical producer left over from the previous century whose success is based on his ownership of theatres rather than on his artistic talents. He elevates Julia to stardom after she submits to his amorous advances.

JOHN WILSON, a young dentist who falls in love with Julia early in her career. She marries him for security, but he dies shortly after.

THOMAS SKANER, a hypocritical, self-righteous playwright who attempts to seduce Julia. Later he leads a movement in Boston to clean up the stage.

TREVOR LOOMIS, a matinee idol who seduces Edwin's wife, Jessamy.

CHARLES EVERETT, a wealthy businessman who supports Julia as his mistress after the death of John Wilson.

FRANK DUVAL, the juvenile lead in Julia Scarlet's company, whom she marries. Later he runs off with a chorus girl and seeks a divorce from Julia.

JULIA SCARLET, the aspiring actress Edwin first meets in Ann Arbor. She attempts to build a career without compromising her virtue, but discovers that she must use men in the way they want to use her if she is to succeed in the theatre. The press eventually refer to Julia as "Our Own Sarah." Towards the end of the novel Julia marries Edwin. It is only then that he learns that her little girl, Mary, is actually his own.

JESSAMY LEE, a pretty but emotional actress with whom Edwin falls in love. Jessamy becomes pregnant and has an abortion. Edwin later marries her, but regrets the action throughout his life. Jessamy leaves Edwin and spends most of her time abroad, where she becomes addicted to drugs and turns to prostitution for support. Although Edwin makes a final attempt to save Jessamy, she is past hope of recovery and dies. Through her death, Edwin experiences a temporary rehabilitation from his own dissipations.

ADELINA KANE, "First lady of the American stage." A recluse, she is secretly married to Daniel Mendoza, by whom she has had a child. Adelina meets Edwin in Europe, where they have an affair.

HELEN SAMPSON, a lesbian who is considered the most influential theatrical agent in New York. When Julia shuns her attentions, Helen drops her from her management.

OTTILIE POTTER, an actress friend of Julia who teaches Julia the "facts of life" about becoming a star.

CHARLOTTA MOORE, a free and independent actress whom Julia greatly admires.

GERTRUDE GRAY, the temperamental star of Edwin's first play, *The Glass of Fashion*.

NATASHE AGENOVA, Amory's "small, dark, divinely slim" second wife who can throw fits that make "Mrs. Leslie Carter in 'Zaza' look like a cooing dove."

HANNAH, Julia Scarlet's aristocratic black maid who is always with her.

MAUD GRANTON, Adelina Kane's possessive and somewhat "mannish" traveling companion.
THE SHELTOFF BROTHERS, theatrical producers who help Julia Scarlet finance the Julia Scarlet Theatre.
WINFIELD AND CAMPBELL, the new theatrical firm that produces Edwin's first play.

It is clear that Edwin Endsleigh is patterned after Hopwood himself, and it may be that the character's surname was taken from Endsleigh Street in London where he had rented rooms during his first trip abroad in 1911. His characterization of Edwin also corroborates the fictional perceptions of himself presented in Van Vechten's *Peter Whiffle* and Ettie Stettheimer's *Love Days*. But some aspects of Edwin's life are far removed from Hopwood's own.

One of the most intriguing plots to be developed in the novel, considering that Hopwood never married, is Edwin Endsleigh's love affair with and eventual marriage to Julia Scarlet, who attains stardom and ultimately owns controlling interest in a theatre that bears her name. In this respect Scarlet shares a similarity with Maxine Elliott, but further comparison seems doubtful. Just as intriguing is Edwin's earlier marriage to musical comedy actress Jessamy Lee, and his affair with the famous, yet very private Adelina Kane. Jessamy Lee may be based on Nesta [Ernestina] de Becker, an actress who had played the ingenue in *The Powers That Be*. Hopwood, it will be remembered, was reportedly engaged to one of the actresses from that play, and, in the novel, Jessamy plays the ingenue role in *Masters of Men,* the revised version of *The Powers That Be.*

The idea of Hopwood's attachment to a music-hall performer is found in an actual incident that occurred in 1924 as he was about to sail for Europe. Before the all-ashore bell sounded, Hopwood told reporters that he was going to marry Miss Rose Rolando, a popular *Music Box Revue* dancer who was there to see him off. When asked when the marriage would take place, Hopwood replied: "That's not decided. An engagement is enough for one day, seems to me."[12] In later years, Carl Van Vechten confirmed that the whole thing had been a practical joke played on the press.[13] Rose Rolando married Miguel Covarrubias, the popular Mexican caricaturist and painter of that time.

In a 1920 letter to Stanley Rinehart, Hopwood also mentioned that he intended to get married, but no wedding took place. The only Cleveland girls that anyone ever associated with him were neighborhood friends, Jane Saunders and Mildred Black, and later Elsie Weitz, all of whom remained single. Van Vechten's Hopwoodian character, Sasha, of the unpublished short story, also toys with marriage, but he too backs out at the last minute. No present evidence exists that Hopwood ever married, or, as some have speculated, that he had a common-law wife.

The conventional love affairs and marriages in Hopwood's novel may point to his need for companionship and family. Edwin echoes "Sasha" when he says that his only motivation for marriage is: "He wanted a child—he

Engaged to be married: Hopwood and Rose Rolando play a little joke on the press, 1924.

wanted children. His instincts were strongly paternal." None of Hopwood's
female characters is as clearly identifiable as some of the male characters, and
more than likely they are all composites.

Of the male characters in the novel, two are easily recognizable. Theatrical
producer Daniel Mendoza is fashioned after David Belasco. Throughout the
book, Mendoza is pictured as what has become the cliché director who
demands favors from his leading ladies. When they don't submit, as in the case
of Julia Scarlet, they are let go. Mendoza's office is characterized as an "oriental
bazaar," where the producer lounges about in his pajamas waiting to make the
next ingenue who enters a "star." Mendoza insists, as Belasco did, that his stars
remain unmarried, and form no "entanglements" of any kind.

The second character that is clearly drawn from Hopwood's life is Edwin's
friend Amory Van Duzen, who is fashioned after Carl Van Vechten. The narrator reveals that Edwin's friendships were "tinged with superficiality. He liked
almost everybody, and he was fond of almost nobody. Amory was one of the
exceptions." The narrator continues:

> He met Amory at a party. It was difficult, indeed, to go to a party *without*
> Amory. At least, in the semi-literary, quasi-theatrical, demi-Bohemian set
> into which Edwin had penetrated. Amory was a character. Or perhaps,
> rather, a personality. He asserted, with some pride, that he did not possess
> a character. Certainly, if he did, he could not be accused of waving it at one.
> He was calmly unmoral. He looked out at the world through large limpid
> eyes—brown, like Edwin's, but rarely eager, and certainly not searching.
>
> Amory was contemplative—at least, when he was sober. When he was
> drunk, which was frequently, he was apt to be anything from a Chinese god
> to a negro at a revival meeting. His countenance, which showed, in its high
> cheek bones, traces of his Dutch ancestry, was ordinarily passive—non-
> committal. Often, when he listened, it was with his mouth slightly open,
> disclosing his teeth, which were formidably large, and set far apart. When
> he was tipsy he liked to bite people. He was at the moment a music critic,
> but concerts and the opera were beginning to pall on him.

Bruce Kellner affirms:

> Amory is certainly Carl Van Vechten.... The physical description is ab-
> solutely accurate, even the biting.... With this appearance, Carl is now in
> the cast of characters in a baker's dozen books, but this is the only one to
> employ his sense of the ridiculous. The others are all slightly and sometimes
> leadenly nasty.[14]

Amory makes two significant appearances in the novel. The first is in episode
four, Chapter IV of Book One, in which he devises a plan to be caught in
adultery in order to obtain a divorce from his wife; this incident is a "more or
less accurate" retelling of Van Vechten's plot to divorce his first wife, Ann. His
second appearance is in Book Fifth, Chapter II, episodes one through three,
in which he talks Edwin into attending a costume party in Brooklyn. Amory

goes as "The Man Who is Visible"—practically naked—and Edwin wears a sailor uniform Amory digs from the closet. At the party the narrator discloses:

> There seemed nothing for anyone to do, except get drunk, or drunker, and dance about madly and foolishly, and shriek dull and meaningless witticisms, or banal vulgarities. It was the latter that succeeded best, and Edwin found himself talking coarsely and obscenely, and joining in the loud laughter that greeted his own obvious efforts at *double entendre*. And he was not ashamed of himself, so long as he kept drinking.

The only other characters that are clearly recognizable as contemporaries of Hopwood's are Gertrude Gray, patterned after Grace George, the star of *Clothes,* and Natashe Agenova, the fictional counterpart to Carl Van Vechten's wife, Fania Marinoff. The theatrical firm of Winfield and Campbell is certainly fashioned after Wagenhals and Kemper, as is the Sheltoff Brothers management based on the Messrs. Shubert. It may be that further research into the mannerisms peculiar to other minor characters in the novel will reveal additional counterparts to contemporaries in the theatre of the period.

The value of Hopwood's novel today rests primarily in passages like the one quoted above relating Edwin's experience at the party that serve to illustrate Hopwood's own thoughts and motivations. The novel is, as Somerset Maugham apparently proclaimed it, a "frank self-revelation." Actual discussion of the theatre during the period is rather superficial. Hopwood only gives the names of three of Edwin's plays, *The Glass of Fashion,* the fictional counterpart to Hopwood's *Clothes; Masters of Men,* the actual title of the revised version of Hopwood's *The Powers That Be;* and *Summer Nights* (?). He assigns the writing of *Thekla Bodnar,* the original character name for Thekla Mueller in *This Woman and This Man,* to another playwright. But Hopwood does not disclose much of the working of the theatre of the period. It is curious that he avoids all mention of Edwin's collaborating with any other playwrights, nor does he make reference to plays like *The Bat, Seven Days,* or *Ladies' Night* that were written with collaborators. Hopwood's record-setting 1920-21 season is completely ignored. Most often specifics about the theatre are dismissed with such comments as: "They discussed the current plays, the popular actors, the merits and demerits of the critics." Throughout the novel, Edwin's plays fall into the background as he struggles to find his purpose in life.

The following excerpts from Hopwood's novel chronicle that struggle in a way that is at once poignant and chilling:

Book Third

P. 352: He had drawn a winning number in the great theatrical lottery. In the twinkling of an eye his condition had changed from actual poverty to affluence. Money poured in. And the newspapers wrote about him, the managers petted him. He had become a Name, on Broadway.

P. 356: In spite of the overwhelming success of his play, Edwin felt, more than ever, that in the drama he could never fully express himself—that he needed the broader reaches of the field of fiction. His first impulse, now that he was no longer dogged by financial necessities, was to sit down, straightway, to work upon his novel. But it was the very success of his play, that for the time at least deterred him.

There was, he found, something very satisfying about making money.... About the mere receiving of it, the mere consciousness of possessing it, there was something fascinating. He experienced a thrill, when he surveyed his weekly royalty check....

P. 360: The trouble, he told himself, was that he seemed to be losing interest, there was nothing to which he eagerly looked forward. Perhaps it was because his work did not sufficiently absorb and satisfy him. Perhaps he ought now, to turn to his novel.

P. 442: It was in my Freshman year, before I had entered a fraternity, and I was very unhappy, for I had been terribly lonely and I was poor, and I'd been very ill—with acute bronchitis, which left a cough that didn't wear away, when Spring came on. The Doctor told me that I had a spot on my lungs. I thought that perhaps I was going to die—what I remember is, standing out, one Spring night, in the yard in front of the little house where I was living, and looking up at the stars, and saying, "Oh, there must be something besides this life—there must be something!" You see, my religious faith was slipping away, and it had meant so much to me now it was gone, there didn't seem to be anything left. Since then, I've got used to living without faith—I mean, the Christian faith—and now, when I look up at the stars, I'm quite resigned to the fact that there's nothing beyond this life. It doesn't seem dreadful any longer—it seems inevitable. I'm not even sure that it's tragic. It makes life all the more wonderful to feel that we're here for only so short a time, in this precious, dreadful, beautiful world. And then we're gone, and that's the end.... (Cf. Hopwood's short story, "J. Brown, Misfit," page 15.)

P. 560: Did people just go on, doing the things that they had always done, because they were afraid to halt long enough to confront reality? Was it because they did not dare to pause, and gaze at their hands, and note, when those hands were idle for a moment, how empty they were? Yes, Edwin reflected, he himself was like that. Almost every day he spent some hours grinding over his play, just because, for many years now, he had grown accustomed to doing something of that sort. And he did not really want to write a play. But he didn't know what else to do. His novel, of course—Oh yes, his novel. But he'd do that later. The play came easier.

There were times when he almost longed for the religious faith which he had once had, and which he knew he could never have again.

To go through life without religion was rather like undergoing a surgical operation without an anaesthetic.

P. 561: Edwin felt the greatness of things impinging upon him. He felt puny and helpless. He could not take refuge in the fairy stories of religion, and he found little solace in the theorizing of the philosophers. But he felt the need of some sort of spiritual chloroform. He found it mainly in alcohol. If he could have kept constantly under its influence—life would not have been so bad. But there was always the awakening.

(6)

He never drank deliberately. Never, that is, set himself with purpose to the task of getting drunk. It was always a process imperceptible to himself, beginning, usually, with a cocktail, taken, if he were alone, as an antidote to fatigue or depression, or if he were in company, as a gesture of conviviality. With the imbibing of that first drink there occurred an invariable transformation in his feelings. . . . His inebriation, for the most part, took a quieter form, so far as outward manifestations were concerned. But within him there occurred a decided metamorphosis. Worry and unhappiness vanished. Gone too, was his sense of world-sadness, and the futility of life and of the human effort. There supervened an unquestioning conviction that all was well with the universe, or that, if it were not, he could quite easily make it so. He felt enormously *[sic]* potential, capable of great work, urged to the highest and most dazzling adventure. Ideas surged in upon him, and true to his writer's habit he scribbled them down on bits of paper, with the feeling that he was not, after all, wasting his time and energy in dissipation—he was really working—or at any rate, laying the foundation for future efforts, and he would resolve that, in the morning, he would set himself to the accomplishment of "something really big." The morning would come, as mornings have the sad habit of doing, and with the aching head he would look at the bits of paper upon which he had jotted down his great ideas of the night before, and scarcely recognize the crazy scrawl which had been his handwriting. And when he did, painfully, succeed in deciphering the splendid, nocturnal inspirations, they proved, always, in the light of day, hysterical, impossible, or merely dull.

P. 564: But it seemed to him, sometimes, as if there were two natures in him, instead of one. There were, at least, strongly contradictory impulses, some of which were momentarily blotted out by alcohol, while others were violently accented by it. It was the latter which, in time, gave him more and more concern. . . . He became truculent, unreasonable, he brooked no interference with his tipsy whims, he provoked fights with strangers; or else, what was worse, he became friendly, even inordinately intimate, with people whom he could not have tolerated when he was in his senses. And on the following day he would have to avoid them, or submit, writhing inwardly, to the terms of companionship which he had so incredibly established with them. Often, to avoid them, he fled from a town, as if he had committed a crime. Sometimes he fled without clearly knowing why, simply a prey to vague but panic apprehension, for his memory of the previous night's events would almost completely fail him, and the little that he did uncertainly recall·was disgusting or terrifying. And for the most part, he was led into these associations, he descended to these depths, not from any desire to wallow in the mire of sensuality. At times, it is true, he was obeying merely the rutty instinct of the male. But more often, he was seeking companionship—love. . . .

Book Fourth

P. 648: He *was* lonely. This, partly, was what made him unhappy, kept him from working, drove him to dissipation. . . . He had been terrified, . . . in his soberer hours, when he realized how, daily, he was stumbling nearer to the black morass of defeat, despair, extinction.

Book Fifth

P. 677: It began to seem to Edwin that he was always running away. But now, upon this latest, abrupt departure, for the first time it dawned upon him that what he was so continually trying to flee from was not some person, or persons, or some complication, or some city. What he was trying vainly to run away from, was himself. . . .

"Where will this end?" he asked himself in his soberer moments, now so unhappily infrequent. He could not believe that he, Edwin Endsleigh, could go on like this. He could not face the fact that he was becoming a confirmed drunkard.

P. 680: He was able to thrust into the background of his consciousness the fact of his changing appearance. . . . He roamed purposelessly about the Continent . . . too depleted physically to attempt any creative work.

P. 683: Significant at this period, was the changing quality of his friends. The best of them he gradually ceased to frequent. He feared their reproaches, although these were mostly tacit. The friends of lesser value left him of their own accord . . . for news of his declension had by this time seeped through the world of the theatre. His new acquaintances were mostly hangers on, given to much talk and few deeds, overfond of drinking, delighting in foolish "parties," which began at midnight, and lasted until morning. Edwin shared their cheapening pleasures, their flabby self-indulgences, conscious often of a great disgust with them and with himself — but still he went on and on. . . . He gave his time, his vitality, the very essence of his being to these futile people, for whom he did not care and who did not care for him. . . . And almost always, when the liquor had taken hold of him, he fled the company of these new found boon companions — he left them, rudely and abruptly, without a word of apology. But he did not, unfortunately, leave them in order that he might go home. He rushed out from these gatherings to seek other, more intimate, dissipations. And again and again it happened to him in New York, as it had in Europe, that he awoke the next morning oblivious of the happenings of the night before, or else remembering only some wild and shameful incident, which made him cover his face with his hands, and cry out, in agony: "How could I? Oh my God, how could I?"

P. 685: But presently he began to experiment in a much more dangerous indulgence. One night in Harlem, when he had been drinking heavily, he purchased a packet of cocaine, and going to the toilet, sniffed the white powder up his nostrils. . . . Before long, he was taking cocaine frequently — perhaps three or four times a week. It had not yet become indispensable to him, and he told himself that it never should, but he found himself thinking more and more often of it — wishing that he had some in hand, to wipe out his fatigue, his dejection.

P. 686: He realized with despair, that he no longer seemed able to write a play which had any vitality in it, any life. He could conceive an idea, he could block out the general course of the action, but when it came to the writing, he felt flat, uncreative. His dialogue which before had always welled up so spontaneously, was forced and wooden. Something within him seemed to have died. And the terrible thing about it all was, that he did not seem able even to be disturbed about it. More and more, all that really interested him was the mood into which he could project himself, with the aid of drink or cocaine.

P. 756: He realized that he no longer had control of himself.... To this he had come, he who had dreamed such high and splendid dreams, who had started out, so confidently, to conquer the world. Conquer the world! He, who could not control his own impulses, who was destroying himself, who had sold his own birthright for a mess of pottage.... He did not know how to check himself. He was lost, lost, irretrievably ruined—unless he changed, and changed at once. But who ever did change? "What an incorrigible romanticist I am!" he thought, "I still have the ideas of a schoolboy. I have learned nothing from life."

P. 862: He would devote two more years to making a "clean-up". Then he would retire from the theatre, with his well-gotten gains, and consecrate himself, at the last, to writing the "something big"—his novel. He told himself that—and he believed it.... Then, as he was starting upon his final year of "potboiling", suddenly, he was interrupted.

Pp. 864-869: The doctor hesitated, for the fraction of a second. "My dear fellow, you have cancer of the rectum." Edwin had a moment of dazed astonishment. Then a wave of something like nausea passed through his abdomen. A nausea of fear.... Cancer!—Cancer! ... His father had died of cancer. Cancer of the stomach.... The opening from the stomach to the intestine had been closed up by this cancer, and he had slowly and miserably perished from hunger.... And the end had been agony—agony!

Hopwood's father died of just such a condition, "carcinoma of pyloris of the stomach."[15] The question that cannot be answered is whether or not Hopwood himself, like Edwin in the novel, had been diagnosed as having cancer. Might this disease have been one of the maladies he referred to during his last visit with Channing Pollock?

P. 880: He had thought of suicide, but now that his years, perhaps his months, were numbered, he did not want to die. Life was precious—and he had so little of it left. He felt an agonized desire to gather to himself, before darkness and nothingness closed in upon him, all the splendor, the beauty, the wisdom of the world.

Pp. 881-883: He thought of his work. Of the work, that is, which he had been doing. And as he thought, he was overwhelmed with a sense of emptiness, of nonaccomplishment. And of shamed wonder at himself.

After all that he had gone through, after his betrayal of his young, high resolves, after his degradation and his recovery, he had returned to this—to what he had been doing for the past two years—the futile amassing of wealth. He had made it, this money which he desired, and now he was to vanish from the earth. The money would remain.... There would be left no memory of him—except a few plays, infrequently produced, in stock companies, and then, later not at all. And that would be the sum of his accomplishment in life's great adventure. It would be for this that he had lived....

He did not comprehend much of existence, but his mind groped toward at least one truth. Character, in its reaction to circumstance, might seem to constitute all of what one called Destiny. And yet, he felt, obscurely but convincedly, that in man lay the power of choice—between the lower and the higher, between the better and the worse. And in the aspiring exercise of that choice subsisted all the divine that man, in this life, was destined to know.

He went to his desk. The manuscript upon which he had been working — an adaptation of a German play — was lying there. He put it aside, and got out the rough draft of his novel.

Could he write a novel? And when he wrote it, would it be good? And would he even live to finish it?

He did not know, but he knew that he must try. He sat down, he began to write.

THE END[16]

With the completion of the rough draft of his novel, Avery Hopwood moved closer than at any point in his career to achieving the kind of work he had aspired to since his earliest days in Ann Arbor. If he had lived to complete the revisions on the manuscript and have it published, he may well have been satisfied that he had finally produced a work of significance. What impact the novel might have had in the literary world is difficult to say — most likely very little. But it seems highly probable that the public would have read about the various disquised theatrical personages with considerable interest. All along Broadway, one imagines the book's "scandalous revelations" stirring up reactions similar to those aroused by stories in the many sensational tabloids of the day. To Hopwood's friends and colleagues, though, one cannot help feeling that the novel's candid self-disclosures would have been genuinely moving.

The significance of the novel today lies not in its "devastating exposé" of the American theatre — for what may have once been considered shocking and eye-opening about the lives of its stage personalities, has since become routine fare for countless books, motion pictures, and television mini-series — but in its painful "self-revelation" and sincere attempt to offer an explanation for what was a successful yet destructive career in the commercial theatre. In this respect, Avery Hopwood's unpublished novel may indeed be his greatest work. It stands as a posthumous vindication; a work that at long last casts light upon Hopwood's deep "sense of emptiness, of nonaccomplishment. And of shamed wonder at himself."

VIII

The Hopwood Awards: The New, the Unusual and the Radical

Avery Hopwood's frustrated ambitions as an author of serious work gained wide public attention a month after his death with the disclosure of the terms of his will: "Avery Hopwood leaves Million; Helps Students ... Wills One-fifth to University of Michigan as Fund for Young Writers ... Would Encourage Unusual," ran the headlines in one newspaper. For the first time, friends, colleagues, and the "many-headed multitude" learned that Hopwood had established a trust that would eventually go to his alma mater in Ann Arbor for the purpose of establishing a program of awards in creative writing. It must have seemed an inconsistency to some that this writer of farces and similar entertainment wished to encourage students in the writing of "the new, the unusual, and the radical"; but as Howard Mumford Jones, then Professor of English at the University of Michigan, told his fellows: "Hopwood, it would seem wished to fulfill in the achievement of others his own unfulfilled ambition."[1]

The bequest, which amounted to $313,836, came to the University shortly after the death of Jule Hopwood in 1929. Accordingly, the Regents of the University were empowered

> to invest and keep the same invested and to use the income therefrom in perpetuity, as prizes to be known as "The Avery Hopwood and Jule Hopwood Prizes," to be awarded annually to students in the Department of Rhetoric of the University of Michigan, who perform the best creative work in the fields of dramatic writing, fiction, poetry, and the essay. The number and value of the prizes shall be in the discretion of the Faculty or other governing body of the University, but the income shall not be allowed to accumulate from year to year. In this connection, it is especially desired that the students competing for prizes shall be allowed the widest possible latitude, and that the new, the unusual, and the radical shall be especially encouraged.[2]

At the time Hopwood had his will drafted in 1921, Rhetoric and Journalism were one department, and his old mentor, F.N. Scott, was still serving as its chairman and encouraging students in his advanced composition courses. In 1929, however, Journalism (later Communication) was made a department

211

separate from Rhetoric, and in 1930 the Department of Rhetoric was joined with the Department of English. It was at the first meeting of the faculties of the new department that the executive secretary of the English Department informed his audience of the Hopwood bequest, adding "that it appeared the English Department had married an heiress."[3] And indeed it had. The amount of the bequest, and the stipulation that the income was to be awarded as cash prizes every year, made the Hopwood Awards one of the largest and most prestigious programs in creative writing in any American university, and perhaps in any university in the world. From the first contest in 1930–31 when $13,000 was awarded to students at Michigan to a low of $5,885 awarded in 1945–46, the prizes have grown to a recent high of $45,925 in 1986–87. Total prizes through 1988 have amounted to $965,055, or an average yearly prize of $16,930.

Beginning with the first contest, the requirement that restricted contestants to the Department of Rhetoric was changed to include all students enrolled in the departments of English Language and Literature, Humanities, or Communication, for at least one course in English composition. Today, the students of the Residential College, which did not exist in Hopwood's time, are also eligible. From the beginning, the awards have been classified as Major Awards, open to graduate students and seniors, and Minor Awards, open to undergraduates, including seniors and freshmen. In both the major and minor contests, cash prizes continue to be awarded in drama, fiction (short story and the novel), poetry, and the essay. Two judges for each area are appointed from writers of national reputation to read the manuscripts and make recommendations, and final selection is made by the Hopwood Committee, which also determines the monetary value of each prize. Contests are now held twice a year, with the Major and Minor Awards being presented in the spring. Along with the announcement of the winners of prizes, an important part of the spring awards ceremony is the delivery of the Annual Hopwood Lecture, given by an influential writer and scholar. Through the years, participants in the contests have heard such distinguished authors as Max Eastman, Zona Gale, Carl Van Doren, John Crowe Ransom, Robert Penn Warren, Stephen Spender, Denise Levertov, Saul Bellow, Robert Corrigan, and Maxine Hong Kingston, to name a few, all of whom have also served as judges for the contests.

Groundwork for the Hopwood Awards was completed under the first director of the program, Professor Bennett Weaver, but it was under the leadership of Professor Roy W. Cowden, who assumed the directorship in 1934, that the awards program developed its distinctive character, and achieved a national reputation for recruiting promising young writers. Cowden opened the first Hopwood Room in 3227 Angell Hall, and immediately began to seek Hopwood manuscripts and memorabilia. Carl Van Vechten was the most helpful in this respect, and it was through his efforts that the Hopwood Room acquired Florine Stettheimer's melancholy portrait of Avery Hopwood — the only known portrait of the playwright to be extant. In 1952, following Cowden's retirement, Professor Arno L. Bader took over leadership

Avery Hopwood from the painting by Florine Stettheimer, ca. 1917.

of the awards program, serving until 1965. During that time, the Hopwood Room was relocated to its present space in 1006 Angell Hall, and Professor Bader compiled a significant collection of play reviews and biographical and critical materials on Hopwood. Since 1965 the awards program has been chaired by Professor Robert F. Haugh (1965–72), co-chaired by Professors Donald Hall and Sheridan Baker (1973–74), Professor John W. Aldridge (1975–1988) and the present chairman, Professor Nicholas Delbanco.

From the early years of the contest until her retirement in 1972, Hopwood Program Secretary was Mary E. Cooley. Along with tending to the Hopwood Room library, Miss Cooley began organizing the extensive collection of prize-winning Hopwood Award manuscripts, of which there are now more than 900

volumes. Also through her efforts Thursday afternoon teas—"just tea!"—
became a tradition, and today students and faculty gather once a week in the
Hopwood Room around F.N. Scott's round oak table to share ideas or just
become acquainted. Miss Cooley was followed as secretary by Sister Hilda
Bonham, and in 1981 Sister Bonham was succeeded by the present Hopwood
Program Coordinator, Dr. Andrea Beauchamp. In addition to carrying on the
traditions of the Hopwood Room, Dr. Beauchamp compiles the *Hopwood
Newsletter,* administers the various contests that have developed in conjunc-
tion with the Hopwood Awards, and maintains an extensive correspondence
with past winners of the awards.

Seventy-one winners of Hopwood Awards have had the manuscripts that
they entered in the contests published. Among the most notable Hopwood
Award-winning publications are Iola Fuller's novel *The Loon Feather* (1940),
Maritta Wolff's novel *Whistle Stop* (1941), Charles Madden's volume of poetry
Bent Blue (1950), X.J. Kennedy's book of poems *Nude Descending a Staircase*
(1968), John Roberts's novel *The Right Trumpet* (1968), and Gillian Brad-
shaw's novel *Hawk of May* (1980).

Past Hopwood Award winners have contributed extensively to all forms
of literature. The most prominent writers of fiction to have won awards include: Betty Smith *(A Tree Grows in Brooklyn),* Glendon Swarthout *(They
Came to Cordura, Where the Boys Are, Bless the Beasts and the Children, The
Shootist,* to name a few), Padma Perera, whose stories frequently appear in the
New Yorker, and Marge Piercy *(The High Cost of Living, Woman on the Edge
of Time, Vida,* and more recently *Gone to Soldiers,* among others).

Perhaps the best known poets to have won Hopwood Awards are John
Ciardi, Howard Moss, Robert Hayden, Frank O'Hara, and Norman Rosten.
Kimon Friar, Emery George, and Jascha Kessler have distinguished themselves in the area of translation of poetry, and among past award winners
noted for serious literature are Martin Green for his controversial literary
studies, and Dorothy McGuigan for *The Hapsburgs* and *Metternich and the
Duchess.*

In the area of drama, Dennis McIntyre has had his *Modigliani* and *Split
Second* produced, and Milan Stitt has had success with two of his plays, *The
Runner Stumbles* and *Back in the Race.* David Newman's screenplays for *Bon-
nie and Clyde, What's Up Doc, Superman, Superman II* and *III,* and *Santa
Claus, the Movie,* have been highly successful, as have Lawrence Kasdan's
screenplays for *Continental Divide, The Empire Strikes Back* (co-scripted),
and, more recently, *Body Heat* and *The Big Chill,* both of which he also directed. But undoubtedly the most eminent Hopwood Award alumnus is Arthur Miller, who won two Minor Awards in drama—the first in 1936, and the
second in 1937.

In 1981, Miller delivered the Annual Hopwood Lecture at the spring
awards ceremony commemorating the Fiftieth Anniversary of the Avery Hopwood and Jule Hopwood Awards. In his talk, "The American Writer: The
American Theatre," Miller spoke of their influence on his early development:

The idea of a university handing out cold cash to students, was, I confess, almost too glorious to contemplate. The money itself was important of course—even on the lowest prize, $250, I would later manage to live for a semester. And, of course, with money so hard to come by in the Depression Thirties, giving it away for nothing more than words on a piece of paper had miraculous overtones when I had been working in industry for years for twelve and fifteen dollars a week. But the central attraction was even more mysterious—the fact that money was given out meant that judges—unlike your mother or your friends—could really tell good writing from bad. Thus, the recognition of an award touched more than the pocket; it might even point the future.[4]

"It is not too far-fetched," wrote John Chapman in the *Daily-News* shortly after Miller won the Pulitzer Prize for *Death of a Salesman* in 1949, "to say that Avery Hopwood, whose *Getting Gertie's Garter, Ladies' Night, Gold Diggers,* and many other Woods and Belasco plays won him the title King of Farce, is responsible—20 years after his death—for Arthur Miller, our current King of Drama."[5]

For the young Arthur Miller and the many other Hopwood contestants, the possibility of a financial boost of a minor or major prize to help them survive their apprentice years was important, but along with the money, these young writers have received encouragement and evaluation from professionals; and, for many who have won, an award has been the determining factor in their decision to pursue a career in writing. Hopwood must have hoped that this is how it would turn out; for, even though his career had been consumed in the production of clever entertainment, his ideal of writing something more significant had never died. One recalls the words of his early years:

I want to write something which an intelligent man can sit down and read and think about. I do not care so much about having him say, "This was written by Hopwood," as to have him say, "This was worth reading."[6]

In the end, it was with the royalties from his frothy farces, the sum of his accomplishments, that Hopwood resolved to pass this ideal on to others by encouraging them to write "the new, the unusual, and the radical."

IX
Conclusion

I am tired of the show! *It was all right, for awhile, but now—I've* had all *that—and I want to go on, to something else!... I want to* live! *I want to see* everything—*be* everything—*know* everything. *I want to be on a high, high hill—where all the winds of Heaven blow—and where I can see—all the kingdoms of this world. And instead, I'm shut in here, in the daily grind, in the awful sameness of this little show—shut in, so that it seems, sometimes, as if I'd go mad! I'm tied to a wheel that's going round and round—always the same! The show—the people in it—they're good enough—but I can't talk to them about the things I love—the things that are my life! When I came here, it was Spring—and somehow, it was Spring in me, too—everything welling up, and bursting into flower—my heart singing—and my soul so free—so that every moment was a job, and I could live—and love—and write! I can't, now! It's all dying in me, day by day! It's being killed! I can't stand it any longer! I must get away!*

The Sideshow
Avery Hopwood[1]

When Avery Hopwood graduated from the University of Michigan in 1905 and headed to New York City to peddle his first play to the managers, the American theatre was about to enter the most exciting and thriving period in its history. It was a theatre in transition, filled with paradoxes, in conflict with itself. The old dramaturgy with its conventional melodramas and formula problem plays, along with the standard musical entertainments continued to be the mainstay of producers who were quick to give their audiences what they wanted. As a result, the popular audience was supporting the theatre in unprecedented numbers. Theatre had become a "Big Business," and it was becoming bigger. In direct conflict with the commercial theatre that inevitably perpetuated the "tried and true" vehicles of popular taste, was the influence in America of the European art theatre in the form of the "new stagecraft," and the innovations of the Little Theatre Movement. George Pierce Baker, among others, was introducing young American dramatists such as Eugene O'Neill and Sidney Howard to the new theories and encouraging them to fight against the limitations imposed upon the playwright by commercialism in the theatre.

For Avery Hopwood at 23, as well educated perhaps as any of the new generation of playwrights, the theatre presented itself as a glamorous and enticing opportunity for success and the acquiring of untold fortunes in royalties. While still in college, he responded to the commercial managers' "call" for more playwrights by writing *Clothes* (1906). This "sartorial" comedy-drama, after being reworked in collaboration with Channing Pollock, became a vehicle for Grace George and was an immediate commercial hit, even if it wasn't a unanimous critical success. In later years Hopwood summed up his feelings towards his fledgling work by quoting from a song popular at the time: "My, Gawd, how the money rolls in!"[2] From that time on, Hopwood seemed obsessed with the money he was able to earn from writing plays. For him, playwriting was not so much an art as a craft.

Hopwood's few attempts at serious drama followed the formula of the social problem play. *The Powers That Be* (1907), although sincere in its intent, was conventional and hackneyed. Its theme of civic corruption proved to be a similar but inferior handling of the idea developed in George Broadhurst's *The Man of the Hour,* which was produced the same season. Consequently, *The Powers That Be* never reached Broadway. Hopwood's second attempt at significant drama was *This Woman and This Man* (1909), produced for Carlotta Nillson at the newly opened Maxine Elliott's Theatre. A play dealing with the hypocrisy of forced marriage as a way of legitimizing a child conceived out of wedlock, *This Woman and This Man* was adjudged to be an artistic success insofar as it showed Hopwood to be a young dramatist full of promise. The play's unevenness, however, led to its commercial failure. Hopwood wrote several other plays of a serious nature, but none were produced. He enjoyed success too much to spend any more time cultivating the serious drama during his journeyman years. Eventually he came to think of the writers of this form as "poseurs." He seemed to resent the critical attention they received simply because they wrote "heavy dray-ma." These attitudes masked his own failure to produce anything of significance in the genre.

Shortly after the failure of his serious works, Hopwood began talking about leaving playwriting and beginning a career as a writer of fiction, a form which he felt was more in keeping with his need for expression. He vowed to quit writing plays just as soon as he had earned enough money to afford him the leisure that good fiction writing demanded. Hopwood's one published attempt at a novel, *Sadie Love* (1915), has been characterized as "curiously inept," and it was in fact a fictionalization of his 1913 comedy *Miss Jenny O'Jones,* which failed during tryouts.

In 1909 Hopwood had his first major success when he collaborated with Mary Roberts Rinehart on *Seven Days,* adapted from her novel, *When a Man Marries. Seven Days,* a boisterous rollicking farce of the old school that many critics proclaimed funnier than the ever-popular *Charley's Aunt,* succeeded in reviving farce as standard Broadway fare during the teens and twenties. Hopwood collaborated with Rinehart twice more in 1920, when he helped her adapt the romantic-melodrama *Spanish Love,* and then on *The Bat,* the most

successful mystery play for more than 50 years. Apart from the monetary success the Hopwood/Rinehart partnership generated, Hopwood regarded his
collaborations with Rinehart as the most satisfying theatrical experiences of his
career.

Hopwood's favorite solo endeavor was, as he termed it, his "sturdy little
bread winner," *Fair and Warmer*. Produced in 1915 after the limited success
of the musical *Judy Forgot* (1910), and the disastrous failure of the musical extravaganza *Somewhere Else* (1913), *Fair and Warmer* capitalized on the
popularity of American bedroom farce that had been piqued by Margaret
Mayo's *Twin Beds* and *Baby Mine*. Hopwood's ability to launder the conven-
tions of French farce in such a way as to make them palatable to "puritanical"
Americans earned him the title of the champion skater over thin ice. In a Hopwood bedroom farce one suspected that adultery might occur, or perhaps had
occurred, but whatever one's suspicions, the play always resolved itself in a conventional and proper way. It was Madge Kennedy as Blanny Wheeler in *Fair
and Warmer* who came to epitomize the Hopwood heroine through her look
of "devilish innocence." But, if *Fair and Warmer* was Hopwood's greatest personal triumph, it was also his "albatross." Throughout his career, critics judged
him by the play, and lamented the fact that he never seemed able to recapture
the brilliancy of its humor.

After the moderate successes of *Sadie Love* (1915), the play, and *Our Little
Wife* (1916), and the failure of *Double Exposure* (1918), Hopwood attained the
high point of his career in the 1920–21 season when he had four plays running
concurrently on Broadway, a record for the post–World War I period. Aside
from the Rinehart collaborations *The Bat* and *Spanish Love,* Hopwood's most
risqué farce to date, *Ladies' Night,* written in collaboration with Charlton Andrews and produced by Al Woods, had its premiere, and his spectacular hit
The Gold Diggers was held over from the previous season. Alexander
Woollcott called Hopwood "Inexhaustible Avery," but added he wished the
playwright would take some time off and come back with a really worthwhile
contribution to the theatre. Hopwood dismissed such criticism by admitting
that he wrote "for Broadway, to please Broadway." His playmaking factory was
built on the idea that the drama was a "democratic art, and that the dramatist
was not the monarch, but the servant of the public."[3]

The most successful comedy to come from the Hopwood playmaking factory, and the one for which his name is most likely to be rememberd, along
with *The Bat,* was *The Gold Diggers* (1919), which starred Ina Claire. This
"sparkling" comedy, that made the slang term "gold digger" a part of the
American idiom, was one of three plays Hopwood wrote for David Belasco.
The first had been in 1910, when the producer had commissioned him to write
Nobody's Widow for Blanche Bates. The last was *The Harem* produced in
1924. This play, a sensational adaptation of a play by Ernö Vadja, like similar
plays of the period, caused the censors to demand that certain lines and situations be removed before it was allowed to continue.

The sex humor of Hopwood's later plays, although naive by today's standards, became more blatant and cynical, in keeping with the recklessness of the time. *Getting Gertie's Garter* (1921) and *The Demi-Virgin* (1921), which had also incurred the wrath of the leagues of decency, went, in the opinion of some, far beyond his most "bed-ridden" of farces, *The Girl in the Limousine* (1919). All of these "titillating" plays had been produced by Al Woods, who was the master of Forty-second Street entertainment. But, by the end of 1921 even Woods had sensed that the public was growing tired of the "same old thing" and he declared that he was placing a seven-year moratorium on the production of bedroom farce.

From 1922 until 1927, when Hopwood had his last play produced on Broadway, he attempted to move with the times by writing comedies that reflected the fads and concerns of the moment. *Why Men Leave Home* (1922), which some considered his attempt at a "moral" bedroom farce, was a moderate success, but it was his last attempt as sole author of a play. Beginning in 1923 Hopwood relied exclusively on collaborations and adaptations of foreign plays. After two rather successful adaptations for French actress/vocalist Irene Bordoni, *Little Miss Bluebeard* (1923) and *Naughty Cinderella* (1925), his New York career had about run its course. *The Best People* (1924), written in collaboration with David Gray, proved to be a much bigger hit in Chicago and San Francisco than on Broadway, and in London it had a particularly long run. Hopwood's last play to be produced in New York was *The Garden of Eden* (1927), adapted from the German. This play, first performed in London as a drama with Tallulah Bankhead in the lead, had scored a tremendous popular success; but, when it reached New York it had been revised for conventional comic appeal, and it fell flat.

During the last years of his life, Hopwood spent most of his time abroad. Always on the move even from his earliest years, he was attempting to flee from himself. Despite the financial success he had achieved in the theatre his life remained lonely and incomplete. His frustration over his sexuality and his inablity to produce significant work began to take their toll. As Hopwood turned to drink and cocaine as a release from his misery, it became increasingly apparent to those around him that his most productive years had come to an end. And yet, during these years, in the hope of finding a meaning and a purpose to his life, he had been working on a novel that chronicled his fears and anxieties. His unpublished, "autobiographical" novel, while not the "devastating theatre exposé" it was once thought to be, is valuable for the light it casts upon his thoughts and the frustrations he experienced throughout his life.

Within a few years of Hopwood's death in 1928, most of what he had contributed to the American theatre had been forgotten. Burns Mantle, writing in 1929, recalled Hopwood "with a playgoers sense of loss." That sense of loss was, however,

> one of sentiment, born of a memory of what he had done, rather than a feeling that, at 46, he still had many active and promisingly productive years ahead of him.

> Mr. Hopwood was rich and self-indulgent. He might have written, or helped to write, several good theatre pieces in the next ten years, but chances are strong that he would not have done so.[4]

Had Hopwood been able to overcome the effects of his initial success, he might have devoted more time during his journeyman years to, as Edwin, his fictional counterpart in his unpublished novel disclosed, the ideals of Ibsen, Shaw, and Strindberg. But,

> Instead of asking himself how he could bring forth that which was finest and best, he had set himself the inferior task of imitating the dramatic "best sellers."
> Instead of sitting at the feet of the Intellectuals, of the truly inspired, and learning from their greatness, he had played the sedulous ape to the masters of box-office popularity. Instead of freeing his imagination and urging it, winged, to unaccustomed heights, he had cribbed and cabined and confined it, and given it, for its furthermost goal, the achievement of "a run on Broadway."[5]

Courted by commercial managers who demanded sure hit formula plays, Hopwood moved further and further from his youthful aspirations to write good fiction. Rather, he became a master at giving theatregoers what they wanted: cleverly built plays that presented characters whose "breezy" dialogue typified the attitudes of the time. Hopwood soon came to realize, however, that his own axiom, "the voice of the public should be considered the voice of the gods,"[6] was destroying him. His talents became stifled and outmoded, unlike the new generation dramatists of the twenties who were able to develop their talents in changing cultural conditions. Lacking sufficient versatility to free himself from the formulae that had made him a success, Hopwood's life deteriorated into a self-indulgent masquerade characteristic of the cynical gaiety of the times.

Between 1915 and 1925, Hopwood's farces ran an average of 168 performances each, compared to the average run of 91 performances for all other farces during the same period.[7] When combined, all of Hopwood's plays ran a total of 4,932 performances, or, an average of 206 performances each — this at a time when 100 performances was still considered a hit. His success was immense, even by today's inflated standards. Yet of the 24 plays that he had produced on Broadway, only one has been revived there during the past thirty years — *The Bat* in 1953 — and it ran only 23 performances. Plans for a 1981 revival with Claudette Colbert never materialized. This prototype of most mystery plays of the past fifty years was simply outmoded compared to such recent psychological thrillers as *Sleuth* and *Deathtrap*. Several of Hopwood's farces were revived in England during the thirties and forties, and the German translations of *Fair and Warmer (Gröna Hissen [The Green Elevator]), Our Little Wife (Unsere Kleine Frau),* and *Why Men Leave Home (Stohwitver)* are said to have remained popular on the Continent. A World War II revival of

Ladies' Night brought up to date by Cyrus Woods as *Good Night Ladies* broke all records in Chicago, running for 100 weeks at the Blackstone Theatre, but it lasted only 78 performances when it reached New York.

Avery Hopwood's success, like that of his lesser rivals, was achieved because his talents were exactly suited to the times. If his "risqué" bedroom farces had been written before the change in social and moral attitudes brought about by World War I, not even Al Woods could have produced them. If they had been written later than the twenties, their coy eroticism would have had no impact on the popular audience. Playwrights such as Philip Barry, George Kelly, Kaufman and Connelly, Noel Coward, and S.N. Berhman were writing a more genuine, mature comedy marked, as Bader has said, by "sophistication that took sex for granted."[8] The appetite for the risqué and titillating, everything that the word "naughty" aroused in the teens and early twenties, had faded. *Vox populi vox Dei.* It seems doubtful that theatre historians will ever consider his plays or his career more than a phenomenon characteristic of the most booming years of the American commercial theatre.

Because Hopwood was convinced that the royalties he had amassed were all that would remain of his accomplishments, he endowed the Avery Hopwood and Jule Hopwood Awards in Creative Writing at his alma mater, the University of Michigan. He wanted to encourage young writers to attempt "the new, the unusual, and the radical" at a time critical in their development. Writing in 1933 about Hopwood's intentions in establishing the awards, Gertrude Stein told then Hopwood Award Chairman Roy W. Cowden:

> Avery Hopwood did several times talk to me of his ardent hope that there would be a great deal of *writing* good writing coming out of America, and that he hoped it would have some connection with modern writing. When he was a young man which was when I first knew him he hoped to achieve this himself and later he always hoped that he still would do something himself. He had a very keen interest in the intellectual life and I imagine this was the origin of his idea of his bequest.[9]

Thus by an irony Hopwood himself would have appreciated, he made his chief contribution to the development of American drama indirectly by extending a helping hand to Arthur Miller, creator of the new tragedy of the common man: Miller was to do the kind of work Hopwood himself had aspired to but never achieved.

Appendix A
Production Lists of the Plays
of Avery Hopwood

The following information was compiled from various sources, including: programs in the Theatre Collection of the Museum of the City of New York, Burns Mantle's *Best Plays* series, *New York Dramatic Mirror,* and *Variety.* Plays marked with (*) have been published by Samuel French, Inc., New York.

Clothes

Play in four acts in collaboration with Channing Pollock. Produced by William A. Brady, by arrangement with Wagenhals and Kemper, at the Manhattan Theatre, New York, 11 September 1906.

Cast: Olivia Sherwood (Grace George), Richard Burbank (Robert T. Haines), Arnold West (Frank Worthing), John Graye (Charles Stanley), Horace Watling (A.H. Stuart), Thomas J. Smith (Douglas Fairbanks), Dean (Richard Wilson), Patience Augusta Fyles (Louise Closser Hale), Mrs. Watling (Jennie A. Eustace), Mrs. Cathcart (Anne Sutherland), Mrs. Maxwell (Dorothy Revell), Mrs. Conningsby-Lowe (Diana Huneker), Alice (Angela Ogden), Louise (Justine Cutting). *Settings by* Robert T. McKee and H. Robert Law. *Costumes by* Van Horn, Lord and Taylor. 113 performances.

The Mills of the Gods

One-act vaudeville sketch written in 1906 for comedian Leon Kohlmer.

The Powers That Be; or, The Grafters

Play in four acts. Produced by E.F. Bostwick at the Shubert Theatre, Columbus, Ohio, 27 February 1907.

Cast: Burton Clark, District Attorney (David Proctor), Jimmie Clark (Albert Latscha), Charles Buntz, "The Boss" (Edwin Holt), F.M. Davis, "The Hyprocrite" (Not known), William, a servant to Davis (Sidney Mansfield), Dorothy Davis (Kathleen Mulkins), Jessie Melville (Nesta de Becker), Mrs. Keane (Anne Sutherland), Aunt Sally (Caroline Newcombe). Also entitled *The Franchise Grabbers.* A slightly revised version, *Masters of Men,* was taken on tour and played in stock, but it was never produced in New York.

This Woman and This Man

Play in three acts. Produced at Maxine Elliott's Theatre, New York, 22 February 1909.

Cast: Thekla Mueller (Carlotta Nillson), Norris Townsend (Milton Sills), Goddard Townsend (Frank Currier), Davy (John Tansey), Herman Johnson (Howard Kyle), Mrs. Ware (Eva Vincent). *Staged by* George Foster Platt. 24 performances. Alternate title: *The Woman Pays.*

Seven Days*

Farce in three acts in collaboration with Mary Roberts Rinehart. Adapted from her novel *When a Man Marries*. Produced by Wagenhals and Kemper at the Astor Theatre, New York, 10 November 1909.

Cast: James Wilson (Herbert Corthell), Dallas Brown, (Allan Pollock), Tom Harbison (Carl Eckstrom), Officer Flannigan (Jay Wilson), Tubby McGirk, a burglar (William Eville), Hobbs, a footman (F.C. Butler), Bella Knowles (ex-Wilson) (Hope Latham), Anne Brown (Florence Reed), Kit McNair (Georgia O'Ramsey), Aunt Selina (Lucille LaVerne), Reporters, Newspaper Photographers, Etc. 397 performances. Produced in London at the New Theatre, 15 March 1915. 16 performances.

Judy Forgot

Musical comedy in two acts. Book and lyrics by Avery Hopwood. Music by Silvio Hein. Produced by Daniel V. Arthur at the Broadway Theatre, New York, 6 October 1910.

Cast: Judy Evans (Marie Cahill), Freddie Evans (Arthur Stanford), Elsa (Ann Ford), Francois (H.P. Woodley), Dr. Kuno Lauberscheimer (James B. Carson), Trixie Stole (Truly Shattuck), Dickie Stole (Joseph Santley), John Mugg (Bert Baker), Rosa (Ethel Johnson), Betty James (Hazel Kingdon), Virginia Ellwood (Emilia Bernabo), Dorothy Lewis (Evelyn Grahame-Smith), Fanny De Kalb (Anna Hoffman). *Staged by* Daniel V. Arthur. 44 performances.

Nobody's Widow

Farcical romance in three acts. Produced by David Belasco at the Hudson Theatre, New York, 15 November 1910.

Cast: Roxana Clayton (Blanche Bates), Betty Jackson (Adelaide Prince), Countess Manuela Valencia (Edith Campbell), Fanny Owens (Dorothy Shoemaker), Duke of Moreland (Bruce McRae), Ned Stephens (Rex McDougall), Baron Reuter (Henry Schuman-Heink), Peter (Westhrop Saunders). *Staged by* David Belasco. 215 performances. Lise-Lone Marker reports in her book, *David Belasco,* that *Nobody's Widow* was the first play in which Belasco used spotlights to follow the lead actors around the stage, unknown to the audience. Produced in London at the Lyric Theatre under the title *Roxana,* 18 September 1918, starring Doris Keane in 219 performances.

Somewhere Else

Musical fantasy in two acts. Book and lyrics by Avery Hopwood. Music by Gustav Luders. Produced by Henry W. Savage at the Broadway Theatre, New York, 20 January 1913.

Cast: Queen Mary Seventh (Cecil Cunningham), Villainus (Will Philbrick), Chloe (Elena Leska), Billy Gettaway (Taylor Holmes), Rocky Rixon (Franklyn Farnum), Hepzibah (Catherine Hayes), Cupid (Violet De Biccai), also Donald Chalmers, Burton Lenihan, Marion Whitney, Saith Powell, Edith Thayer, Melville Anderson, George Healy and chorus. *Staged by* Frank Smithson. 8 performances.

Miss Jenny O'Jones

Comedy in three acts produced by William A. Brady at the Cort Square Theatre, Springfield, Massachusetts, 27 November 1913.

Cast: Jenny O'Jones (Grace George), Baron Von Hanau (Julian L'Estrange), Mrs. Allingby [Comtesse de Miraball] (Jane Evans), Jim Wakeley (William Morris), Mrs. Warrington (Carolyn Kenyon), Lillah Wakeley (Belle Daub), Mumford Crewe (Edgar Norton), The Butler (Warren Munsell). Withdrawn after three performances when it was determined to be unsuitable for Grace George. It was later reworked, and in 1915 presented by Morosco as *Sadie Love*. See *Sadie Love* cast list.

Fair and Warmer

Comedy farce in three acts. Produced by Selwyn and Company at the Eltinge Theatre, New York, 6 November 1915.

Cast: Billy Bartlett (John Cumberland), Laura Bartlett (Janet Beecher), Jack Wheeler (Ralph Morgan), Blanche ("Blanny") Wheeler (Madge Kennedy), Phillip Evans (Hamilton Revelle), Harrigan (Robert Fisher), Tessie (Olive May), Pete Mealy (Harry Lorraine). *Staged by* Robert Milton. Moved to the Harris Theatre, 24 July 1916. 377 performances. Earlier version entitled *The Mystic Shrine*. Produced in London at the Prince of Wales's Theatre, 14 May 1918. Starring Fay Compton. 498 performances. German translation, most likely by Beatrice Pogson, known as *Gröna Hissen (The Green Elevator)*.

Sadie Love

Farce in three acts. Produced by Oliver Morosco at the Gaiety Theatre, New York, 29 November 1915.

Cast: Sadie Love (Marjorie Rambeau), Prince Luigi Pallavicini (Pedro de Cordoba), Comtesse de Mirabold (Betty Callish), Jim Wakeley (Franklyn Underwood), Lillian Wakeley (Ivy Troutman), Mrs. Warrington (Ethel Winthrop), Mumford Crewe (Alwyn Lewis), Detective Maloney (William Morris), Edward, butler to Mrs. Warrington (John Lyons), Giovanni, steward (John Ivan). *Staged by* Robert Milton. Moved to Harris Theatre 17 January 1916. 80 performances. Preliminary title: *Compromising Sally*. See *Miss Jenny O'Jones* above.

Our Little Wife

Comedy farce in three acts. Produced by Selwyn and Company at the Harris Theatre, 18 November 1916.

Cast: "Dodo" Warren (Margaret Illington), Herbert Warren (Lowell Sherman), "Bobo" Brown (Walter Jones), Angie (Gwendolyn Piers), Doctor Elliott (Charles Hampden), Tommy Belden (Effingham Pinto), Francois (Robert Fisher), Fanny Elliott (Rae Selwyn), Burke (Thomas F. O'Malley), George Haywood (Lyle Clement). *Staged by* Edgar Selwyn. 41 performances. Produced in London at the Comedy Theatre, 8 May 1928. 6 performances. The German translation, *Unsere Kleine Frau* (1924) by Beatrice Pogson, was very popular for many years.

Just for Tonight

Copyrighted 3 June 1916. Produced as a motion picture in 1918 by Samuel Goldwyn. Reviewed in *Variety*, 20 September 1918, p. 46.

Pete

Copyrighted 7 August 1917. Revised version, *Don't Be Afraid*, was being readied for production 11 June 1920, but never reached Broadway.

The Little Clown*

Copyrighted 10 May 1918. Although the piece was originally written for Billie Burke, she never appeared in it. Produced as a motion picture in 1921, starring Mary Miles Minter.

Double Exposure

Play of personalities in three acts. Produced by Selwyn and Company at the Bijou Theatre, New York, 27 August 1918.

Cast: Tommy Campbell (John Westley), Lecksy Campbell (Francine Larrimore), Sybil Norton (Janet Beecher), Jimmie Norton (John Cumberland), Baba Mahrati (J. Harry Irvine), Maggie (Grace Hayle), William (William Postance), Officer O'Brien (Dan Moyles). *Staged by* Edgar Selwyn. 15 performances.

The Gold Diggers

Comedy in three acts. Produced by David Belasco at the Lyceum Theatre, New York, 30 September 1919.

Cast: Stephen Lee (Bruce McRae), James Blake (H. Reeves-Smith), Barney Barnett (Frederick Tuesdell), Wally Saunders (Horace Braham), Freddie Turner (Austen Harrison), Fenton Jessup (Harold Christy), Tom Newton (D. Lewis Clinton), Marty Woods (Frank Lewis), Jerry Lamar (Ina Claire), Mabel Munroe (Jobyna Howland), Violet Dayne (Beverly West), Mrs. Lamar (Louise Galloway), Topsy St. John (Ruth Terry), Cissie Gray (Pauline Hall), Trixie Andrews (Lilyan Tashman), Eleanor Montgomery (Luella Gear), Gypsy Montrose (Gladys Feldman), Dolly Baxter (Katherine Walsh), Sadie (Louise Burton). *Staged by* David Belasco. 720 performances. Produced in London at the Lyric Theatre, 14 December 1926, starring Tallulah Bankhead in 179 performances.

The Girl in the Limousine

Farce in three acts in collaboration with Wilson Collison. Produced by A.H. Woods at the Eltinge Theatre, New York, 6 October 1919.

Cast: Kargan (Edward Butler), Benny (Dann Malloy), Betty Neville (Doris Kenyon), Dr. Jimmie Galen (Charles Ruggles), Tony Hamilton (John Cumberland), Riggs (Barnett Parker), Freddie Neville (Frank M. Thomas), Bernice Warren (Vivian Rushmore), Lucia Galen (Claiborne Foster), Aunt Cicely (Zelda Sears), Giles (Harry Charles). Staged by Bertram Harrison. 137 performances.

I'll Say She Does

The musical version of *Our Little Wife.* Announced in *Variety,* 26 September 1919, p. 13, as a farce in three acts featuring Lynn Overlord due in New York in October after a successful Washington, D.C., stock run. Bader lists it as a musical comedy which failed in Stamford, Connecticut, and Wilmington, Delaware, tryouts, 1920. Nothing more is known about it.

Ladies' Night

Farcical comedy in three acts in collaboration with Charlton Andrews. Produced by A.H. Woods at the Eltinge Theatre, New York, 9 August 1920.

Cast: Suzon (Adele Rolland), Bob Stanhope (Vincent Dennie), Dulcy Walters, (Claiborne Foster), Jimmy Walters (John Cumberland), Alicia Bonner (Allyn King), Fred Bonner (Charles Ruggles), Mimi Tarlton (Evelyn Gosnell), Cort Craymer (Edward Douglas), Mrs. Shultz (Mrs. Stuart Robson), Mrs. Green (Pearl Jardinere), Josie (Grace Kaber), Tillie (Helen Barnes), Miss Murphy (Eleanor Dawn), Rhoda Begova (Judith Vossellie), Lollie (Nellie Fillmore), A Policewoman (Julia Ralph), A Fireman (Fred Sutton), Babette (Eda Ann Luke). *Staged by* Bertram Harrison. 375 performances. A revival entitled *Good Night, Ladies** adapted by Cyrus Woods and produced by

Lang and Rosen at the Blackstone Theatre in Chicago, ran from April 1942 through 11 March 1944, a total of 100 weeks, breaking all records in that city. Produced later in New York (1/17/45) at the Royale, it lasted only 78 performances. Last revived Off Broadway, March 1961.

Spanish Love (from the Spanish classic, *Maria del Carmen*)
Drama in three acts with music in collaboration with Mary Roberts Rinehart. Adapted from *Aux Jardins de Merci* by José Felice y Codina, Carlos de Battle, and Antonia Lavergne. Incidental music by H. Maurice Jacquet. Produced by Wagenhals and Kemper at Maxine Elliott's Theatre, New York, 17 August 1920.
Cast: Roque (Wallace Hickman), Alvarez (Manolo Ihestino), Andres (Paul Huber), Tonete (Victor Hammond), Pepuso (Ben Hendricks), Romero (Richard Morrise), Anton (Frank Peters), Don Fulgencio (Russ Whytal), Maria del Carmen (Maria Ascarra), Fuensantica (Ione Bright), Concepsion (Kenyon Bishop), Migalo (Gus C. Weinberg), Domingo (Henry Stephenson), Javier (William H. Powell), Pencho (James Rennie), A Singer (Jasper Mangione), A Singer (Ofelin Calvo). Marked William Powell's Broadway debut in a major speaking role. 308 performances.

The Bat*
Mystery drama in three acts in collaboration with Mary Roberts Rinehart. Loosely adapted from her novel *The Circular Staircase*. Produced by Wagenhals and Kemper at the Morosco Theatre, New York, 23 August 1920.
Cast: Lizzie (May Vokes), Miss Cornelia Van Gorder (Effie Ellsler), Billy (Harry Morvil), Brooks (Stuart Sage), Miss Dale Ogden (Anne Morrison), Dr. Wells (Edward Ellis), Anderson (Harrison Hunter), Richard Fleming (Richard Burrows), Reginald Beresford (Kenneth Hunter), An Unknown Man (Robert Vaughn). *Staged by* Collin Kemper. 878 performances. Entitled *A Thief in the Night* during tryouts. Produced in London at the St. James's Theatre, 23 January 1922. 327 performances. A 1953 revival at the National with Lucille Watson, ZaSu Pitts, and Shepherd Strudwick ran only 23 performances.

The Great Illusion
Adapted from Sasha Guitry's *L'Illusioniste* (1917). Completion of script announced in *Variety,* 8 August 1919, p. 15. Rehearsal announced in *Variety* 17 September 1920, p. 12. Tryout scheduled for Chicago never materialized. Typescript in the possession of Hollywood Plays, Inc.

Getting Gertie's Garter
Farce comedy in three acts in collaboration with Wilson Collison. Produced by A.H. Woods at the Republic Theatre, New York, 1 August 1921.
Cast: Pattie Walrick (Dorothy Mackaye), Billy Felton (Lorin Raker), Nanette (Adele Rolland), Gertie Darling (Hazel Dawn), Allen (Walter Jones), Ken Walrick (Donald MacDonald), Teddy Darling (Louis Kimball), Barbara Felton (Eleanor Dawn), Algy Riggs (Ivan Miller). *Staged by* Bertram Harrison. 120 performances. Performed in England as *Night of the Garter.*

The Demi-Virgin
Farce comedy in three acts, loosely based on a French original, *Les Demi-Vierges,* by Marcel Prévost. Produced by A.H. Woods at the Times Square Theatre, New York, 18 October 1921.

Cast: A Movie Director (Charles Mather), Owen Blair (John Maroni), Jack Milford (Ralph Glover), Rex Martin (John Floyd), Estelle St. Marr (Marjorie Clements), Gladys Lorraine (Mary Salisbury), Fay Winthrop (Helen Flint), Cora Montague (Constance Farber), Bee La Rose (Sascha Beaumont), Amy Allenby (Peggy Coudray), Wanda Boresca (Mildred Wayne), Aunt Zeffle (Alice Hegeman), Betty Wilson (Helen Cunningham), Chicky Belden (Charles Ruggles), Gloria Graham (Hazel Dawn), Sir Gerald Sydney (Kenneth Douglas), Wally Dean (Glenn Anders). *Staged by* Bertram Harrison and Charles Mather. 268 performances.

Why Men Leave Home

Comedy in three acts. Produced by Wagenhals and Kemper at the Morosco Theatre, New York, 12 September 1922.

Cast: Butler (Minor Watson), Grandma (Jessie Villars), Tom (John McFarlane), Fifi (Florence Shirley), Nina (Theresa Maxwell Conover), Betty (Audrey Hart), Sybil (Isabel Leighton), Artie (Herbert Yost), Sam (Paul Everton), Doris (Wauna Lorraine), Maid (Peggy Lytton), Billy (Norval Keedwell). *Staged by* Collin Kemper. 135 performances. Produced in London at the Royalty Theatre, 2 June 1924 under the title *Bachelor Husbands.* 13 performances. Successfully translated into German in 1927 by Beatrice Pogson under the title *Strohwitver.*

The Return

Adapted with Charlton Andrews from the French, *Le Retour,* by Robert de Fleurs and Francis de Croisset. Produced by Al Woods. *New York Times,* 22 July 1923, sec. 7, p. 1: "On all sides there was manifest evidence of a greater desire to see Mr. Hopwood, personally, than to give really serious consideration to the new play." Washington, D.C., tryout. Nothing more is heard about the play.

Little Miss Bluebeard*

Comedy in three acts adapted from *Der Gatte des Fräuleins* by Gabriel Dregeley. Produced by Charles Frohman, Inc. in association with E. Ray Goetz at the Lyceum Theatre, New York, 28 August 1923.

Cast: Larry Charters (Bruce McRae), Eva Winthrop (Margaret Linden), Smithers (William Eville), Sir John Barstow (Arthur Barry), The Hon. Bertie Bird (Eric Blore), Bob Talmadge (Stanley Logan), Colette (Irene Bordoni), Gloria Talmadge (Jeannette Sherwin), Lulu (Eva Leonard-Boyne), Paul Rondel (Burton Brown). *Staged by* W.H. Gilmore. 175 performances. Produced in London at Wyndham's Theatre, 15 April 1925. Starring Irene Bordoni. 13 performances.

The Alarm Clock*

Comedy in three acts from *La Sonnette d'alarme* by Maurice Hennequin and Romain Coolus. Produced by A.H. Woods at the Thirty-ninth Street Theatre, New York, 24 December 1923.

Cast: Wills (John Troughton), Lulu Deane (Helen Flint), Charlie Morton (Ernest Lambart), Mrs. Dunmore (Gail Kane), Dr. Wallace (George Alison), Bobby Brandon (Bruce McRae), Mrs. Susie Kent (Blanche Ring), Mary Kent (Marion Coakley), Homer Wickham (Harold Vermilye), Theodore Boom (Charles Abbe), Reggie Wynne (Vincent Serrano). *Staged by* David Burton. 32 performances.

The Best People*

Comedy in three acts in collaboration with David Gray from his unproduced play *Goodness Knows*. Produced by Charles Frohman, Inc. at the Lyceum Theatre, New York, 19 August 1924.

Cast: Mrs. Bronson Lenox (Margaret Dale), Bronson Lenox (Charles Richman), Marion Lenox (Frances Howard), Butler (Roy Cochrane), Lord Rockmere (William Valentine), Henry (James Rennie), Miss Tate (Eva Condon), Footman (Charles Adams), Bertie Lenox (Gavin Muir), A Waiter (Joseph Burton), Millie (Florence Johns), Alice O'Neil (Hope Drown), Another Waiter (Lichfield Owen). *Staged by* Bertram Harrison. 143 performances. Produced in London at the Lyric Theatre, 16 March 1926. 308 performances.

The Harem

Comedy in three acts by Ernö Vadja. Adapted by Avery Hopwood. Produced by David Belasco at the Belasco Theatre, 2 December 1924.

Cast: Roland Valetti (William Courtney), Carla (Lenore Ulric), Manon (Virginia Hammond), Petri (Lennox Pawle), Prince Hilmi (Robert Fischer), Juci (Marjorie Vonnegut), Lulu (Arthur Bowyer). *Staged by* David Belasco. 183 performances.

The Cat Came Back (Pretty Little Pussy)

A play by Larry E. Johnson and Beulah King; revised by Avery Hopwood. Produced by A.H. Woods at the Adelphi Theatre, Chicago, 29 December 1924.

Cast: Mrs. Gray (Louise Mackintosh), Isobel West, her niece (Claudette Colbert), Mildred, their maid (May Vokes), Bill Halliday (Charles Lawrence), George Tuttle (Frank Lalor), Smeersey (Louis Kimball), The Captain (Harry Hanlon), The Steward (Ralph Sipperly). *Staged by* Bertram Harrison. Failed during tryouts. Typescript in possession of Hollywood Plays, Inc. shows title, *Pretty Little Pussy* "(The Cat Came Back)," a play by Avery Hopwood. *Burns Mantle's Best Play Series, 1924-1925,* p. 17: "*Pretty Little Pussy,* author forgotten — Avery Hopwood sent on to fix it up, took a look, and advised A.H. Woods to throw it into the lake. Mr. Woods threw it into the lake." — Fred Donaghey, *Chicago Tribune* Drama Critic. The *New York Public Library Catalog of the Theatre and Drama Collection, Pt. III: Non-Book Collection* lists *Pretty Little Pussy; or The Cat Came Back* by Lawrence E. Johnson and Beulah King. This last version was adapted as a musical May 1937 entitled *Sea Legs.*

Naughty Cinderella*

Romantic Song-Farce in three acts "far" from the French of René Peter and Henri Falk's *Pouche*. Produced by Charles Frohman, Inc. in association with E. Ray Goetz at the Lyceum Theatre, New York, 9 November 1925.

Cast: Gerald Gray (Henry Kendall), Jacques (Eugene Redding), Claire Fenton (Evelyn Gosnell), Bunny West (John Deverell), Thomas Fenton (Orlando Daly), Germaine Leverrier (Irene Bordoni), Chouchou Rouselle (Adele Windsor), K.O. Bill Smith (Nat Pendleton), An Italian Policeman (Alfred Ilma). *Staged by* W.H. Gilmore. 121 performances.

The Duchess of Elba

Adaptation of Rudolph Lothar's and Oscar Ritter-Winterstein's *Die Herzogin von Elba*. Unsuccessful tryout in Chicago, 1926. Produced in London at the Arts Theatre, 2 October 1927. 8 performances.

The Garden of Eden

Comedy in three acts from the German of Rudolph Bernauer and Rudolph Oester-reicher. Produced by Arch Selwyn at the Selwyn Theatre, New York, 27 September 1927.

Cast: Adele (Barbara Barondess), Diane (June Leslie), Cleo (Betsy Jane Southgate), Rosa (Alison Skipworth), Revard (Stapelton Kent), Toni Lebrun (Miriam Hopkins), A Call Boy (Daniel Wolf), Durand (Harlan Briggs), Madame Rimsky (Camilla Dalberg), Henri Glessing (C. Stafford Dickens), Count de Mauban (Gordon Ash), Baron Laperau (A.G. Andrews), Count de L'Esterel (T. Wigney Percyval), Richard Lamont (Douglass Montgomery), Maitre d'Hotel (Alfred A. Hesse), Professor Rossio (Ignacio Martinetti), Aunt Matilde (Doris Rankin), Uncle Herbert (Ivan F. Simpson), Prince Miguel de Santa Rocca (Russ Whytal), Servant of the Prince (Walter Geer). *Staged by* Edwin H. Knopf. *Designed by* Joseph Mullen. 23 performances. First produced in London at the Lyric Theatre, 30 May 1927 with Tallulah Bankhead in the lead. 232 performances.

The Sideshow

Typescript in the Billy Rose Theatre Collection, New York Public Library at Lincoln Center, shows: "A Comedy in Three Acts by Avery Hopwood. Laura Wilck 1939 B'Way. American Play Co." No date. No production known.

The following titles appear on lists at the Hopwood Room at the University of Michigan: *Four Stuffed Shirts, His Mother's Son* (1910), *Paulette, A Weak Woman.* No further information on these plays has been found. The titles, which do not appear in the U.S. *Register of Copyrights,* may be alternate titles to certain of his plays. There is also a possibility that Hopwood produced motion picture scenarios by these titles. According to a statement by his executors, the picture rights to twenty-seven of his plays had been sold at the time of his death.

Appendix B
Hopwood Filmography

Motion pictures based on plays by Avery Hopwood as listed in the *New York Times Directory of the Film*, the *Library of Congress Film Superlist, Vol. 8*, and the *American Film Institute Catalog: 1921–1930*.

1914 *Clothes*, Famous Players, Lasky Productions.
1915 *Judy Forgot*, Broadway Universal Special.
1918 *Just for Tonight*, Samuel Goldwyn Pictures. Starring Lucy Fox and Tom Moore.
 Our Little Wife, Samuel Goldwyn Pictures. Starring Madge Kennedy.
1919 *Fair and Warmer*, Screen Classics, Inc. Starring May Allison.
 Sadie Love, Paramount Picture Corporation. Starring Billie Burke.
1920 *Clothes*, Metropolitan Picture Corporation.
 Guilty of Love, Paramount/Artcraft adaptation of *This Woman and This Man*.
1921 *The Little Clown*, Realart Pictures. Starring Mary Miles Minter.
1923 *The Gold Diggers*, Warner Bros., a David Belasco Production.
1924 *The Girl in the Limousine*, Chadwick Pictures. Starring Oliver Hardy.
 Why Men Leave Home, Louis B. Mayer Productions. Starring Hedda Hopper.
1925 *The Best People*, Famous Players, Lasky Productions.
 Miss Bluebeard, Famous Players, Lasky Productions.
 Seven Days.
1926 *The Bat*, Feature Productions/United Artists.
 Good and Naughty, adapted from *Naughty Cinderella*. Starring Pola Negri.
1927 *Getting Gertie's Garter*, Metropolitan Picture Corporation.
 Nobody's Widow, DeMille Pictures.
1928 *Ladies' Night in a Turkish Bath*, Asher-Small Rogers.
1929 *Gold Diggers of Broadway*, Warner Bros., Vitaphone, Technicolor. Musical starring Nick Lucas, Ann Pennington, and Conway Tearle. Songs include: "Painting the Clouds with Sunshine," "Song of the Gold Diggers," and "Tip Toe Through the Tulips with Me." Directed by Mervyn LeRoy.
1930 *The Bat Whispers*, Art Cinema Corporation/United Artists. Starring Una Merkle and Chester Morris.
 Fast and Loose, Paramount adaptation of *The Best People*. Starring Miriam Hopkins.
 Her Wedding Night, Paramount adaptation of *Little Miss Bluebeard*. Starring Clara Bow and Charles Ruggles.
1932 *This Is the Night*, Paramount adaptation of *Naughty Cinderella*. Starring Lily Damita, Cary Grant (debut), Charles Ruggles, and Roland Young.
1933 *Gold Diggers of 1933*, Warner Bros. Musical starring Joan Blondell, Ruby Keeler, Dick Powell, Ginger Rogers, and Warren Williams. Songs include: "Remember My Forgotten Man," "Shadow Waltz," and "We're In The

Money." Directed by Mervyn LeRoy. Musical numbers created and staged by Busby Berkeley. Spin-offs: *Gold Diggers of 1935* and *1937, Gold Diggers in Paris* (1938) with Rudy Valle, and *Painting the Clouds with Sunshine* (1951) with Virginia Mayo.

1934 *Night of the Garter,* British & Dominion Films adaptation of *Getting Gertie's Garter.*

1939 *Solo per Donne,* Italian-German adaptation of *Our Little Wife.* Released in the United States 1940.

1946 *Getting Gertie's Garter,* United Artists. Starring Binnie Barnes, Marie McDonald, Dennis O'Keefe, and J. Carrol Nash.

1952 *The Gold Diggers,* adapted for the Broadway Television Theatre, December 29. Starring Gloria McGhee and John Newland.

1953 *The Bat,* television adaptation of the 1953 revival. Starring Lucille Watson and ZaSu Pitts.

1959 *The Bat,* Allied Artists. Starring Agnes Moorehead and Vincent Price.

1960 *The Bat,* adapted for the Dow Great Mystery Theatre. Starring Helen Hayes and Jason Robards, Jr.

Appendix C
Selected Letters to
Mary Roberts Rinehart

French Lick Springs Hotel
French Lick, Indiana
June 9th, 1913

Dear Mrs. Rinehart: —

I suppose you've often wondered what became of "Seven Days", in England, and why that darned Hop didn't write and tell you all about it. I could offer you all the excuses which you would offer in a similar situation, but I won't. I merely hereby give you permission to call me all the names you want to, and I will content myself with narrating, as veraciously as possible, at this late date, just what happened.

When I arrived in England it was six days before the first performance, in Harrogate. During those six days, one thing and another prevented a dress rehearsal, or any other kind of a rehearsal, so they told me not to come to the first performance as it would be too rough. But it turned out that the first performance had to be postponed a couple of days, as [James] Welch was ill, so when I did go down to Harrogate I saw what was practically a premiere, as there had been only one performance before, — a matinee, on the same day. Well, the performance was bad beyond words. No one seemed to have his lines, and things were dragged out until I wanted to yell. The first act, for instance, played about ten minutes longer than it did in America, — though that was partly due to the fact that the DeMilles sent over the ORIGINAL version of the play, — without any of the cuts in the first two acts, and with THE OLD THIRD ACT! I wished you could have been there, to share with me the experience of seeing at least one performance of an act which we wrote, but never played, — you remember, — the bath cabinet etc. It appears that some months after the DeMille office sent over that old version, Welch wrote over for a prompt copy, as the old version MS., of course, had no stage directions. Well, when the prompt copy arrived, it was, of course, the authentic version, but by that time the mischief had been done.

Welch had learned his part, and as there was more for "Jim" to do in the old third act than the new, he decided to stick to the old version!

I was overcome by that first performance, and showed it so plainly that Welch begged me to go away and let them have a free hand, for a few weeks, until he could whip things into shape. I did go away, and did not come back until "Seven Days" was playing Manchester. By that time, they had restored the original third act, which went much better than the old one, but they had not quickened their tempo, nor improved their company, which was not good with the exception of Welch (who, however, was far from up to his mark) and Mrs. Welch [Audrey Ford], who played Bella, and the girl who played Anne. The part of Anne, however, had been cut down, as it was scoring too heavily for a star play. At least, that seemed the only ostensible reason. Other changes had been liberally made in the script, both in the Harrogate and the Manchester performances. The love scene between Tom and Kit (played by two absolutely colorless persons) — the love scene between them, in the first act, had been entirely cut out (by the way, it *wasn't* exactly a love scene, was it! — but you know the scene I mean — and the scene between them, in the second act, — the cooking scene, had been taken away from them, and boiled down, and what was left of it shoved into the scene between Kit and Jim.

After the Manchester performance, Ernest Mayer and I had a long talk with Welch, and advised him not to go into London until he had bettered his cast, and until he had got hold of a stage manager who knew how to produce a farce. You see, Welch, in addition to playing "Jim", had staged the production, and as he is not a great stage director, things naturally went to pot, for as you know, it's no easy thing to play a principal part, and, at the same time, direct oneself and the rest of the company. Welch said he thought we were entirely right, and that he had made a mistake in undertaking to stage manage the production, but neither he nor Mayer could think of anyone in London who would do to undertake the job. All the competent stage directors they could think of were men like Weedon Grossmith, who are also actor managers, and will not put on other people's productions. Then Welch suggested that the play be put on in the Autumn, with himself and an improved cast, and with an American stage director. I said I would try to find a good man to put the play on for them. Mayer told Welch that we would waive a further payment down, if he held the London production over until the Autumn, but that, in case he did so, and then, for any reason, failed to produce, he must pay us a forfeit of three hundred pounds. When I left England, they were arranging a new contract to cover this point. But now that I am back here, I have received a letter from Mayer (I will enclose it, if I find that I have it here) saying that changes must be made in the third act. I knew, before I left, that Welch considered that he hadn't enough to do in the authentic third act — though he acknowledged that it was superior, in every other point, to the act which he first tried out. I suppose there is something in his contention, for, after all, in England, "Seven Days" is an unknown quantity, and Welch is a big drawing card, and people who go to see him will be disappointed to find he has so little to do in the last act. I've written, asking just what changes are desired, in the script. As soon as I get a reply, I'll communicate with you.

Whew! What a long letter! That's the *real* reason I didn't write you before!

I had a wonderful time on the other side, and did some work, too. I'm going from here to Ann Arbor, for a few days, and then to Cleveland, so, if you should write me, you can address me at 1817 W. 44th St., Cleveland.

Very best regards to you, and to the Doctor, and to the boys.

Your's, most sincerely,
Hop

P.S. You'll be glad to know that, badly produced and handicapped as it was, the play made good seventy five percent of the time. I think it will make good one hundred per cent of the time, if they only give it a fighting chance.

The Copley-Plaza
Boston, Massachusetts

Dear Mary:

Kemper . . . claims that you and I, that day in the office (the Doctor was present, too)—agreed to give him & Wagenhals [an] increase on their salaries for *all* of the *big cities* companies—that is—next year they would be getting this extra salary for Chicago, Boston, & Philadelphia companies, as well as for the New York company.—I told Kemper that I was quite positive we did not make any such arrangement. Wagenhals said I was right, but he also said that he thought such an arrangement should be made *now*. —I told him that I would talk it over with you & the Doctor, when I went to Pittsburgh. —As I shall not be going there, I am writing this to you. —
Personally, I do not see why W.&K. should get any more money. —I have an agreement with Woods, for a ¼ business interest in a play, and he charges only $100 a week, for office & managerial expenses—and the same amount for any additional companies. —I'm afraid that W.&K. can't get over being worried because we are making more money than *they* are—but I think we *should* be making more, & I don't think its fair, now, to cut into us for additional sums, —at least that's how it seems to me. . . .
All good wishes to you & to the Doctor.

Cordially
[October 1921]   Hop

475 Fifth Avenue, New York City
Sept. 8, 1921

Dear Doctor and Mary: —

Wagenhals and Kemper and myself have been very much upset by the fact that a moving picture theatre, in Chicago, in the Loop, quite close to where "The Bat" is playing, is showing the motion picture of "The Circular Staircase" under the title of "The Bat". I believe that measures have been taken to restrain them from using the title, "The Bat", but I do not know if they can be prevented from showing the picture under the title of "The Circular Staircase". It looks as if some man owns, or claims to own, the rights to this picture for seven of the Middle Western States. He must have acquired these rights from Selig—to whom we paid seven thousand dollars for all the motion picture rights to "The Circular Staircase".
I am hoping that the thing can be stopped and of course W. and K. are working night and day to do it. Everything, however, has to be negotiated through [R. Larry] Giffen, or George Doran, as the contract with Selig went through them.
The other day I noticed in "The Review of Reviews" an advertisement of Mary's collected works, in which the statement was made that "The Circular Staircase" had been dramatized as "The Bat". I think that if the Doran company are responsible for this, they should be told that it is not a fact, and that this linking of the novel and the play should be discontinued. You see, it simply plays into the hands of whoever had got hold of any part of the film rights to "The Circular Staircase", and it creates in the mind of the public the impression that the play and the novel are the same—which, as we know, is not the truth.
Since the showing of the film in Chicago Selig has wired that he would refund our money if we were dissatisfied. I suppose this means either that he does not want to

stop the film being shown in Chicago—or that he wants to get out of his contract with us—which would permit of the whole country being flooded with "The Circular Staircase" film—which, of course, might mean the loss of hundreds of thousands of dollars to us.

In New Haven, this week, two book stores are making big window displays of "The Circular Staircase"—advertising it as the novel from which "The Bat"—now playing New Haven—is taken. This sort of thing, also, serves, of course, to make the public think that the play and the book are identical—and prepares more trouble for us, should the film of "The Circular Staircase" appear upon the scene.

I hate to bother you with all this, but it is very serious. "The Bat" has opened so well on the road—but if the film of "The Circular Staircase" is allowed to be shown, I am afraid we will be done for.

All good wishes to you both, from

Your's sincerely,
Hop

Notes

Introduction

1. Avery Hopwood, "Is the Undraped Drama Unmoral?" *Theatre Magazine*, January 1921, p. 6.
2. "Rebuilding *Powers That Be*," *Cincinnati Times-Star*, 7 March 1907. (Arno L. Bader's collection of dramatic reviews and biographical materials, Department of Rare Books and Special Collections, University of Michigan, Ann Arbor.)

I. The Call for the Playwright and Before (1882–1905)

1. Glen Loney, *20th Century Theatre*, 2 vols. (New York: Facts on File Publications, 1983), 1:5, 55.
2. Ibid., p. 51.
3. Louis Vincent De Foe, "The Call for the Playwright," *Michigan Alumnus* (January 1904): 176.
4. Avery Hopwood, "The Play-Writing Business," *Green Book Album*, August 1912, p. 222.
5. Alexander Woollcott, "Second Thoughts on First Nights," *New York Times*, 5 September 1920, sec. 6, p. 1.
6. "Hopwood, the Playmaker," *Detroit News*, 26 February 1920, sec. 2, p. 4.
7. Archie Bell, "A Dramatist Who Writes His Plays in a Tent," *Theatre*, August 1910, p. 62.
8. Ibid., p. 64.
9. *My Maiden Effort*, with an introduction by Gelett Burgess (New York: Doubleday, Page & Company, 1921), p. 105.
10. Avery Hopwood, "Avery Hopwood Bares Secrets of His Early Life," *Detroit News*, 8 October 1916, p. 1.
11. Ibid.
12. Bell, "Tent," p. 62.
13. Thomas C. Monks to the author, 6 April 1983.
14. "Avery is Great! Says Kate," *Cleveland Leader*, 26 Feb. 1909. (Robinson Locke Coll., ser. 2, Billy Rose Theatre Collection, New York Public Library at Lincoln Center.)
15. "Hopwood's Strange Fancy," Hopwood clipping folder, Harvard University Library, Cambridge, Massachusetts.
16. Leonard Hall, "Show Stopping," *New York Telegram*, 6 July 1928. (Players' Collection, Billy Rose Theatre Collection, New York Public Library at Lincoln Center.)
17. Bell, "Tent," p. 62.
18. "Few Knew True Hopwood Back of His Drunken Pose," clipping in the files

of the Hopwood Room, University of Michigan, Ann Arbor. Hereafter cited as Hopwood Room.

19. "Mrs. Hopwood Dies; Dramatist's Mother," *New York Times,* 2 March 1929, p. 17.

20. Avery Hopwood Papers, Department of Rare Books and Special Collections, University of Michigan, Ann Arbor. Hereafter cited as Michigan.

21. Marjorie Wilson, "Your Laughs Earn $200,000 a Year for This Man," *Cleveland Sunday News-Leader,* 30 November 1919, sec. 4, p. 1.

22. Bell, "Tent," p. 62.

23. Michigan. Carl Van Vechten, then drama critic for *The New York Press* (from August 1913 to May 1914), had hired Djuna Barnes to draw Hopwood for an upcoming interview. The article, "Playwriting Attracts Second-Rate Intellectuals, Says Hopwood, Who's Going to Quit" by Harold E. Stearns, and the accompanying drawing, were published January 4, 1914. Djuna Barnes, who had developed a reputation as a perspicacious and creative interviewer herself, went on to write poetry, plays (as one of the original members of the Theatre Guild), and fiction, principally: *The Book of Repulsive Women,* 1915; *A Night Among the Horses,* 1929; and *Nightwood,* 1936.

24. Bruce Kellner to the author, 5 October 1983.

25. William Forrest Dawson, "Some Notes About Playboy Playwright," *Phi Gamma Delta,* January 1958, p. 184.

26. Gertrude Atherton, *Adventures of a Novelist* (New York: Liveright, Inc., 1932), p. 237.

27. Gertrude Stein, *The Autobiography of Alice B. Toklas* (New York: Harcourt Brace and Company, 1933), p. 70.

28. "Chapter Correspondence," *Phi Gamma Delta,* October 1902, p. 101.

29. *Phi Gamma Delta,* May 1903, p. 580.

30. Bell, "Tent," p. 62.

31. Dawson, "Playboy Playwright," p. 184.

32. Thomas Henry Read, Letter to the Editor, *Phi Gamma Delta,* May 1958, p. 347.

33. Hopwood Room.

34. Read, Letter.

35. "Avery Hopwood Interviewed," *Phi Gamma Delta,* February 1923, p. 474.

36. Roy W. Cowden, "Creative Writing and the Hopwood Awards," *Michigan Alumnus,* 48 (Spring 1942): 468.

37. Avery Hopwood, "When Alicia Played," *Inlander,* June 1905, p. 339.

38. Avery Hopwood, "After the Hop is Over," *Inlander,* vol. 15, no. 6 (souvenir edition), p. 194.

39. Avery Hopwood, "J.B. Brown, Misfit," *Inlander,* January 1904, pp. 339-340.

40. "Avery Hopwood's *Clothes,*" *Phi Gamma Delta,* March 1907, p. 402.

41. Hopwood Room.

42. Dawson, "Playboy Playwright," p. 347.

43. Hopwood, "Play-Writing," p. 222.

II. A Dramatist Full of Promise (1906–1908)

1. Channing Pollock, *Harvest of My Years* (Indianapolis: Bobbs-Merrill Company, 1948), p. 149.

2. Ibid., p. 150.

3. Ibid.

4. "Something of the New Play Called *Clothes,*" *New York Dramatic News,*

14 July 1906. (Robinson Locke Collection, ser. 2, Billy Rose Theatre Collection, New York Public Library at Lincoln Center. Hereafter cited as Locke Collection.)

5. Avery Hopwood and Channing Pollock, *Clothes.* (Typescript-Promptbook, n.p., 1906), Billy Rose Theatre Collection, New York Public Library at Lincoln Center, Act II, pp. 17-18. Hereafter cited as Billy Rose Collection.

6. Ibid., Act III, pp. 18-19.

7. Archie Bell, "Miss George Wins New Laurels," *Cleveland News,* 29 January 1907. (Arno L. Bader's collection of dramatic reviews and biographical materials, Department of Rare Books and Special Collections, University of Michigan, Ann Arbor. Hereafter cited as Bader's collection.)

8. "*Clothes,*" *New Dramatic Mirror,* 22 September 1906, p. 3.

9. Ibid.

10. Ibid.

11. "Avery Hopwood's *Clothes,*" *Phi Gamma Delta,* March 1907, p. 405.

12. "Gospel of *Clothes,*" *Cincinnati Times-Star,* 5 March 1907, Bader's collection, p. 8.

13. "*Clothes,*" *Theatre,* October 1906, p. xi.

14. "Hopwood's *Clothes,*" p. 401.

15. "Mr. Hopwood's Career," *Toledo Blade,* June 1916, Locke Collection.

16. Pollock, *My Years,* p. 211.

17. "Hopwood's *Clothes,*" p. 401.

18. Ibid.

19. Clipping fragment, 24 October 1906, Locke Collection.

20. "Hopwood's *Clothes,*" p. 407.

21. Avery Hopwood, "The Supermen and Superwomen of the Stage," *Theatre Magazine,* May 1906, pp. 120-122.

22. Avery Hopwood, "Where They Try Out Voices for the Operatic Stage," *Theatre Magazine,* April 1906, pp. 96-98.

23. "*The Powers That Be,*" *Columbus* (Ohio) *Evening Disptach,* 28 February 1907, p. 4. Hopwood's literary agent at this time, Mrs. H.C. De Mille, widow of David Belasco's former associate and mother of William and Cecil B. De Mille, had recently entered the playbroking field. During this period, each of the major playbrokers, Sanger & Jordan, Selwyn & Co., Elizabeth Marbury, Alice Kauser, Bellows and Gregory, and, of course, Samuel French & Son, had his own specialty. Kauser's was stock companies, and Marbury's foreign authors. Mrs. De Mille's specialty was the encouragement of new American playwrights. She evidently saw promise in Hopwood after *Clothes,* and represented him in the production of *The Powers That Be.*

24. "*The Powers That Be,*" *Ohio State Journal,* 28 February 1907, p. 9. The time-worn "curtain speech" that audiences had come to expect from authors on opening nights was still popular, but New York critics were beginning to decry it. Hopwood himself was rather reticent about making such speeches, especially after his first attempt at one on the opening night of *Clothes.* He and Pollock had graced the stage at the close of the show, but when he stepped forward to make a few remarks, Pollock abruptly pulled him back, letting the Act Curtain obliterate him. According to Pollock, Hopwood frequently joked about this "song and dance act" throughout his life.

25. Avery Hopwood, "On Dramatizing Life," *Ohio Sun,* February 1907, Locke Collection.

26. Ibid.

27. Avery Hopwood Letters, Literature Department, Cleveland Public Library, Cleveland, Ohio. Hereafter cited as Cleveland.

28. Avery Hopwood, "The Play-Writing Business," *Green Book Album,* August 1912, p. 222.

29. "An American Play," *Cincinnati Enquirer,* 4 March 1907, p. 7.

30. Avery Hopwood, *The Powers That Be* (Typescript-Promptbook, n.p., 1907), Billy Rose Collection, Act I, p. 16.

31. Hopwood, "Play-Writing," p. 223.

32. "Rebuilding *Powers That Be,*" *Cincinnati Times-Star,* 7 March 1907, Bader's collection, p. 25.

34. "Author Engaged to 1 of These 3," 12 April 1907. (Locke Collection.)

35. Cleveland.

36. Marjorie Wilson, "Your Laughs Earn $200,000 a Year for This Man," *Cleveland Sunday News-Leader,* 30 November 1919, sec. 4, p. 1.

37. *New York Telegraph,* 2 September 1908. (Locke Collection.)

38. F.N. Scott Papers, Bentley Historical Library, University of Michigan, Ann Arbor.

39. Avery Hopwood, *This Woman and This Man* (New York: c. 1909; Washington, D.C.: Library of Congress, MIC RR 82/6720), Act III, p. 19.

40. "*This Woman and This Man,*" *Theatre Magazine,* April 1909, p. ix.

41. Ibid., Act I, p. 22.

42. Ibid., Act III, pp. 21-22.

43. "*This Woman and This Man,*" production clipping folder, Harvard University Library, Cambridge, Massachusetts. The success of Davy's scenes may have been due, in part, to Hopwood's professed fondness for children, at least other people's children. One interviewer of the time reported that he had "a supreme and beautiful devotion to the little tots of this world," something which is reiterated in other articles. His unproduced play, *Pete (Don't Be Afraid),* the story of a little boy whose father scolds him for being a "scaredy cat," also contains scenes of childhood sincerity and simplicity.

44. "*This Woman and This Man,*" Harvard.

45. "*This Woman and This Man,*" *New York Dramatic Mirror,* 6 March 1909, p. 3.

46. Clayton Hamilton, "The Promise of New Playwrights," *Forum,* April 1909, p. 333.

47. Archie Bell, "A Dramatist Who Writes His Plays in a Tent," *Theatre,* August 1910, p. 62.

48. John Van Doren, "How To Write a Play," *Theatre Magazine,* October 1921, p. 212.

III. *"The Play-Writing Business" (1909–1914)*

1. Ernest F. Giffin, ed., *Westchester County and Its People,* 2 vols. (New York: Lewis Historical Publishing Co., Inc., 1946), 2:367-370.

2. Avery Hopwood Letters, Literature Department, Cleveland Public Library, Cleveland, Ohio. Hereafter cited as Cleveland.

3. Avery Hopwood, "Avery Hopwood Writes Plays on Fresh Air," *Chicago Tribune,* 13 February 1910. (Robinson Locke Collection, ser. 2, Billy Rose Theatre Collection, New York Public Library at Lincoln Center. Hereafter cited as Locke Collection.)

4. Mary Roberts Rinehart, *My Story,* 2nd ed. (New York: Rinehart & Company, Inc., 1948), p. 109.

5. Unidentified clipping, *Green Book Album,* January 1911, Locke Collection.

6. Ibid.

7. Rinehart, *My Story,* p. 109.

8. James T. Nardin, "A Study in Popular American Farce, 1865–1914" (Ph.D. dissertation, University of Chicago, 1950), p. 6.

9. Rinehart, *My Story*, p. 10.

10. Ibid.

11. Walter P. Eaton, "The Return of Farce," *American Magazine*, December 1910, p. 264.

12. Channing Pollock, "Seven Days," *Green Book Album*, January 1910, p. 77.

13. Avery Hopwood and Mary Roberts Rinehart, *Seven Days* (New York: Samuel French, Inc., 1931), Act II, pp. 64-65.

14. LeRoy D. Haberman, "American Farce on Broadway, 1914–1950" (Ph.D. dissertation, Stanford University, 1959), p. 278.

15. "Hopwood's Profits," *New York Times*, 24 September 1922, sec. 6, p. 1.

16. Jan Cohn, *Improbable Fiction, The Life of Mary Roberts Rinehart* (Pittsburgh: University of Pittsburgh Press, 1980).

17. Channing Pollock, "Something About 'First Nights,'" *The Footlights Fore and Aft* (Boston: The Gorham Press, 1911), p. 284.

18. Ibid., p. 286.

19. Shirley J. Burns, "The Day of Young Dramatists," *Green Book Album*, January 1911, p. 187.

20. Cleveland.

21. Ibid.

22. Ibid.

23. Ibid.

24. "Avery Hopwood Ill," *New York Telegraph*, 4 October 1910. (Locke Collection.)

25. James S. Metcalfe, *"Judy Forgot," Life*, 20 October 1920, p. 660.

26. Ibid.

27. *"Judy Forgot," New York Dramatic Mirror*, 12 October 1910, p. 7.

28. *"Judy Forgot," Theatre*, November 1910, p. 133.

29. Metcalfe, *"Judy,"* p. 660.

30. Avery Hopwood, *Judy Forgot* (Typescript, n.p., n.d.), Billy Rose Theatre Collection, New York Public Library at Lincoln Center, Act I, p. 74.

31. Ibid., Act. II, pp. 19-23.

32. *"Judy Forgot," New York Dramatic Mirror*, 30 November 1910, p. 10.

33. Avery Hopwood, "Two Theatrical Memories," *Theatre Magazine*, May 1920, p. 368.

34. Avery Hopwood, "The Play-Writing Business," *Green Book Album*, August 1912, p. 225.

35. Marjorie Wilson, "Your Laughs Earn $200,000 a Year for This Man," *Cleveland Sunday News-Leader*, 10 November 1911. (Locke Collection.)

36. William E. Sage, "News, Views and Reviews of the Spotlight People," *Cleveland Leader*, 10 November 1911. (Locke Collection.)

37. Craig Timberlake, *The Bishop of Broadway* (New York: Library Publishers, 1954), p. 315.

38. Channing Pollock, *"Nobody's Widow," Green Book Album*, February 1911, p. 316.

39. James Metcalfe, "Blanch Bates' New Play," 23 November 1910, Locke Collection.

40. "Blanch Bates in *Nobody's Widow," New York Times*, 16 November 1910. (Locke Collection.)

41. Ibid.

42. Hopwood, "Play-Writing," p. 226.

43. William Winter, *The Wallet of Time*, 2 vols. (New York: Moffat, Yard & Company, 1913), 2:245.

44. Pollock, *"Widow,"* p. 316.

45. *"Nobody's Widow,"* Theatre, December 1910, p. 162.

46. Channing Pollock, *Harvest of My Years* (Indianapolis: Bobbs-Merrill Company, 1948), pp. 192-194.

47. Rennold Wolfe, "Showing Author Hopwood To Be More Discreet Than Colleagues," *New York Telegraph*, 17 November 1910. (Locke Collection.)

48. Cleveland.

49. "Hopwood to Quit Play Wrighting," *New York Telegraph*, 26 October 1910. (Locke Collection.)

50. William E. Sage, "News, Views and Reviews of the Spotlight People," *Cleveland Leader*, 10 November 1911. (Locke Collection.)

51. Cleveland. Wyndham and Moore never played in *Nobody's Widow*, but Wyndham finally offered the rights to Doris Keane, after denying them to Olga Nethersole and Lily Langtry, and the play was premiered 18 September 1918 at the Lyric under the title *Roxana*—it ran for 219 performances. The *Illustrated London News*, 28 September 1918 reported: "It is not as deep as a well, or as wide as a churchdoor, this play of Avery Hopwood's entitled *Roxana*, which supplies Miss Doris Keane with her new part; but since it does that much—why, in Mercutio's words, 'twill serve.'"
It is not known to what extent Hopwood may have adapted the play to suit Doris Keane's abilities.
The libretto manager Col. Henry W. Savage had "gotten hold of" was *Somewhere Else*, a musical fantasy that Hopwood had never been too pleased with from the beginning. Hopwood's frustration over having to return for a production is significant in light of his vow to quit playwriting and begin the long-awaited novel. A similar scenario brought him back from Europe in the spring of 1913.

52. "Hopwood Abroad," Locke Collection.

53. Clipping fragment, 16 May 1911, Locke Collection.

54. Cleveland.

55. "He Represented a Sponge," 25 November 1911, Locke Collection.

56. Bruce Kellner, *Carl Van Vechten* and the *Irreverent Decades* (Norman: University of Oklahoma Press, 1968), p. 43.

57. Ibid., p. 78.

58. Edward Lueders, *Carl Van Vechten* (New York: Twayne Publishing, Inc., 1965), p. 143.

59. Kellner, *Van Vechten*, p. 131.

60. Ibid., p. 45.

61. Ibid., p. 57.

62. Ibid., p. 78.

63. Mabel Dodge Luhan, *Intimate Memories*, vol. 1: *Movers and Shakers* (New York: Harcourt, Brace and Company, 1936), p. 45.

64. *Flowers of Friendship*, ed. Donald Gallup (New York: Alfred A. Knopf, 1953), p. 151.

65. Ibid., p. 152.

66. Gertrude Stein, *The Autobiography of Alice B. Toklas* (New York: Harcourt, Brace and Company, 1933), p. 138.

67. Kellner, *Van Vechten*, p. 78.

68. "Avery Hopwood Recovering," *New York Telegraph*, 23 January 1912. (Locke Collection.)

69. "New Comedy by Hopwood," *Phi Gamma Delta*, April 1912, p. 597.

70. Cleveland.

71. Hopwood, "Play-Writing," p. 226.

72. Cleveland. By this time, Hopwood had become a member of The Lambs Club on West Forty-fourth Street and this was the permanent mailing address he used when in New York; he took rooms in various hotels from time to time, as well as rented apartments and summer homes, but he never settled at one location.

73. Unidentified clipping, 1912, Locke Collection.

74. Cleveland.

75. Avery Hopwood, *Somewhere Else* (Typescript, 1913), in the possession of Hollywood Plays, Inc., Glen Rock, New Jersey.

76. *"Somewhere Else," New York Dramatic Mirror,* 22 January 1913, p. 9.

77. Heywood Broun, *"Somewhere Else," New York Tribune,* 21 January 1913, p. 9.

78. *"Somewhere Else," Variety,* 24 January 1913, p. 20.

79. "Gustave Luder's Death," *New York Times,* 25 January 1913, p. 25.

80. Cleveland.

81. Ibid.

82. Ibid.

83. Wilson, *Your Laughs,* p. 1.

84. "Hopwood's Strange Fancy," Hopwood clipping folder, Harvard University Library, Cambridge, Massachusetts.

85. Channing Pollock Correspondence, Box 2, Folder 12, Princeton University Library Collections, Princeton, New Jersey.

86. *"Miss Jenny O'Jones," Springfield* (Massachusetts) *Republican,* 28 November 1913, p. 6.

87. Ibid.

88. "Grace George Collapses," *Jenny O'Jones* production folder, Harvard.

89. "Hopwood Tired of Stage Limitations," *Cleveland Leader,* 16 January 1914. (Locke Collection.)

90. "Why Avery Hopwood Writes Plays," *Green Book Album,* March 1914, p. 387.

91. Ibid.

92. Ibid., p. 389.

IV. *Skating on Thin Ice (1915–1918)*

1. "Hopwood Missing," *New York Telegraph,* 27 August 1914. (Robinson Locke Collection, ser. 2, Billy Rose Theatre Collection, New York Public Library at Lincoln Center. Hereafter cited as Locke Collection.)

2. Avery Hopwood Papers, Department of Rare Books and Special Collections, University of Michigan Library, Ann Arbor. Hereafter cited as Michigan.

3. Michigan.

4. Mary Roberts Rinehart Collection, Hillman Library Special Collections, University of Pittsburgh, Pittsburgh, Pennsylvania. Hereafter cited as Hillman Library.

5. Avery Hopwood Letters, Literature Department, Cleveland Public Library, Cleveland, Ohio. Hereafter cited as Cleveland.

6. *"Sadie Love," New York Times Book Review,* 2 April 1916, sec. 7, p. 12.

7. Arno L. Bader, "Avery Hopwood, Dramatist," *Michigan Quarterly Review* 66 (Autumn 1959): 68.

8. Avery Hopwood, *Sadie Love* (Typescript, n.p., n.d.), Billy Rose Theatre Collection, New York Public Library at Lincoln Center, Act I, p. 52. Hereafter cited as Lincoln Center. At the time Hopwood signed the contract for *Sadie Love,* 26 June 1915, it was entitled *Sally Love;* he affixed his signature as sole author, and T. Daniel Frawley

signed as agent for Oliver Morosco. Hopwood's literary representative was now John W. Rumsey of the American Play Company, Inc., which had purchased Mrs. De Mille's agency in 1912. There has been some speculation that Hopwood was a founding member of the organization, but, to date, this has not been substantiated.

9. Ibid., p. 56.

10. Channing Pollock, "Sugar and Spice," *Green Book Album*, February 1916, p. 317.

11. "Sadie Love," *New York Dramatic Mirror*, 4 December 1915, p. 8.

12. *"Sadie Love," New York Telegraph*, 18 September 1915. (Locke Collection.)

13. Gertrude M. Price, "Women Demand the Naughty Plays! Says Avery Hopwood, Who Has Just Written a 'Naughty' One," *Toledo News*, 28 September 1915. (Locke Collection.)

14. Ibid.

15. "Avery Hopwood Scorns Women," *New York Telegraph*, 18 September 1915. (Locke Collection.)

16. Price, "Women Demand," Locke Collection.

17. Ibid.

18. George Jean Nathan, "The Commercial Theatre Mismanagers," in *Mr. George Jean Nathan Presents* (New York: Alfred A. Knopf, 1917), pp. 55-58.

19. Heywood Broun, "Another Play About Pajamas," *New York Tribune*, 30 November 1915, p. 9.

20. Ibid.

21. Nathan, *Presents*, p. 60.

22. "Extravagant Farce by Avery Hopwood," *New York Times*, 30 November 1915, p. 13.

23. *"Sadie Love," Vogue*, 15 January 1916. (Locke Collection.)

24. *Theatre*, January 1916, p. 6.

25. Pollock, "Sugar and Spice," p. 316.

26. Nathan, *Presents*, p. 58.

27. Ibid.

28. Avery Hopwood, *Fair and Warmer* (Typescript in the possession of Hollywood Plays, Inc., Glen Rock, New Jersey), Act I, p. 4. Hereafter cited as Hollywood Plays.

29. *"Fair and Warmer," Vogue*, 15 Dec. 1915. (Locke Collection.)

30. *"Fair and Warmer," Harper's Weekly*, 27 November 1915, p. 515.

31. *Vogue*, Locke Collection. The "pink"-haired Robert Milton, who also directed *Sadie Love*, established himself as a successful stager of farce comedies during this period.

32. *"Fair and Warmer,"* 15 November 1915, Locke Collection.

33. "Personal Triumphs of the Season," *Green Book Album*, April 1916, p. 691.

34. "Fair and Warmer is Highly Diverting," *New York Times*, 8 November 1915, p. 13.

35. Interview with Madge Kennedy, Hollywood, California, 16 June 1983.

36. Avery Hopwood, *The Mystic Shrine* (Typescript-Promptbook, n.p., 1915), Lincoln Center, Act I, p. 45.

37. "Fijis Boost Hopwood," *Phi Gamma Delta*, April 1916, p. 643.

38. Bader, *Hopwood*, p. 64.

39. *Who's Who in the Theatre*, 4th ed., comp. & ed. by John Parker (Boston: Small, Maynard & Co., 1922), p. 1141.

40. 18 January 1915, Hillman Library.

41. 29 January 1915, Hillman Library.

42. 16 March 1915, Hillman Library.

43. Hillman Library.

44. 19 March 1915, Hillman Library.

45. Cleveland.

46. Ibid. By this time, Archie Bell, as well as being drama critic for the *Cleveland Leader*, had also established himself as an important Travel Journalist, often sending Hopwood his latest books on where he had vacationed. Pep-Squeak, the monkey, remained Hopwood's pet throughout his life, and was passed on to his mother, who set up a ten-thousand-dollar trust for its care after her death.

47. Avery Hopwood, *Our Little Wife* (Typescript-Promptbook, n.p., 1916), Lincoln Center, Act I, p. 50.

48. George Jean Nathan, *Comedians All* (New York: Alfred Knopf, 1919), p. 107.

49. Nathan, *Presents,* p. 297.

50. *The Oxford Companion to the Theatre,* 3rd ed., 1967, s.v. "Nathan, George Jean," by Thomas Quinn Curtiss.

51. Nathan, *The Popular Theatre* (New York: Alfred A. Knopf, 1928), p. 47.

52. Nathan, *Comedians,* p. 108.

53. Ibid., p. 110.

54. Ibid. In an unidentified newspaper fragment entitled "Avery Hopwood Writes of the New York Critics," in the "Avery Hopwood" folder of the Robinson Locke Collection, Billy Rose Theatre Collection, New York Public Library at Lincoln Center, one is able to read what the playwright had to say about Nathan:

> He is as nea[rly infal]lible as a critic can be. W[henever] he praises a play of mine I kn[ow that] it is doomed to a run of four [weeks, months]. If he damns my product I f[ind] that I can bank upon several pr[ofitable] seasons. But, please observe, [I do] not offer this as a reflection upo[n his] taste. The best plays do not alw[ays] run the longest. And Mr. Nathan [knows] his predilections in the theatre evidences a strong leaning to the unusual. He is fond of dramatic caviare. He also [has] a liking for being found unusual. Take the period when he chose to criticize adversely the, to me, so admirable Mrs. Fiske. I could not help feeling that he had reasoned somewhat in this manner: "If I praise Mrs. Fiske no one will pay any attention to me, for every critic in the country praises her. But if I comment adversely upon her people will exclaim, 'Who is this fellow Nathan, who dares criticize the great Mrs. Fiske?' Then they will begin to talk about me instead of about her, and they will end up by thinking that I am a very clever young fellow."
>
> Which, indeed, he is. And he succeeded in his purpose. For here we are talking about him.

55. "Some Facts on Farce," *Detroit Free Press,* 8 October 1916, p. 3.

56. Nathan, "The American Dramatist—Why He Isn't," *Theatre Magazine,* March 1917, p. 136.

57. Untitled article, January 1917, p. 118.

58. "Polyandrous Farce by Avery Hopwood," *New York Times,* 20 November 1916, sec. 10, p. 3.

59. *"Our Little Wife,"* *New York Dramatic Mirror,* 25 November 1916, p. 7.

60. Carl Van Vechten, "Two American Playwrights," *The Merry-Go-Round* (New York: Alfred A. Knopf, 1918), p. 236.

61. "Hopwood and His Plays," *Columbus* (Ohio) *Dispatch,* 26 November 1916. (Locke Collection.)

62. *Sadie Love* agreement, Lincoln Center.

63. Karl K. Kitchen, "Avery Hopwood Writes Another 'Naughty-Nice' Farce, Gets Away With It," *Cleveland Plain Dealer,* 26 November 1919, p. 2.

64. Untitled article, *St. Paul* (Minnesota) *Dispatch,* 23 March 1917. (Locke Collection.)

65. Bruce Kellner, *Carl Van Vechten and the Irreverent Decades* (Norman: University of Oklahoma Press, 1968), p. 119.

66. Michigan. Hopwood is referring to Ettie Stettheimer's Ph.D. dissertation, "The Will to Believe as a Basis for the Defense of Religious Faith; a Critical Study" (1907). Ettie, Carrie, and Florine Stettheimer enjoy a unique place in the High Bohemia of New York City in the twenties and thirties. In their rooms at the Renaissance Alwyn Court, this trio of eccentric sisters established a kind of cultural salon, where they entertained their friends who just "happened to be celebrated," among them the artists Duchamp, Lachaise, and O'Keefe; the photographers Steichen and Stieglitz; the writers Mencken, Anderson, and on occasion Stein; the critics McBride and Rosenfeld; the composer Virgil Thompson; and writer/critic Van Vechten, whom Hopwood had introduced to the sisters. Ettie Stettheimer aspired to writing herself, and penned some poetry and a novel, *Love Days,* under the pseudonym Henri Waste (Henrie[tta] Wa[lter] Ste[ttheimer]). Florine became a painter of portraits and murals — works which John Richardson has characterized as a combination of *"fausse naïveté,* high camp, and wit" — and on one occasion, she applied her imagination to the stage, receiving critical recognition for her fanciful cellophane and tarlatan settings for Gertrude Stein and Virgil Thompson's opera, *Four Saints in Three Acts* (1934). Happily, the sophisticated and whimsical world of the Stettheimer sisters and their friends was captured in miniature by Carrie Stettheimer, who devoted many hours in her early years to building and decorating a doll-house representation of the sisters' artistic-social drawing rooms; one need only travel to the Museum of the City of New York to enjoy them. See *Florine Stettheimer: a Life in Art* by Parker Tyler. NY: Farrar, Straus and Company, 1963.

67. Cleveland.

68. Ibid.

69. 26 December 1916, Locke Collection.

70. 6 January 1917, Hillman Library.

71. "Hopwood Here After Illness," *New York Telegraph,* 12 May 1917. (Locke Collection.)

72. Hillman Library.

73. 27 June 1917, Hillman Library.

74. Cleveland. *Bab* was eventually produced in October of 1920 as adapted for the stage by Edward Childs Carpenter. It featured Helen Hayes in her first starring role on Broadway as Bab the 18-year-old subdeb, who raises "havoc . . . when she fabricates a love affair for herself"; it ran for 88 performances.

75. Ibid.

76. *"Sadie Love* with Music," *Variety,* 16 January 1920, p. 15.

77. *"I'll Say She Does* in October," *Variety,* 26 September 1919, p. 13.

78. "Hopwood on Reincarnation," *Variety,* 11 June 1920, p. 15.

79. Avery Hopwood, *Pete* (Hollywood Plays), Act I, p. 7.

80. Ibid., p. 19.

81. Ibid., p. 25.

82. Ibid., Act III, p. 35.

83. Avery Hopwood, *Don't Be Afraid* (Typescript, n.p., n.d.), Lincoln Center.

84. Mary Miles Minter made fifty films between 1912 and 1923. Unfavorably compared with Mary Pickford, Minter's career was on the wane at the time of *The Little Clown;* and, in 1922, her career was all but destroyed by the scandal surrounding the murder of film director William Desmond Taylor, with whom she was in love. For an account of one of Hollywood's classic, unsolved crimes, see *A Cast of Killers* by Sidney D. Kirkpatrick, New York: E.P. Dutton, 1986.

85. Burns Mantle, *Best Plays 1909–1919* (New York: Dodd, Mead & Co.), pp. viii-ix.

86. Hillman Library.

87. Unidentified clipping, Locke Collection.

88. Hillman Library.

89. Nathan, *Comedians,* p. 108.

90. James T. Nardin, "A Study in Popular American Farce, 1865–1914" (Ph.D. dissertation, University of Chicago, 1950), p. 22.

91. *"Double Exposure," New York Dramatic Mirror,* 31 August 1918, p. 301.

92. Heywood Broun, "New Farce by Hopwood Is Seen at Bijou Theatre," *New York Tribune,* 28 August 1918, p. 7.

93. "Hopwood Writes a High Moral Farce," *New York Times,* 28 August 1918, p. 5.

94. *"Double Exposure* Is Clever Farce," production folder, Harvard University Library, Cambridge, Massachusetts.

95. Nathan, "American Playwright—Why He Isn't," p. 136.

96. Broun, "New Farce," p. 7.

97. Hillman Library.

98. Mary Roberts Rinehart, *My Story,* 2nd. ed. (New York: Rinehart & Company, Inc., 1948), p. 220.

99. Hillman Library.

100. Ibid.

101. 25 February 1919, Hillman Library.

102. Hillman Library.

103. N.d., Hillman Library.

104. *"Tumble In," Theatre,* May 1919, p. 274.

V. Inexhaustible Avery (1919–1921)

1. Glen Loney, *20th Century Theatre,* 2 vols. (New York: Facts on File Publications, 1983), 1:104.

2. LeRoy D. Haberman, "American Farce on Broadway, 1914–1950" (Ph.D. dissertation, Stanford University, 1959), p. 88.

3. Mary Roberts Rinehart Collection, Hillman Library Special Collections, University of Pittsburgh, Pittsburgh, Pennsylvania. Hereafter cited as Hillman Library.

4. Ibid.

5. Mary Roberts Rinehart, *My Story,* 2nd ed. (New York: Rinehart & Company, Inc., 1948), p. 303.

6. Hillman Library.

7. Alfred Harding, *The Revolt of the Actors* (New York: William Morrow & Company, 1929), p. 162.

8. Channing Pollock, *Harvest of My Years* (Indianapolis: Bobbs-Merrill Company, 1948), p. 259.

9. Ward Morehouse, "The Broadway Season: 1919 Album," *Theatre Arts,* September 1950, p. 20.

10. Avery Hopwood, "How Avery Hopwood Discovered the Gold Diggers and Induced Them to the Stage," *Cleveland Plain Dealer,* 16 November 1919, sec. D, p. 3.

11. Ibid.

12. "Belasco's *Gold Diggers," Variety,* 6 June 1919, p. 14.

13. Avery Hopwood, *The Gold Diggers* (Typescript in the possession of Hollywood Plays, Inc., Glen Rock, New Jersey, 1919), Act I, pp. 23-26.

14. "Belasco Presents Miss Claire as *The Gold Diggers* Star," *New York Herald,* 1 October 1919, sec. 2, p. 1.

15. "Miss Claire on 'Gold Digging' and the Non-Commissioned Girls of the Stage," *New York Herald,* 5 October 1919, Robinson Locke Collection, ser. 2, Billy Rose Theatre Collection, New York Public Library at Lincoln Center.

16. Heywood Broun, "Avery Hopwood's *The Gold Diggers* Has First Peformance at Lyceum," *New York Tribune,* 1 October 1919, p. 11.

17. *"The Gold Diggers," Forum,* December 1919, p. 622.

18. *"The Gold Diggers," Variety,* 10 October 1919, p. 6.

19. John Van Doren, "How to Write a Play," *Theatre Magazine,* October 1921, p. 212

20. "Second Thoughts on First Nights," *New York Times,* 5 October 1919, sec. 4, p. 2.

21. Broun, *Avery Hopwood's "The Gold Diggers,"* p. 11.

22. Alexander Woollcott, "The Play," *New York Times,* 1 October 1919, p. 20.

23. *"Gold Diggers* Till September," *Variety,* 14 May 1920, p. 14.

24. "Ina Claire Leaving Belasco's Banner?" *Variety,* 25 February 1921, p. 1.

25. William C. Young, *Famous Actors and Actresses on the American Stage,* 2 vols. (New York: R.R. Bowker Co., 1975), 1:187.

26. "Hopwood's Profits," *New York Times,* 24 September 1922, sec. 7, p. 1.

27. William Torbert Leonard, *Theatre: Stage to Screen to Television,* 2 vols. (Metuchen, N.J.: Scarecrow Press, 1981), 2:614.

28. Hillman Library.

29. Harding, *Revolt,* p. 126.

30. Allen Churchill, *The Theatrical Twenties* (New York: McGraw Hill Book Co., 1975), p. 238.

31. "Inside Stuff," *Variety,* 3 September 1920, p. 11.

32. "Our Greatest Playwright, Avery Hopwood," *Phi Gamma Delta,* December 1919, p. 376.

33. "Bedroom Farce to the Limit," *New York Times,* 7 October 1919, p. 22.

34. Ibid.

35. *Life,* September 1918, p. 381.

36. Kenneth Macgowan, "America's Best Season," *Theatre Arts,* April 1920, p. 92.

37. Moorehouse, "1919 Album," p. 14.

38. *Theatre Arts,* January 1920, p. 1.

39. Avery Hopwood Letters, Literature Department, Cleveland Public Library, Cleveland, Ohio. Hereafter cited as Cleveland.

40. Hillman Library.

41. Ibid.

42. Jan Cohn, *Improbable Fiction* (Pittsburgh: University of Pittsburgh Press, 1980), p. 140.

43. Rinehart, *My Story,* p. 306.

44. Hillman Library.

45. Cohn, *Improbable Fiction,* p. 141.

46. Rinehart, *My Story,* p. 309.

47. Howard Haycraft, *Murder for Pleasure: The Life and Times of the Detective Story* (London: Peter Davies, 1942), p. 88.

48. *"The Bat* Receipts," *Variety,* 25 June 1920, p. 13.

49. *"The Bat," Life,* 9 September 1920, p. 456.

50. *New York Times,* 14 November 1920, sec. 6, p. 1.

51. "A Rinehart Mystery Staged," *New York Times,* 24 August 1920, p. 6.

52. Cohn, *Improbable Fiction,* p. 142.

53. Hillman Library.

54. Ibid.

55. 15 September 1921, Hillman Library.

56. Cohn, *Improbable Fiction*, p. 143.

57. Ibid., p. 143.

58. Rinehart, *My Story*, p. 315.

59. *"Thrills from Spain,"* New York Times, 18 August 1920, p. 6.

60. Rinehart, *My Story*, p. 315.

61. *"Spanish Love* Brings Color to the Stage," New York Tribune, 18 August 1920, p. 6.

62. *"Spanish Love," Life,* 2 September 1920, p. 408.

63. Woollcott, *"Thrills from Spain,"* p. 6.

64. Ibid.

65. Rinehart, *My Story*, p. 316.

66. Hillman Library.

67. Percy Hammond, *But—Is It Art?* (Garden City: Doubleday, Page & Company, 1927), p. 107.

68. Bernard Sobel, *"Ladies' Night* Turkish Bath House Turns on Comedy Steam," New York Dramatic Mirror, 14 August 1920, p. 283.

69. *"Ladies' Night," Theatre,* October 1920, p. 186.

70. Avery Hopwood, "Is The Undraped Drama Unmoral?" *Theatre Magazine,* January 1921, p. 6.

71. "Second Thoughts on First Nights," *New York Times,* 15 August 1920, sec. 6, p. 1.

72. "Second Thoughts on First Nights," *New York Times,* 5 September 1920, sec. 6, p. 1.

73. Ibid.

74. Archie Bell, "A Dramatist Who Writes His Plays in a Tent," *Theatre,* August 1910, p. 6.

75. Avery Hopwood Papers, Department of Rare Books and Special Collections, University of Michigan, Ann Arbor. Hereafter cited as Michigan.

76. Kevin Brownlow, *The Parade's Gone By* (New York: Alfred A. Knopf, 1969), p. 276.

77. Pollock, *My Years*, p. 231.

78. Hillman Library.

79. 29 October 1920, Michigan.

80. 29 November 1920, Hillman Library.

81. 2 December 1920, Hillman Library.

82. Cleveland.

83. Ibid.

84. Michigan.

Hôtel de Paris

Monte Carlo

Yes, my buddy—here I am—& how I miss buddy, in Monte—not to mention Carlo!—And *Oh* how I miss Fania & Mabel Dodge! . . .—your dear friend [feminine], the precious little darling George Brandt is in Berlin—and Sacha is here, with the accent on the see.

There are great things to see and to have in Monte Carlo—I've seen some of them [feminine] and had several of them [feminine]—

But why the feminine?—asks little Buddy—Oh well—it's all part of the game.

I return to the states stripped [of money] towards June 11—(on the Aquitania)—and I hope—I'll return alone [feminine]—This time little Buddy doesn't ask why the feminine!

I leave tomorrow for Florence — where I 'opes to 'ave many h'adventures — and probably shall & will not (When in doubt, include all available forms of the verb).

I thought of you in Paris in the street of the cat which fishes. [If Hopwood has deliberately omitted the accent in *peche*, he may be punning on *pêche* = fishes and *péché* = sins.]

And now I must away to the gambling well, & sell myself to the lowest biter.
so long, my Carlo

A thousand kisses — everywhere — for my adored Fania.

May 13 [1921]   Avery

85. "Inside Stuff," *Variety*, 29 April 1921, p. 13.

86. Cleveland.

87. Ibid.

88. "Hazel Dawn Steps Out," *Variety*, 1 April 1921, p. 13.

89. "The Season in Chicago," in Burns Mantle's *The Best Plays of 1920–1921* (New York: Dodd, Mead & Company, 1922), p. 17.

90. "*Getting Gertie's Garter*," *Life*, 18 August 1921, p. 18.

91. "New Woods Farce Fails to Shock Anybody Much," *New York Tribune*, 2 August 1921, p. 6.

92. *Life*, p. 18.

93. Untitled article, *Variety*, 7 October 1921, p. 17.

94. Ibid.

95. "*Demi-Virgin* Storm Grows on Broadway," *New York Herald*, 15 November 1921, p. 8.

96. Ibid.

97. Ibid.

98. Ibid.

99. "M'Adoo Indicts *The Demi-Virgin*," *New York Morning Telegraph*, 15 November 1921, *Demi-Virgin* clipping folder, Museum of the City of New York.

100. "*Demi-Virgin* Wins in Appellate Court," *Demi-Virgin* clipping folder, Harvard University Library, Cambridge, Massachusetts.

101. Harding, *Revolt*, p. 332.

102. "Criticizing Clergy in Censorship," *New York Times*, 10 May 1922, p. 18.

103. Untitled *Demi-Virgin* advertisement, *New York Times*, 31 May 1922, p. 12.

104. *New York Dramatic Mirror*, 22 October 1921, p. 593.

105. *Life*, 10 November 1921, p. 18.

106. *New York Times*, 19 October 1921, p. 22.

107. *Life*, p. 593.

108. *Theatre*, May 1924, p. 10.

109. Burns Mantle, *American Playwrights of Today* (New York: Dodd, Mead & Company, 1929), p. 159.

110. Gertrude Atherton, *Adventures of a Novelist* (New York: Liveright, Inc., 1932), p. 537.

111. Cleveland.

112. Last Will and Testament of James Avery Hopwood, 30 December 1921, Michigan.

113. Archie Bell, "Committee Seeking To Encourage Youth," *Cleveland News*, 13 November 1931. (Cleveland.)

VI. The Playmaking Factory and Final Years (1922–1928)

1. Untitled article, *Toledo Blade*, Robinson Locke Collection, ser. 2, Billy Rose Theatre Collection, New Public Library at Lincoln Center. Hereafter cited as Locke Collection.

2. "Some American Plays May Be Tried Out Abroad," *Toledo Blade*, 4 May 1922. (Locke Collection.)

3. Avery Hopwood Papers, Department of Rare Books and Special Collections, University of Michigan, Ann Arbor. Hereafter cited as Michigan.

4. Avery Hopwood Letters to Archie Bell, Literature Department, Cleveland Public Library, Cleveland, Ohio. Hereafter cited as Cleveland.

5. "Author of 'The Wooden Kimono,'" biographical clipping in the Billy Rose Theatre Collection, New York Public Library at Lincoln Center.

6. Memo in the Hopwood Files, Hopwood Room, University of Michigan, Ann Arbor.

7. Sheldon Cheney, "Who Are the American Playwrights and Why?" *Theatre Magazine*, December 1922, p. 360.

8. Al Woods, "Why I Produce Bed Room Farces," *Theatre Magazine*, June 1922, p. 406.

9. Montrose J. Moses, "The Metamorphosis of Owen Davis," *Theatre Magazine*, May 1922, p. 300.

10. Avery Hopwood, "Why I Don't Write More Serious Plays," *Theatre Magazine*, April 1924, p. 56.

11. Ibid., p. 10.

12. Avery Hopwood, "How To Write Plays," *Theatre Magazine*, August 1921, p. 212.

13. Carl Van Vechten, *Peter Whiffle: His Life and Works* (New York: Alfred A. Knopf, 1922), pp. 224–246.

14. Ibid., p. 4.

15. Ibid., p. 244.

16. Avery Hopwood, *Why Men Leave Home* (Typescript in the possession of Hollywood Plays, Inc., Glen Rock, New Jersey, 1922). Hereafter cited as Hollywood Plays.

17. Robert Benchley, "*Why Men Leave Home*," *Life*, September 1922, p. 18.

18. Lawrence Reamer, *New York Herald*, 17 September 1922, sec. 6, p. 3.

19. "Blushing Material Skillfully Handled in Hopwood Play," *New York Herald*, 13 September 1922, p. 6.

20. Kenneth Macgowan, "Hopwood as a Moralist," *New York Globe*, 13 September 1922. (Locke Collection.)

21. Percy Hammond, "Hopwood Says Men Leave Home After Women," *New York Tribune*, 13 September 1922, p. 6.

22. Avery Hopwood to Lee Shubert, 15 March 1919, Private Collection. Copy in the possession of the author.

23. Avery Holpwood to Mr. Morris, 29 August 1919, Private Collection. Copy in the possession of the author.

24. George Jean Nathan, *The World In False Face* (New York: Alfred A. Knopf, 1923), p. 148.

25. Michigan.

26. Ibid.

27. "Gossip on the Rialto," *New York Times*, 22 August 1923, sec. 7, p. 1.

28. *American Mercury*, February 1924, p. 247.

29. Cleveland.

30. Avery Hopwood, "Avery Hopwood Has a Change of Mind," *New York Times,* 28 October 1923, sec. 7, p. 2.

31. Ibid.

32. Cleveland.

33. *New York Times,* 29 August 1923, p. 18.

34. *Life,* 20 September 1923, p. 18.

35. *Theatre,* October 1923, p. 50.

36. LeRoy D. Haberman, "American Farce on Broadway, 1914–1950" (Ph.D. dissertation, Stanford University, 1959), p. 278.

37. Avery Hopwood, "A Playwright's First Night Palpitations," *New York Herald,* 7 October 1923, Locke Collection.

38. Cleveland.

39. David Gray, "Avery Hopwood Reshapes Play," *New York Times,* 19 October 1924, sec. 8, p. 3.

40. Ibid.

41. September(?) 1924, Cleveland.

42. *Theatre,* October 1924, p. 16.

43. *American Mercury,* October 1924, p. 247.

44. *Theatre,* October 1924, p. 16.

45. *New York Times,* 20 August 1924, p. 8.

46. "The Season in San Francisco," *Burns Mantle's Best Plays 1925–1926* (New York: Dodd, Mead & Company, 1921), p. 24.

47. Ian Herbert, ed., *Who's Who in the Theatre,* 16th ed. (London: Pitman Publishers, 1977), p. 1288.

48. P. 78.

49. *New York Times,* 3 December 1924, p. 24.

50. Ibid.

51. "Belasco to Rewrite Two Plays by Tuesday," *New York Times,* 21 February 1925, p. 1.

52. "The Season in Chicago," *Burns Mantle's Best Plays 1924–1925* (New York: Dodd, Mead & Company, 1926), p. 17.

53. "Smut Bores Avery Hopwood," *Phi Gamma Delta,* April 1925, pp. 649–650.

54. "The Mirror of the Stageland," *Theatre Magazine,* March 1923, p. 12.

55. Carl Van Vechten Collection, Beinecke Rare Book and Manuscript Library, Yale University, New Haven, Connecticut. Hereafter cited as Yale.

56. Ibid.

57. "Few Knew True Hopwood Back of His Drunken Pose," clipping in Files of the Hopwood Room, University of Michigan, Ann Arbor.

58. Cleveland.

59. Michigan.

60. September(?) 1924, Cleveland.

61. "Avery Hopwood in Clash with Police," *Asbury Park Evening Press,* 15 August 1924, p. 1.

62. 4 April 1925, Michigan.

63. Haberman, "American Farce," p. 133.

64. Leonard Hall, "Show Shopping," *New York Telegraph,* 6 July 1928, p. 12.

65. Cleveland.

66. Yale.

67. Beverley Nichols, *All I Could Never Be* (New York: E.P. Dutton & Company, Inc., 1952), pp. 191–192. Beverley Nichols (1899–1984), novelist, interviewer, essayist, and playwright, was twenty-five when he met Hopwood, and already the author of three books, including an autobiography, *Twenty-Five.* Known for his witty and

impudent epigrams, he was quoted everywhere during the era of "Bright Young Things." He once remarked: "I believe in doing things too soon." In later years, along with writing, he devoted himself to house and garden.

68. Alice B. Toklas, *What Is Remembered* (Chicago: Holt, Rinehart and Winston, 1963), p. 126; Nichols, *All I Could Never Be*, pp. 192–193.

69. Beverley Nichols to the author, 6 July 1983.

70. Gertrude Stein Collection, Beinecke Rare Book and Manuscript Library, Yale University, New Haven, Connecticut. Hereafter cited as Stein. Printed in *Flowers of Friendship: Letters Written to Gertrude Stein,* edited by Donald Gallup (New York: Alfred A. Knopf, 1953), p. 195.

71. Bruce Kellner to the author, 29 July 1983.

72. Edward Burns, ed., *The Letters of Gertrude Stein and Carl Van Vechten, 1913–1946* (New York: Columbia University Press, 1986), p. 82.

73. Stein.

74. Michigan.

75. Robin Douglas, *Well, Let's Eat* (London: Cassell and Company Limited, 1929), pp. 127–128.

76. Carl Van Vechten to Mary E. Cooley, 14 November 1946, Yale.

77. Ettie Stettheimer [Henrie Waste], *Love Days (Susanna Moore's)* (New York: Alfred A. Knopf, 1923), p. 250.

78. Ibid., p. 299.

79. Ibid., p. 309.

80. Yale.

81. Brendan Gill, *Tallulah* (New York: Holt, Rinehart and Winston, 1972), p. 117.

82. Tallulah Bankhead, *Tallulah* (New York: Harcourt Brace, 1952), p. 13.

83. Ibid.

84. December 1926, Yale. Jobyna Howland had originated the role of the man-chasing Mabel Munroe in the New York Production.

85. December 1926, Yale.

86. Yale.

87. Gill, *Tallulah*, p. 129.

88. R.D. Charques, "The London Stage," *New York Times,* 26 June 1927, sec. 8, p. 1.

89. "A Slice of Cinderella Life," *New York Herald Tribune,* 28 September 1927, p. 14.

90. September 1927, Cleveland.

91. 15 October 1927, Michigan.

92. *Phi Gamma Delta,* November 1927, p. 138.

93. Cleveland.

94. Bruce Kellner, *Carl Van Vechten and the Irreverent Decades* (Norman: University of Oklahoma Press, 1968), p. 160.

95. Ibid., p. 161.

96. "Fitzgerald's Commentary on New York, 1926," in Arthur Turnbull, *Scott Fitzgerald* (New York: Charles Scribners Sons, 1962), p. 183.

97. Cleveland.

98. F. Scott Fitzgerald, *The Great Gatsby* (New York: Charles Scribners Sons, 1925), p. 21.

99. Channing Pollock Correspondence, Box 2, Folder 12, Princeton University Library Collections, Princeton, New Jersey.

100. Channing Pollock, *Harvest of My Years* (Indianapolis: Bobbs-Merrill Company, 1948), pp. 360–361.

101. "Our Little Wife," *The Times* (London), 9 May 1928, p. 4.
102. Stein. Printed in *Flowers of Friendship,* p. 207, but the letter has been misdated as Wednesday May 25, 1927.
103. Gertrude Stein, *The Autobiography of Alice B. Toklas* (New York: Harcourt Brace and Company, 1933), p. 170.
104. Toklas, *What Is Remembered,* p. 127.
105. Stein, *Toklas,* p. 171.
106. Burns Mantle, *American Playwrights of Today* (New York: Dodd, Mead & Company, Inc., 1929), p. 159.
107. Yale.
108. Michigan.
109. Michigan.
110. Official Death Certificate, Antibes. Photocopy in the possession of the author.
111. Hopwood v. Globe Indemnity, #3051/29, Hall of Records, New York City. Photocopy in the possession of the author.
112. 30 July 1928, Yale.
113. Edward Lueders, *Carl Van Vechten* (New York: Twayne Publishing, Inc., 1965), p. 111.
114. Toklas, *What Is Remembered,* p. 126.
115. Bruce Kellner, ed., *Letters of Carl Van Vechten* (New Haven: Yale University Press, 1987), p. 104.
116. "Plan Paris Funeral for Avery Hopwood," *New York Times,* 3 July 1928, p. 21.
117. William F. McDermott, "Critic and Writer Praise Cleveland Man," *Cleveland Plain Dealer,* 19 August 1928, sec. 6., p. 1.
118. *New York Times,* 3 July 1928, p. 21.
119. "Avery Hopwood Drowns Off Nice," *Cleveland Plain Dealer,* 2 July 1928, p. 1.
120. McDermott, "Critic and Writer," sec. 6, p. 1.
121. Kellner, *Letters of Carl Van Vechten,* p. 104. Carl Van Vechten and Fania Marinoff would eventually each receive about $40,000 from the trust.
122. William Dawson, "Some Notes on Playboy Playwright," *Phi Gamma Delta,* January 1958, p. 184.
123. Archie Bell, "Devastating Theatre Exposé, Avery Hopwood's Last Work," *Cleveland News,* 11 March 1929. (Hopwood Folder, Literature Department, Cleveland Public Library, Cleveland, Ohio.)

VII. The Hopwood Novel: The Great Bordel, or, This Is Life

1. Archie Bell, "Devastating Theatre Exposé, Avery Hopwood's Last Work," *Cleveland News,* 11 March 1929. (Hopwood Folder, Literature Department, Cleveland Public Library, Cleveland, Ohio.)
2. Walter Winchell, "Crosses Trail of 'Greatest Novel' by Hopwood," *Cleveland News,* 24 July 1940. (Cleveland.)
3. Carl Van Vechten Collection, Beinecke Rare Book and Manuscript Library, Yale University, New Haven, Connecticut. Hereafter cited as Yale.
4. Jule Hopwood's Death Certificate, copy in the possession of the author.
5. Elsie M. Weitz to Mrs. M.W. Hornberger, 31 July 1933, Avery Hopwood Papers, Department of Rare Books and Special Collections, University of Michigan, Ann Arbor.

6. 11 January 1945, Yale.

7. Gertrude Stein, *Everybody's Autobiography* (New York: Random House, 1937), p. 226.

8. Sol Jacobson to the author, 11 September 1982.

9. Winchell, "Crosses Trail."

10. Bell, "Devastating Theatre Exposé."

11. Avery Hopwood, unfinished, unpublished manuscript of novel. (Carbon typescript in the possession of Hollywood Plays, Inc., Glen Rock, New Jersey. Photocopy in the possession of the author.)

12. "Avery Hopwood in Own Romance," *Phi Gamma Delta*, May 1924, p. 800.

13. *Michigan Quarterly Review*, v. 21, no. 1, p. 1.

14. Bruce Kellner to the author, 29 July 1983.

15. Saxton Funeral Home, Cleveland, Ohio, to the author, 29 April 1983.

16. Hopwood, unfinished novel.

VIII. The Hopwood Awards: The New, the Unusual and the Radical

1. Howard Mumford Jones, "Hopwood Awards Lead in their Field," *Michigan Alumnus*, 2 April 1932, p. 465.

2. Last Will and Testament of James Avery Hopwood, 30 December 1921, Department of Rare Books and Special Collections, University of Michigan, Ann Arbor. For complete information about the Hopwood Awards Program write to: Dr. Andrea R. Beauchamp, Hopwood Program Coordinator, 1006 Angell Hall, University of Michigan, Ann Arbor, Michigan 48109.

3. Roy W. Cowden, "Creative Writing in the Making," *Michigan Alumnus*, July 1948, p. 294.

4. Arthur Miller, "The American Writer: The American Theatre," *Michigan Quarterly Review*, vol. 21, no. 1 (Winter 1982), pp. 4-5.

5. John Chapman, "With Avery Hopwood's Help Arthur Miller is Cleaning Up This Season," *New York Daily-News*, 8 May 1949. (Clipping files of the *Daily-News* Library, New York City, New York.)

6. "Rebuilding *Powers That Be*," *Cincinnati Times-Star*, 7 March 1907. (Arno L. Bader's collection of dramatic reviews and biographical materials, Department of Rare Books and Special Collections, University of Michigan, Ann Arbor.)

IX. Conclusion

1. Avery Hopwood, *The Sideshow* (Typescript, n.p., n.d.), Billy Rose Theatre Collection, New York Public Library at Lincoln Center, Act I, sc. ii, p. 38.

2. Burns Mantle, *American Playwright of Today* (New York: Dodd, Mead & Company, Inc., 1929), p. 159.

3. Avery Hopwood, "Is the Undraped Drama Unmoral?" *Theatre Magazine*, January 1921, p. 6.

4. Mantle, *American Playwrights*, p. 156.

5. Avery Hopwood, unfinished, unpublished manuscript of novel. (Carbon typescript in the possession of Hollywood Plays, Inc., Glen Rock, New Jersey. Photocopy in the possession of the author), pp. 44–45.

6. Hopwood, "Undraped Drama," p. 6.

7. LeRoy D. Haberman, "American Farce on Broadway, 1914 to 1950" (Ph.D. dissertation, Stanford University, 1959), p. 278.

8. Arno L. Bader, "Avery Hopwood, Dramatist," *Michigan Alumnus* **66**, December 1959, pp. 60-68.

9. Gertrude Stein Collection, Beinecke Rare Book and Manuscript Library, Yale University, New Haven, Connecticut.

Sources Consulted

Primary Sources

Plays of Avery Hopwood — Single Author

The Alarm Clock. New York: Samuel French, 1930.

The Cat Came Back. N.d. (In the possession of Hollywood Plays, Inc., Glen Rock, New Jersey.)

The Demi-Virgin. 1921. The Billy Rose Theatre Collection, New York Public Library at Lincoln Center.

Don't Be Afraid. N.d. The Billy Rose Theatre Collection, New York Public Library at Lincoln Center.

Double Exposure. 1918. The Billy Rose Theatre Collection, New York Public Library at Lincoln Center.

Fair and Warmer. 1915. (In the possession of Hollywood Plays, Inc., Glen Rock, New Jersey.)

The Garden of Eden. 1927. The Billy Rose Theatre Collection, New York Public Library at Lincoln Center.

The Gold Diggers. 1919. (In the possession of Hollywood Plays, Inc., Glen Rock, New Jersey.)

The Great Illusion. N.d. (In the possession of Hollywood Plays, Inc., Glen Rock, New Jersey.)

Judy Forgot. 1910. The Billy Rose Theatre Collection, New York Public Library at Lincoln Center.

The Little Clown. New York: Samuel French, 1934.

Little Miss Bluebeard. New York: Samuel French, 1935.

Naughty Cinderella. New York: Samuel French, 1934.

Nobody's Widow. 1910. The Billy Rose Theatre Collection, New York Public Library at Lincoln Center.

Our Little Wife. 1916. The Billy Rose Theatre Collection, New York Public Library at Lincoln Center.

Pete. 1917. (In the possession of Hollywood Plays, Inc., Glen Rock, New Jersey.)

The Powers That Be. 1907. The Billy Rose Theatre Collection, New York Public Library at Lincoln Center.

Sadie Love. 1915. The Billy Rose Theatre Collection, New York Public Library at Lincoln Center.

The Sideshow. N.d. The Billy Rose Theatre Collection, New York Public Library at Lincoln Center.

Somewhere Else. 1913. (In the possession of Hollywood Plays, Inc., Glen Rock, New Jersey.)

This Woman and This Man. Washington, D.C.: Library of Congress, MIC RR 82/6720.

257

Why Men Leave Home. 1922. (In the possession of Hollywood Plays, Inc., Glen Rock, New Jersey.)

The Plays of Avery Hopwood—Collaborations

Collison, Wilson. *Getting Gertie's Garter.* 1921. (In the possession of Hollywood Plays, Inc., Glen Rock, New Jersey.)
————. *The Girl in the Limousine.* 1919. (In the possession of Hollywood Plays, Inc., Glen Rock, New Jersey.)
Gray, David. *The Best People.* London: Samuel French, Ltd., 1928.
Pollock, Channing. *Clothes.* 1906. The Billy Rose Theatre Collection, New York Public Library at Lincoln Center.
Rinehart, Mary Roberts. *The Bat.* New York: Samuel French, 1932.
————. *Seven Days.* New York: Samuel French, Inc., 1931.
————. *Spanish Love.* 1920. The Billy Rose Theatre Collection, New York Public Library at Lincoln Center.
Wood, Cyrus. *Good Night Ladies* (based on *Ladies' Night* by Avery Hopwood and Charlton Andrews). New York: Samuel French, Inc., 1946.

Novels, Short Stories and Poems of Avery Hopwood

"After the Hop Is Over." *Inlander,* v. 15, no. 6 (souvenir ed.), pp. 190–194.
"The Awakening." *Adelbert,* March 1903, p. 158.
"Beside the Summer Sea." *Adelbert,* November 1902, pp. 41–47.
"A Comic Tragedy: A Story of an Unimaginative Man." *Inlander,* September 1904, pp. 11–16.
"Hallowe'en." *Adelbert,* May 1903, pp. 217–218.
"A Hint." *Adelbert,* December 1902, p. 77.
"J.B. Brown, Misfit." *Inlander,* January 1904, pp. 207–213.
"Parting." *Adelbert,* November 1902, p. 48.
"The Plotters." *Adelbert,* February 1903, pp. 128–133.
Sadie Love. New York: John Lane Company, 1915.
"A Trifle Too Early." *Adelbert,* April 1903, pp. 185–187.
Unfinished, unpublished novel in five books, circa 1928. (Carbon typescript in the possession of Hollywood Plays, Inc., Glen Rock, New Jersey.)
"What Might Have Been." *Adelbert,* December 1902, pp. 79–80.
"When Alicia Played." *Inlander,* June 1905, pp. 336–339.
"The Whole Way." *Inlander,* January 1904, pp. 207–213.
"The Writing on the Wall." *Adelbert,* January 1903, p. 101.

Newspaper, Magazine and Miscellaneous Articles of Avery Hopwood

"Avery Hopwood." *My Maiden Effort,* comp. with an introduction by Gelett Burgess. Garden City: Doubleday, Page & Company, 1921.
"Avery Hopwood Bares Secrets of His Early Life." *Detroit News,* 8 October 1916, p. 1.
"Avery Hopwood Writes of the New York Critics." *Robinson Locke Collection,* The Billy Rose Theatre Collection, New York Public Library at Lincoln Center.
"'How Avery Hopwood Discovered the Gold Diggers and Induced Them to the Stage." *Cleveland Plain Dealer,* 16 November 1919, sec. D, p. 3.
"Is the Undraped Drama Unmoral?" *Theatre Magazine,* January 1921, p. 6.
"Little Miss Bluebeard: A Change of Mind." *New York Times,* 28 October 1923, p. 2.
"The Play-Writing Business." *Green Book Album,* August 1912, pp. 222–226.

"A Playwright's First Night Palpitations." *New York Herald,* 7 October 1923.

"The Supermen and Superwomen of the Stage." *Theatre Magazine,* May 1906, pp. 120–122.

"Two Theatrical Memories." *Theatre Magazine,* May 1920, p. 368.

"Where They Try Out Voices for the Operatic Stage." *Theatre Magazine,* April 1906, pp. 96–98.

"Why I Don't Write More Serious Plays." *Theatre,* April 1924, pp. 10 and 56.

Interviews with Avery Hopwood

Bell, Archie. "A Dramatist Who Writes His Plays in a Tent." *The Theatre,* August 1910, pp. 62–64.

Burns, Shirley. "The Day of Young Dramatists." *Green Book Album,* January 1911, pp. 187–188.

Chapple, Bennett. "The Creator of *Somewhere Else.*" *National Magazine,* March 1913, pp. 1105–1106.

"Hopwood, the Playmaker." *Detroit News,* 26 September 1920, sec. 2, p. 4.

Van Doren, John. "How to Write a Play." *Theatre Magazine,* October 1921, pp. 212 and 276.

Webber, John E. "A New School of Playwrights." *The Canadian,* September 1911, pp. 443–453.

"Why Avery Hopwood Writes Plays." *Green Book Album,* March 1914, pp. 387–388.

Wilson, Marjorie. "Your Laughs Earn $200,000 a Year for This Man." *Cleveland Sunday News-Leader,* 30 November 1919, sec. 4, p. 1.

Letters of Avery Hopwood

Avery Hopwood Letter. Rare Books and Special Collections, Temple University, Philadelphia, Pennsylvania.

Avery Hopwood Letters to Archie Bell. Literature Department, Cleveland Public Library, Cleveland, Ohio.

Avery Hopwood Papers. Department of Rare Books and Special Collections, University of Michigan, Ann Arbor, Michigan.

Channing Pollock Correspondence, Box 2, Folder 12. Princeton University Library Collections, Princeton, New Jersey.

F.N. Scott Papers. Bentley Historical Library, University of Michigan, Ann Arbor, Michigan.

Gelett Burgess Papers. The Bancroft Library, University of California, Berkeley, California.

Gertrude Stein Collection. The Beinecke Rare Book and Manuscript Library, Yale University, New Haven, Connecticut.

Kate F. Elkins Papers. Special Collections, Stanford University Library, Stanford, California.

Mary Roberts Rinehart Collection. Hillman Library Special Collections, University of Pittsburgh, Pittsburgh, Pennsylvania.

Van Vechten Collection. The Beinecke Rare Book and Manuscript Library, Yale University, New Haven, Connecticut.

Secondary Sources

Books That Mention Avery Hopwood

Appelbaum, Stanley, ed. *The New York Stage: Famous Productions in Photographs, 1883–1939.* New York: Dover Publications, Inc., 1976.

Atherton, Gertrude. *Adventures of a Novelist.* New York: Liveright, Inc., 1932.

Atkinson, Brooks. *Broadway.* Rev. ed. New York: Macmillan Company, Inc., 1974.

Bankhead, Tallulah. *Tallulah.* New York: Harper & Brothers, 1952.

Benchley, Nathaniel. "Do I Hear Twenty Thousand?" In *The Benchley Roundup: A Selection by Nathaniel Benchley of His Favorites.* New York: Harper & Brothers, 1954.

Bernstein, Eve. *Gold Diggers of Broadway.* New York: Efrus & Bennett, Inc., 1929.

Brownlow, Kevin. *The Parade's Gone By.* New York: Alfred A. Knopf, 1969.

Burns, Edward, ed. *The Letters of Gertrude Stein and Carl Van Vechten, 1913–1946.* New York: Columbia University Press, 1986.

Churchill, Allen. *The Great White Way.* New York: E.P. Dutton & Co., Inc., 1962.

_____. *The Theatrical Twenties.* New York: McGraw Hill Book Co., 1975.

Clark, Barrett H., and George Freedley, eds. *A History of Modern Drama.* New York: Appleton-Century-Crofts, Inc., 1947.

Cohn, Jan. *Improbable Fiction, The Life of Mary Roberts Rinehart.* Pittsburgh: University of Pittsburgh Press, 1980.

DeMille, Cecil B. *Autobiography.* Edited by Donald Haynes. Englewood Cliffs, New Jersey: Prentice-Hall, 1959.

Douglas, Robin. *Well, Let's Eat.* London: Cassell and Company Limited, 1929.

Gagey, Edmond M. *Revolution in American Drama.* New York: Columbia University Press, 1947.

Gallup, Donald, ed. *Flowers of Friendship, The Letters Written to Gertrude Stein.* New York: Alfred A. Knopf, 1953.

Gill, Brendan. *Tallulah.* New York: Holt, Rinehart & Winston, 1972.

Griffen, Ernest F., ed. *Westchester County and Its People.* 2 vols. New York: Lewis Historical Publishing Company, Inc., 1946.

Hammond, Percy. *But—Is It Art.* Garden City: Doubleday, Page & Company, 1927.

Harding, Alfred. *The Revolt of the Actors.* New York: William Morrow & Company, 1929.

Haycraft, Howard. *Murder for Pleasure: The Life and Times of the Detective Story.* London: Peter Davies, 1942.

Israel, Lee. *Miss Tallulah Bankhead.* New York: B.P. Putnam's Sons, 1972.

Kellner, Bruce. *Carl Van Vechten and the Irreverent Decades.* Norman: University of Oklahoma Press, 1968.

Kellner, Bruce, ed. *Letters of Carl Van Vechten.* New Haven: Yale University Press, 1987.

Kohler, John. *Damned in Paradise: The Life of John Barrymore.* New York: Atheneum, 1977.

Krows, Arthur Edwin. *Playwriting for Profit.* New York: Longmans, Green and Company, 1928.

Krutch, Joseph Wood. *The American Drama Since 1918.* New York: George Braziller, Inc., 1957.

Laufe, Abe. *Anatomy of a Hit.* New York: Hawthorne Books, Inc., 1966.

_____. *The Wicked Stage: A History of Theatre Censorship and Harassment in the United States.* New York: Frederick Ungar Publishing Co., 1978.

Leonard, William Torbert. *Theatre: Stage to Screen to Television.* 2 vols. Metuchen, N.J.: Scarecrow Press, 1981.

Loney, Glenn. *20th Century Theatre, Vol. 1.* New York: Facts on File Publications, 1983.

Lueders, Edward G. *Carl Van Vechten.* New York: Twayne Publishing, Inc., 1965.

_____. *Carl Van Vechten and the Twenties.* Albuquerque: University of New Mexico Press, 1955.

Luhan, Mabel Dodge. *Intimate Memories, Vol. 3: Movers and Shakers.* New York: Harcourt, Brace and Company, 1936.

Mantle, Burns. *American Playwrights of Today.* New York: Dodd, Mead & Company, 1929.

_____. *The Best Plays of 1899–1909; 1909–1919; 1919–1920; 1920–1921; 1927.* New York: Dodd, Mead & Company, 1930–1934.

Marker, Lise-Lone. *David Belasco: Naturalism in the American Theatre.* Princeton: Princeton University Press, 1975.

Middleton, George. *These Things Are Mine.* New York: The Macmillan Company, 1947.

Mordden, Ethan. *The American Theatre.* New York: Oxford University Press, 1981.

Morehouse, Ward. *Just the Other Day.* New York: McGraw-Hill Book Company, Inc., 1953.

_____. *Matinee Tomorrow.* New York: Whittlesey House (McGraw-Hill), 1949.

Morosco, Helen M., and Leonard Paul Dugger. *The Life of Oliver Morosco: Oracle of Broadway.* Caldwell, Idaho: Caxton Printers, Ltd., 1944.

Nathan, George Jean. *Comedians All.* New York: Alfred A. Knopf, 1919.

_____. *"Good Night Ladies,* January 17, 1945." *The Theatre Book of the Year 1944–45.* New York: Alfred A. Knopf, 1945.

_____. *Mr. George Jean Nathan Presents.* New York: Alfred A. Knopf, 1917.

_____. *The Popular Theatre.* New York: Alfred A. Knopf, 1928.

_____. *The Theatre, The Drama, The Girls.* New York: Alfred A. Knopf, 1921.

_____. *The World in False-Face.* New York: Alfred A. Knopf, 1923.

Nichols, Beverley. *All I Could Never Be.* New York: E.P. Dutton & Company, Inc., 1952.

Parker, John, comp. and ed. 4th ed. *Who's Who in the Theatre.* Boston: Small, Maynard & Co., 1922.

_____. 11th ed. Boston: Small, Maynard & Co., 1952.

Poggi, Jack. *Theatre in America: The Impact of Economic Forces 1870–1967.* Ithaca: Cornell University Press, 1968.

Pollock, Channing. *Harvest of My Years.* Indianapolis: Bobbs-Merrill Company, 1948.

_____. *"Something About 'First Nights.'"* In *The Footlights Fore and Aft.* Boston: The Gorham Press, 1911.

Rinehart, Mary Roberts. *My Story.* 2nd ed. New York: Rinehart & Co., Inc., 1948.

Sayer, Oliver M. *Our American Theatre.* New York: Brentano's Publishers, 1923.

Shipley, Joseph T. *Guide to Great Plays.* Washington, D.C.: Public Affairs Press, 1956.

Simon, Linda. *The Biography of Alice B. Toklas.* Garden City: Doubleday and Co., 1977.

Stein, Gertrude. *The Autobiography of Alice B. Toklas.* New York: Harcourt, Brace and Company, 1933.

_____. *Everybody's Autobiography.* New York: Random House, 1937.

Stettheimer, Ettie [Henrie Waste]. *Love Days (Susanna Moore's).* New York: Alfred A. Knopf, 1923.

Timberlake, Craig. *The Life & Work of David Belasco the Bishop of Broadway.* New York: Library Publishers, 1954.

Toklas, Alice B. *What Is Remembered.* Chicago: Holt, Rinehart & Winston, 1963.

Van Vechten, Carl. "Two American Playwrights." In *The Merry-Go-Round.* New York: Alfred A. Knopf, 1918.

_____. *Peter Whiffle: His Life and Works.* New York: Alfred A. Knopf, 1922.

Winter, William. *The Wallet of Time.* 2 vols. New York: Moffat, Yard & Co., 1913.

Related Books and Dissertations

Allen, Frederick Lewis. *Only Yesterday: An Informal History of the Nineteen-Twenties.* New York: Harper & Row, Publishers, 1931.

Bell, Archie. *The Clyde Fitch I Knew.* New York: Broadway Publishing Company, 1909.

Bentley, Eric. *The Life of the Drama.* New York: Atheneum, 1964.

_____. "The Psychology of Farce." In *"Let's Get a Divorce!" and Other Plays.* Ed. by Eric Bentley. New York: Hill and Wang, Inc., 1958.

Bermel, Albert. *Farce: A History from Aristophanes to Woody Allen.* New York: Simon and Schuster, 1982.

Bronner, Edwin. *The Encyclopedia of the American Theatre: 1900–1975.* New York: A.S. Barnes & Company, Inc., 1980.

Caputi, Anthony. *Buffo: The Genius of Vulgar Comedy.* Detroit: Wayne State University Press, 1978.

Davis, Owen. *My First Fifty Years in the Theatre.* Boston: Walter H. Baker Co., 1950.

Fitzgerald, F. Scott. *The Great Gatsby.* New York: Charles Scribners Sons, 1925.

Gassner, John and Quinn, Edward, eds. *The Reader's Encyclopedia of World Drama.* New York: Thomas Y. Crowell Company, 1969.

Gelb, Arthur and Barbara. *O'Neill.* New York: Harper & Brothers, 1962.

Gordon, Ruth. *My Side.* New York: Harper & Row, Publishers, 1976.

Haberman, LeRoy D. "American Farce on Broadway, 1914–1950." Ph.D. dissertation, Stanford University, 1959.

Hartnoll, Phyllis, ed. *The Oxford Companion to the Theatre.* 3rd ed. S.v. "Nathan, George Jean," by Thomas Quinn Curtis.

Hemingway, Ernest. *A Moveable Feast.* New York: Charles Scribner's Sons, 1964.

Hewitt, Barnard. *Theatre U.S.A.: 1668–1957.* New York: McGraw-Hill Book Company, Inc., 1959.

Knapp, Margaret May. "A Historical Study of the Legitimate Playhouses on West Forty-Second Street Between Seventh and Eighth Avenues in New York City." Ph.D. dissertation, City University of New York, 1982.

Nardin, James T. "A Study in Popular American Farce, 1865–1914." Ph.D. dissertation, University of Chicago, 1950.

Nathan, George Jean. *Another Book on the Theatre.* New York: B.W. Huebsch, 1925.

Powell, George. *The Victorian Theatre: 1792–1914.* London: Cambridge University Press, 1978.

Quinn, Arthur Hobson. *A History of the American Drama: From the Civil War to the Present Day.* Rev. ed. New York: Appleton-Century-Crofts, Inc., 1936.

This Fabulous Century: 1920–1930. New York: Time-Life Books, 1969.

Turnbull, Andrew. *Scott Fitzgerald.* New York: Charles Scribners Sons, 1962.

Wilson, Garff B. *Three Hundred Years of American Drama and Theatre.* Englewood Cliffs, N.J.: Prentice-Hall, Inc., 1982.

Young, William C. *Famous Actors and Actresses on the American Stage.* 2 vols. New York: R.R. Bowker Co., 1975.

Periodicals

Archer, William. "The Development of American Drama." *Harper's Magazine* **142** (1920): 75–86.

"Avery Hopwood's Sense of Humor." *Green Book Album,* June 1913, p. 1007.

Bader, Arno L. "Avery Hopwood, Dramatist." *Michigan Alumnus* **66** (December 1959): 60–68.

"Bedroom Farces Are Passé, Declares Their Leading Producer." *Current Opinion,* September 1922, p. 364.

Brown, Ivor. "Broadway in London," *The Saturday Review* (London), 27 March 1926, p. 399.

Cheney, Sheldon. "Who Are the American Playwrights — And Why?" *Theatre Magazine*, December 1922, pp. 360 and 408.

Cooley, Mary E. and Beauchamp, Andrea R. "Hopwood Awards (Revised July, 1980)." In the files of the Hopwood Room, University of Michigan, Ann Arbor, Michigan.

Cowden, R.W. "Creative Writing and the Hopwood Awards." *Michigan Alumnus* **48** (1942): 465–475.

————. "Creative Writers in the Making." *Michigan Alumnus* **54** (July 1948): 293–300.

Crocker, Lionel. "Note on Comedy." *Nation*, 25 September 1920, pp. 347–348.

Dawson, William Forrest. "Some Notes About Playboy Playwright." *The Phi Gamma Delta*, January 1958, pp. 184–188.

Defoe, Louis Vincent. "The Call for the Playwright." *The Michigan Alumnus*, January 1904, pp. 176–181.

Dukes, Ashley. "Mask of Comedy." *Theatre Arts*, August 1925, pp. 503–510.

Eaton, Walter P. "Return of Farce." *American Magazine*, December 1910, pp. 264–273.

Findon, B.W. "Roxana." *The Play Pictorial* (London), vol. 33, no. 201, p. 82.

Hamilton, Clayton. "Melodramas and Farces." *Forum*, January 1909, pp. 23–32.

Hamilton, E. "Comedy." *Theatre Arts*, July 1927, pp. 503–512.

Hartley, Randolph. "New Dramatists Who Have Captured Broadway." *Theatre Magazine*, September 1910, pp. 81–83.

Jones, Howard Mumford. "Hopwood Awards Lead in Their Field." *The Michigan Alumnus*, 2 April 1932, pp. 465–466.

Lavine, Stephen D. Introduction to "A Special Issue: The Writer's Craft — 50 Years of the Hopwood Awards." *Michigan Quarterly Review* (Winter 1982): 1–3.

Macgowan, Kenneth. "America's Best Season." *Theatre Arts*, April 1920, pp. 91–104.

————. "American Drama Mid-Channel." *Theatre Arts*, January 1920, pp. 1–5.

Miller, Arthur. "The American Writer: The American Theatre." *Michigan Quarterly Review* (Winter 1982): 4–20.

Moorehouse, Ward. "The Broadway Season: 1919 Album." *Theatre Arts*, September 1950, pp. 10–20.

Nathan, George Jean. "The American Dramatist — Why He Isn't." *Theatre Magazine*, March 1917, pp. 135–136.

Olendorf, Donna. "Academic Plums: The Hopwood Awards." *Monthly Detroit*, April 1980, pp. 27–28.

Quinn, Arthur Hobson. "The Significance of Recent American Drama." *Scribner's Magazine*, July 1922, pp. 97–108.

"*Roxana* at the Lyric." *The Illustrated London News*, 28 September 1918, p. 378.

Sherwood, R.E. "The Silent Drama: *Up in Mabel's Room.*" *Life*, 22 July 1926, p. 172.

Shubert, Lee. "The Truth About Commercialism in the Theatre." *Theatre Magazine*, April 1924, pp. 9 and 72.

Stewart, Henry T. "The Playbrokers of New York." *Theatre Magazine*, July 1905, pp. 163–165.

Theatre Magazine, untitled article, September 1921, pp. 142–143.

Theatre Magazine, March 1923, p. 12. S.v. "The Mirrors of Stageland," by The Lady with the Lorgnette.

Turner, W.J. "The Theatre." *The Spectator* (London), 4 February 1922, pp. 143–144.

Waldman, Milton. "The Drama." *London Mercury*, May 1926, p. 78.

The Writer's Craft: Hopwood Lectures, 1965–81. Edited with an introduction by Robert A. Martin. Ann Arbor: University of Michigan Press, 1982.

Newspaper Articles

"Anti-Theatre Novel Credited to Hopwood." *New York Times*, 12 March 1929, p. 24.

"Author's Four Plays Make B'Way Record." *New York Times*, 3 September 1920, p. 13.

"Avery Hopwood Dies in the Sea — American Dramatist Stricken While Bathing on the French Riviera." *Variety*, 2 July 1928, p. 19.

"Avery Hopwood in Clash with Police." *Asbury Park Evening Press*, 15 August 1924, p. 1.

"Belasco Presents Miss Claire as *The Gold Diggers* Star." *New York Herald*, 1 October 1919, sec. 2, p. 1.

"Belasco to Rewrite Two Plays by Tuesday." *New York Times*, 21 February 1925, p. 1.

"Belasco's *Gold Diggers*." *Variety*, 6 June 1919, p. 14.

Bell, Archie. "Committee Seeking to Encourage Youth." *Cleveland News*, 13 November 1931. (In the Hopwood file of the Literature Department, Cleveland Public Library, Ohio.)

_____. "Devastating Theatre Exposé, Avery Hopwood's Last Work." *Cleveland News*, 11 March 1929. (In the Hopwood file of the Literature Department, Cleveland Public Library, Ohio.)

Bower, Helen. "The Book Rack." *Detroit Free Press*, January–February? 1944. (In the clipping files of the Hopwood Room, University of Michigan, Ann Arbor, Michigan.)

Chapman, John. "*Best People* Is Played Again at the Waldorf." (In *The Best People* folder, Theatre Collection, The Museum of the City of New York.)

_____. "With Avery Hopwood's Help, Miller Is Cleaning Up This Season." (In the clipping files of the *Daily-News* Library, New York City.)

Charques, R.D. "The London Stage." *New York Times*, 26 June 1927, sec. 8, p. 1.

"Cocktail Comedy." *The Outlook* (London), 24, December 1926, p. 629.

Coleman, Robert. "*Best People* Revived with All Old Laughs." (In *The Best People* folder, Theatre Collection, The Museum of the City of New York.)

"Criticizing Clergy for Censorship." *New York Times*, 10 March 1922, p. 18.

Cuppy, Will. "*The Bat:* A Novel from the Play." *New York Herald Tribune*, 6 June 1926, p. 17.

"*The Demi-Virgin*." *Variety*, 21 October 1921, p. 16.

"*The Demi-Virgin* Farce Is Usually Dull, Always Vulgar." *New York Herald*, 19 October 1921, p. 10.

"*Demi-Virgin* Must Be Closed To-night." *New York Herald*, 24 November 1921, p. 12.

"*Demi-Virgin* Storm Grows in Broadway." *New York Herald*, 15 November 1921, p. 3.

"*Demi-Virgin* To Be Kept On To Test Law." *New York Herald*, 25 November 1921, p. 11.

"*Demi-Virgin* Trial May Mean Prison Term, Says Swann." *New York Herald*, 18 November 1921, p. 12.

"Few Knew True Hopwood Back of His Drunken Pose." (In the clipping files of the Hopwood Room, University of Michigan, Ann Arbor, Michigan.)

Garland, Robert. "*The Best People* Back in Full Vigor After Long Repose." (In *The Best People* folder, Theatre Collection, The Museum of the City of New York.)

"*Getting Gertie's Garter* New Woods Farce Risque but Funny." (In the *Getting Gertie's Garter* folder, Theatre Collection, The Museum of the City of New York.)

"*The Gold Diggers*." *Variety*, 10 October 1919, p. 16.

"*Gold Diggers* Till September." *Variety*, 14 May 1920, p. 14.

"Gossip on the Rialto." *New York Times*, 22 July 1923, sec. 7, p. 1.

Gray, David. "Avery Hopwood as Joint Author Reshapes Play." *New York Times*, 19 October 1924, sec. 3, p. 1.

"Gustave Luder's Death." *New York Times*, 25 January 1913, p. 25.

"Hazel Dawn Steps Out." *Variety*, 1 April 1921, p. 13.

"Hopwood on Reincarnation." *Variety*, 11 June 1920, p. 15.

"Hopwood's Profits." *New York Times*, 24 September 1922, sec. 6, p. 1.

"Ina Claire Leaving Belasco's Banner?" *Variety*, 25 February 1921, p. 1.

"Inside Stuff." *Variety*, 3 September 1920, p. 11.

"Inside Stuff on Legit." *Variety*, 29 April 1921, p. 13.

Kitchen, Karl K. "Avery Hopwood Writes Another 'Naughty-Nice' Farce, 'Gets Away With It.'" *Cleveland Plain Dealer*, 26 November 1916, p. 2.

"Ladies' Night Is Broad Farce with Turkish Bath Scene." *New York Herald*, 10 August 1920, p. 12.

"Lost Hopwood Motion—Mother of the Late Actor [*sic*] Failed in Court Move Just Before Her Death." *New York Times*, 3 March 1929, p. 5.

"Managers Move to Cleanse Stage and Avoid Censor." *New York Herald*, 19 November 1921, p. 8.

Materka, Pat. "U–M Writers Share Legacy of Hopwood." *Detroit News*, 6 April 1971. (In the clipping files of the Hopwood Room, University of Michigan, Ann Arbor, Michigan.)

McDermott, William F. "Avery Hopwood's Heirs Elusive . . ." *Cleveland Plain Dealer*, 12 January 1942. (In the Hopwood file of the Literature Department, Cleveland Public Library, Ohio.)

"Miss Ina Claire on 'Gold Digging' and the Non-Commissioned Girls of the Stage." *New York Herald*, 5 October 1919.

"Miss Jenny O'Jones for Three Days at Court Theatre." *Springfield* (Massachusetts) *Republican*, 23 November 1913, p. 9.

"Miss Jenny O'Jones. Springfield (Massachusetts) *Republican*, 28 November 1913, p. 6.

"Miss Keane's New Part." *The Times* (London), 19 September 1918, p. 9.

"Mrs. Hopwood Dies; Dramatist's Mother." *New York Times*, 2 March 1929, p. 17.

"Mrs. Hopwood Left Fund to University." *New York Times*, 5 March 1929, p. 27.

Nichols, Lewis. "Good Night!" *New York Times*, 18 January 1945, p. 16.

"1,000,000 Is Left by Avery Hopwood. Playwright's Will Gives Bulk of Estate to Mother and Sets Up Trusts For Friends—University to Get $150,000." *New York Times*, 28 July 1928, p. 13.

Osborn, E.W. "The New Plays: *The Best People.*" *Evening World* (New York), 20 August 1924, p. 8.

"Plan Paris Funeral for Avery Hopwood." *New York Times*, 3 July 1928, p. 21.

"Police Close *Ladies Night.*" *New York Dramatic Mirror*, 1 October 1921, p. 478.

Reamer, Lawrence. "Blushing Material Skillfully Handled in Hopwood Play—*Why Men Leave Home* Amusing and Finished Specimen of Writing." *New York Herald*, 13 September 1922, p. 6.

Sauer, Lou. "Hopwood Play Royalties Aid 'U' Literary Writers." *The Michigan Daily*, 5 December 1954. (In the clipping files of the Hopwood Room, University of Michigan, Ann Arbor, Michigan.)

"Spanish Love Has Striking Scenes and Notable Dancing." *New York Herald*, 18 August 1920, p. 7.

"Somewhere Else." *Variety*, 24 January 1913, p. 20.

Stearns, Harold E. "Playwriting Attracts Second-Rate Intellectuals, Says Hopwood, Who's Going to Quit." *New York Press*, 4 January 1914.

Untitled article. *Variety*, 7 October 1921, p. 16.

Untitled *Demi-Virgin* advertisement. *New York Times*, 31 May 1922, p. 12.

Winchell, Walter. "Walter Winchell Crosses Trail of 'Greatest Novel' by Hopwood." *The Cleveland News*, 24 July 1940. (In the Hopwood file of the Literature Department, Cleveland Public Library, Ohio.)

Woollcott, Alexander. *"The Best People* Presented." *New York Sun,* 20 August 1924, p. 13.

————. "Second Thoughts on First Nights." *New York Times,* 5 September 1920, sec. 6, p. 1.

————. "The Stage." *The World,* 28 September 1927, p. 13.

Selected Reviews

Clothes

Bell, Archie. "Miss George Wins New Laurels in Avery Hopwood's Play." *Cleveland News,* 29 January 1907. Cited in A.L. Bader, comp. "Avery Hopwood, Dramatist 1882–1928: A Collection of Dramatic Reviews and Biographical and Critical Materials," p. 7. (Typescript in the possession of the Department of Rare Books and Special Collections, University of Michigan, Ann Arbor.) Hereafter cited as Bader.

Hillhouse, Lewis J. "Extravagantly Staged Is Grace George's Play." *Cincinnati Times-Star,* 5 March 1907. (Bader, p. 8.)

New York Dramatic Mirror, 22 September 1906, p. 3.

Sage, William E. "Sartorial Drama of Hopwood a Hit." *Cleveland News,* 29 January 1907. (Bader, p. 5.)

Theatre, October 1906. (Bader, p. 4.)

The Powers That Be

"An American Play." *Cincinnati Enquirer,* 4 March 1907, p. 7.

Cincinnati Enquirer, 10 March 1907, sec. 3, p. 2.

Columbus Evening Dispatch, 28 February 1907, p. 4.

Hillhouse, Lewis J. "Applauded the Political Boss." *Cincinnati Times-Star,* 4 March 1907. (Bader, p. 17.)

"New Play Knocking Graft Makes Hit." *Columbus Citizen,* 28 February 1907, p. 3.

Ohio State Journal, February 1907, p. 9.

"Play by Hopwood Hit in Columbus." *Cleveland Leader,* 28 February 1907. (Bader, p. 16.)

"Rebuilding *Powers That Be.*" *Cincinnati Times-Star,* 7 March 1907. (Bader, p. 25.)

Simms, Phil. "Oh! Oh! Hopwood! Why'd You Do It!" *Cincinnati Post,* 4 March 1907. (Bader, p. 21.)

"The Powers That Be, A New Play Given at the Lyric." *Cincinnati Tribune,* 4 March 1907. (Bader, p. 19.)

This Woman and This Man

Hamilton, Clayton. "The Promise of New Playwrights." *Forum,* April 1909, pp. 333–336.

New York Dramatic Mirror, 6 March 1909, p. 3.

Theatre, April 1909, p. ix.

Seven Days

Goodman, Edward. "The American Dramatic Problem." *Forum,* February 1910, pp. 183–184.

Harper's Weekly, 27 November 1909, p. 25.

Metcalfe, J.S. *"Seven Days." Life,* 25 November 1909, p. 54.

New York Dramatic Mirror, 20 November 1909, p. 5.

Pollock, Channing. *"Seven Days." Green Book Album,* January 1910, pp. 77–79.

Theatre, December 1909, pp. xv, xvii.

Judy Forgot
"A Charge of Plagiarism." *New York Dramatic Mirror*, 23 November 1910. (Bader, p. 49.)
Hampton's Magazine, December 1910, p. 830.
Metcalfe, J.S. *"Judy Forgot." Life*, 20 October 1910, p. 660.
New York Dramatic Mirror, 12 October 1910, p. 7.
New York Dramatic Mirror, 30 November 1910, p. 10.
Theatre, November 1910, pp. 133–134.

Nobody's Widow
Hamilton, Clayton. "Plays, Home-Made and Imported." *Bookman*, February 1911, pp. 595–597.
Hampton's Magazine, March 1911, p. 360.
Metcalfe, J.S. *"Nobody's Widow." Life*, 8 December 1910, p. 1064.
New York Dramatic Mirror, 23 November 1910, p. 7.
Pollock, Channing. *"Nobody's Widow." Green Book Album*, February 1911, pp. 315–316.
Theatre, December 1910, pp. 162, xvii.

Somewhere Else
New York Dramatic Mirror, 22 January 1913, p. 7.
New York Tribune, 21 January 1913, p. 9.

Fair and Warmer
DeFoe, Louis V. "Personal Triumphs of the Season." *Green Book Album*, April 1916, p. 691.
"Fair and Warmer Is Highly Diverting." *New York Times*, 8 November 1915, p. 13.
Harper's Weekly, 27 November 1915, p. 515.
Metcalfe, J.S. *"Fair and Warmer." Life*, 18 November 1915, p. 961.
New York Dramatic Mirror, 13 November 1915, p. 8.
Theatre, December 1915, p. 279.

Sadie Love
Broun, Heywood. "Another Play About Pajamas." *New York Tribune*, 30 November 1915, p. 9.
"Extravagant Farce by Avery Hopwood." *New York Times*, 30 November 1915, p. 13.
New York Dramatic Mirror, 4 December 1915, p. 8.
Pollock, Channing. "Sugar and Spice." *Green Book Album*, February 1916, pp. 316–318.
Theatre, January 1916, p. 16.

Our Little Wife
Broun, Heywood. "Avery Hopwood Goes Overboard." *New York Tribune*, 21 November 1916, p. 7.
Metcalfe, J.S. "Our Little Wife." *Life,* 30 November 1916, p. 948.
New York Dramatic Mirror, 25 November 1916, p. 7.
"Polyandrous Farce by Avery Hopwood." *New York Times,* 20 November 1916, sec. 10, p. 3.
Theatre, January 1917, pp. 21–22.

Double Exposure
Broun, Heywood. "New Farce by Hopwood Is Seen at Bijou Theatre." *New York Tribune*, 28 August 1918, p. 7.

"Hopwood Writes a High Moral Farce." *New York Times,* 28 August 1918, p. 5.
Metcalfe, J.S. *"Double Exposure." Life,* 12 September 1918, p. 381.
New York Dramatic Mirror, 31 August 1918, p. 301.
Theatre, October 1918, p. 212.

The Gold Diggers
Broun, Heywood. "Avery Hopwood's *The Gold Diggers* Has First Performance at
    Lyceum." *New York Tribune,* 1 October 1919, p. 11.
"The Gold Diggers Sprightly Comedy of Chorus Girls by Avery Hopwood." *New York
    Dramatic Mirror,* 9 October 1919, p. 1579.
Hornblow, Arthur, ed. *"The Gold Diggers." Theatre,* December 1919, p. 436.
Savage, C. Courtenay. *"The Gold Diggers." Forum,* December 1919, p. 622.
Woollcott, Alexander. "The Play." *New York Times,* 1 October 1919, p. 20.
_____. "Second Thoughts on First Nights." *New York Times,* 5 October 1919, sec.
    4, p. 2.

The Girl in the Limousine
"Bedroom Farce to the Limit." *New York Times,* 7 October 1919, p. 22.
"The Girl in the Limousine, Another Bedroom Farce." *New York Tribune,* 7 October
    1919, p. 13.
"The Girl in the Limousine, Bedroom School of Farce Continues to Hold Its Own."
    New York Dramatic Mirror, 16 October 1919, p. 1610.
Savage, C.C. *"The Girl in the Limousine." Forum,* December 1919, pp. 623–624.
Woollcott, Alexander. "Second Thoughts on First Nights." *New York Times,* 12 Oc-
    tober 1919, sec. 4, p. 2.

Ladies' Night
Hornblow, Arthur. *"Ladies' Night." Theatre,* October 1920, pp. 185–186.
"Ladies' Night Lacks Beds, But Little Else." *New York Tribune,* 10 August 1920, p. 16.
Sobel, Bernard. *"Ladies' Night* Turkish Bath House Turns On Comedy Steam." *New
    York Dramatic Mirror,* 14 August 1920, p. 283.
Woollcott, Alexander. *"Ladies' Night." New York Times,* 10 August 1920, p. 10.
_____. "Second Thoughts on First Nights." *New York Times,* 15 August 1920, sec.
    6, p. 1.

Spanish Love
Benchley, Robert. *"Spanish Love." Life,* 2 September 1920, p. 408.
Broun, Heywood. *"Spanish Love* Brings Color to the Stage." *New York Tribune,* 18
    August 1920, p. 6.
Kelley, Richard. *"Spanish Love* Tempestuous Melodrama of Love and Hate Presented."
    New York Dramatic Mirror, 21 August 1921. Bader, p. 124.
Theatre, October 1920, p. 242.
"The Week's New Offerings." *New York Times,* 5 August 1920. Bader, p. 122.
Woollcott, Alexander. "Thrills from Spain." *New York Times,* 18 August 1920, p. 6.

The Bat
Benchley, Robert. *"The Bat." Life,* 9 September 1920, p. 456.
Broun, Heywood. *"The Bat* Brings Thrills in Plenty to Broadway." *New York Tribune,*
    24 August 1920, p. 10.
Independent, 4 September 1920, p. 261.
Reid, Louis B. *"The Bat* Thrilling Melodrama with Scene Laid in Haunted House." *New
    York Dramatic Mirror,* 28 August 1920, p. 371.

Theatre, October 1920, p. 240.

Woollcott, Alexander. "A *Rinehart* Mystery Staged." *New York Times*, 24 August 1920, p. 6.

_____. "Second Thoughts on First Nights." *New York Times*, 5 September 1920, sec. 6, p. 4.

_____. "Second Thoughts on First Nights." *New York Times*, 14 November 1920, sec. 6, p. 1.

_____. "Second Thoughts on First Nights." *New York Times*, 30 April 1922, p. 1.

Getting Gertie's Garter

Benchley, Robert. "*Getting Gertie's Garter*." *Life*, 18 August 1921, p. 18.

Broun, Heywood. "New Woods Farce Fails to Shock Anybody Much." *New York Tribune*, 2 August 1921, p. 6.

Hammond, Percy. "The Season in Chicago." In *The Best Plays of 1920–21*, p. 17. Edited by Burns Mantle. New York: Dodd, Mead, & Co., 1930.

Kaufman, S. Jay. "*Getting Gertie's Garter* Hopwood-Collison Farce Is Stale and Unprofitable." *New York Dramatic Mirror*, 6 August 1921, p. 193.

"New Risque Farce Rapid and Noisy..., Has Moments of Broad Hilarity." *New York Times*, 2 August 1921, p. 16.

Theatre, October 1920, pp. 233–234.

The Demi-Virgin

Benchley, Robert. "*The Demi-Virgin*." *Life*, 10 November 1921, p. 18.

Hammond, Percy. "Mr. Hopwood in *The Demi-Virgin* Is Naughty, But at the Same Time He Is To Many Dramagoers, as Camille Was, Good Company." *New York Tribune*, 19 October 1921, p. 8.

Kaufman, S. Jay. "*The Demi-Virgin*." *New York Dramatic Mirror*, 22 October 1921, p. 593.

Mantle, Burns. *The Best Plays of 1921–22*. Boston: Small, Maynard & Co., Publ., 1922, pp. 5–6.

Wolfe, Elizabeth. "*The Demi-Virgin* Hopwood Farce Produced in Atlantic City." *New York Dramatic Mirror*, 1 October 1921, pp. 484–485.

Woollcott, Alexander. "*The Demi-Virgin*." *New York Times*, 19 October 1921, p. 22.

Why Men Leave Home

Benchley, Robert. "*Why Men Leave Home*." *Life*, 28 September 1922, p. 18.

"Hopwood Play Says Men Leave Home After Wives." *New York Tribune*, 13 September 1922, p. 6.

"*Why Men Leave Home* Told in Hopwood Play." *New York Times*, 13 September 1922, p. 18.

Little Miss Bluebeard

Benchley, Robert. "*Little Miss Bluebeard*." *Life*, 20 September 1923.

Corbin, John. "*Little Miss Bluebeard*." *New York Times*, 29 August 1923, p. 12.

Hammond, Percy. "*Little Miss Bluebeard* Is Mildly Diverting, and Miss Irene Bordoni Is Much More Than That." *New York Tribune*, 29 August 1923, p. 8.

Theatre, October 1923, p. 50.

The Alarm Clock

"*The Alarm Clock* Rings." *New York Times*, 25 December 1923, p. 26.

Hammond, Percy. "*The Alarm Clock* Was Presented Last Night at the 39th Street Theatre." *New York Tribune*, 25 December 1923, p. 12.

Nathan, George J. *"The Alarm Clock."* *American Mercury,* February 1924, pp. 246–247.

The Best People
Benchley, Robert. *"The Best People."* *Life,* 11 September 1924, p. 18.
Hammond, Percy. *"The Best People,* Like Its Principal Character, Is An Amusing Gold-Digger." *New York Tribune,* 20 August 1924, p. 3.
Nathan, George J. *"The Best People."* *American Mercury,* October 1924, p. 247.
Theatre, October 1924, p. 16.
Warren, George C. "The Season in San Francisco." In *The Best Plays of 1925–26,* p. 24. Edited by Burns Mantle. New York: Dodd, Mead, & Company, 1930.
Young, Stark. *"The Best People." New York Times,* 20 August 1924, sec. 8, p. 1.

The Harem
Bromfield, Louis. *"The Harem." Bookman,* February 1925, p. 742.
"It May Be Said of *The Harem* That It Is Carnal, Though Harmless." *New York Tribune,* 3 December 1924, p. 16.
Nathan, George J. *"The Harem." American Mercury,* February 1925, pp. 245–246.
Theatre, February 1925, p. 19.
Young, Stark. "More Vajda's Betrayals." *New York Times,* 3 December 1924, p. 24.

Naughty Cinderella
"Irene Bordoni Triumphs in *Naughty Cinderella." New York Tribune,* 10 November 1925, p. 19.
"Naughty Cinderella Full of Piquancies." *New York Times,* 10 November 1925, p. 23.
Theatre, January 1926, p. 16.

The Garden of Eden
Atkinson, J. Brooks. "Among Peers of Highest Station." *New York Times,* 28 September 1927, p. 28.
Hammond, Percy. "Another Slice of Cinderella Life Carved by Avery Hopwood in *The Garden of Eden." New York Tribune,* 28 September 1927, p. 14.
"New Plays Out of Town." *New York Times,* 14 August 1927, sec. 7, p. 2.

Clipping Collections
Avery Hopwood Clipping Folder. The *Daily-News* Library, New York City.
Avery Hopwood Clipping Folder. The Fraternity of Phi Gamma Delta, Lexington, Kentucky.
Avery Hopwood Clipping Folder. The Harvard Theatre Collection, Harvard Library, Cambridge, Massachusetts.
Avery Hopwood Clipping Folder. The Hopwood Room, University of Michigan, Ann Arbor.
Avery Hopwood Clipping Folder. The Literature Department, Cleveland Public Library, Cleveland, Ohio.
The Demi-Virgin Clipping Folder. The Harvard Theatre Collection, Harvard Library, Cambridge, Massachusetts.
Double Exposure Clipping Folder. The Harvard Theatre Collection, Harvard Library, Cambridge, Massachusetts.
Miss Jenny O'Jones Clipping Folder. The Harvard Theatre Collection, Harvard Library, Cambridge, Massachusetts.
This Woman and This Man Clipping Folder. The Harvard Theatre Collection, Harvard Library, Cambridge, Massachusetts.

Miscellaneous

Assignment of Copyright. Hopwood Plays, Inc. Vol. 282, pp. 240–245, 29 January 1932. Copyright Office, Washington, D.C. (Photocopy in the possession of the author.)

Bader, Arno L., comp. "Avery Hopwood, Dramatist 1882–1928: A Collection of Dramatic Reviews and Biographical and Critical Materials." June 1959. (Carbon typescript in the possession of the Department of Rare Books and Special Collections, University of Michigan, Ann Arbor.)

Gordon, Ruth. Letter to the author, 16 April 1983.

Hopwood, Henry W. Letter to the author, 13 May 1982.

Housum, Robert. Letter to the author, 27 January 1983.

Interrogatories, Hopwood v. Globe: #3051/29. Hall of Records, New York City. Photocopy in the possession of the author.

Isherman, Chris, Manager of the Lyric Theatre, London. Letter to the author, 1 December 1983.

Jacobson, Sol. Letter to the author, 11 September 1982.

Kellner, Bruce. Letter to the author, 10 September 1982.

_____. Letter to the author, 1 July 1983.

_____. Letter to the author, 29 July 1983.

_____. Letter to the author, 5 October 1983.

Kennedy, Madge. Hollywood, California. Interview, 16 June 1983.

Kirk, Flora Bruce. Euclid, Ohio. Interview, 27 January 1983.

Last Will and Testament of James Avery Hopwood, 30 December 1921. (Copy in the possession of the author.)

Monks, Thomas C. Letter to the author, 6 April 1983.

Mordden, Ethan. Letter to the author, 24 April 1983.

Nichols, Beverley. Letter to the author, 6 July 1983.

Reed, Ilse Gehring. Letter to the author, 14 September 1983.

_____. Letter to the author, 4 January 1983.

Riverside Cemetery. Letter to the author, Cleveland, Ohio, 10 November 1982.

Sadie Love agreement. The Billy Rose Theatre Collection, New York Public Library at Lincoln Center.

Saxton Funeral Home. Letter to the author, Cleveland, Ohio, 29 April 1983.

Van Vechten, Carl. "Undecided Sasha," 9 January 1917. Carl Van Vechten Collection, Manuscript Division, New York Public Library.

Weissberg, Albert O. (A.H. Woods's great-nephew.) Letter to the author, 8 December 1982.

Index

273

musical version *(Tumble In)* 108–10,
112; royalties 43, 90; synopsis 40–43
Severn, Margaret 163
Seymour, Anne ix
"Shadow Waltz" (song) 231
Shakespeare, William 47, 80
Shattuck, Truly 224
Shaw, George Bernard 92, 152, 168, 181
Shean and Gallagher 173
Sheldon, Edward 36
Shenandoah (Howard) 50
Sheridan, Clare 163
Sherlock Holmes (Gillette) 50
Sherman, Lowell 225
Sherwin, Jeannette 228
Sherwood, Robert E. 163
Shipman, Samuel 140
Shirley, Florence 228
Shoemaker, Dorothy 224
Shootist, The (Swarthout) 214
Show Boat (musical) (Hammerstein
II/Kern/Ferber) 184
Shubert, Lee 156; Hopwood letter to
156–57
Shubert Theatre (Columbus, OH) 26,
223
Shuberts, Messrs. 18, 26, 33, 99, 101,
199, 205
Sideshow, The 101–03, 216, 230
Siegfried (Wagner) 82
Sills, Milton 34, 223
Silver Fox, The (Hamilton/Herczeg) 144
Simple Life, The (Dickson) 47
Simpson, Ivan F. 230
Sins of Society, The (play) 47
Sipperly, Ralph 229
Siska, William C. ix
Size, Patricia Angelin viii
Skinner, Cornelia Otis 193
Skinner(s), Otis 193
Skipworth, Alison 230
Slaight, Craig ix
Sleeping Partners (Guitry/Hicks) 106
Sleuth (Shaffer) 220
Smart Set, The (periodical) 73, 74, 78,
92
Smith, Betty 214
Smith, C. Aubrey 91
Smith, Mrs. Harry B. 25
Smith, MaryAnn vii
Smith, Winchell 93, 107, 113, 144
Smithson, Frank 224
Snyder, Ann see Van Vechten, Ann
So Much for So Much (Mack) 80

"So This Is Love" (song) 160, 161
Social Register, The (Loos) 168
Solo per Donne (film) *(Our Little
Wife)* 231
Solomon, Joseph x
"Some Notes About Playboy Playwright"
(Dawson) 13
Sometime (Young/Friml) 106
Somewhere Else (Hopwood/Luders)
(musical) 1, 56, 58, 62ff, 69, 218,
242n; cast 224; synopsis 65
"Song of the Gold Diggers" (song) 231
Sonnette d'Alarme, La (Hennequin/
Coolus) 158, 228; see also *Alarm
Clock, The*
Sothern, E.H. 5, 40
Sothern-Marlowe Company 5, 80
Southgate, Betsy Jane 230
Southwind (Douglas) 178
Spanish Love (Hopwood/Rinehart) 2, 43,
131–33, 136, 218; cast 227
Spender, Stephen 212
Spider Boy (Van Vechten) 189
Spite Corner (Craven) 86
Split Second (McIntyre) 214
Springfield [MA] *Sunday/Daily
Republican*, (newspaper) 69, 74
Spring's Awakening (Wedekind) 181
Stage Writers' Protective Association 113
Stanford, Arthur 224
Stanley, Charles 223
"Star Factory, The" (song) 46
Starr, Francine 54
Stearns, Harold E. 238n
Steichen, Edward 246n
Stein, Gertrude viii, 3, 12, 60–61, 170,
176, 187–88, 189, 190, 193, 246n;
Hopwood letters to 177, 178, 187–88;
on Hopwood's bequest 221; on Hop-
wood's novel 199
Stephenson, Henry 227
Stettheimer, Carrie 246n
Stettheimer, Florine 212, 213, 246n
Stettheimer, Ettie viii, 96, 179, 202,
246n
Stieglitz, Alfred 246n
Stitt, Milan 214
Strange, Michael 162
Straton, John Roach 144, 163
Strauss, L.A. 17
Strauss, Richard 149
Strindberg, August 92
Strohwitver 228; see also *Why Men Leave
Home*